INTERNATIONAL STUDIES OF THE

COMMITTEE ON INTERNATIONAL RELATIONS

UNIVERSITY OF NOTRE DAME

The Russian Revolution and Religion, 1917–1925. Edited and translated by Bolesław Szcześniak.

Soviet Policy Toward the Baltic States, 1918–1940. Albert N. Tarulis.

Introduction to Modern Politics. Ferdinand Hermens.

Freedom and Reform in Latin America. Fredrick B. Pike, ed.

What America Stands For. Stephen D. Kertesz and M. A. Fitzsimons, eds.

The Representative Republic. Ferdinand Hermens.

Theoretical Aspects of International Relations. William T. R. Fox, ed.

Catholicism, Nationalism and Democracy in Argentina. John J. Kennedy.

Christian Democracy in Western Europe, 1820–1953. Michael P. Fogarty.

The Fate of East Central Europe. Stephen D. Kertesz, ed.

German Protestants Face the Social Question. William O. Shanahan.

Soviet Imperialism: Its Origins and Tactics. Waldemar Gurian, ed.

The Foreign Policy of the British Labour Government, 1945–1951. M. A. Fitzsimons.

Diplomacy in a Whirlpool: Hungary between Nazi Germany and Soviet Russia. Stephen D. Kertesz.

Bolshevism: An Introduction to Soviet Communism. Waldemar Gurian.

Theory
and
Practice

Theory

and

Practice:

History of a Concept

from Aristotle to Marx

NICHOLAS LOBKOWICZ

UNIVERSITY OF NOTRE DAME PRESS
NOTRE DAME—LONDON

Library of Congress Catalog Card Number: 67-22145
Manufactured in the United States of America

To I. M. Bochenski
in thankful admiration

PREFACE

The basic nature and aim of this first volume of a study of the origins and history of the Marxist notion of "revolutionary practice" may be best explained by saying a few words on its genesis. Several years ago I contemplated writing a small study on the treatment of theory and practice in contemporary Soviet philosophy. As I worked in the field of "philosophical Sovietology" before, I was from the very beginning aware of the fact that such a study, due to its very subject, inevitably would become utterly boring if it did not take into account Marx's original ideas on this question* and consequently trace the intricate development of the problem from Marx to contemporary Marxism-Leninism. As I began to gather materials for this study, I gradually realized that the period most important for an adequate understanding, not to speak of evaluation, of the Marxist treatment of theory and practice is the relatively brief period between Hegel's deăth in 1831 and the emergence of Marx's mature thought in the *German Ideology* in 1845.

In consequence, what I originally meant to be a brief introductory section on the origins of the treatment of theory and practice in contemporary Marxism-Leninism became a detailed study of Hegel, the left Hegelians, and the young Marx. Moreover, after the sections on the Hegelians and the young Marx were written—that is, the *second* and *third* part of the present volume—I felt that it would be interesting to contrast this early nineteenth-century speculation on theory and practice with earlier ideas on the same subject. The result was the *first* part of this study, which traces the problem of theory and practice from the Greeks to about the end of the eighteenth century.

* I have indicated my views on this subject in an article published in *Studies in Soviet Thought*, 6 (1966), 25-36.

Of course, while the second and third parts contain a relatively thorough treatment, in fact a detailed history of the development from Hegel to Marx, the first part had to remain very sketchy. It contains only a collection of *materials for a prehistory* of the treatment of theory and practice in Marx and the Marxists. As the reader will notice, I somewhat arbitrarily concentrated on what seemed most important to me in each period: the opposition between philosophy and politics in the Greeks; the dissociation of theory proper from contemplation in Neoplatonism; the opposition between "contemplative" and "active" life in medieval Christianity; the gradual transformation of a basically atheoretical "practical philosophy" in the Greeks into the "practical philosophy" of the post-Cartesian period, which actually is only an "applied theory"; the emergence of a "theory" involved in "making" and "production"; etc. To do anything more than this would have required writing another volume—a temptation I resisted in spite of the fact some of my friends urged me to do so.

I am fully aware of course that as a result the present volume is somewhat unbalanced. The first part covers the more than two thousand years from Aristotle to Kant; the second covers only forty years, namely, the development from Hegel through the Left Hegelians to Moses Hess; and the third part (which incidentally is also the longest) covers no more than five years, namely, the brief period during which the thought of Karl Marx matured. My hope is that in the near future I will be able to smooth over this obvious disproportion by adding a second volume in which I shall discuss the features of Marx's philosophy not touched upon in this first volume, such as his notion of "materialism" and the relationship between Marx's "historical materialism" and Engels' "dialectics of nature." This volume hopefully will also contain what I originally set out to write, namely, a history of the development of the notion of practice from Marx through Engels and Lenin to contemporary Soviet philosophy.

In order to avoid misunderstandings, I may do well to emphasize that this study deals only with the history of two *notions*. That is to say, it does not pretend to throw significant light upon how actual theory and actual practice, as well as their interrelationship, developed through the ages. This study restricts itself to the history of the *ideas* concerning theory and practice, and in this sense it may be described as a history of the *theory of* theory and practice. Occasionally it was unavoidable to take a glance at actual theories and actual practices as well. Thus, Aristotle's distinction between theoretical and practical life cannot be appreciated without taking into account the actual structure of a Greek city-state; the theoretization of practical philosophy in Descartes cannot be understood without considering the emergence of a mathematical theory in the fourteenth, fifteenth, and sixteenth centuries; and the development of the Left Hegelian notion of *Praxis*, from Cieszkowski through Bruno Bauer and Moses Hess to Marx, cannot be explained without considering the political situation in Prussia during the late 1830's and early 1840's. But I have consciously refrained from implying that the development of the *notions* of theory and practice is but a reflection of the development of *actual* theories and *actual* practices. In fact, I even suspect that there does not exist anything resembling a genuine history of theory and practice themselves— a topic which I hope to discuss in a later volume.

Throughout this study I have refrained as far as possible from criticizing. This should not be taken to mean that I consider most of Marx's ideas correct, for example. On the contrary, I consider them theoretically unsound and entailing truly tragic consequences if applied in practice. But it seemed to me that a faithful and objective exposition usually is the best criticism. Occasional critical passages ought to be seen in this light: a false idea cannot really be understood without realizing that it is false, that is, without explaining why it was conceived in spite of the fact that it has little to do with reality as it is.

This study never would have been completed without the generous help of many patrons and friends. In particular, I should like to extend my thanks to Rev. C. A. Soleta, former academic vice-president at the University of Notre Dame, for granting me a quite undeserved leave of absence during which I gathered various materials at the *Bayerische Staatsbibliothek* at Munich; to Professor E. Voegelin, University of Munich, who permitted me to use the truly unusual library of his *Institut für Politische Wissenschaften* and with whom I discussed a number of problems which I could not have tackled without his help; to Rev. E. McMullin, head of the Department of Philosophy at the University of Notre Dame, whose unflinching critical views again and again forced me to rewrite certain sections, especially in the first part; to Dr. H. Deku, University of Munich, presently visiting professor at Notre Dame, whose insights into the Greeks, and into the basically ideo-logical character of modern philosophy have been a constant inspiration to me; to Professor G. L. Kline, Bryn Mawr College, who carefully read the second and third part of the manuscript and offered a number of invaluable criticisms and suggestions; to Mr. John Redmond, graduate student at Notre Dame, and Mrs. J. Robinson, Los Angeles, who took upon themselves the ghastly effort to amend my English and to whom I cannot but apologize for the many awkward passages which I insisted should remain unchanged; and *above all* to Professor Stephen Kertesz, chairman of the Committee on International Relations at the University of Notre Dame, under whose auspices the present volume is publish-ed, for his constant encouragement and the almost unbelievable patience with which he watched the slow progress of my work.

I am dedicating this volume to my former teacher, Rev. I. M. Bochenski, Professor of Modern and Contemporary Philosophy, and presently *rector magnificus*, at the University of Fribourg, Switzerland. It is from him that I learned that a philosopher may ascend to the heights of abstractions and abandon himself to the vast fields of pure scholarship without at the same time loosing his connection with the pressing problems of the day. I wish that he would accept this dedication as an excuse for the fact that for various personal reasons I was unable to contribute to the *Festschrift* commemorating his sixtieth birthday in 1962.

CONTENTS

Part I:

Materials for a Prehistory

Man is that substance which re-
fracts, that is, polarizes, the whole
of nature.

Novalis, II, 85.

1: *GENERA VITAE*

When today we oppose "practice" to "theory," we usually have in mind lived life as opposed to abstract ideas, or else man's acting as opposed to his "mere" thinking and reflecting. Almost nothing in this distinction which today is found in all European languages, reminds us of the fact that it is a last relic of several categories in terms of which the Greeks tried to tackle a question highly characteristic of their culture, namely, which is the best and most desirable of lives. For when the Greeks opposed to each other θεωρία and πρᾶξις, they did not have in mind abstract doctrines in contrast to their concrete application[1]; nor did they, without further ado, think of the two most obvious facets of man's conscious life, his thinking and his acting. Rather, what they had in mind was a distinction between various kinds or walks of life— a distinction which permitted them to tackle the kind of questions which of yore it was customary to ask at the Delphic oracles: Who is the most pious, the most happy, the wisest, the best man?

When Aristotle distinguishes three kinds of life from which a man free of the immediate necessities of life may choose (the life of enjoyment, political life, and the life of contemplation[2]) he simply resumes an old Greek tradition. As we shall see, the tri-

---

[1] Plato, it is true, sometimes uses the expression 'ἐν ταῖς πράξεσιν' in the sense of 'in practice,' 'in lived life,' as opposed to 'in theory,' e.g. *Phaedrus* 271 E ; *Epistola* VII, 343 A ; etc. *For the abbreviations used in this volume see the Bibliography, BELOW p.* 427.

[2] *Nic. Eth.* I, 5, 1095 b 17-19 ; *Eud. Eth.* I, 4, 1215 b 36; *Pol.* VII, 2, 1324 a 15 ff.; *Magna Moralia* I, 3, 1184 b 5.

3

partition just mentioned probably goes back to Pythagoras. But
the basic idea is much older; as R. Joly has shown, it already is
intimated in early Greek poetry—and continues to be one of the
main themes of Greek thought later taken up by Roman thinkers
such as Cicero and Seneca and eventually handed down to the
Middle Ages.

That which we call "theory" today corresponds to what Aristotle
called "contemplative life"; and what we call "practice" has its
origins in Aristotle's analysis of "political life." In fact, Aristotle
seems to have been the first Greek thinker to reduce the many
different walks of life to three and in a sense to two, thus becoming
the first explicitly to contrast "theory" and "practice."

Plato still operated with a much more complex and therefore
far less articulate scheme. Thus in the *Phaedo* the philosopher who
is the embodiment of Aristotle's "contemplative life" is contrasted
with a "lover of the body (φιλοσώματος)," who in turn is either a
"lover of power and fame (φίλαρχος καὶ φιλότιμος)" or a "lover
of riches (φιλοχρήματος)."[3] In the *Republic*[4] two kinds of "lovers
of pleasure (φιλήδονος)" are added; and Plato proceeds to an
ingenious correlation between the various kinds of life, on the
one hand, and parts of the soul, political constitutions, and social
classes, on the other hand.

In Aristotle this complex scheme is reduced to a tripartition.
In fact, it is reduced to an opposition between "practical" and "theoretical" life. For, as Aristotle indicates in the first book of the
Nicomachean Ethics, only the vulgar mob which identifies the
Good with pleasure is content with the βίος ἀπολαυστικός, the
voluptuous life; men of refinement (οἱ χαρίεντες) take only two
kinds of life seriously into consideration, namely, the "practical"
life of politics, whose representatives identify the Good with honor,
and the "theoretical" life of the philosopher, ·who strives for the
contemplation of eternal truths.[5]

---

[3] *Phaedo* 68 B-C; cf. *Rep.* 581 C ff.

[4] Cf. *Rep.* 555 ff.

[5] *Nic. Eth.* I, 5, 1095 b 14-1096 a 6. To illustrate his opinion that the life
of pleasure is a "life for cattle," Aristotle sometimes refers to the Assyrian
king, Sardanapallus, who is supposed to have said: "I only have what I ate, what

In the *Politics*[6] Aristotle characterizes the difference between these two more "refined" ways of life as follows: "practical" life is the life of active citizenship (συμπολιτεύεσθαι), of active participation in the life of the πόλις; "theoretical" life, on the contrary, is a life of detachment from political partnership, the life of someone who is alien to the πόλις. In order to appreciate this distinction, we shall have to say a few words about the origin and the exact meaning of the two expressions 'θεωρία' and 'πρᾶξις.'

"THEORY"

If we may believe Cicero and Jamblichus, who in turn rely upon a lost treatise of Heracleides of Pontus, Aristotle's distinction between three basic kinds of life as well as his emphasis on "theoretical" life goes back to Pythagoras. When Pythagoras (we are told) was asked what he meant calling himself a "philosopher" (a neologism which he is said to have invented), he replied by telling the following simile. Men enter their lives somewhat like the crowd meets at a festival. Some come to sell their merchandise, that is, to make money; some come to display their physical force in order to become famous; while there is a third group of men who only come to admire the beautiful works of art as well as the fine performances and speeches. In a similar way we meet each other in this life of ours; it is as if each of us were coming from afar, bringing along his own conception of life. Some desire nothing except wealth; some only strive for fame; while a few wish nothing except τῶν καλλίστων θεωρίαν, to watch or to contemplate the most beautiful things. But what are the most beautiful things? Certainly the universe as a whole and the order according to which the heavenly bodies move around are beautiful. But their beauty is merely a participation in the beauty of the First Being which can only be reached

---

wantonness I have committed, what joys I received through passion" (Athenaeus, *Deipnosoph.* VIII, 336 a). In his *Protrepticus*, Aristotle seems to have argued that this inscription might be found on the tomb of a bull; cf. Cicero, *Tusc.* V, 35, 101; cf. *Magna Moralia* II, 7, 1204 a 38.

[6] *Pol.* VII, 1, 1324 a 15 ff.

by thought. Those who contemplate this First Being (which Pythagoras seems to have described as the number and the proportion
constituting the nature of all things) are the philosophers, the
"lovers of wisdom." For wisdom is the knowledge of things beautiful, first, divine, pure, and eternal.[7]

We need not concern ourselves with the question whether it
really was Pythagoras who invented the expression ' φιλόσοφος '
and whether he really did explain it in the manner just described.
In fact, as the story is told by Cicero and Jamblichus, Pythagoras
did not explain what being a "lover of wisdom" amounts to. Rather, he explained what "theoretical" life is—so much so that recently it has been suggested that he should have called himself φιλο-
θέωρος, "lover of contemplation." For the whole story ultimately
is based upon a play with the many connotations of the expression
' θεωρία. '

It is well known that the expression ' θεωρός ' means "spectator
at games"; ' θεωρία, ' then, would mean what a spectator at games
does, namely, watching. However, ' θεωρός ' originally referred to
the envoy sent to consult an oracle; ' θεωρία ' was the official title
of the group of state-ambassadors which a city-state delegated
to the sacral festivals of another city-state. As such sacral festivals
were usually connected with sports and games, ' θεωρός ' simply
came to mean "spectator"; and as the delegation just mentioned
had to travel, and often to travel far to reach its destination, ' θεωρός '
also came to refer to a traveler who visits foreign countries to
learn something about their customs and laws. Thus Pythagoras
did not have to be concerned that his hearers would mistake the
"spectator" and in consequence the philosopher for the screaming
and applauding mob which, even today, remains one of the less
pleasant features of games and sports. For his hearers, and all
Greeks who subsequently read the story, were aware of the fact
that the "festival" in question was a sacral event and that the
spectators had come from afar to take part in a feast with religious
significance.[8] In fact, as he used the expression ' θεωρία, ' Pytha-

---

[7] Cf. Cicero, *Tusc.* V, 3, 8-9; Jamblichus, *De vita Pyth.* 58-59.

[8] Cf. Plato's *Laws* 650 A, where the festival of Dionysius is called a θεωρία.

goras could expect that his hearers associated the events to be watched with something divine; for this expression reminded the Greek of the expression 'θεός,' 'god.'[9]

Thus it transpires that "theory" appeared to the Greeks as a particularly sublime way of life which was less shallow than that of mere pleasure-seekers and less hectic than that of "politicians." Pythagoras described the "spectator" as a man who is most similar to a truly free man (liberalissimus, ἐλευθεριώτατος): he is free of the unrest and the agitation of those who yearn for money or fame. In a similar way the philosopher is removed from the agitation and transitory character which life has for ordinary man: he contemplates the divine order and takes part in its eternity, thus somehow succeeding in transcending what the Greeks experienced as man's most distinctive character, his "mortality."[10] Placed between an ever-changing but nevertheless everlasting Nature, on the one hand, and gods who never grew old, on the other hand, man was the only mortal being in a cosmos of immortal reality. In the philosopher's contemplation of the eternal this human condition somehow was transcended; since the only activity conceivable in the gods was contemplation, a man who lived the "theoretical" life had to be considered dearest to the gods and therefore happiest. In fact, as Aristotle says in the last book of the Nicomachean Ethics, this kind of life was beyond the properly human level; man could only reach it in virtue of something within him that was divine. "... nor ought we obey those who enjoin that a man should have man's thought and the mortal the thoughts of mortals, but we ought so far as possible achieve immortality."[11]

---

[9] Cf. Pseudo-Plutarch, De Musica 27, where the expressions 'θεωρεῖν' and 'θέατρον (theater)' are said to derive from 'θεός.' This erroneous etymology will be repeated by Greek Christians, e.g. Gregory of Nyssa, Basil, Pseudo-Dionysius, etc. Incidentally, the Latin expression 'contemplatio' originally had a religious connotation, too. It derives from 'templum' which originally referred to the place which the augur delimited as the field of observation relevant to the prophecy.

[10] Cf. Arendt, 18 ff.

[11] Nic. Eth. X, 7, 1177 b 33 ff.; cf. 1178 b 8 ff., 1179 a 24, etc.

However, one must not mistake the Greek "theoretical" life for
something similar to the monastic *vita contemplativa* of the Middle
Ages. In a sense, the object of Greek contemplation was not God
but his manifestation in the visible world, in particular, the awe-
inspiring regularity of the movement of heavenly bodies to which
Aristotle still refers as "those among divine things which appear
to us."[12] Pythagoras, as we have seen, described "the totality
of the universe and the order of the stars which move within it"
as the immediate object of contemplation. Anaxagoras, when
he was asked the reason for which one ought to desire to be born
and to live is said to have replied: "To contemplate the heaven and
its stars, the moon and the sun"; another text reads " ... the heaven
and the whole order of the universe."[13] And when Aristotle distinguishes three "theoretical sciences," he in fact is speaking about
three objects of contemplation: the universal and therefore un-
perishable features of nature, the mathematical realm which Plato
had placed among the Ideas and which Aristotle himself sometimes
seems to identify with the heavenly bodies (in any case, we sometimes find him mentioning astronomy instead of mathematics[14]), and
the First Causes, which of all things divine obviously are the most
eternal ones.[15] Thus "theoretical" life included what today would
be called "scientific inquiry"; after all, the philosopher was the only
Greek counterpart to the modern scientist. But the "scientific
inquiry" in question was rooted neither in mere curiosity nor in
"practical necessity." As Aristotle put it, it was owing to their
wonder that men began to philosophize; one philosophizes in
order to escape from ignorance, not because on expects some use
from philosophy. Therefore, according to Aristotle the very possession of this knowledge is beyond what is human; if the gods ever
envied mortal men, they would envy this king of knowledge rather
than anything else. For it is a knowledge which it would be most

[12] φανερόν τῶν θείων, *Met. E*, I, 1026 a 18; *Phys.* II, 4, 196 a 33.

[13] *Protrept.* Fr. 11 Walzer; *Eud. Eth.* I, 5, 1216 a 11.

[14] *Phys.* II, 7, 198 a 29-31. Cf. Ph. Merlan, *From Platonism to Neoplatonism*
(The Hague, 1960) 59 ff.

[15] *Met. E*, 1, 1026 a 13-19; *K*, 7, 1064 b 1-3; *Phys.* II, 2, 193 b 22-26, and
194 b 14; *Nic. Eth.* VI, 8, 1142 a 17-18.

meet for God to have—a knowledge of what is divine (τῶν θειών) and therefore divine knowledge (θεία τῶν ἐπιστημῶν).[16]

"PRACTICE"

About the origins of the notion of practice much less can be said. In fact, Aristotle seems to have been the first to use it as a technical term, but even he also frequently uses it as a term of vernacular Greek. The verb 'πράσσω' has a number of closely related meanings such as "I accomplish (e.g., a journey)," "I manage (e.g., state affairs)," "I do or fare (e.g., well or ill)," and, in general, "I act, I perform some activity." 'Πρᾶξις,' then, refers to almost any kind of activity which a free man is likely to perform; in particular, all kinds of business and political activity. Only activities involving bodily labor seem to be excluded from the range of its meaning, and also to some extent merely intellectual activities such as thinking and reflecting.

Aristotle several times opposes πρᾶξις to ποίησις.[17] The distinction is not easily rendered in English; what comes closest to it is the difference between "doing" and "making." We *do* sports or business or politics, and we *make* ships or houses or statues. Aristotle himself illustrates the difference between these two kinds of activity by saying that while "making" aims at an end different from the very act of "making," the end of "doing" is nothing else but the act of "doing" itself performed well. At first sight this distinction is far from being clear. For though it may be true that we "make" a house but refer to the playing of the flute as a "doing" rather than a "making," we nonetheless "produce" something when we play the flute (e.g., sounds) or when we perform political activities (e.g., changes in the state). And as a matter of fact, in a passage in which he wants to emphasize that a philosopher is not inactive, Aristotle himself distinguished between "external actions (ἐξωτεριχαὶ πράξεις)" which have an effect upon others and

16 *Met. A*, 2, 982 b 17 to 983 a 7.
17 *Nic. Eth.* VI, 4, 1140 a 2 ff.; 5, 1140 b 3 ff.; *Magna Moralia* I, 34, 1197 a 3 ff.; II, 12, 1211 b 27 ff.; *Pol.* I, 2, 1254 a 6.

πϱάξεις such as contemplating and reflecting which are αὐτοτελεῖς, have their end in themselves.[18] Still, it would seem possible to give meaning to this distinction by saying, as Aristotle himself does say in the *Magna Moralia*,[19] that playing the flute is both the end and the activity of the flute player, while a builder of a house has a different end beyond his activity. Also we may add that "making" has not achieved its end until it has reached the point at which it may stop, while "doing" only fulfils its end while it is being done. An activity such as building a house would never be considered satisfactory if it did not stop, that is, resulted in a house built and finished. As opposed to this, εὐπϱαξία, "doing something well," is in itself an end;[20] playing the flute obviously has achieved its end a long time before it stops. In fact, once it has stopped, it is no longer of any value—precisely because it does not aim at a result beyond the mere "doing" it.[21]

When the distinction is seen from this point of view, there is an interesting and significant kinship between πϱᾶξις and life. As Aristotle says in the *Politics*, "life is πϱᾶξις, not ποίησις."[22] If we assume that life may be described as some kind of an activity, it obviously is not an activity which reaches its completion by stopping and leaving behind something different from itself. To live is like playing a flute, not like building a house. It is therefore not by chance that the expression 'πϱᾶξις' time and again occurs in Aristotle's biological writings: procreation and feeding are called πϱάξεις;[23] indeed, all the life activities of animals are described as

---

[18] *Pol.* VII, 2, 1325 b 16 ff.

[19] *Magna Moralia* II, 12, 1211 b 27 ff.

[20] *Nic. Eth.* VI, 4, 1140 b 6; cf. *Magna Moralia* I, 34, 1197 a 3 ff.; II, 12, 1211 b 27 ff.; *Pol.* I, 2, 1254 a 6.

[21] This would seem to be the meaning of the passage *Met.* Θ, 6, 1048 b 23 ff., where Aristotle says that we at the same time are seeing and have seen, are understanding and have understood, are thinking and have thought, while one cannot say of a house that it has been built while it is being built. Cf. *De Sensu* 6, 446 b 2; *Soph. El.* 22, 178 a 9 ff.

[22] *Pol.* I, 2, 1254 a 7 ff. Aristotle uses this statement to show that a slave is an instrument of action, such as a dress or a bed which one uses without getting from it something beside and beyond the use.

[23] *Hist. an.* VII, 1, 589 a 3, cf. *Problemata* III, 2, 872 b 23 ff.

πράξεις,[24] in terms of which, among other things, animals ought to be distinguished from each other.[25] And even about the πράξεις of the stars Aristotle argues that they should be considered analogous to those of animals.[26]

However, there is a more technical sense of the expression 'πρᾶξις' which restricts its use to strictly anthropological rather than biological phenomena. Not incidentally Aristotle once refers to his whole "practical philosophy" as ἡ περὶ τὰ ἀνθρώπινα φιλοσοφία, the part of philosophy concerned with the problems of man.[27] Indeed, we find him explicitly stating that no animal beside man can truly be said to act; for man alone of all animals is πράξεών τινών ἀρχή, the true source of some activity.[28] The reason is simple: the efficient cause of all activity is προαίρεσις, purposeful choice; and such a choice, in turn, is not possible without desire and a λόγος ὁ ἕνεκά τινος, a reasoning directed to some end.[29] In this sense, then, 'πρᾶξις' refers to rational and purposeful human conduct.

Of course, "making" as well as mere thinking is rational and purposeful human conduct as well. And in fact, Aristotle sometimes seems to use 'πρᾶξις' in so wide a sense that one gets the impression that it is supposed to cover "making" as well; and sometimes he describes contemplation[30]—indeed seeing, thinking, and intellection[31]—as specific kinds of πρᾶξις. Still, in its most technical sense the expression 'πρᾶξις' only covers those human actions and activities which Aristotle discusses in his ethical and political writings: moral conduct and political activity. And as Aristotle explicitly states that ethics is only a part of the ἐπιστήμη πολιτική, of political science, we may simply say that 'πρᾶξις' is Aristotle's term for man's free activity in the realm of political life.

[24] De part. an. II, 1, 646 b 14 ff.
[25] Hist. an. I, 1, 487 a 11 ff.
[26] De caelo II, 12, 292 b 1 ff.
[27] Nic. Eth. X, 9, 1181 b 15.
[28] Eud. Eth. II, 5, 1222 b 19; cf. Nic. Eth. VI, 1, 1139 a 16 ff.
[29] Nic. Eth. VI, 1, 1139 a 32 ff.
[30] Pol. VII, 2, 1325 b 17 ff.
[31] Met. Θ, 6, 1048 b 18 ff.

Before discussing Aristotle's conception of the relationship between political and philosophical life and thus the Greek version of the opposition between "practice" and "theory," we must mention one more point, namely, that Aristotle explicitly excludes the realm of πρᾶξις from the objects of contemplation. Overstating a bit, we may say that Aristotle admits a "practical knowledge" but rejects the notion that there exists a "theoretical knowledge," and thus an ἐπιστήμη in the strict sense of the term, of πρᾶξις.

Even though Aristotle's justification of this claim is not very articulate, two lines of argument may be distinguished.[32] First of all, the end of an inquiry into πρᾶξις is not knowledge but πρᾶξις itself; "for we do not wish to know what bravery is but to be brave, nor what justice is but to be just, just as we wish to be in health rather than to know what being in health is, and to have our bodies in good condition rather than to know what good condition is."[33] Taken by itself, this argument against there being a theoretical knowledge of πρᾶξις is not overly convincing, for must not the philosopher know what justice or bravery, or the Good to be pursued, is in order to deliberate about the moral and "political" aspects of such activities? And in fact, Aristotle often at length discusses *what* the various virtues are or *what* the end of man is, and in some instances he certainly discusses questions of this type at greater length than their being ordered toward the question "What ought to be done?" would seem to justify. Still, there can be no doubt that Aristotle held that the study of πρᾶξις aims only at so much of knowledge as is required for εὐπραξία, "doing something well": "we are not investigating the nature of virtue in order to know what it is, but in order that we may become good, without which result our investigation would be of no use."[34] The idea found in Thomas Aquinas—namely, that one may *operabilia modo speculativo considerare*, consider things doable with the detached attitude of someone only

[32] *Nic. Eth.* I, 3, 1094 b 11 to 1095 a 13.
[33] *Eud. Eth.* I, 6, 1216 b 21-25.
[34] *Nic. Eth.* II, 3, 1103 b 27-29.

interested in their properties[35]—certainly is not present in Aristotle.

All the more important is the second argument. It amounts to saying that the ὕλη, the subject matter, of ethics and political science—"actions which occur in life (αἱ κατὰ τὸν βίόν πράξεις)"—do not lend themselves to the amount of precision (ἀκρίβεια) which one ordinarily would, and Aristotle certainly does, expect from an object of contemplation. For things noble and just (about which political science inquires) involve much difference of opinion and uncertainty, in fact so much so that some people argue that they are only conventional.[36]

What Aristotle intends to say here is something much more precise and far-reaching than the claim that the subject matter of ethics and political science is so complex and difficult that adequate analysis of the facts and formulation of the laws in this sphere has not yet been achieved, and perhaps never will. What he suggests is that only those things can be *known* in the strict sense of the term and thus contemplated which cannot be other than what in fact they are (μὴ ἐνδέχεσθαι ἄλλως ἔχειν); all objects of knowledge and contemplation exist of necessity and therefore are eternal.[37] As Aristotle puts it in one of his biological writings, only things eternal and divine (ἀΐδια καὶ θεῖα) are objects of contemplation.[38]

One might, of course, object that physics, which Aristotle describes as a "theoretical" science, studies things which come to be and pass away and thus are contingent. But Aristotle probably would have replied, as Thomas Aquinas did centuries later, that even though physics is concerned with the realm of things generable and corruptible, it studies them with respect to universal patterns which are eternal and do not change.[39] Yet ethics and political

35 *S. Th.* I, 14, 16.
36 *Nic. Eth.* I, 3, 1095 b 14 ff.
37 *Nic. Eth.* VI, 6, 1140 b 31; cf. *Pol.* VII, 6, 1328 a 19 ff.
38 *De gen. an.* I, 23, 731 b 24. Cf. *Nic. Eth.* III, 3, 1112 a 19 ff., where Aristotle says that one does not deliberate (and therefore think "practically") about eternal realities.
39 *In VI. Eth.* 3, 1146 Spiazzi; cf. 1, 1123 Spiazzi.

science are supposed to result in εὐπραξία, and as they thus are
supposed to guide human action, and human action always deals
with particular things, they cannot avoid entering the realm of
the particular and contingent which does not lend itself to "precise"
knowledge.[40] All the more is this so since human actions are free.
As Aristotle explains in the eighth book of the *Metaphysics*, potentialities of the rational part of the human soul are δυνάμεις τῶν
ἐναντίων, potentialities of alternative and contrary realization.
While nonrational potentialities can be actualized only in one
determinate way and therefore necessarily produce their effects
as soon as certain conditions are satisfied, rational potentialities
may be realized in this way or that and therefore require a further
determining factor—choice (προαίρεσις).[41]

This doctrine about a lack of "scientific precision" in ethics and
political science obviously has important implications. It amounts
to saying that neither ethics nor political science can decide what
ought to be done in each particular instance, and that laws cannot
possibly cover everything. In fact, whatever the moral philosopher,
the political scientist, or the lawgiver promulgate only takes into
consideration the majority of cases (ἐπὶ τὸ πλέον), even though
it is not unaware of the defectiveness this involves. "And this
does not make it a law which is less right; for the defect is not in
the law or in the lawgiver, but in the nature of the case: the subject
matter of things doable and done (τῶν πρακτῶν ὕλη) simply is
of this kind."[42]

This notion, we may add, is not peculiar to Aristotle. Already
Plato argued that a law cannot determine what is noblest and most
just, since the irregularities (ἀνομοιότητες) of men and actions
do not admit of a simple rule for all and valid for all time. Laws
are like the rules at gymnastic contests: they are not precision
work like that of joiners and turners, for example.[43] In fact, they

[40] *Nic. Eth.* VI, 7, 1141 b 14 ff.

[41] *Met.* Θ, 5, 1047 b 35 to 1048 a 24. For a more detailed analysis, see H. H.
Joachim, *The Nicomachean Ethics* (Oxford, 1951) 108 ff.

[42] *Nic. Eth.* V, 10, 1137 b 17-19.

[43] *Politicus* 294 D: λεπτουργεῖν, an expression which Plutarch, *Aem. Paulus*
37, 2. 997 d, uses for turners and joiners.

only roughly prescribe what in most cases applies to the majority. It is almost exactly the same words that Aristotle uses in the first book of the *Nicomachean Ethics*: in political science we have to be content if we are able to present that which, roughly and in outline, applies to most cases, and to reach conclusions proportionate to such premises.[44]

---

[44] *Politicus* 294 E; *Nic. Eth.* I, 3, 1094 b 20. Cf. E. Kapp, "Theorie und Praxis bei Aristoteles und Platon," *Mnemosyne* 5 (1937) 179-194, here 183.

2: CONTEMPLATION AND POLITICS: THE TWO DIMENSIONS OF MAN

We said earlier that the Greek version of the opposition between "theory" and "practice" originally amounted to an opposition between two "ways of life," political life and philosophic life. To this statement, however, we have to add an explanation and a qualification. An *explanation* is required because today we have a hard time understanding how anyone possibly could identify the realm of the practical with that of the political.

Certainly even the Greeks, one will argue, were aware of the fact that political activity is not the only kind of activity characteristic of man. This undoubtedly is true. We have already referred to the distinction between πρᾶξις and ποίησις, and we hardly have to add that Aristotle, when he explained what this distinction amounts to, was relying on the educated Greek's feeling for correct idiom rather than artificially introducing a distinction where the Greek saw none. In fact, there was still a third notion (which, however, plays a very insignificant role in the thinking of Greek philosophers): 'πόνος,' an expression which meant not only hard labor and toil but also, and by no means incidentally, distress, suffering, and even sickness.[45]

Now one might argue that in discussing the Greek conception of the relationship between "theory" and "practice" we should oppose to contemplative life the life of πρᾶξις, ποίησις, and πόνος, *taken into one.* But, first of all, this would amount to introducing into Greek thought a contrast where precisely the Greeks saw no

---

[45] St. Augustine was still aware of this ambiguity. Cf. *De Trin.* XXII, 18; *PL* XLII, 410.

contrast. As far as I can see, no Greek ever contrasted πόνος and θεωρία.[46] And as to ποίησις, the Greeks probably would have argued that it is at least as different from πρᾶξις as πρᾶξις is different from θεωρία; we shall come back to this point in the next section. Secondly, the truly interesting aspect of the subject under discussion is precisely the fact that what originally was an opposition between philosophy and politics later became an opposition between "theoretical thought" and almost any kind of human activity, in particular, productive activity.

Still, a few remarks would seem to be in place to explain why the Greeks most often and most explicitly opposed philosophic to political life rather than, for example, commercial life. When in the *Nicomachean Ethics* Aristotle distinguishes the life of (mainly bodily) enjoyment which is pursued by the πολλοὶ καὶ φορτικώτατοι, the multitude and the most vulgar, from the political and contemplative life which is pursued by the χαρίεντες, the men of refinement,[47] one is easily misled into believing that this tripartition is supposed to cover the life of all human beings; in particular, the life of all inhabitants of the Greek city-state. But this certainly is not what Aristotle had in mind. In the *Eudemian Ethics* he introduces the same tripartition by premising that there of course exist other ways of life as well—the life of those who pursue "vulgar arts" (Aristotle seems to have in mind people only living for the sake of money), or the life of the retailers who buy in markets and huckster in shops, or finally the life of those who pursue wage-earning occupations (probably day-laborers). Yet all these ways of life are only mentioned in order to be dismissed immediately as uninteresting, since they are pursued τῶν αναγκαίων χάριν, for the sake of the necessities of life.[48]

In other words, the Aristotelian tripartition (and the same would seem to apply to all Greek discussions concerning the various

[46] Christian thinkers, it is true, sometimes will describe contemplation as a laborious effort. Thus Gregory of Nyssa speaks of a πόνος τῆς θεωρίας, *In eccles. Salom.*; *MG* XLIV, 617 A; also St. Augustine, *Contra Faustum* II, 52; *PL* XLII, 432.
[47] *Nic. Eth.* I, 2, 1095 b 14 ff.
[48] *Eud. Eth.* I, 4, 1215 a 20 ff.

"ways of life" and the "best of lives") only covers the lives of those
who can afford to spend very little time with "necessary" activities,
that is, the lives of full-fledged citizens of some means. Why this
is so may be explained to some extent at least by referring to the
social structure of a Greek πόλις. All hard manual labor such as
mining, loading and unloading ships, domestic work, and even
agricultural labor to a lesser extent, was carried out by slaves who
usually formed almost one-half the inhabitants of ancient Greece.
Thus manual labor was not considered a sufficiently meaningful
occupation to constitute a special "walk of life." There was only
one exception: agricultural labor as carried out by the αὐτουργοί,
the husbandmen who owned a little ground and usually had a
few slaves helping them. The husband of Euripides' Electra,
for example, is an αὐτουργός, and Euripides certainly describes
him as a very likable fellow; Xenophon's *Oeconomicus* even contains a eulogy on agricultural labor based on the belief that it
not only produces the necessities of life and thus is the mother
and nurse of all other arts but also forms the body as well as the
soul.[49] Nevertheless, the very fact that agricultural labor was an
activity which slaves could and did perform seems to have excluded
it from the number of "lives" which could claim to be "truly happy."

As to artisans, they usually were foreigners who, even though
legally free, were not citizens and in fact could be taken as slaves
as soon as they were no longer able to pay the μετοίκιον, a special
tax to which these men owed their names; the same applies to the
great majority of merchants and retailers. Moreover, the μέτοικοι,
as they were called, formed the great majority of day-laborers whom
undertakers hired on the market, be it for a day or for a longer period.
As a great number of such "foreigners" were Phoenicians, Phrygians,
Egyptians, and even Arabs—that is, foreigners properly speaking
and not only resident aliens from other Greek city-states—their
activities almost automatically were considered disreputable. This
applied in particular to those who "huckster in shops," the retailers
who were always suspected of cheating. As to the artisans, many

---

[49] Xenophon, *Oec.* V, 4-17. Cf. Plutarch, *Lycurgus* 24, 3, and *Solon* 2, 5 ff.;
also Antipater, *Anth. Palat.* IX, 23.

of whom were great artists, their activity was considered much more reputable. Yet Aristotle compares even them to slaves as far as their need for virtue is concerned (even though he grants that there exist natural slaves, while no shoemaker or other craftsman is under his "limited slavery" by nature[50]). Indeed, he argues that citizenship should not be granted to artisans (even though at this time most Greek-born artisans already were citizens[51]). His argument is very revealing: if artisans were permitted to become citizens, then the "citizen's virtue"—that is, his being capable of participating in the government—would not belong to every citizen; only those released from the ἔργα ἀναγκαία, from necessary and menial occupations, have the leisure required for governing.[52]

This, of course, does not mean that all Greek citizens were wealthy. In fact, some of them were so poor that during the Peloponnesian War a special pecuniary indemnity had to be granted to the θητές, the small peasants whose land produced less than 150 medimni (about 180 bushels) of corn per annum, in order to enable them to participate in the frequent political meetings. But as the πόλις did not offer an indemnity for the time and effort spent in public office, the poor obviously could not afford to be "politicians," that is, active citizens properly speaking; in fact, it would seem fair to suggest that the great majority of the many nameless who, according to Aristotle, only led a life of enjoyment were such proletarians among citizens. For those who were rich enough almost necessarily took part in politics; public opinion and custom prevented them from leading an "apolaustic" life, from simply enjoying their wealth.

Thus, on the one hand, those actively taking part in political life were almost exclusively landed proprietors, either smaller peasants who had a few slaves and therefore could occasionally afford to accept one of the less burdensome offices, or owners of large estates such as Ischomachus (Socrates' interlocutor

---

[50] *Pol.* I, 5, 1260 b 1 ff.
[51] As Aristotle himself admits, *Pol.* III, 3, 1278 a 6-8.
[52] *Ibid.* 1278 a 8-11.

in Xenophon's *Oeconomicus*, whose only connection with the necessities of life consisted in his supervision of his many slaves), or finally men such as Pericles, who had a supervisor, usually a slave, manage their estates so that they could spend their entire lives as "politicians" in Athens. On the other hand, such landed proprietors could not avoid being politicians—and almost their whole lives were dominated by political activities.

Already from this social survey[53] it becomes obvious that the most prominent activity of a relatively well-to-do citizen was political activity. But even the lives of citizens who were too poor ever to receive important offices were dominated by such activities. The πόλις was governed by the Assembly, which consisted of all citizens[54] and usually convened three times a month; the numerous wards and tribes had assemblies of their own, which were summoned much more often. Every citizen could count on becoming a member of the Senate at least twice during his life; each second or third year he could expect to be nominated ἡλιαστής, a juryman of the court; moreover, several hundred magistrates had to be nominated for the πόλις, the wards, and the tribes—and in each case the Greek had to count on spending a whole year in office. If, in addition, one takes into account that nonfulfillment of one's duties as a citizen was punishable by loss of citizenship and that citizens without office, who happened to be in town when an assembly was summoned, were driven by special police consisting of slaves to the assembly point in order to fulfill their political duties, it becomes quite understandable that the average Greek citizen considered politics his most prominent activity. As Fustel de Coulanges put it: "Men passed their lives by governing themselves. The democracy could not last unless all citizens worked incessantly at it."[55]

---

[53] Cf. G. Glotz, *Le travail dans la Grèce ancienne* (Paris, 1920); R. Flacelière, *La vie quotidienne en Grèce au siècle de Périclès* (Paris, 1959) 45 ff., 147 ff.

[54] Even though only a small fraction of the citizens took part in each individual meeting. According to Plutarch, *Aristeides* 7, 6, the *quorum* for really pressing decisions was 6,000 electors (of a total of about 40,000).

[55] *La Cité Antique* (Paris, 1866) 437.

Nevertheless, the Greeks viewed their political life as *the* realm of freedom, but not solely because they were legally free and equal before the law. More basically, they identified politics and freedom—or politics and the most truly human activity— because in order to take part in the political life just described a man had to be freed from all struggle for survival, that is, released from all or almost all activities concerned with the procurement of the necessities of life. It is against this background that the Greek distinction has to be understood, between ζῆν and εὖ ζῆν, between "mere life," in the sense of a mere maintaining and preserving of one's physical existence, and a "good life," which achieved man's ultimate destination. There were activities which simply did not belong to a "good life," even though they were indispensable preconditions of any life and thus also of a "good life": labor of all kinds, handicraft, commerce, in fact, all activities except those of which "political life" consisted and to which the philosophers added a further "activity," that of contemplation. One almost would be tempted to say that the Greeks considered all "prepolitical" activities prehuman and that only in the political life were they able to see a way of life which transcended the animal realm.

As O. Gigon [56] has pointed out recently, it is on this conception that Aristotle's ill-famed justification of slavery, as something almost intended by nature itself, is based: no man is capable both of struggling with the necessities of life and of pursuing a "good" life which aims at virtue and ultimately at happiness. Thus, if at least a few are to be able to fulfill the true destination of man, there must exist human beings who by their very nature are not capable of doing anything except to procure the ἀναγκαῖα. Such men are the φύσει δοῦλοι, the "natural slaves." When in the *Politics*[57] Aristotle argues that not all persons who are necessary for the existence of the πόλις are to be deemed citizens, one of the implications of this statement certainly is that some

[56] "Die Sklaverei bei Aristoteles," in *La Politique d'Aristote*, Fondation Hardt, Entretiens, XI (Vandoeuvres-Genève, 1964) 247-276, especially 272 ff. Cf. also J. A. Stewart, *Notes on the Nicomachean Ethics* (Oxford, 1892) I, 20 ff.

[57] *Pol.* III, 3, 1278 a 2-3.

humans, even though their existence and activity is an indispensable precondition of a truly human life, are not to be deemed "men" in the full sense of the term.

In view of the involvement in and esteem for the political life characteristic of the citizens of the πόλις, the philosophers could not expect that they would agree with the apolitical ideal of a contemplative life. Most of Aristotle's arguments for the supremacy of contemplative life have to be understood against this background. In the context of ancient Greece, the superiority of the contemplative life could be defended only by arguing that it is the *activity* of the best part of us, the νοῦς, and that it is therefore an activity in accordance with the highest virtue;[58] to justify contemplation as an ἀπρακτεῖν, or *inaction*, seemed utterly impossible to Aristotle.[59] Contemplation had to be an activity transcending "political life" almost to the same degree as politics transcended all activities concerned with the necessities of life; whatever constituted the supremacy of "political life" over the ἔργα ἀναγκαῖα had to be found in "contemplative life" as well, and to a higher degree.[60] For example, contemplation had to be described as less tiring and therefore more "continuous" than politics: no one could be expected to till the ground as intensively and incessantly as he discussed and argued at the Assembly; but contemplation could be carried on even more continuously. Or again, contemplation was an activity least similar to and least involved with activities related to the necessities of life: while certainly both the philosopher and the political man required the necessities of life, the philosopher, unlike the politician, did not need other men and therefore was the least dependent of all—the man most sufficient in himself (αὐταρκέστατος). Or again, politics presupposed leisure from the procurement of the necessities of life.[61] Already Plato had said that

---

[58] *Nic. Eth.* X, 7, 1177 a 12 ff.

[59] Cf. *Pol.* VII, 3, 1325 a 31 ff.

[60] For the rest of the paragraph see *Nic. Eth.* X, 7, 1177 a 27 to b 26.

[61] Even though the expression 'σχολή' usually referred to freedom from political activities (cf. Arendt, 303), Aristotle often uses it as referring to a

a business is not disposed to wait until the businessman is at leisure;[62] Aristotle had no difficulty in convincing his hearers that political business was at least as unleisured as menial occupations. In any case, contemplation certainly required a greater leisure than politics.

In short, the argument of the philosophers consisted in saying that all positive aspects of politics—that it was an activity relatively free from fatigue, an activity entailing independence and leisure, and thus a free activity—were found in contemplation as well, and that they were found in contemplation in a significantly superior way. In addition to that, in contemplation man succeeded in actualizing that wich has most divine within himself—a virtue of the νοῦς.[63] Even though it seemed small in bulk, such a virtue surpassed all other human perfections both in power and in worth. As Aristotle explained in one of his biological writings, man was the only animal to whose share had fallen a "good life" as opposed to mere "life"; and this share had fallen to man because he alone of all animals partook of the divine.[64] Yet of all man's faculties certainly the νοῦς was the most divine; in fact, this part of man was so divine that it had to be considered as entering man from outside (θύραθεν) and thus as being a direct participation in God. The vegetative as well as the nutritive and sensitive part of the soul came into being in the embryo without existing previously outside it, but the νοῦς entered the soul from outside, thus granting to man a kind of activity which had no connection with the activities of the body.[65]

---

freedom from activities concerned with the necessities of life, e.g., 1334 a 13 ff., 1329 a 1 ff.

[62] Cf. *Rep.* 370 B-C: τὸ πραττόμενον ... τοῦ πράττοντος. That Aristotle had no difficulty in saying, on the one hand, that contemplation is an activity and, on the other hand, that it is completely leisured, may be due to the circumstance that the Greek language expresses 'to be leisured' as an activity: 'σχολὴν ἄγειν.'

[63] *Nic. Eth.* X, 7, 1177 a 15-16.

[64] *De part. an.* II, 10, 656 a 5-8.

[65] *De gen. an.* II, 3, 736 b 5-29. For an analysis of this difficult passage see M. de Corte, *La doctrine de l'intelligence chez Aristote* (Paris, 1934) 286 ff.

At this point it becomes obvious that we also have to *qualify* our earlier statement that to the Greeks the distinction between the "theoretical" and the "practical" was only a distinction between two kinds of life. For as soon as the various walks of life were related to various parts of man's composite nature, the "theoretical" and the "practical" almost inevitably came to be considered as two *dimensions* in the existence of each and every man. Plato, it is true, had related the various walks of life to different parts of the soul without, thereby, at all abandoning his notion that the walks of life are strictly incompatible. In fact, it almost seems as if by relating the walks of life to parts of the soul he wanted to substantiate his idea of the *incompatibility* of the walks of life. Thus, for example, in the *Republic* the identification of the lover of wisdom, the lover of honor, and the lover of gain, with reason, the heart, and appetite, respectively,[66] seems precisely to aim at showing that each man's life is ruled by one of the human faculties, it being presupposed that the question as to *which* faculty is the ruling one is predetermined by man's birth.[67]

Aristotle, however, beginning with his early dialogue *Protrepticus*, seems to have mainly been interested in showing that philosophic knowledge can be *acquired*, that one can *become* a philosopher. Contrary to the unknown author of the postscript to Plato's *Laws*, who argued that wisdom (which, incidentally, later turns out to be astronomy) is reserved to a very few special persons,[68] Aristotle from the very beginning of his career seems to have been convinced that virtually any man was capable of embracing philosophy and philosophic life.

But as soon as one begins to write a hortatory essay inviting others to philosophize and thus to become philosophers (and Aristotle's *Protrepticus* obviously was such an essay), as soon as one begins to argue that there is a sense in which no one who wishes to be a man properly speaking can avoid being a philos-

---

[66] Especially 580 E ff.
[67] Though not by his heredity; cf. Joly, 84 ff.
[68] Cf. *Rep.* 494 A: φιλόσοφον πλῆθος ἀδύνατον εἶναι.

opher (and Aristotle in the *Protrepticus* seems to have claimed precisely this), it becomes impossible to think only of θεωρία and πρᾶξις as two distinct ways of life, not to speak of walks of life which are incompatible with each other. After all, Aristotle could not meaningfully argue that all citizens should abandon their political activities and become contemplators of truth, for this would have amounted to inviting the Greeks to let the πόλις fall apart. In other words, the idea that each walk of life is related to a particular part of the soul eventually resulted in the notion that the various walks of life are compatible, which, in turn, led to the conception that θεωρία and πρᾶξις are dimensions of human existence rather than realizable types of existing.

Thus, what originally was thought of as several distinct ways of life, each of which can be embodied by a human being, became a set of abstract ideals which no one truly could embody and in each of which, nevertheless, every man participated to some degree. The Pythagorean and Platonic notion of a "pure" philosopher, who in no way was a man of action or else was a politician by being a philosopher (like Socrates in the *Gorgias*[69] or the philosopher-king of the *Republic*), gradually gave way to the notion that a good politician could not avoid being a philosopher, and vice versa.

Thus, for example, in the *Nicomachean Ethics*, after having extolled contemplative life and shown that political life with all its virtues is not comparable with it, Aristotle explicitly acknowledges that even the philosopher, as a man living in a society with others, cannot avoid engaging in πρᾶξις.

Thus "theory" and "practice" became two dimensions or poles of human existence. But it is important to see in what this polarity ultimately consisted for the Greeks. It certainly was not an opposition between abstract knowledge and concrete application; nor was it an opposition between "theoretical" endeavors, such as science, and "lived life." Rather, it was an opposition (and tension) between what was strictly human

---

[69] 521 D, where Socrates claims to be the only Athenian practicing the true art of politics, indeed the only Athenian who presently practices politics at all.

and what was divine in man. When Aristotle extols contemplation, he speaks of an ἀθανατίζειν, a sort of active immortality; when he speaks of politics, he qualifies it by the verb 'ἀνθρω-πεύεσθαι,' which means "existing and acting as a man."[70] The politician is the truly human man, but man cannot restrict himself to being a mere man but rather "ought as far as possible to achieve immortality and do all that he may to live in accordance to what is highest in him."

Again, however, one has to be careful not to mistake the contrast between ἀθανατίζειν and ἀνθρωπεύεσθαι as a contrast between man's animal and his godlike features. For "existing and acting as a man" is nothing else but maintaining the precarious balance between the two extremes, man's animality and his divinity. When Aristotle discusses what he calls "bestiality," he hesitates on whether he should describe it as a vice or a subhuman character; but his reason for hesitating is by no means only the fact that a bestial character is rare among men, that it is found most frequently among barbarians, and that among men, properly speaking, it only occurs as a result of disease or mutilation. His central point would seem to be that just as bestiality is too much beneath man to be a vice in the proper sense of the term, the virtue opposed to bestiality is too much above man to be a virtue properly speaking. In fact, the "virtue" opposed to bestiality is without name, since it is only found in gods and demigods, to whom one ascribes an eternally perfect nature, not acquired dispositions.[71]

Thus to be a man is to be something in between wild beasts and gods. But to be a man is to be a "political animal"; thus politics is both *the* human activity and the activity which distinguishes man from animals and subhumans, and from the gods. A human being who by his nature, not solely by some chance, is outside the πόλις is either beneath or above man;[72] "a man

---

[70] ἀθανατίζειν, 1177 b 33 (cf. *Theaetetus* 176 A-B); ἀνθρωπεύεσθαι, 1178 b 7. On this point see J. v. d. Meulen, *Aristoteles—die Mitte in seinem Denken* (Meisenheim/Glan, 1951) 269 ff.

[71] *Magna Moralia* II, 5, 1200 b 8-19; *Nic. Eth.* VII, 1, 1145 a 18-32.

[72] *Pol.* I, 1, 1253 a 3-4.

incapable of entering into ("political") partnership or so sufficient in himself that he has no need to do so, is no part of the πόλις, like either a wild beast or a god."[73]

Only those humans who by their very nature are capable of being a μέρος πόλεως, a constitutive part of a "city-state," are men in the full sense of the term; this and nothing else is what Aristotle means by saying ὅτι ἄνθρωπος φύσει πολιτικὸν ζῷον ἐστί, that man is by nature a "political animal."[74] And if one remembers that for the Greeks the πόλις was neither a geographical, nor an economic, nor even a "social" unit, but a "political" unit defined in terms of the members which constituted it; if one notices Aristotle's argument that a collection of slaves would constitute a πόλις as little as a collection of "other animals"[75] and that "barbarians" are more slavelike (δουλικώτεροι) than Greeks[76] (indeed have the same nature as slaves[77]); if one observes, finally, that to the tillers of the ground, to craftsmen, and generally to all those who pursue menial occupations the honorary title of a "part of the πόλις" is denied, so that eventually only the military and deliberative classes really constitute the πόλις[78]

---

[73] *Ibid.* 27-29.

[74] *Ibid.* 2-3; cf. *Nic. Eth.* I, 7, 1097 b 11; IX, 9, 1169 b 18. However, it seems that H. Arendt somewhat overstates the point when she argues that for the Greeks "sociability" was something which man had in common with animals, while "politicality" stood in direct opposition to all "natural associations." Thus in the *Nic. Eth.* VII, 10, 1242 a 22-28, Aristotle relates man's being public to his being a household-maintaining animal, describing both features as distinctly human. Apart from this, the fact that Aristotle believed it important to stress that there is a basic difference between the πόλις and a household indicates that this was not a commonly accepted notion. In fact, the opening sentences of the *Politics* clearly are a polemic against Socrates as presented in Xenophon's *Oeconomicus*. In a sense, even for Aristotle "sociability" and "politicality" are not opposites at all; their mutual relationship is that between something imperfect and something perfect. On the other hand, however, Arendt certainly is right in stressing that in Aristotle the "social" is *outside* the "political" in the same way in which the ἀναγκαία are *outside* the εὖ ζῆν.

[75] *Pol.* III, 5, 1280 a 32 ff.

[76] *Pol.* III, 9, 1285 a 20 ff.

[77] *Pol.* I, 1, 1252 b 9; cf. 1255 b 29.

[78] *Pol.* VII, 8, 1329 a 35-39.

— then it becomes obvious that Aristotle wants to say that only active "citizens" arrive at full humanity, that is, are men.

Of course this statement requires some qualification at which we, however, can only hint. First of all, the fact that he considers only citizens as men does not mean that Aristotle was inclined to throw slaves, barbarians, and legally free hirelings into one pot. He was well aware of the difference between slaves and hired artisans; the former render menial services to individual citizens, while the latter may be said to serve the community;[79] the slavery of the former usually is one by nature, while the "limited slavery" of the artisan certainly is not one due to his very nature;[80] etc. He also was aware of the fact that the barbarians cannot without further ado be likened to slaves: even though he argues that Greece, because of its natural superiority, is capable of ruling all mankind,[81] he knew well that in their way the barbarians, too, were "free men."[82]   Secondly, one will have to distinguish what Aristotle says about the slave as well as the artisan *taken as such* from what he might have said, and in fact sometimes says, about the man who *happens* to be a slave or an artisan. His distinction between men who are slaves by their very nature and men who happen to be slaves is well known;[83] and in the *Nicomachean Ethics* there is a passage in which Aristotle says that even though there can be no friendship with a slave, since *as* slave he is only an "ensouled tool," there can very well be friendship with a slave in so far as he is a man—"for there seems to be something of justice involved in the relationship of every man to every other who is capable of participating in law and conventional agreements, and hence also friendship in so far as the other is a man."[84]   Indeed, even in relation to "natural slaves" the same Aristotle who likens the slaves to domestic animals[85] will point out that they differ from animals; for even

[79] *Pol.* III, 3, 1278 a 11-13.
[80] *Pol.* I, 5, 1260 a 41 ff.
[81] *Pol.* VII, 6, 1327 b 29 ff.
[82] *Pol.* I, 2, 1255 a 33 ff.
[83] *Ibid.* 1254 a 13 ff.
[84] *Nic. Eth.* VIII, 11, 1161 b 5-8.
[85] *Pol.* I, 2, 1254 b 26.

though the natural slave has as little λόγος as an animal, he at least apprehends it while animals are only subservient to impressions.[86] Finally, when Aristotle distinguishes men from animals, he does not mention man's "being a citizen"; rather, he mentions that man alone of all animals stands erect,[87] that he alone has hands which he can use at will as "talon, hoof or horn,"[88] and the like.

Yet in spite of all this the Greeks of the fourth and the third century B.C. still had a long way to go to reach what today is called "the idea of the unity of mankind." And the reason why they were so far removed from this idea, oddly enough, seems to have been their much praised insight that λόγον δὲ μόνον ἄνθρωπος ἔχει τῶν ζῴων, that man alone of the animals possesses λόγος, or, as it was later put, that man is an *animal rationale*.[89] For 'λόγος' to the Greeks certainly did not primarily refer to some "cognitive faculty"; it meant rationality as it expresses itself in articulate speech. And this rationality a Greek did not precisely see either in the slave or in the barbarian; rational and articulate speech for the Greek was embodied in politics—arguing and persuading one another and reaching rational decisions based on common agreement. Thus, what today seems to us a characteristic distinguishing the biological species "man" from all other animals, to the Greeks often amounted only to a distinction between the men who are capable of leading a truly human life and all the rest. Or, to put it another way, the distinction between those who *used* the λόγος and those who did *not use* it was more important than either the "virtual" possession of the λόγος by all men or the difference between men and animals.

But if what we are saying is true, if the Greeks identified "being a man" with "being a member of the πόλις" and only considered as true members of the political community those who actively

---

[86] *Ibid.* 22-24.

[87] See, e.g., *De part. an.* 653 a 30, 656 a 10, 662 b 20, 669 b 5, etc.

[88] *Ibid.* IV, 10, 687 b 1 ff.

[89] *Pol.* I, 1, 1253 a 10. Cf. H. C. Baldry, "The Idea of the Unity of Mankind," *Grecs et Barbares*, Fondation Hardt, Entretiens, VIII (Vandoeuvres-Genève, 1961) 169-195.

took part in its life, then the philosophers with their apolitical ideal obviously were and in any case felt themselves in conflict with the "human realm." We shall refrain from discussing the many conflicts, be they existential as in the case of Socrates or merely intellectual as in the case of Plato, which this situation inevitably produced. It must suffice here to point out that it was not a clash between two conceptions of what was truly human; rather, it was and was acknowledged to be a conflict between those who wished to remain human in the fullest sense of the term and the philosophers who strove for something which they knew was above man and who therefore considered themselves aliens among men. In the *Republic* Plato at one point gives a moving description of those who are likely to consort with philosophy: a few noble persons who are overtaken by exile, or scorn and disregard the parochial affairs of their πόλις, or are too infirm to take part in politics. The philosopher is like one who, in the midst of the madness of the multitude which itself is like a storm cf dust and sleet, retires under a shelter; for he has realized that there is nothing sound in what the πόλις does.[90] Of course, as far as Plato is concerned, one might always point out that he had a complex about his not having participated and later not being able actively to participate in politics. But even Aristotle once describes the life of the philosopher as a βίος ξενικός, the life of an alien who detaches himself from the κοινωνία,[91] the partnership which Aristotle himself had elaborated as the realm in which man achieves his humanity. It certainly is not by chance that the main interlocutor of the three late Platonic dialogues, which take up the philosopher's relationship to the πόλις, is both a "stranger" and a "divine man."[92] The philosopher was a "stranger among men." *Qua* philosopher, he

---

[90] *Rep.* 496 B ff.

[91] *Pol.* VII, 2, 1324 a 16.

[92] In the *Sophist*, which begins by discussing the difference between the sophist, the statesman, and the philosopher, the stranger is first suspected to be a god and then declared to be divine, since he is a philosopher (216 A-D). The *Politicus* proceeds from the same problem and the "stranger," in all likelihood, is identical with that in the *Sophist*; in the *Laws*, the "stranger" is said to be named after the goddess Athene, since he reduces arguments to their principles (626 D).

felt himself closer to the divine than to his politically minded
fellow men, and the latter quite naturally reciprocated by considering him either a madman or an egoist.

At the same time, however, the philosopher could not avoid
being a man who lived in a society with others. Both Plato and
Aristotle realized this. Yet while Plato suffered from this insight
and considered his remaining among men a mission and a painful
duty, for Aristotle it was already obvious that, duty or no duty,
the incompleteness of contemplative life was rooted in the philosopher's very human nature. "Theory" and "practice," philosophy
and politics, no longer were separable simply because the philosopher was a man, and a man had to remain in the public realm
even though, *qua* philosopher, he strived for something radically
transcending the political order and thus the human level.

To later Greek philosophers this unity of "theory" and "practice"
will be so obvious that instead of proclaiming the absolute superiority
of contemplative life they will support the ideal of a life composed
of both philosophy and politics. A passage in Arius Didymus,
an eclectic who lived two centuries after Aristotle and of whose
synopsis of Peripatetic ethics a few fragments have been handed
down to us by Stobaeus, illustrates this development better than
any interpretation:

> The wise man will choose a life in accordance with virtue, be
> it that, by favor of circumstances, he has become ruler, or that
> he has to live at the court of a king, or is making laws, or is
> politically active in some other way. If none of these possibilities
> offer themselves to him, he will retire to private life and either
> contemplate or, going midway, teach. He will like both to act
> and to contemplate things beautiful. And if the circumstances
> prevent him from doing both, he will take one—preferring con-
> templation but, because of the common link (διὰ τὸ κοινωνικὸν),
> pressing for political actions. This [namely, the common link]
> is also the reason why he will marry, produce children, do politics,
> like temperate love, occasionally get himself drunk without
> previously having decided to do it, and, in general, be virtuous
> and nevertheless remain in this life .... There are three types
> of life: one practical, another theoretical, and still another
> composed of both. The life of enjoyment is beneath men and
> contemplative life is preferable to all other lives. But the wise
> man also will do politics, having decided so in advance and

not only in critical times; for practical life is the same as political life. The best life is a life in accordance with virtue in the midst of natural things (ἔν τοῖς κατὰ φύσιν).[93]

In Roman philosophers such as Seneca and Cicero this doctrine will be repeated with explicit references both to Aristotle and to human nature. Thus, for example, Seneca writes in his dialogue *De otio*: "The supreme good is to live in accordance with nature; and nature has made us both for the contemplation of things and for action." And again: "Thus I live in accordance with nature ... but nature wants me to do both, to act as well as to contemplate. Thus I do both, in particular, since there is no contemplation without action."[94] And Cicero, in his *De finibus*, which contains some of antiquity's most explicit statements about the "theoretical ideal," writes: "just as it has made the horse for racing, the ox for tilling, and the dog for hunting, nature has made man for two things, as Aristotle says, for thinking and acting—as if man were a mortal god."[95]

---

[93] Stobaeus, *Eclogues* II, p. 143 ff. We are translating from the text as quoted in Joly, 148 ff.

[94] *De otio* V, 1 and 8.

[95] *De finibus* II, 13, 40. The phrase *quasi mortalem deum* goes back to Aristotle, *Protrept*. Fr. 10 c Walzer.

3: "THINKING AND ACTING"

Up to now, our discussion of the Greek understanding of "theory" and "practice" centered around the meaning of the two expressions 'θεωρία' and 'πρᾶξις.' But there is also another context in which we might want to seek an understanding of the Greek origins of the distinction between "theory" and "practice," namely the relationship between thinking, on the one hand, and "making," "doing," and also "lived life," on the other hand.

However, we must emphasize once more that in this case we will no longer contrast that which the Greeks used to distinguish as θεωρία and πρᾶξις. For the relationship between θεωρία and πρᾶξις, as the Greeks understood these terms, was precisely not that between abstract ideas and their concrete application or realization. Rather, as we saw in the previous chapter, it was a relationship between two activities which constituted two distinct walks of life and which since Aristotle were considered as expressive of two levels of human existence. Yet even apart from this, when Aristotle speaks of a διάνοια or ἐπιστήμη θεωρητική, of "theoretical" thinking or knowledge, he has in mind precisely that kind of thinking which is not concerned with the doable or makable and which therefore cannot meaningfully be contrasted either with "doing" or with "making." For the Greeks θεωρία was opposed to political life and its activities, and "theoretical knowledge" was opposed *to other kinds of knowledge*, not to "doing" or "making."

Following an idea which probably goes back to Plato,[96] Aristotle several times distinguishes between three kinds of thinking or knowledge: "theoretical," "practical," and "productive." While theoretical knowledge is concerned with things which cannot be otherwise than in fact what they are, both practical and productive knowledge are concerned with things dependent on man's "doing" and "making," respectively. Practical knowledge is concerned with human actions which, both for their coming to be and with respect to their distinctive character, depend upon deliberate choice; productive knowledge is concerned with artifacts which depend upon human "art."[97] Accordingly, theoretical knowledge is a complete end in itself; it is pursued for its own sake; it aims at truth alone and has no obvious relationship either to "doing" or to "making"; it is right or wrong according to whether it is true or false. Practical knowledge, on the contrary, aims at "practical truth," that is, at conclusions whose sole purpose is to guide human actions; it is right or wrong according to whether it succeeds or fails in leading man to true "happiness." *Mutatis mutandis*, the same applies to productive knowledge.

Thus the only opposition found for the Greeks is that between the knowledge which a cultured and reflective politician, physician, or architect has with respect to his distinctive activities—and these activities themselves. And the knowledge of a politician, physician, or architect, taken as such, is not precisely "theoretical," since it is thoroughly ordered toward political activities, healing, or building. One might of course object that as it is the guiding principle of the philosopher's life, "theoretical knowledge" at least might be contrasted with the concrete life which the philosopher leads. But the Greeks probably would have answered that, strictly speaking, contemplation *is* the philosopher's life and that he performs other activities only in so far as he is also a politician, a physician, and, last but not least, a man.

But was not Aristotle aware of the fact that both practical and productive knowledge require some theoretical foundation? The

[96] Cf. Diog. Laertius, III, 84.
[97] *Met. E*, 1, 1025 b 18 ff.

answer to this question largely depends on whether one uses the expression 'theoretical' in its original Greek sense (= 'contemplation') or in the modern sense (= 'abstract'). For if the question had been, "Does not ethics, for example, entail some knowledge of what things are?", Aristotle probably would have answered affirmatively, even though he would have added that in this case the knowledge of the "what" only has the purpose of bringing about normative knowledge. But if the question had been, "Does not ethics entail some contemplation of eternal and unchanging realities?", Aristotle certainly would have answered in the negative. For neither the morality of human actions, which political science tries to uncover, nor the artifacts, which are the concern of productive knowledge, are eternal and unchanging; in fact, even their basic patterns are not unchanging and timeless.

This may sound surprising in view of the fact that Aristotle anticipates the notion of "natural law" by speaking of a "political justice" which is based on nature rather than on human conventions. However, he takes care to point out that 'natural' and 'unchanging' are not equivalent expressions; "for even things which exist by nature get their share of change."[99] The example which Aristotle uses to illustrate this point is quite revealing, since it indicates how far he was from identifying the "natural" foundation of ethics and politics with an unchanging "divine law": certainly our right hand is by nature stronger than our left hand, and still it is possible for any man to make himself ambidextrous. As the author of the *Magna Moralia* (either Aristotle himself or one of his immediate pupils) adds, to state this is not to deny that our being right-handed is by nature. It only amounts to saying that even that which is by nature only holds "for the most part and for the greater length of time."[100]

Let us pursue this question a little further. One might want to ask questions such as, Was not the Greek architect aware of the fact that his "art"[101] entailed a knowledge of mathematics, that is,

[99] *Nic. Eth.* VI, 2, 1139 a 27-28.
[99] *Magna Moralia* I, 33, 1194 b 32 ff.
[100] *Ibid.* 38. Cf. *Nic. Eth.* V, 7, 1134 b 18-35.
[101] For Aristotle's constant identification of "productive knowledge" and "art" see, e.g., *Met.* Θ, 2, 1046 b 3.

theoretical knowledge in the *Greek* sense? or the Greek physician, of the fact that his "art" entailed a great amount of knowledge of what Euripides had called the "ageless order of deathless Nature"?[102] The problem raised by these questions is of course far too complex and difficult to be discussed here in detail. We must restrict ourselves to three remarks.

First of all, it cannot be denied that at least as far as political action is concerned, both Plato and the young Aristotle[103] felt that the action of a perfect statesman is guided ultimately by his insight into eternal realities. Yet even apart from the fact that Aristotle soon abandoned this idea and that even Plato did not adhere to it consistently, one has to be careful not to mistake this conception for the claim that the ideal politician draws concrete political conclusions from abstract statements derived from the contemplation of eternal truths. Rather, what is meant here, is both much simpler and much more vague: the perfect statesman "imitates" the eternal in the sense that, being in contact with the divine, he simply and without further ado *knows* what ought to be done in each case. As Socrates puts it in the *Republic*[104]: in heaven there is set up a pattern of the ideal city which he who desires may behold and, beholding, may set his own house in order. The relationship involved here cannot possibly be reduced to that between abstract premises and concrete conclusions. It is the relationship between a man's being in contact with the divine and his almost instinctively doing what is right.

Secondly, it certainly is true that the Greeks occasionally were aware of the fact that the contemplative knowledge characteristic of the mathematician and the philosopher of nature is useful for productive knowledge. This is most obvious in the case of medical science (which, as it "produces" health, was taken to be a "productive" knowledge[105]). Cornelius Celsus, writing three centuries after

---

[102] Fr. 910 Nauck.

[103] Cf. *Protrept.* Fr. 13 Walzer.

[104] *Rep.* 592 B.

[105] Cf. *Nic. Eth.* I, 1, 1094 a 8 ff., where medicine is mentioned together with the "science" of shipbuilding, military sciences, and economics; *Met. Λ*, 4, 1070 b 33, mentioned together with the building arts; *Topics* VI, 5, 143 a 3:

Aristotle, tells us that originally the science of healing was held to be a part of philosophic wisdom, so that the treatment of disease and the contemplation of the nature of things began through the same authorities; and he adds that even after Hippocrates had separated medical science from the study of philosophy proper, that part of medicine which cures diseases by diet remained bound to a *naturae cognitio*, without which it seemed stunted and weak.[106] This notion is not an invention of a Roman living in the reign of the Emperor Tiberius. Already in his small treatise *On Breathing* Aristotle argued that "physicians of culture who really are interested in their work discourse to a certain extent about nature and claim to derive their principles from it, while the most refined among natural philosophers usually lead up to medical principles."[107] One of the oldest parts of the Hippocratic corpus, the treatise *On Decorum*, goes even further: the best physician is one who knows (natural) philosophy.[108] The relatively early Hippocratic treatise *On Airs, Waters, and Places*[109] even suggests a close connection between medical art and so "contemplative" a science as astronomy, since "with the seasons man's diseases, like their digestive organs, undergo change"— a statement which seems later to have induced some Greek theoreticians to consider medical science a part of mathematics.[110]

The connection with mathematics of production properly speaking, or technology as we would call it today, was somewhat less obvious to the Greeks. Of course the Greeks were aware of the distinction between "pure" and "applied" mathematics. Plato seems to have known of mathematicians who had recourse to mechanical devices for the solution of geometrical problems; according to Plutarch

ἰατρικὴ ... ὑγίειαν ποιῆσαι; *ibid.* I, 2, 101 b 6: medicine is likened to rhetorics, another "productive science."

[106] *De medecina,* prooem. 6-9.

[107] *De respir.* 21, 480 b 26-30. Cf. *De sensu* 1, 436 a 17 ff. On this whole point see W. A. Heidel, *The Heroic Age of Science* (Baltimore, 1935) 57 ff.

[108] Περὶ εὐσχημοσύνης V, 4 ff.

[109] Περὶ ἀερων ὑδάτων τόπων II, 24 ff.

[110] Cf. Proclus, *In I. Euclidis Elementorum librum commentarium,* prologus I, ed. Friedlein (1873) 38, 10 ff.

he accused them of corrupting the excellency of mathematics by turning back from intelligible to sensible realities and thus concerning themselves with things which required vulgar handicraft.[111] Aristotle several times distinguishes between mathematics and sciences such as optics, harmonics, and astronomy, which he describes as "the more physical among mathematical sciences."[112] Around the first century B.C. the Stoic philosopher and mathematician Geminus already made a clear-cut distinction between a kind of mathematics concerned only with contemplative objects obtained by the soul from itself and another kind of mathematics dealing with forms in matter and applied to sensible realities; the latter was said to consist of mechanics, astronomy, optics, geodesy, harmonics, and logistics, or the art of calculation.[113]

However, none of these types of applied mathematics was connected with the "making of things." The only possible exception was mechanics. For example, the law of the lever, which was discussed both by the Peripatetic school[114] and by Archimedes,[115] certainly was relevant to technology; in the fourth century A.D., Pappus of Alexandria mentions the art of lifting great weights by mechanical devices as one of the most important mechanical arts "useful in life." The various military engines devised by Archimedes[116] and later discussed by Greek "engineers" such as Hero of Alexandria and Philo of Byzantium and by Roman architects such as Vitruvius are further examples of applied mechanics.[117]

---

[111] Plutarch, *Marcellus* XIV, 5-6.

[112] τὰ φυσικώτερα τῶν μαθημάτων, *Phys.* II, 2, 194 a 7-8. Cf. the discussion in *Met. M*, 2.

[113] Proclus, *op. cit.* 38, 1 ff.

[114] *Mechanica* 3, 850 a 30 ff.

[115] *On the equilibrium of planes* I, 1-7. While Aristotle treats the problem in terms of the general laws of motion, Archimedes bases his deduction on assumptions concerning the equilibrium and the centers of gravity. In the late nineteenth century, there has been considerable discussion on the advantages and limitations of the two approaches.

[116] Cf. Plutarch, *Marcellus* XIV, 7 ff.; Ioh. Tzetzes, *Chiliades* II, 103-144.

[117] Cf. the texts collected and translated in M. I. Cohen and I. E. Drabkin, *A Source Book in Greek Science* (Harvard, 1958) 318 ff.

Still—and this is the third point which we wish to make—neither the physician's occasional use of natural philosophy nor the ingenuity of "engineers" applying mathematics and mechanics to the "making of things" seems to have been an occasion striking enough to make the Greeks truly aware of the importance of "contemplative thought," or science, for the "making of things." Most of the inventions of the "engineers" were little more than toys; one only has to think of the various gadgets invented by Hero of Alexandria, which include curiosities such as an altar, at the side of which figures offer libations when a fire is raised on it, or a temple whose doors open automatically when a fire is lit and shut again when the fire is extinguished. Even Pappus of Alexandria, who is often mentioned as a Greek who did not despise applied mechanics, mentions "the art of those who contrive marvelous devices" and the "art of the sphere makers ... (who) construct a model of the heaven (and operate it) with the help of the uniform circular motion of water" as a subdivision of the mechanical arts most necessary for the purposes of practical life.[118] The science of mirrors, or catoptrics, is described by Hero as a science worthy of study, since it produces spectacles which excite wonder in the observer, for example, the view of one's own back. Even though they were usually interested in such inventions, the Greeks easily dismissed them just as Aristotle once dismissed the rattle devised by Archytas, the great Pythagorean mathematician and contemporary of Plato: "a nice invention which people give to children in order that while occupied with this they may not break anything in the house."[119]

It is somewhat more difficult to explain the slight impact of the fact that "theoretical" knowledge of nature obviously played an important part in Greek medicine. In a way, however, it is this instance more than any other which illustrates the feeling common to all Greeks and Romans, namely, that experience and skill are much more important in the realm of the practical and productive than the occasional usefulness of "theoretical knowledge." From about the middle of the third century B.C. the "empiricists" among

[118] *Mathematical Collection* VIII, 1 ff., ed. Hultsch 1022, 3 ff.
[119] *Pol.* VIII, 6, 1340 b 27-29.

the physicians contended that all inquiries about "hidden causes" and thus also all philosophical knowledge were superfluous as far as the art of healing was concerned.   And even though they were opposed by "dogmatists" who emphasized the relevance of philosophical theorizing to medicine, both sides probably would have agreed with Cornelius Celsus, who at one point argues that all theorizing should be rejected *non ab cognitione artificis sed ab ipsa arte*, from the practice of the art, although not necessarily from the practitioner's private studies.[120]

In short, what today we would call "applied science" was more or less unknown to the Greeks.   Either a knowledge was theoretical in the strong sense of the term, and then it was concerned with the universal and timeless and had no application to the realms of "doing" and "making"; or else it was applicable to "doing" and "making" and thus was not theoretical in any sense relevant to the Greek mind.   In fact, when a knowledge was applicable to "doing" and "making," it was not truly scientific; and in any case it was closer to everyday experience than to "contemplation." As Aristotle puts it in the *Posterior Analytics*,[121] the most essential character of truly scientific knowledge is the contemplation of the "why"; for Aristotle, and in fact for all Greeks, contemplation, "theory," the knowledge of the "why,"   and "science" in the true sense of the term, were only different facets of one and the same thing.   But what counted in practical and productive knowledge was the familiarity with the facts, or experience, not the "why."[122] Commenting on the *Nicomachean Ethics*, Thomas Aquinas was later to express this idea as follows:

> In moral inquiries, one has to take as one's starting point the fact that things are such and such. And this one learns by experience and habit .... And once the facts are manifest, a man, supposed to act, no longer really needs to know the "why." For a physician to heal it is enough to know that this herb helps against that disease. To know the "why" is required only for

[120] *De medecina* I, 74.
[121] *Anal. post.* I, 14, 79 a 29.
[122] Cf. *Nic. Eth.* I, 2, 1095 b 7.

knowledge in the strong sense of the term which mainly is intended by speculative sciences.[123]

It is true of course that Aristotle, and with him all Greeks, did not adhere to this conception consistently. Seneca once writes that *quaedam moralibus rationalia immixta sunt*, some theoretical elements are included in moral issues;[124] though he never explicitly admits it, Aristotle certainly discusses ethical and political issues often as if it was meaningful to know the "why" after all; and the author of the pseudo-Aristotelian *Mechanics*, who even writes that "by art we prevail where we are vanquished by nature,"[125] certainly seems to have been aware of the fact that productive knowledge leads to success only if one knows the "causes."

Still, the Greeks and later the Romans stuck to this conception consistently enough to make it rather difficult for us to discuss the relationship between "practical and productive knowledge," as they understood it, and "doing and making" in terms of the notions of "theory" and "practice." For, in a sense the most significant thing that can be said about the Greek treatment of the relationship between thought relevant to action and action itself is that it cannot truly be subsumed under the heading "theory and practice." Productive knowledge to the Greeks was certainly not "applicable theoretical thought." The ease with which Aristotle time and again identifies productive knowledge with art, and art with the skill of an experienced artisan, indicates how misleading it would be to view productive knowledge in this way. In the end this kind of knowledge is little more than accumulated experience based on past "making," either one's own or that of others, which is sufficiently articulate to be useful to further "making." The same applies to practical knowledge, though to a somewhat lesser degree. When, in the *Metaphysics*[126] Aristotle states that in regard to action men with experience succeed better than those who have a "λόγος without experience," he certainly has in mind the politician

---

[123] *In I. Eth. Nic.* 4, 53 ff., Spiazzi.
[124] *Epist. morales* 102, 4.
[125] *Mech.* 847 a 11-21.
[126] *Met. A*, 1, 981 a 14 ff.

as well as the artisan. And one only has to remind oneself of the
fact that ethics and politics for Aristotle is a knowledge oriented
almost exclusively toward action, in order to realize immediately
that the moral philosophy in question is not an abstract normative
science but rather a reasoned articulation of experience sufficient
to serve as a guide in the realm of "doing."

One might of course proceed to ask why the Greeks did not
discover what today we would call "abstract but applicable theory."
As far as ethics and politics is concerned, it would seem fair to
suggest that the Greeks did not discover it because it does not exist;
the belief that such a theory is possible and that man would be
better off if it existed would seem to be one of the great confusions
of modern times. Yet quite apart from that, it would appear that
the Greeks argued for an atheoretical practical and productive
knowledge because they viewed productive knowledge from the
point of view of a moral and political knowledge in which "theory"
is out of place, just as later ages were inclined to look at ethics and
politics from the point of view of a productive knowledge literally
impregnated by "theory." It was the pre-eminence of moral and
political life, with only a pure θεωρία reaching beyond it, which
prevented the Greeks from taking seriously the notion, later so
prominent, of a "theory" which is the essential element of a progressive "practice." For in the realm of ethics and politics properly
speaking, such a "theory" does not exist; in any case the Greeks
did not feel that it existed.

We may conclude this section by pointing out that in spite of
all this neither the notion of progress nor the notion of a collaboration necessary to further progresss was wholly absent among the
ancients.[127] Already in the sixth century B.C. Xenophanes seems
to have argued that the gods certainly did not reveal everything
to mortals from the very beginning, but inquiring mortals themselves gradually have to discover what is best for them.[128] By

[127] For the following, as well as some of the preceding references, see L. Edel-
stein, "Recent Trends in the Interpretation of Ancient Science," *Journal of
the History of Ideas* 13 (1952) 5˜3-604; *idem*, "Motives and Incentives for Science
in Antiquity," *Scientific Change*, ed. A. C. Crombie (London, 1963) 15-41.
[128] Fragm. 21 B 18 Diels-Kranz.

the times of Plato and Aristotle this notion of a gradual progress due to the collaboration of many seems to have been quite generally accepted; Aristotle's "historical" introductions to many of his works obviously arose out of his conviction that it is meaningful to investigate what predecessors did well and where they committed errors in order to learn from them and then to proceed to further discoveries. Sometime in the third century Philo of Byzantium uses a phrase which indicates that "engineers" were well aware of such a progress and even reflected upon its causes; discussing the importance for artillery of adequately determining the diameter of the bore, he writes that "the ancients did not succeed in determining this magnitude by test, because their trials were not conducted on the basis of many different types of performance, but merely in connection with performance needed at the time. But the engineers who came later, noting the errors of their predecessors and the results of subsequent experiments, reduced the principle of construction to a single basic element."[129] As if to anticipate the modern claim that only Greek practitioners, not the scientists, were aware of progress and its necessity, Archimedes writes around the same time that he is explaining his "method" because "I apprehend that some, either of my contemporaries or of my successors, will, by means of the method when once established, be able to discover other theorems in addition, which have not yet occurred to me." And three centuries later, in words which are still timely, Seneca describes science as a patrimony left to us by earlier generations, which we administer and should leave enriched to those who come after us:

> There will arrive a time, where the day and the diligence of a later age will bring to light those things which now are still hidden. Even if we would study the heavens exclusively, the span of one human life could not possibly suffice to exhaust such an immense subject. We unequally divide the few years at our disposal between study and vice. Thus, such questions can be solved only by a long succession of researchers. A time will come, when our descendants will wonder how it was possible that we ignored so many of the things which to them are

[129] Cf. M. I. Cohen and I. E. Drabkin, *A Source book*, etc., 318.

obvious .... How many animals have we only just discovered!
And how many things have we still not discovered at all! The
people of coming ages will know many things which we do not
know; many discoveries are reserved to future ages when we
no longer shall be remembered. In fact, the world would be a
poor wretched thing if all future ages did not find it a subject
of research .... Thus we have to be indulgent toward the ancients.
Nothing is perfect from the very beginning.[130]

[130] *Naturales quaestiones* VII, 24 ff.; 30, 5; VI, 5.

4: THEORY AND CONTEMPLATION

A reader familiar with Greek and Roman philosophy will certainly agree that almost any of the several themes which up to now we have touched upon might be supplemented by details, some of which would probably force us to correct our analyses as far as a number of individual thinkers or even certain philosophical schools are concerned. Thus, for example, we said nothing about the Stoics, who were rather reluctant to subscribe to the absolute priority of contemplative life and in whom θεωρία became a wisdom which centered around practical behavior in everyday life rather than the contemplation of eternal realities. Nor did we say anything about the Epicureans, the only Greek philosophical school which opposed active participation in politics and therefore usually was accused of defending a base hedonism, even though their ideal seems to have been a relatively ascetic life of moral and aesthetic studies rather than an ordinary life of enjoyment.

However, as we stated at the outset, in this introduction we can dwell only on the major turning points in the development of the notions of "theory" and "practice." Accordingly we shall restrict ourselves to register the radical change which was initiated by Neoplatonism sometime between the second and the fourth century A.D. The fact that Plotinus has been chosen to illustrate this change is not intended to suggest that it is due only to this greatest of all Greek thinkers after Aristotle. Not everything in Plotinus is thoroughly original; in fact, Plotinus himself was accused of plagiarism while he still was alive.[131] Furthermore, the changes

---

[131] Cf. Porphyrius, *Vita Plotini* 17 ff.

which we have in mind cannot be explained by philosophical ideas alone; as we shall see, they are just as much due to socio-political developments. But they are more obvious in Plotinus than in other Neoplatonics before him or, for that matter, several centuries after him.

The two major changes which we wish to discuss here may be summed up as follows. First, Neoplatonism discovered a new kind of contemplative knowledge, and this discovery resulted in the separation, more or less explicit, of "theoretical thought" from contemplation proper. Secondly, the discovery of a previously unknown kind of θεωρία resulted in such a major degradation of political life that it ceased to be considered as meaningful in its own right and became a life of catharsis that prepared man for the ecstatic union with the Absolute. For the sake of clarity we shall discuss these two changes separately, even though they obviously are closely connected.

The reader may have noticed that up to now much of what was said about the Greek notion of θεωρία was encumbered by a curious sort of ambiguity. On the one hand, we said that the expression θεωρία originally meant "watching" and that the Greek philosophers used it to refer to a *contemplation* of whatever they considered unchanging and eternal, and therefore divine. On the other hand, we saw that mathematics, astronomy, philosophy of nature, and even mechanics, were instances of a θεωρία so understood. The ambiguity which we have in mind is not concerned with the fact that much of what the Greeks considered an object of θεωρεῖν we no longer view as eternal and unchanging, not to mention divine. What we have in mind is the fact that in the Greek notion of θεωρία there is no distinction between the intuitive gazing which today we would associate with the expression 'contemplation' and the discursive "theorizing" connected with "scientific" endeavors.

It is of course true that thinkers such as Aristotle were fully aware of the fact that philosophy of nature and mathematics, and also "First Philosophy," are a predicative as well as discursive "knowing about" rather than an immediate vision. But the ease with which Aristotle and others continued to use the expression θεωρία would seem to indicate that the distinction between an intuitive vision, or contemplation, and a discursive theorizing was not as obvious to them as it today is obvious to us. At first sight it is not easy to decide whether they lacked a clear notion of theoretical thought and therefore identified it with contemplation more easily than we do, or whether they lacked a clear insight into the nature of contemplative gazing and therefore tended to confuse it with theorizing. But it certainly is worth noticing that "contemplation" and "theory" did not become clearly distinct until Neoplatonism introduced the notion of a contemplative union with a strictly transcendent Absolute.

In addition to the ambiguity just mentioned there is a further and related ambiguity. Earlier, when speaking about the original meaning of '$\theta\varepsilon\omega\varrho\acute{\iota}\alpha$,' we intimated that this expression had something of a religious connotation. However, it is very difficult to say exactly what this means. Most authors, when asked what they mean by saying that the $\theta\varepsilon\omega\varrho\acute{\iota}\alpha$ of the Greeks had a religious connotation, probably would reply that the object of this "activity" was believed to be something divine and that therefore the "watching" in question was accompanied by an awe which today is usually associated with activities other than profane. This certainly is true. But what did the Greeks mean by saying that $\theta\varepsilon\omega\varrho\acute{\iota}\alpha$ was concerned with the divine?

The problem emerges quite clearly in Plato. Certainly we find in Plato the idea that philosophy aims at God.[132] Contemplative wisdom is even described as a sort of rapture, as when Socrates suddenly stops in the middle of the market place and, thinking about something which he cannot resolve, remains standing for a full twenty-four hours, surrounded by his puzzled fellow citizens.[133] Elsewhere this kind of rapture is said to arrive suddenly, like lightning, even though it presupposes a long and laborious process of self-purification and elevation; and it is suggested that in such a rapture man becomes possessed by the contemplated object instead of taking it into his possession—as if contemplative wisdom were

[132] E. g. *Theaetetus* 176 A ff.
[133] Cf. *Symposium* 220 C.

a madness[134] comparable to the inspiration which a poet receives from a deity.[135]

All this would seem to suggest that in Plato philosophic contemplation is something very close to an immediate experience of God. And yet one remains sceptical as to whether all this may be described as a religious experience in the strict sense of the term. For what is Plato's God? 'Divine' in Plato would seem to be only a predicate of all truly intelligible and unchanging realities, of the ideas; only in terms of these ideas is Plato's God what in fact he is.[136] And just as his God is nothing more than an epiphenomenon of the intelligibility with which the philosopher or "scientist" is concerned, this contemplative wisdom and its rapturous character would seem to be nothing more than a concomitant symptom of a knowledge not yet distinctly "theoretical," but certainly closer to "science" than to what today we would call "contemplation."

As for Aristotle, his God cannot be described as a mere epiphenomenon of intelligibility, it is true. While the Platonic God is a dimension of the realm of the intelligibles, which themselves are nothing but "formal causes" of reality, Aristotle's God is clearly an ἀρχὴ τῆς κινήσεως, a cause of change, and therefore unambiguously a subsistent entity; that the causality of this God is due to his being desired rather than to his being an efficient cause in the strict sense is here of little importance. The θεωρία concerned with this God is clearly a "knowledge about," not a mere "watching"; Aristotle explicitly states that man cannot contemplate without sensible images. But the fact that Aristotle does not conclude that therefore God cannot possibly be an object of contemplation again indicates that he does not have a clear-cut distinction between "contemplating" and "theorizing."

Finally, in the Stoics as well as in their Roman followers such as Cicero and Seneca θεωρία became a wisdom which was practical rather than "theoretical" or even "contemplative." The "logical life" which the Stoics are said[137] to have preferred both to the

---

134 E.g., *Phaedrus* 249 D ff.
135 Cf. *Ion* 534 B.
136 Cf. *Phaedrus* 249 C.
137 Diog. Laert. VII, 130.

strictly "theoretical" and to the merely "practical" life, and which was virtuous life by being in conformity with nature, no longer permitted a θεωρία in the sense, both pretentious and ambiguous, of earlier Greek thinkers. It is true that this "logical life" was said to entail both θεωρία and πρᾶξις, and thus was similar to the 'mixed life' of the Peripatetics. But as the emphasis was on the "practical," the θεωρία of the Stoics was little more than the knowledge required for the κατὰ φύσιν ζῆν, the life according to nature; it was reasonable thinking rather than either contemplation or "theory." In fact, except for logic and the study of nature the Stoics no longer were interested in the intelligible order, and even their study of nature was not an end in itself—it was only pursued in so far as it was relevant to living a life in accordance with nature. "The virtuous man is both theoretical and practical with respect to things to be done (τῶν ποιητέων)," as Diogenes Laertius sums up the Stoic position.[138] Cicero repeats the same doctrine when, following Chrysippus, he writes that man is born to contemplate and to imitate the world; the prime purpose of θεωρία is to imitate nature, that is, to lead a life in accordance with it.[139] And when Seneca writes that the Aristotelian tripartition of lives is artificial since it is impossible to pursue pleasure or to act *sine contemplatione*, just as it is impossible to contemplate *sine voluptate* and *sine actione*, the expression 'contemplation' seems to mean little else than the thinking characteristic of a cultured and virtuous man.[140]

In short, it was not until Plotinus used 'θεωρία' to refer to an intuitive union with an absolutely transcendent God that contemplation and "theorizing" became clearly distinct. Unfortunately we have to refrain from discussing the details of Plotinus' very complex notion of the relationship between θεωρία and πρᾶξις;[141] nor can we discuss here the almost mystic and, in any case, definitely ecstatic connotations of 'θεωρεῖν' in this great metaphy-

---

[138] *Ibid.* 126.

[139] *De natura deorum* II, 14, 17: "Ipse autem homo ortus est ad mundum contemplandum et immitandum."

[140] *De otio* VII, cf. Joly, 168.

[141] See R. Arnou, Θεωρία et Πρᾶξις. *Une étude de détail sur le vocabulaire et la pensée des Ennéades de Plotin* (Paris, 1921).

sician.[142] It must suffice to point out that it was in Plotinus that
the momentous separation of contemplation from "theorizing"
occurred.

Certainly, Plotinus still describes the vision of the One as γνῶσις,
knowledge. But this knowledge is clearly not Aristotle's ἐπιστήμη
θεωρητική. It is a contact far more immediate than any ἐπιστήμη
ever could achieve, and in fact it can be reached only by transcending
and even abandoning all ἐπιστήμη. Compared to this union which
Plotinus describes as "contemplation," "vision," a "seeing in which
nothing is seen," a "touching (ἐπαφή)," or simply a "presence," all
theoretical "knowing about" is only a means. The following passage
from the sixth *Ennead* illustrates this break-through of *pure* contemplation and the ensuing profanation of "theoretical knowledge":

> One cannot become aware of the One by scientific knowledge
> (ἐπιστήμη), in the way in which one reaches other intelligible
> realities by pure thought; rather, one only reaches it by an
> immediate presence (παρουσία) surpassing all scientific knowl-
> edge. When our soul acquires scientific knowledge, it deserts
> oneness and is not wholly one. For scientific knowledge is dis-
> cursive and conceptual (λόγος γὰρ ἡ ἐπιστήμη), and discourse
> and concept are a manifold (πολλὰ δὲ ὁ λόγος); thus the soul
> misses the One and plunges into number and multiplicity.
> Therefore it must transcend scientific knowledge, never abandon-
> ing the One; it must desert scientific knowledge as well as its
> object, indeed any other object of knowledge, be it ever so
> beautiful. For everything beautiful follows the One and derives
> from it like daylight from the sun. It is "neither to be spoken
> of nor to be written about," as he [Plato] says. We only speak
> and write about it in order to lead toward it, to awaken from
> discourse and concepts to vision—as if showing the way to
> those who desire to see.[143]

The distinction between θεωρία and λόγος, contemplation and
conceptual thought, which this passage suggests hardly requires
further explanation. To avoid misunderstanding, however, it may
be useful to emphasize that it has nothing to do with the distinction

---

[142] See the excellent summary in the *Dictionnaire de Spiritualité*, fascicules
14-15, pp. 1727-1738.

[143] *Enneads* VI, 9, 4, 24-26. The phrase "neither to be spoken of, etc." probably
refers to Plato's seventh letter, 341 C ff.

between a human operation and a "set of propositions" which is suggested by the two *English* expressions. Today when we speak of contemplation, we have in mind something which a man does or which, possibly, "happens to him"; while when we speak of science and, in particular, of a theory, we rather think of a result of some intellectual activities and, in any case, of a "noema" rather than a "noesis" (to use Husserl's terminology). Quite obviously Plotinus does not have in mind such a distinction between cognitive *activities* and their *noematic correlates*; in fact, though it was fore-shadowed by the Stoic notion of the λεκτόν, this distinction did not emerge clearly until about the fourteenth century. What Plotinus has in mind is the difference between two radically different types of intellectual activities: a knowledge which does not need to articulate itself into demonstrations and propositions, since it amounts to an immediate contact and union with its object; and another knowledge which, being predicative as well as discursive, never can measure up to the wealth and immediacy of a lived intellectual experience and in fact is likely to become an obstacle to it. This is particularly obvious from Plotinus' description of metaphysics, or, as he himself calls it, "dialectics." In terms if this metaphysics which is described by Plotinus as the ability to say about each thing what it is, the philosopher transcends the realm of sensible things and settles down among intelligible realities, working up to the First Principle. Once he has reached this First Principle, he rests; no longer busy about many things, he rests in unity and contemplates; all logic with its premises and syllogisms he leaves to others, even though acknowledging that much of it was a necessary means.[144]

It is easy to see why this new concept of a contemplative union with the Absolute resulted in a degradation of "political life." Compared to an encounter with God himself, all other walks of life necessarily appeared more or less insignificant. One therefore is not astonished to find in Plotinus a reinterpretation of Aristotle's tripartition of lives in which political life, instead of being a lower walk of the life characteristic of men of refinement, has become

[144] *Ibid.* I, 3, 4.

a higher type of the life characteristic of the many vulgar. While
in Aristotle contemplative and political life were truly perfect
lives sharply distint from the vulgar life of the multitude, in Plotinus
political life is almost as imperfect as the life of enjoyment and,
together with it, is opposed to the only life which is truly meaningful,
the life of contemplation. Thus in the second *Ennead* Plotinus
distinguishes between the life of the sage and two kinds of life
characteristic of the multitude. The sage is intent upon the "realm
above," while those in the crowd are either reminiscent of some
virtue and thus in some kind of contact with the Good, or else they
are mere populace whose only purpose is to provide more virtuous
men with what they need.[145]

   That Plotinus' life of the upper class of the multitude corresponds
to Aristotle's "political life" is easy to show; for example, whenever Plotinus speaks of the virtues of this class, he uses the expres-
sion '$\dot{\alpha}\varrho\varepsilon\tau\acute{\eta}$ $\pi o\lambda\iota\tau\iota\varkappa\acute{\eta}$,' 'political virtue.' While in Aristotle the
practical virtues of political life were a genuine alternative for
men of refinement (and later philosophers always argued that
even the philosopher has to acquire such virtues, that is, to engage
in politics), in Plotinus the political men have become an upper
class of the many vulgar to whom Aristotle had ascribed a life of
enjoyment, hardly different from that of cattle. More precisely,
while in Aristotle political life was a truly perfect life in its own
right, even though it did not attain to the ultimate perfection of
philosophizing, in Plotinus the same public life has become the
waiting room for those among the multitude who at least can
hope to reach true perfection. For according to Plotinus the purpose
of practical virtues is only to achieve the purification presupposed
by contemplation. Aristotle's virtues have ceased to be ends in
themselves and have become $\varkappa\alpha\vartheta\acute{\alpha}\varrho\sigma\varepsilon\iota\varsigma$, purifications; the only
purpose of practical life is to achieve the separation from the evil
of this world, a separation without which the union with the One
is unthinkable. As Plotinus puts it, referring to a passage in Plato's
Theaetetus[146]:

[145] *Ibid.* II, 9, 9.
[146] *Theaet.* 176 A ff.

Since "evil" is here in this world and "by necessity haunts this place," yet the soul desires to escape evil, "we must escape from here." But what is this escape? "To become like God," he says. And this we reach "by becoming just and holy and wise" and, in general, by acquiring virtue.... Yet in which sense do we call virtues purifications and how is it that we best become like God by purifying ourselves? Indeed, as the soul is evil by being involved with the body and therefore sharing its states and fancies, it is good and possessed by virtue if it does not share in the body's fancy but itself is the only actuality (this is understanding, νοεῖν, and thoughtfulness, φρονεῖν); if it does not share in its states (this is temperance, σωφρονεῖν); if it knows no fear at the parting of the body (this is courage); if λόγος and νοῦς rule without anything opposing them (and this is justice).[147]

The political dimension of ethics so characteristic of Aristotle has completely disappeared. All the practical virtues have lost their political connotation and become purifications helping to abandon the body and, by implication, the material world; insofar as they are *political* virtues, Plotinus puts them on the same level with the arts "concerned with material objects and making use of perceptible instruments."[148]

In the Neoplatonists after Plotinus, especially in Iamblichus and Proclus, this conception resulted in the outright tendency to identify political life with the life of enjoyment as well as in the notion that the life opposed to contemplation is a καθαρτική ζωή, a life of catharsis. Eventually the Aristotelian tripartition was replaced by a tripartition into "apolaustic," *or* practical, life; cathartic life; and the life of contemplation.[149] Nothing opposed to contemplation was any longer a perfection in its own right; only contemplative life truly counted and everything else was either its radical absence or a path leading toward it. Virtue and human perfection were now divorced from all sociopolitical context. The basic division no longer was that between citizens and non-citizens; what distinguished the "practically" virtuous man from

---

[147] *Enneads* I, 2, 1 and 3.
[148] *Ibid.* VI, 3, 16.
[149] Cf. Joly, 184 ff.

the vulgar mob was his proximity to contemplative life. He was
one of those in the mob who purified himself to become a sage.
And he purified himself by abstaining from passion, by turning
his back on the world, not by performing noble political deeds.

This Neoplatonic degradation of political life and practical
virtues, of course, was not due solely to the discovery of a quasi-
mystical union with the Absolute. It was also a reaction against
the exaltation of practical virtues by the Stoics, to whom Plotinus
often refers as those men who are not capable of seeing the things
above and therefore, "together with the expression 'virtue,'
fall back upon πρᾶξις, that is, upon the option of the things here
below from which at first they sought to escape."[150] Above all,
however, the Neoplatonic degradation of politics was due to the
fact that the πόλις, in which alone the ideal of political life was
meaningful, did not turn out to be as lasting as earlier thinkers
had believed.

Hannah Arendt has suggested that the philosophers' discovery
of a life of contemplation may have been helped by their "very
justified doubt of the chance of the *polis* for immortality or even
permanence."[151] Be that as it may, the gradual fading away of
the ideal of political life quite certainly was also due to the disappearance of the Greek πόλις and, later, of its Roman counterpart.
In a sense, even Aristotle's analyses of the πόλις bore already
the mark of unreality. For in spite of the fact that Athens was
still relatively independent in his time, the majority of the relatively small and self-contained city-states which had served as
Aristotle's model had already been incorporated into the growing
Macedonian Empire. Aristotle himself, living at the court of
Alexander the Great, spent his life in an environment in which
the direct participation in politics of the great majority of adult
citizens was already fiction rather than reality. Six hundred years
later, when Plotinus wrote his treatises and Proclus edited them,
such independent units in which everything was decided by citizens
no longer existed; they had long dissolved into the tight unity of

[150] *Enneads* V, 9, 1; cf. I, 4, 2.
[151] Arendt, 21.

the Roman Empire. Apart from that the social stratification had become infinitely more complex than it was at Plato's or Aristotle's time. Slaves became philosophers, men of the lowest origins became emperors, and some emperors, in turn, were philosophers. This does not mean to say that social classes no longer existed, but people moved much more easily and quickly from one social class to another, thus making it impossible to identify perfection and virtue with a definite social status and forcing the philosophers to develop a notion of virtue less related to public life.

5: CHRISTIANITY:
THE AMBIGUITIES OF ACTION

At first sight the message of the Gospel would seem to contain little to support the exaltation of theoretical endeavors and contemplative life found in the Ancients. For as far as man and his tasks are concerned, this message centers around loving forgiveness and charity, not contemplation. Yet to those whose mind had been formed by Greek thought and its Roman aftermath a number of statements in the Gospel appeared as a last articulation of Greek ideals. Had not Christ himself rebuked Martha for being angry with her sister, Mary, who only sat at the Lord's feet and lovingly followed each of his words? "Martha, Martha, you care and trouble about many things; but only one thing is necessary. Mary has chosen the better part which shall not be taken away from her" (Luke 10:41-42).

The first Christians to reflect explicitly on our problems were the third-century representatives of the Alexandrian school (Clement of Alexandria and Origen) and their fourth-century disciples and followers (in particular, Gregory of Nyssa). At first glance their analyses of "theory" and "practice" are only a slightly Christianized version of the Neoplatonic ideas sketched in the preceding chapter. All emphasize the superiority of a contemplative knowledge of God over a life of action, most of them are aware of the distinction between a pure contemplation of God and a theoretical "knowing about" other timeless realities, and all are inclined to believe that the main, if not the only, purpose of practice is to prepare man for a cognitive and eventually contemplative, even mystical, union with God. Clement of Alexandria, for example, time and again extols the perfections of a contemplative $\gamma\nu\tilde{\omega}\sigma\iota\varsigma$ $\tau o\tilde{\upsilon}$ $\Theta\epsilon o\tilde{\upsilon}$,

knowledge of God. At one point in his *Stromata* he even goes so far
as to say that if someone was to ask a Christian thinker whether
he prefers eternal salvation or knowledge of God, "and supposing
that the two were separable while in fact they are the same," the
Christian sage unhesitatingly would choose the latter.[152] Origen
repeats basically the same doctrine and for the first time introduces
the interpretation of the two sisters, Mary and Martha, as instances
of θεωρία and πρᾶξις.[153] Clement of Alexandria, even though
he usually tends to describe the contemplative knowledge of God
in such a way that it almost reminds one of a savant's scholarly
endeavor, on one occasion mentions a difference between θεωρία
and λόγος,[154] thus clearly anticipating the Plotinian distinction
mentioned earlier. In Gregory of Nyssa one already finds an emphatic distinction between two kinds of θεωρία, one corresponding
to Plotinus' "dialectics" and the other being an immediate "seeing
of God in the darkness."[155] Finally, as regards the relationship
between contemplative and active life all Greek Fathers of the
Church probably would have subscribed to Origen's statement
that the "active life is the stirrup to contemplation."[156]

However, if one looks closer, one soon discovers a quite important
shift of emphasis. For as much as the Alexandrian theologians
may have been engrossed in Greek ideals, the Gospel forced them
to abandon the basic notion of Greek philosophy, namely, that in
this world of ours man's ultimate perfection consists in cognitive
operations transcending and in a sense divorced from all interhuman
relationships. The statements of the Gospel simply were too explicit
to permit them without further ado to embrace the extreme in-

[152] *Stromata* IV, 22; *PG* VIII, 1348 A.

[153] *In Lucam fragmentum* 171, ed. M. Rauer, in Origines, *Die Homilien zu
Lukas, etc.* (Berlin, 1959) 298.

[154] *Stromata* V, 1; *PG* IX, 10 B. Cf. VII, 12, *ibid.* 499 A: "Just as death is a
separation of the soul from the body, so knowledge (γνῶσις) is like a death
of discursive thought (λογικὸς θάνατος), leading the soul away and separating
it from all change."

[155] See, in particular, the eleventh homily to the Song of Songs; *PG* XLIV,
1000 C-D; and *De vita Mosis, PG* XLIV, 328 ff.

[156] *In Lucam fragmenta*, ed. M. Rauer, in Origines, *Werke*, Vol. IX (Leipzig,
1930) 26 ff.

tellectualism of the pagans. After all, St. Paul had written that if he knew all secrets and had all knowledge, yet lacked charity, he would be worth nothing (I Cor. 13:2); and St. John had spelled out that the charity in question concerned one's relationship to other men (I John 2:9). Indeed, Christ himself had pointed out that the commandment to love one's neighbor resembles and is thus inseparable from the first and greatest of all commandments, to love God (Matthew 22:37-39).

It certainly was not easy to combine this unambiguous teaching of the Gospel with the Neoplatonic conception that all activities other than contemplation were nothing but "purifications." For statements such as those just referred to gave to certain types of action a weight which made it very difficult to consider them only a stirrup to knowledge. Certainly it is possible to say that all these actions were only a stirrup to a contemplation to be achieved and, in any case, completed in heaven. Yet as far as their life on earth was concerned, Christians had to admit that contemplation was not the only achievement expected from them; in fact, they had to admit that even if in principle contemplation was the greatest human achievement, a Christian sometimes had to give it up in order not to offend the Lord.

The Alexandrians, it is true, still tended to minimize this point.[157] Certainly Clement of Alexandria time and again stresses that the Christian's ultimate perfection consists in both ἔργα καὶ γνῶσις, in deeds and knowledge. But when it comes to saying what the deeds in question are, he restricts himself to mentioning the fulfilment of the commandments and missionary activities: "Our [Christian] philosopher shall strive for three things: first, contemplation; second, the fulfilment of the commandments; third, the instruction of good men. These three, when they meet, complete the Christian sage."[158] Still, even the simple fulfilment of the commandments entailed much more than Greek philosophers

[157] As far as the Alexandrians are concerned, see the studies by W. Völker: *Das Volkommenheitsideal des Origines* (Tübingen, 1931); *Der wahre Gnostiker nach Clemens Alexandrinus* (Berlin, 1952), especially 301 ff., 446 ff.; and *Gregor von Nyssa als Mystiker* (Wiesbaden, 1955).
[158] *Stromata* II, 10; *PG* VIII, 981 B.

had ever dreamt. Some of the commandments, it is true, could
be reduced to the Stoic and Neoplatonic ideal of a "want of passions
(ἀπάθεια)," which had been ascribed to Christ the Glorified from
the time of Ignatius of Antioch, was considered one of the basic
predicates of God since the apologists of the second century
(Justin, Athenagoras), and by the Alexandrians was extended
to the ideals of Christian life. Up to this point it was possible to
handle the notion of the active life in terms of the "catharsis"
of the Neoplatonics. Yet what about deeds of charity? Were
they not infinitely more than "purifications" preparing for the
knowledge of God?

Here begins to emerge what one might want to call the Christian
discovery of the ambiguities of "practice." How much of what
the Christian *did* was meaningful in itself and how much of it
was meaningful only with respect to a contemplation whose ultimate
completion could not possibly be achieved in this life? Was it
possible to say that *all* "practice" was only a ladder which eventually
the Christian would leave behind? Was it not inevitable to say
that at least in this life a number of actions were an integral part
of Christian perfection rather than only a step leading toward it?
Had not St. Paul intimated that of the perfections of Christian
life, charity was more than just a virtue of the age in which
the Christian speaks, knows, and thinks like an infant (I Cor.
13:11-13)?

In Clement of Alexandria the main function of Christian charity
still seems to be to free man from his commitment to the world;
as he once puts it, the Christian sage, loving "gnostically," rightly
remains in one and the same unchanging attitude.[159] Origen, too,
seems to think in a similar way: those committed to contemplation
are "in the house of God," while those committed to action are
still "in the courtyard of the house of our God."[160] At one point,
however, Origen already formulates an idea which shall be repeated
by St. Augustine and later will become common property of Christian
thought, namely, that most men have to restrict themselves to

---

[159] *Stromata* VI, 9; *PG* IX, 293 D ff.
[160] *In Ps.* 133; *PG* XII, 1652 C.

leading a life of "practice" and expect contemplation as the ultimate reward of afterlife:

> "The starting point of the good path is doing what is just" (Prov. 16:5). As the good path happens to be the longest, the dimension of doing (τὸ πρακτικόν) is among the first things to be grasped, as the words "doing what is just" indicate. As for contemplation (τὸ θεωρητικόν) which succeeds it, I believe it to be the end and completion of all doing in what is called the "ultimate restitution (ἀποκατάστασις)," since eventually not even one of the things inimical will be left.[161]

It is·in St. Augustine that this ambiguous character of Christian "practice," its standing midway between grievous purification and shining perfection, becomes most obvious. As H. Arendt has pointed out, this greatest of the Latin Fathers of the Church probably was the last to know at least what it once meant to be a member of a πόλις and thus to lead a "political life."[162] However, even though St. Augustine still knew of the political implications of the *vita actuosa* or *negotiosa*,[163] after his conversion to Christianity he was interested relatively little in this particular walk of life. As he himself indicates, he owed his knowledge of the (late Peripatetic) tripartition of the walks of life to M. Terrentius Varro, a learned contemporary of Cicero. But Varro's extended discussions of the value of each of the walks of life seemed to St. Augustine to miss the essential point: "A man can lead a life of faith in any of these three lives and reach the eternal rewards. What counts is whether he lovingly holds to truth and does what charity demands.

---

[161] *In Joan.* I, 16; *PG* XIV, 49 C. Cf. also the beautiful passage on the Lord's being both active and contemplative in Origen's second homily to the Song of Songs, 11; *PG* XIII, 56 C. The passage ends with the words: "Maybe my Savior is a roe with respect to θεωρία, a deer with respect to his works," the roe having been described as having keen sight, and the deer as killing serpents, the symbol of evil.

[162] Arendt, 15.

[163] *De civ. Dei* XIX, 2: "in contemplatione vel inquisitione veritatis otioso, altero in gerendis rebus humanis negotioso"; VIII, 4: "activa ad agendam vitam, id est, ad mores instituendos, pertinet." On the other hand, however, see XVIII, 37: "quae moralis vel activa dicitur." On St. Augustine's notion of moral philosophy see the excellent discussion in Th. Deman, *Le traitement scientifique de la morale chrétienne selon St. Augustin* (Montréal-Paris, 1957).

Indeed, one has to avoid being committed to leisurely life so as to give no thought to one's neighbor's needs as well as being so absorbed in action as to dispense with the contemplation of God."[164]

The fundamental difference between the classical Greek idea and the Christian notion of contemplative and active life could hardly be intimated in clearer terms. It no longer counts whether one is a philosopher, a politician, or a combination of both; what counts, regardless of one's walk of life, is the right balance between one's contemplative striving for God and one's actions of charity. Here, *vita activa* is no longer Aristotle's life of active participation in the life of the πόλις, nor is it simply the life of purification of the Neoplatonics. It has become a life of Christian charity.

But what exactly is the right balance between actions of charity and contemplation ? In a sense the answer given by St. Augustine is quite surprising. For he would seem to suggest that actions of charity are "necessities" comparable to the ἔργα ἀναγκαία which the Greeks had excluded from the ideal of a perfect life. In any case they are a *burden* in which no one possibly could see the end of his life and which nevertheless the Christian is expected willingly to accept:

> The love of truth seeks holy leisure; only the compulsion of charity (*necessitas charitatis*) shoulders equitable unleisure. If no such burden is placed on one's shoulder, time should be passed in study and contemplation; but once the burden is here, it should be carried because charity demands it (*propter charitatis necessitatem*). Yet it should not be carried in such a way as to lead to an abandonment of the delight in truth, for then the sweetness of the latter may be lost and the burden become overwhelming.[165]

In other words, actions of charity are a necessity imposed upon man; there is no reason to desire them for their own sake—and still they have to be carried without protest. That St. Augustine, when he wrote this, had in mind the whole realm of Christian deeds of charity, not only activities imposed by public office (as the context of the above quotation might suggest), becomes obvious

---

[164] *De civ. Dei* XIX, 19; *PL* XLI, 647.
[165] *Ibid.*

when one surveys his discussion of the two biblical sisters, Mary and Martha.[166] If it is true that Mary chose the role which never shall be taken away from her, then Martha, representing the life of active charity, obviously chose a part which eventually *will* be taken away from her. Indeed, what does Martha do? She attends to the Lord's bodily needs; she is the symbol of those who serve the "saints of God." Yet this kind of service will end one day. "Whom does she serve except weakness, except mortality, except those who have hunger and thirst? As soon as the perishable becomes imperishable and the mortal, immortal, all this will cease to exist. *Cum enim transierit ipsa necessitas, nullum erit minister-ium necessitatis*: all service out of necessity will disappear with necessity itself."[167] This of course does not mean that Martha's part is worthless. On the contrary, her activities are excellent: "we summon you to pursue them, in the name of the Lord we implore you not to be reluctant to serve the saints.... And still the part chosen by Mary is better. *Illud enim habet ex necessitate occupationem, istud autem ex charitate suavitatem*: Martha's doing is necessary while Mary's doing carries the sweetness of love."[168] In fact, the ultimate reason why Mary chose the better part is that she chose the role which no one ever will take away from her: her contemplation will grow and eventually find its completion in heaven. Martha's part, on the contrary, will be taken away from her; and her reward will be the contemplation with which Mary chose to begin. *Quod agebat Martha, ibi sumus, quod agebat Maria, hoc speramus*: while that which Mary did is what we hope for, Martha's doing is where we are now.[169]

Thus Mary is the fulfilment of Martha. And yet no Christian may abstain from following Martha whenever charity demands it. Charity forces the Christian to do things which he cannot regard as and which even seem to remove him from his ultimate end. On the other hand, however, the Christian may never follow Martha so as to abandon the ideal, Mary; for this would amount to succumb-

---

[166] See, in particular, *Sermones* 103, 104, and 179, 4 ff.
[167] *Sermo* 179, 4; *PL* XXXVIII, 963 ff.
[168] *Sermo* 103, 5; *ibid.* 615.
[169] *Sermo* 104, 4; *ibid.* 618.

ing to the world. Thus "we have to orient some part of our mind toward the handling of things bodily and changing without which this life of ours is impossible. Yet we should not do this so as to conform to the world. We never should see in worldly things the end of our life and deflect our desire for beatitude toward them. Whatever we do with respect to the temporal order, we should do it for the sake of eternal rewards, passing through the former and adhering to the latter."[170]

These ideas certainly are not ambiguous in the sense that one would not understand what St. Augustine means. Yet they surround the notion of "practice" with peculiar existential ambiguities unknown to the pagans. Even in this world, contemplation is man's greatest achievement, and yet charity may demand that one temporarily give it up. Actions are bitter necessity, and yet the Christian should pursue them without bitterness whenever charity demands it. Gone is the unambiguous superiority of contemplative over active life; gone is the notion that all necessary activities are beneath the freedom and dignity of a perfect life; gone, finally, is the notion that all human doing is either an activity thoroughly meaningful in itself or else only a "purification." For Christian deeds of charity serve a world which is not the Christian's homestead, and yet they have to be carried out almost as if they were the only thing which really counted.

Exactly how far, then, is the Christian supposed to serve the world of perishable reality? As far as charity demands it. But how much does charity demand? How much of his effort, indeed of his lifeblood, is the Christian expected to grant to a reality which in the last account only separates him from his true homestead? Certainly he has to care for the most basic needs of those whom he happens to meet; he has to give bread to the hungry, to offer hospitality to travelers, to clothe the naked, to visit the sick, to redeem captives, to reconcile those who quarrel, to bury the dead.[171]

---

[170] *De Trin.* XII, 14 (21); *PL* XLII, 1009.

[171] For this enumeration, see *Sermo* 104, 3; *PL* XXXVIII, 617. Cf. *Sermo* 103, 4; *ibid.* 615: "Bona sunt ministeria circa pauperes, et maxime circa sanctos Dei servitia debita, obsequia religiosa." Here begins to emerge the idea that

But may not charity demand from him activities which result in cultural products and values such as those enumerated in one of St. Augustine's early writings?

> The many handicrafts, the cultivation of soil, the erecting of towns and of miracles of architecture, the inventing of signs in writing, speech and gesture, in music, painting and sculpture; the many languages and institutions, old or new; the many books and monuments reminiscent of the past; the care of posterity; the hierarchy of offices, ranks and dignities in the home and in the state, in war and in peace, in secular and in sacral affairs; the power of researching and inventing, the flows of eloquence, the diversity of poetry, the thousand forms of playing and jesting, the dexterity in playing instruments, the exactness of measuring, the art of counting, the inferring of the past and the future from the present....[172]

Or should a Christian argue, as one of St. Augustine's more severe contemporaries seems to have argued,[173] that such activities and in fact all excessive attention to the practical order are dangerous, since they inevitably prevent one from contemplating God?

We have to refrain from elaborating on St. Augustine's remarks concerning this involved question;[174] suffice it to say that as he became the bishop of poor North African fishermen, thus removing himself from the seductive wealth of Roman culture, he seems to have been increasingly inclined to restrict the notion of a Christian *vita activa* to activities of serving either a neighbor's more basic needs or else those connected with religious service. Yet it must be added that this development was due not only to an increasingly ascetic attitude on the part of the great Bishop of Hippo but also to the fact that St. Augustine made explicit a dimensison of the notion of the practical, or active, life which never had been tho-

the most central dimension of "active life" is religious service, from preaching through dispensing the sacraments to burying the dead.

[172] *De quantitate animae* 33 (72); *PL* XXXII, 1075.

[173] Cf. Cassianus, *Collatio* 23, 4; *PL* XLIX, 492: "Merita tribulum... theoricae claritatis comparatione fuscantur. Multos enim sanctos quamvis bonorum operum terrenis tamen studiis occupatos, a contemplatione summi illius boni retrahunt ac retardant."

[174] The best discussion of this point is still J. Mausbach, *Die Ethik des hl. Augustinus* (Freiburg, 1909) I, 264 ff.

roughly absent, namely, that active life basically was a *walk of perfection*.

Aristotle, it is true, never defined practical life in terms of its being virtuous. Yet even though he probably would have argued that even a vicious politician may lead a political life, he ascribed political life to men of refinement who were not satisfied with the various forms of existence common to men and animals (the "apolaustic" life, the life concerned with necessities, etc.). The Neoplatonists never really could make up their mind as to whether cathartic, or rather "apolaustic," life was "practical life" properly speaking; yet they viewed practice as a catharsis and thus as a set of activities which at least prepared one for perfection. In St. Augustine this implicit connotation resulted in the notion that "active life" is a life of Christian perfection, that is, a walk of life *to be defined* in terms of this perfection. In any case, since about the fifth century, and clearly through St. Augustine's influence, nobody ever spoke of vices of active life, since active life by definition was believed to be a saintly walk of life, that is, the whole of non-contemplative activities characteristic of a Christian striving for saintliness. And since saintly life was moreover rather unambiguously identified with monastic life, from the fifth to about the twelfth century discussions about the active and contemplative life became the prerogative of specialists in ascetic and mystical theology.

The influential treatise *On Contemplative Life* by Julianus Pomerius,[175] the last-recorded rhetor of Gaul and abbot at Arles at the end of the fifth century, is a good example. In the first part Julianus discusses the union of contemplative and active life in the ministry; in the second part he treats of active life proper and in this connection discusses topics such as the conduct of priests toward laymen and sinners, the proper use of possessions of the Church, the excellence of detachment, the nature of abstinence, etc.; and in the third part he discusses virtues and vices, clearly indicating that the latter have to be overcome before one can even aspire to an active life. One century later, in his homily on

[175] Cf. *De vita contemplativa*, e.g., in the translation by M. J. Sulzer, Ancient Christian Writers 4 (Maryland, 1947).

Ezekiel (which in the Middle Ages became one of the authoritative texts on the subject), Pope Gregory the Great describes active life as one of the lives of Christian perfection "in which Almighty God instructs us by His holy word"; among the activities characteristic of this way of life he mentions "to give bread to the hungry, to teach the ignorant the word of wisdom, to correct the erring, to recall to the path of humility our neighbor when he waxes proud, to tend the sick, to dispense to all what they need, and to provide all those entrusted to us with the means of subsistence."[176] Even though it certainly would be an exaggeration to say that these activities are characteristic only of a monk, they clearly are a set of actions which a Christian is obliged to perform even when he strives for contemplation and which therefore he may perform without staining his soul by the dirt of the "world."

On the other hand, however, most Christian thinkers were familiar with the Greek division of lives, at least in the form in which it had been handed down to them by Romans such as Cicero, Seneca, Varro, Quintilianus, and others. But they no longer were able to see the difference between what the Peripatetics, the Stoics, the Neoplatonists, and the Fathers of the early Church had written. At the end of the sixth century the learned Isidor of Sevilla seems to have had a last glimpse of what "practical life" originally amounted to; he defines it as a life concerned with works of justice and the welfare of others,[177] a definition which will be repeated by most medieval thinkers. Yet at the same time he calls it "the right use of worldly things,"[178] thus identifying it with the *scientia* which St. Augustine had opposed to the contemplation of things divine or *sapientia*. At the beginning of the twelfth century the difference between what the ancients had meant and what the Fathers of

[176] *Super Ezechielem* II, 2; *PL* LXXVI, 952 D ff.

[177] *Differentiae* II, 34, 130; *PL* LXXXIII, 90: Activa vita est quae in operibus iustitiae et proximi utilitate versetur.

[178] *Sententiarum liber* III, 15; *PL* LXXXIII, 690: "Activa vita mundanis rebus bene utitur, contemplativa vero mundo renuntians soli Deo vivere delectatur." For St. Augustine's distinction between *sapientia* and *scientia* see *De Trin.* XV, 10 (17); *PL* XLII, 1069 ff. (St. Augustine bases this distinction upon I Cor. 12:8).

the Church had said had already become so obliterated that Hugh
of St. Victor can describe active life as both "public" and concerned
with charity.[179] And in the thirteenth century Thomas Aquinas
unhesitatingly puts side by side Aristotle's distinction between
"civil" and theoretical life, the Neoplatonic opposition between
catharsis and contemplation, St. Augustine's distinction between
scientia and *sapientia*, and Gregory's contrast between a life of active charity and a life of contemplation and prayer, as if all these
oppositions ultimately would amount to one and the same.[180] Politics, ascetic exercises, administration of sacraments, teaching, and
acts of Christian charity have become different aspects of one and
the same active life which in its totality is concerned with the *necessitas praesentis vitae*, the burdensome necessities of life on earth.[181]

When in the twelfth and thirteenth centuries translations both
from the Arabic and from the Greek made possible a more direct
contact with Greek thought, especially with Aristotle, the incompatibility of the Greek and the Christian ideas became too obvious
to permit the theologians simply to leave it at that. Even though
no one was in a position to realize clearly that for Aristotle the
paradigmatic instance of practice had been political activities, it
soon became obvious that while the Christian distinction between
active and contemplative life almost exclusively referred to *saintly*
walks of life, Aristotle's division pretended to cover all lives that
were distinctly *human*. St. Thomas, in any case, seems to have
realized this; he explicitly raised the question as to whether the
division of human walks of life into active and contemplative was
exhaustive. And even though the combined authority of the Gospel
(in particular, the story of Mary and Martha), of the Christian
tradition, and of Aristotle, compelled him to admit that there were
no properly human walks of life beside the two mentioned,[182]

[179] *Allegoriae in Novum Testamentum* III, 3; *PL* CLXXV, 804: "Duae sunt
vitae, activa et contemplativa. Activa est in labore, contemplativa in requie.
Activa in publico, contemplativa in deserto. Activa in necessitate proximi,
contemplativa in visione Dei."
[180] *In III. Sent.* d. 35, qu. 1, a. 1 ff.
[181] Cf. *S. Th.* II-II, 179, 2 ad 3.
[182] E.g., *S. Th.* II-II, 179, 2.

he obviously felt it necessary to enlarge the Christian notion of *vita activa* so as to make it cover all human activities other than mere thinking for its own sake. *Activa vita consistit in omnibus agibilibus, sive sint at seipsum, sive ad alium*: to active life belongs all "doing," both that concerned with oneself (e.g., activities aiming at overcoming passions) and that directed toward others.[183] Having stated this, Aquinas even proceeds to a sort of "ontological justification" of the division of lives:

> Orderly human life (for we do not speak about inorderly lives such as the voluptuous one which is animal rather than human) depends upon the operation of the intellect and of reason. Yet man's intellectual part has two operations: one which is proper to the intellect taken by itself (*quae est ipsius secundum se*), another which is proper to the intellect in so far as it rules inferior faculties. Thus there are two human lives: one which centers around the operation which is proper to the intellect taken by itself, and this is contemplative life; and another which centers around the operation of the intellect and of reason in so far as it orders and rules and commands inferior parts, and this is active life.[184]

Yet while for Aquinas active life still centers around activities which are in accordance with *right* reason (and thus virtuous), in Duns Scotus there emerges for the first time the notion of a practice which, taken by itself, is extraethical. In fact, Scotus seems to have been the first medieval thinker[185] explicitly to ask the question *Quid sit praxis*? What exactly is practice? This question alone is significant enough to mention his discussion. For, as far as I can determine, no Latin author before Scotus ever used the expression '*praxis*' in a philosophical or theological context; though the adjective '*practicus*' occasionally was used

[183] *In III. Sent.* d. 35, qu. 1, a. 3, solutio.

[184] *Ibid.* a. 1; ed. Moos, III, 1173.

[185] After Scotus, the question *quid sit praxis* became commonplace; it was raised either in connection with the question originally asked by Scotus (the nature of theology: Is it practical or theoretical) or in connection with subtleties about *habitus*, e.g., in Suarez, *Disp. Met.*, XLIV, 13, 20 ff., ed. Paris (1866) II, 728 ff. Some thinkers, among them Thomists such as Capreolus (e.g., *Defensiones theologicae*, prologus, q. 2, conclusio 4) and Ockham (*Ordinatio*, prologus, qu. 4, a. 1) argued, however, that intellectual operations are *praxis* as well.

as early as in the fifth century[186] and in the twelfth century began
to replace the classical expression '*activus*,' Aristotle's technical
term '$\pi\varrho\tilde{\alpha}\xi\iota\varsigma$' usually was translated by expressions such as
'*actio*' or '*operatio*,' which were somewhat ambiguous, since they
applied to "activities" of animals and even things as well.

The emergence of a new expression almost always indicates the
awareness of something which previously had escaped notice.
What in this case had escaped notice was the simple fact that there
are in man activities other than those of the intellect which are
generically different from analogous activities in animals. As we
saw earlier, Aristotle had already stated that only man has $\pi\varrho\tilde{\alpha}\xi\iota\varsigma$
properly speaking, since no animal besides him is a true source of
its activity. However, no one before Scotus articulated this notion
as clearly as he did:

> *Praxis*, to which practical cognition extends, is the act of a
> faculty other than the intellect which, by its very nature, succeeds
> intellection and may be elicited in accordance with right intellec-
> tion so as to become right.[187]

Practice must be the act of a faculty different from the intellect,
for it is something to which intellectual considerations *extend*
whenever they cease to be theoretical and become practical. If
the extension of one intellectual act to another would suffice for
calling the first act "practical cognition" and the second act
"practice," then logical considerations which bring order into
acts of reasoning would have to be called "practical"—which
Scotus rightly considered absurd.[188] Secondly, practice must by
its very nature follow intellection. For practice is human activity,
and all activities which either precede intellection or are otherwise
beyond its reach are common to man and animals. In short, only
conscious and deliberate actions other than purely intellectual
ones are *praxis*. Finally, practice must be an activity which
may be wrong or right by being conformable to right intellection.

---

[186] E.g., Cassianus, *Collatio* XIV, 1; *PL* XLIX, 953. In the sixth century,
cf. Fulgentius, *Mythologiae* 2, 1.

[187] *Ordinatio*, prologus, pars V, qu. 2, no. 1, ed. Vaticana (1950 ff.) I, 155 ff.

[188] The notion that logic is a "practical science" may, however, be found in
Robert Kilwardby.

However, as Scotus himself stresses, this must not be taken to mean that only those activities which in fact do conform to right intellection are practice. It is only essential to practice to have a *relatio aptitudinalis ... conformitatis* [*ad cognitionem practicam*], to be in principle capable of conforming to the "practical intellect."[189] For if one were to say that practice conforms to the judgement of the "practical intellect" by its very nature, how could one say that the "practical intellect" directs and rules practice?

Of course, when he speaks of *praxis*, Scotus still has primarily in mind what today we would call "acts of the will"; his whole treatment of the notion of practice is still inserted in a strictly theological context—his aim is to show that by generating love of God theology can be "practical" without thereby being "moral theology."[190] Still, his definition of practice is incomparably more articulate than anything said before him on this subject: practice is conscious and deliberate post-theoretical human action which even though it may be morally right or wrong, is as such outside the realm of the ethical. In a sense this is nothing but a purified and more abstract notion of what Aristotle had called '$\pi\varrho\tilde{\alpha}\xi\iota\varsigma$'; however, the political as well as the cathartic connotation has disappeared, and the difference between "doing" and "making" has become rather secondary, even though the accent still is on "doing," in fact on a "doing" of the will alone.[191]

Moreover, Scotus' notion of *praxis* contains an element which later turned out to be highly explosive. His declared aim is to show that theology is a *practica cognitio* in the sense that it precedes and prepares a love of God, which itself is the culminating point of all theological theorizing. As such this doctrine was not new. Already two generations before Scotus the abbot of Vercelli, Thomas Gallus, had argued that instead of only applying the *intellectus*

---

[189] Loc. cit., no. 2, ed. Vaticana I, 161 ff.

[190] Cf. M. Müller, "Die Theologie als Weisheit nach Scotus," *Sechste und Siebte Lektorenkonferenz der deutschen Franziskaner für Philosophie und Theologie* (Werl in Westphalen, 1934) 40-51.

[191] Several centuries later Suarez will already stress that "quicquid sit de hac distinctione actionis (doing) et factionis (making) ... utraque comprehenditur sub nomine *praxis*," loc. cit., no. 39, ed. Paris II, 731.

theoricus, the human mind ought to reach God by the *summus affectionis apex*, the "tip of the will": "It is by this communion (*unitio*) that we have to know things divine, not in terms of the sobriety of our intellect."[192] Bonaventure had followed this doctrine by arguing that sapiential contemplation *in cognitione inchoatur et in affectione consummatur* starts with knowledge and reaches its completion in love.[193] But Scotus went a step further when he replaced the innocuous notions of affection and "affective knowledge" by the notion of "practice" and argued that in some sense theology had to be "practical" even though it was concerned with God Himself. According to him Aristotle was right in claiming that ethics and politics are concerned with less "knowable" subjects than contemplative sciences, but as he did not know theology, Aristotle wrongly inferred that the absolute knowable, God, could not be the object of practice and practical knowledge. "As opposed to this, we state that God is the 'doable knowable' (*cognoscibile operabile*), that is, that object of knowledge which may be reached by a doing which is true *praxis*."[194] One only has to forget for a second that for Scotus the ultimate secret of will, and thus of practice, is love, in order to be reminded of statements such as: the only knowledge able to reach God is practical, not theoretical (Kant); the only source of meaning in the whole universe is *praxis* (Marx). Of course, Scotus is infinitely far from saying anything of this kind. Still, his statement that God is a *cognoscibile operabile* anticipates, and in a sense paves the way for, the notion that man's ultimate achievement is practice, not theory, and that it is an atheoretical practice in which God is encountered or missed, the meaning of the universe fulfilled or failed. This is more than an instance of Scotus' often-referred-to "voluntarism": the Christian emphasis upon charity and love as opposed to mere knowledge has resulted, and from now on evermore radically will result, in an emphasis upon practice as opposed to theory until eventually practice will become the sole source of meaning and salvation.

[192] *Paraphrasis in De divinis nominibus* 7; in *Dionysii Carthusiani opera omnia* (Montreuil, 1902) XVI, 267 b A.
[193] *In III. Sent.* d. 35, qu. 1; ed. Quaracchi III, 774.
[194] *Ordinatio*, prologus, pars V, No. 6; ed. Vaticana I, 230.

6: PRACTICA THEORIAE

In the sixth book of the *Nicomachean Ethics*[195] there is a passage in which Aristotle states, without further explaining exactly what he means, that the truth of "practical thinking" in terms of which we decide what to pursue and what to avoid consists in the conformity of the practical intellect to a "right desire." Commenting upon this passage, Aquinas remarks that this statement seems to be circular: as we have to determine the rightness of a desire by comparing it to some intellectual insight, Aristotle's invitation to judge the practical intellect in terms of its correspondence to a right desire would seem to amount to an outright invitation to commit a vicious circle. In order to tackle this difficulty, Aquinas advances the following analysis:

> One has to distinguish between the desire for an end and the desire for whatever leads to that end. The end is predetermined by man's very nature; only those things which lead to that end are not predetermined and hence may be investigated by [practical] reason. Thus it becomes obvious that the rightness of the desire for the end is the measure of the truth of practical reason, and in this sense, the truth of practical reason depends upon its agreement with right desire. On the other hand, however, the truth of practical reason is the measure of the rightness of a desire which aims at things which lead to the end; and in this sense one calls "right" a desire which follows whatever right reason says.[196]

[195] *Eth. Nic.* 1139 a 29-31.
[196] *In VI. Eth.* 2, 1131 Spiazzi; cf. *In III. De an.* 15, 821 Pirotta.

What Aquinas would seem to mean here is that there are two
kinds of desire and thus also two meanings of the expression 'right
desire.' There is first man's desire for his ultimate end. As to
this desire man has no choice; all men by nature desire to be happy
and it is not up to them to decide wherein the ultimate fulfilment
of this basic desire should consist. Consequently, this desire is
only "right" in the sense in which everything "natural" is right,
that is, everything which belongs to or immediately follows a
thing's very nature. It certainly is not "right" in the sense in which
we call a decision right, for it makes no sense to ask whether man
should or should not pursue happiness, and should or should not
find the ultimate fulfilment of his desire for happiness, say, in
beatific vision. This kind of question—should one or should one
not?—only makes sense with respect to a different type of desire,
namely, those desires which aim at ends which in fact only are
means. Accordingly, the judgment of the intellect which tells us
what to pursue or avoid only extends to desires which aim at
"intermediary" ends. And the practical intellect judges such
desires by comparing them to man's desire for his ultimate end.

We have no reason to believe that Aristotle would have disagreed
with this interpretation. But as he did not spell it out, he could
leave in the dark a point which anyone reading Aquinas' analysis
no longer can overlook, namely, that ethics cannot be exclusively
practical. For who is to decide what is man's basic "right desire"
and what is the fulfilment of this natural desire? Certainly not
the practical intellect, for it only tells us what to pursue or avoid.
It does not tell us "what is the case." This only the theoretical
intellect can determine, that is, the intellectual operation whose
right and wrong functioning, in Aristotle's own words, consists
of the attainment of truth and falsehood respectively.

Aquinas did not explicitly draw the conclusion that Aristotle's
claim that ethics is only practical is an oversimplification. But in
another context[197] he introduced the distinction between at least
two meanings of the expression 'practical knowledge': a knowledge
may be practical in that its ultimate end is to guide human action,

[197] E.g., *S.Th.* I, 14, 16; *In Boet. De Trin.* V, 2.

but it also may be practical in the sense that its subject matter is something which man may change. Now all ethical considerations obviously are made for the purpose of telling man what he ought to do or not to do. But not all ethical considerations are concerned with a subject matter on which man has a hold. For example, the basic "right desire," the nature of the ultimate fulfilment of this desire, as well as a number of general features of the means leading man to his ultimate end, are not matters of choice. They may only be discovered by a "theoretical" insight which does not basically differ from theoretical insights operative in physics or metaphysics.

Thus, even though Aquinas never drew this conclusion, we may say that by trying to understand a passage in Aristotle he arrived at the notion of a "theory" immediately relevant to "practice." As we indicated earlier, the Greeks only knew of an indirect guidance of human "doing" by theoretical insights: contemplating the eternal, they felt, man begins to desire to be like intelligible realities and changes his life accordingly. This is something very different from what Aquinas seems to suggest. For his analysis amounts to saying that there are insights which, because of their subject matter, have to be considered theoretical and yet are the basic premises for practical knowledge.

Of course, we have to repeat that Aquinas never put it as explicitly as that. One reason for his reluctance to spell out this point may be the fact that the theoretical insights in question are not really theoretical after all. First of all, they only amount to · a knowledge of *what* is the case; even though ethics certainly has to say what man's ultimate end is, it does not have to bother about questions such as *why* man desires happiness or *why* this rather than that is his ultimate end. Secondly, moral philosophy aims at guiding action; but in order to pursue good or avoid evil, one does not need theoretical insights properly speaking; in most instances a "theoretical" knowledge embedded in and almost identical with experience is enough. To put it in another way; ethics is not a master plan according to which man acts, just as logic is not a master plan according to which man thinks; both are reflections upon what in most instances man does almost instinctively.

However, there can be no doubt that Aquinas realized that Aristotle's clear-cut distinction between theoretical and practical knowledge was not as simple as it seemed at first sight. And he certainly
was not the first to realize this. Almost three hundred years earlier
Avicenna had made several statements which obviously aimed at
removing certain ambiguities in Aristotle's division. That at one
occasion he claimed that all arts and sciences have both a theoretical
and a practical part may simply be due to the fact that he was
discussing medicine; in any case this statement occurs in Avicenna's
famous *Liber canonicus*, the copious methodological reflections
introducing the monumental *Codex totius medecinae*.[198] But even
at the beginning of his *Metaphysics* Avicenna explains the distinction between theoretical and practical science in a way which
cannot be traced back to the explicit tradition of classical Greek
thought, even though possibly Aristotle would not have objected
to it.

According to Avicenna's *Metaphysics* theoretical knowledge aims
at perfecting man's theoretical faculties by "actualizing" the
intellect; such an "actualization" is reached whenever the intellect
has acquired ideas of things "which are not our actions or attitudes."
Yet already the next sentence suggests that Avicenna wants to exclude from theoretical philosophy only the *ethical dimension* of human activities. For he adds that the end of theoretical philosophy
is to acquire ideas which do not concern "the quality of the principle
of an action insofar as this action is ethical." In other words, while
Aristotle was inclined to say that only those cognitions which are
concerned with an eternal and unchanging subject matter are
theoretical, and therefore felt that human actions should be approached only by a knowing which aims at guiding these actions,
Avicenna admits the possibility of a *strictly theoretical knowledge
of the strictly human.*

This becomes important when Avicenna proceeds to explain the
nature of practical philosophy. As he puts it, practical philosophy
first aims at completing the theoretical faculty of the soul; basically
it is a theoretical knowledge of our actions. But insofar as it is

[198] Cf. *Liber canonicus*, reprographical reprint (Hildesheim, 1964) 1.

practical, this knowledge is not pursued for the sake of knowledge alone: it aims at helping us "to acquire through this knowledge a perfection of our practical faculties."[199]

In spite of the succinctness of this analysis it is obvious that Avicenna intends to say that those parts of theoretical philosophy which relate to human actions become the axioms of practical philosophy as soon as they are striven for or considered with the intention to make a man and his actions morally better. This is why Avicenna occasionally distinguishes practical from theoretical knowledge by saying that *both* are concerned with things which we have to *know*, but only practical knowledge is concerned with things according to which, *moreover*, we ought to *act*. "The science which treats of things practical, that is, of things which we ought to know and in accordance with which we ought to act, is called practical science."[200] Both theoretical and practical knowledge are concerned with truth in the strict sense of the term. In some cases this truth is relevant to the morality of human actions. As long as this relevance remains implicit, one is doing "theory"; when this relevance becomes explicit, one begins to think "practically." As Duns Scotus puts it several centuries later, practical truth and knowledge are an "extension of theoretical truth and knowledge."

What begins to disappear here is the Greek idea that theoretical and ethicopolitical knowing are radically different; instead there begins to emerge the notion that ethics and politics are simply a "practical application" of apractical, purely theoretical insights. After this, one no longer will be surprised to hear, as Roger Bacon tells us in his *Ethics*,[201] that the anonymous Mohammedan author who translated the *Nicomachean Ethics* into Arabic added an explanation explicitly stating that moral philosophy contains two parts, one theoretical and another practical. When in the thirteenth century Aquinas intimated that ethics contains theoretical in-

---

[199] *Die Metaphysik Avicennas*, tr. M. Horten (Frankfurt, 1960) 3 ff.; cf. the Latin translation *Metaphysica*, ed. Venice (1495), photoprint Louvain (1961) 1.

[200] Cf. A.-M. Goichon, *Lexique de la langue philosophique d'Ibn Sina* (Paris, 1938) 89 ff.

[201] Roger Bacon, *Moralis Philosophia* V, 1, ed. Massa (1953) 249. This is a critical edition of the seventh part of the *Opus Majus*.

sights, he only repeated something which the Arabs had already considered obvious and upon which most of his contemporaries were in agreement, more or less explicitly.

It is somewhat more difficult to say to what extent medieval thinkers also reached the notion of a "theory" immediately relevant to what Marx later called "material practice," that is, the whole realm of human actions concerned with making, changing and handling things. One would expect to find an answer to this question by studying the numerous medieval treatises concerned with classifying sciences and arts, from Alfarabi's *On the Origin of Sciences* and Avicenna's *On the Division of Sciences* through Hugh of St. Victor's *Eruditiones didascalicae*, his brother Richard's *Exceptiones allegoricae*, Dominic Gundisalvi's *De divisione philosophiae*, Michael Scot's introduction to philosophy, partially preserved in Vincent of Beauvais' *Speculum doctrinale*, and Robert Kilwardby's *De ortu et divisione philosophiae*, to the various *opera* of Roger Bacon. Yet it must be noticed that all these treatises which attest to the great interest of the Middle Ages both in methodological questions and in programs of studies are very difficult to evaluate.

Even though the body of human knowledge and skills had increased considerably since ancient times, thus adding to the complexity of the interrelation both between various disciplines and between "theory" and "practice," most of the authors mentioned continued to work with the few simple categories of classification devised by the ancients. Taken by itself, this would not have been as serious as in fact it was had it not been for the additional circumstance that the scholastics were not satisfied with rough classifications but went out of their way to justify the applicability of obsolete *schemata* to realities which meanwhile had significantly changed. In consequence most of their analyses only attest to their ingenuity in making sense of what no longer made sense, indeed often never had made sense in the way in which the scholastics conceived of the classical divisions.

Occasionally, it is true, their attempts to make sense of the classical divisions resulted in important new analyses. A case in point is Aquinas' justification of Aristotle's division of theoretical knowledge into physics, mathematics, and metaphysics. When

Aristotle advanced this tripartition, he seems to have succumbed to a Platonic scheme which could not possibly apply to his own philosophy, and yet Aquinas, when trying to justify this tripartition, developed a theory of "types of abstraction" whose value is quite independent of Aristotle's original division.[202] In most cases, however, the medieval classifications of arts and sciences are easily misleading; very little in them corresponds either to existing programs of studies or to existing sciences.

As a matter of fact, most medieval thinkers operated with a division of philosophy which was even more narrow than that of the Greeks. As we have seen, Aristotle had divided knowledge into theoretical, practical, and productive. Yet the third member of this division seems to have fallen into oblivion soon after Aristotle's death, the main reason probably being that Aristotle had tended to identify productive knowledge with arts and thus had suggested that it was not a genuine type of *knowledge* in the strong sense of the term. In any case most of the Greek Peripatetics already distinguished only between theoretical and practical knowledge, either treating productive knowledge as an insignificant subdivision of the latter or else simply forgetting about it.

Accordingly, when the Arabs and early medieval thinkers wished to classify quasi-sciences such as medicine, alchemy, or navigation, they were in the somewhat embarrassing situation of either having to treat them as theoretical sciences somewhat comparable to mathematics and metaphysics, or else being forced to place them in practical philosophy beside politics and ethics. If the first alternative was chosen, such "sciences" could only be treated as parts or subparts of the knowledge of nature, an interpretation which most Arab thinkers seem to have followed. Thus in his widely read *On the Origin of Sciences* Alfarabi spoke of eight parts of the section of natural science which were concerned with the sublunar realm: the science of symptoms and the science of medicine (probably diagnostics and therapeutics which the Arabs considered two relatively independent branches of medicine); the "science of necromancy according to physics" (which Michael

[202] Cf. *In Boet. De Trin.* V, 3.

Scot took to be a "description of the properties of natural things"[203]); the science of images and the science of navigation, the latter including all information concerning trade and commerce; and the science of alchemy, which Alfarabi himself describes as a science concerned with the transformation of substances into each other.[204]

If, on the other hand, one preferred to consider such quasi-sciences as practical, one had to treat them as subparts of the "art of family government," or economics, which, quite contrary to Aristotle's original intention, had become the third member of practical philosophy beside ethics and politics. This interpretation is found in Dominic Gundissalvi's *De divisione philosophiae*, a compilation of various Arab and patristic sources written around 1150. According to Gundissalvi, fabrile or mechanical arts concerned with making out of matter something useful to man (the matter used coming either from living things such as wood, wool, linen, or bones, or from dead things such as metals and stones) are parts of economics.[205]

It is easy to see that both classifications are quite unsatisfactory. In Alfarabi one misses a clear awareness of the fact that several of the eight quasi-sciences are concerned with production and "making"; in consequence, Alfarabi lumps together purely theoretical sciences such as optics, and sciences essentially ordered toward production such as agriculture. Gundissalvi, on the other hand, simply reduces all "productive sciences" to skills, thus perpetuating the Greek notion that production and theoretical insight have little to do with each other.

The only twelfth-century thinkers who realized that the mechanical arts are neither theoretical nor practical and therefore deserve a slot of their own was Hugh of St. Victor, whose *Didascalion* and *Epitome Dindimi in philosophiam* contain what undoubtedly is the most sophisticated division of the sciences of his era.

[203] Cf. the fragments published by L. Bauer as an appendix to his edition of Dominicus Gundissalvi's *De divisione philosophiae*, in *Beiträge zur Geschichte der Philosophie des Mittelalters* IV, 2-3 (Münster, 1903) 399.

[204] *De ortu scientiarum*, ed. Cl. Bäumker, in *Beiträge zur Geschichte etc.* XIX, 3 (Münster, 1916), 20.

[205] Cf. the edition referred to in fn. 203, p. 108.

According to Hugh, "philosophy" consists of four divisions: *logica*, *theorica*, *practica*, and *mechanica*. The *logica* includes grammar and the art of discourse, which in turn is subdivided into rhetorics and dialectics, so that the *logica* embraces the whole traditional *trivium*; the *theorica* includes mathematics (embracing the four branches of the *quadrivium*: arithmetics, harmonics, geometry, and astronomy), physics, and theology; the *practica* includes ethics, economics, and politics; and the *mechanica* includes *omnium rerum fabricam*, all kinds of production—from manufacturing cloth through the manufacture of instruments, navigation, agriculture, hunting, and medicine, to the "science of theatrical performances."[206]

In spite of this elaborate division, however, Hugh himself contributed to later confusions by introducing the notion of a "practical geometry." In his division of sciences the expression '*practica*' (probably an abbreviation of an expression such as '*pars practica philosophiae*') only referred to those sciences which traditionally were associated with "doing" as opposed to "making"; in fact, when he introduced the distinction between *theorica*, *practica*, and *mechanica*, he explicitly associated the *practica* with virtue.[207] Yet just around the time when he wrote his *Didascalion*, Hugh also published a small treatise entitled *Practica geometriae*, which

[206] For a detailed analysis, cf. R. Baron, *Science et sagesse chez Hugues de Saint-Victor* (Paris, 1957) 47-96. Cf. also Richard of St. Victor's *Liber Exceptionum*, ed. J. Chatillon (Paris, 1958) 106-111, which contains a summary of Richard's analysis.

[207] Hugh and Richard of St. Victor give a pseudo-historical account of the origin of arts and sciences which is worth mentioning. The creator granted to man three basic goods: he created man in his image, made him similar to himself, and gave him an immortal body. Original sin resulted in a corruption of these three goods and made emerge three evils: ignorance as to what is good, concupiscence of the evil, and bodily infirmity. To these three evils, in turn, correspond three remedies: wisdom, virtue, and "necessary activities without which we cannot survive but by the help of which we would live better." All arts and sciences (except for logic, which Richard considers a later invention) were invented for the sake of these remedies: the *theorica* dispels ignorance and helps us to find wisdom, the *practica* fights vice and strengthens virtue, and the *mechanica* tempers the distress due to the defectiveness of the body; cf. the summary in Richard's *Liber Exceptionum* 104 ff.

had nothing to do with any relationship of geometry to ethics and virtue. Rather, it contained a discussion of the measuring of distances, surfaces, and volumes, such as a land surveyor or an architect would be likely to use. In this treatise Hugh distinguished between a "theoretical" and a "practical" geometry, describing the latter in a way which makes one wonder why he did not call it "mechanical geometry."[208]

While no thinker of the twelfth century seems to have taken seriously Hugh's suggestion that besides the *theorica* and the *practica* there is a *mechanica*, this distinction between a "theoretical" and a "practical" part of basically theoretical disciplines had tremendous success. Thus Dominic Gundissalvi, writing only a few decades after Hugh, already spoke of a practical part of arithmetic— the counting and reckoning of material things, as in commerce by means of the abacus—and of a practical part of harmonics concerned with the production of sounds by voice and instruments. Moreover, he introduced into the theoretical science par excellence, mathematics, two "sciences" which obviously were not theoretical at all: a science of weights (concerned with principles of balance and with instruments by which heavy things were lifted and carried) and a science called *De ingeniis*, "On Devices," which adopted the principles of other branches of mathematics to useful purposes, as, for example, for stone masonry, the making of musical and optical instruments, carpentry, and other mechanical arts.

From this brief survey, we may draw two important conclusions: first, in the twelfth century the notion of an immediate relevance of theoretical insights to "practice" certainly was not absent and, second, from about the same time the expression 'practical' ceased to refer exclusively to the ethicopolitical realm.

As to the first point, one will of course have to add that the ideas concerning the relationship between theory and "making" were still rather vague and in some cases even confused. For example, it is sometimes difficult to say whether the authors in question

---

[208] "Hugonis de Sancto Victore *Practica Geometriae*," introduced and edited by R. Baron, *Osiris* 12 (1956) 176-224. Cf. by the same author, "Note sur les variations au XIIe siècle de la Triade Géometrique, Altimetria, Planimetria, Cosmimetria," *Isis* 48 (1951) 30 ff.

clearly realized that the "practical" part of a science drew its premises from the theoretical part. When Hugh of St. Victor introduces his distinction between a theoretical and a practical geometry, he seems to suggest that the connection between these two geometries lies in their common subject matter rather than in a direct dependence of the practical upon the theoretical part. In any case he distinguishes the two parts by arguing that theoretical geometry investigates spatial magnitudes by the help of reason alone, while practical geometry uses instruments and infers from one given magnitude to another.[209]

Gundissalvi, it is true, already states that theoretical geometry "is the principle of the rules (doctrinarum) of practical geometry."[210] On the other hand, however, throughout his treatise he constantly confuses the distinction "theoretical-practical" with the Aristotelian, or rather Avicennian, notion of different degrees of abstraction. For example, even while he says that theoretical geometry aims at understanding and practical geometry at doing something (aliquid agere), he also distinguishes the two by saying that theoretical geometry studies spatial magnitudes "as they are intellected outside matter" and practical geometry studies them prout in materia senciuntur, as they are sensed in matter.[211]

Last but not least, Gundissalvi does not seem to realize that he split productive knowledge into two disconnected parts: on the one hand, it is found in economics; on the other hand, it is a subdivision of theoretical sciences. This point seems to have been noticed by Michael Scot, it is true, whose introduction to philosophy was written early in the thirteenth century. For Scot enumerates the eight parts of natural science mentioned by Alfarabi as parts of economics and adds that "they have a relationship to that part of theoretical philosophy which is called natural science and in fact belong to it tamquam practica eiusdem, as its practical manifestation."[212]

---

[209] Cf. Osiris 12 (1956) 187.
[210] De divisione philosophiae (cf. fn. 203) 108: "Geometria theorica docet operationem et est principium doctrinarum practice quae manibus exercuntur."
[211] Ibid. 91.
[212] Cf. the fragments quoted by L. Baur, 399.

The fact that in the twelfth century the expression 'practical' came to refer both to the deontological realm of ethics and politics and to the twilight zone in which strictly theoretical science met with the purposeful handling and making of things is even more noteworthy. For this ambiguity did not disappear when in the thirteenth century the newly translated writings of Aristotle drew the philosophers' attention to the Greek distinction between a knowledge guiding ethicopolitical action and a quite different kind of knowledge guiding "making." Thomas Aquinas in many instances uses the term 'practicus' as referring both to the virtuous man and politician and to the artisan;[213] and Robert Kilwardy, in his widely read and highly influential *De ortu et divisione scientiarum*, even makes "morals" (which includes ethics, economics, and politics) and "mechanics" two main subdivisions of practical science.[214]

There certainly is more to this development than only an innocuous shift in terminology. Earlier, we suggested that this shift was due to the twelfth century's unfamiliarity with the third member of the original Greek tripartition of knowledge. But it would be an oversimplification to say that this whole development simply is due to a lexicographic embarrassment. After all, Hugh of St. Victor, by introducing his *mechanica*, had reinvented Aristotle's notion of a "productive science."

But as far as I can see, no medieval thinker ever followed Hugh's suggestion. And it is not difficult to see why: one no longer was aware of a basic difference between the knowledge involved in ethicopolitical activities and the knowledge characteristic of an artisan. This simple fact, we may add, may be looked upon in two quite different ways. On the one hand, one might argue that the Middle Age was faithful to the Greek spirit, even though it was not faithful to the letter of Aristotle: to admit a *mechanica* beside the *theorica* and the *practica* seemed to most medieval thinkers to amount to granting to the mechanical arts more of a scientific

[213] E.g., S.*Th.* I, 14. 16,
[214] For Kilwardby's division of philosophy, cf. D. E. Sharp, "The *De ortu scientiarum* of Robert Kilwardby," *The New Scholasticism* 8 (1943) 1-30.

character than in fact they had. This is the reason why Robert
Kilwardby, for example, polemized against Hugh of St. Victor's
raising the *mechanica* to the rank of a primary division of philosophy.
As Kilwardby explained, the mechanical arts were primarily the
concern of manual workers and common people and thus outside
the realm of philosophy proper, except for a few fundamental
principles to be discussed in practical philosophy.[215]

In other words, the subsumption of mechanical arts under the
notion of practical philosophy *may* be taken to have been rooted
in the conviction that such arts were based upon the experience
of a skilled man in much the same way as ethics and politics were
based upon the ethical or political experience of a virtuous man or
politician. However, this fusion of the deontological and technological permitted, and later increasingly invited, a treatment of the
deontological in terms of categories applicable to an artisan—to a
man who has a well-weighed masterplan and then carries it out.
In fact, one might even want to suggest that this fusion of two
radically different realms was due to the fact that for centuries
Christianity had conceived of God himself as a supreme artisan
and therefore was inclined to describe man as an artisan even in
those cases where this image did not really apply.

Aquinas, for example, only rarely patterns his analysis of ethical
knowledge on the model of an artisan when he comments upon
Aristotle. But when he speaks in his own name, his primary instance of the "practical" usually is an artisan. Of course, neither
Aquinas nor, for that matter, any other thinker of the thirteenth
century would have dreamt of suggesting that ethical and political
knowledge is an abstract masterplan according to which a virtuous
man or a ruler should act. But then they also would have questioned
that this description applies to an ordinary artisan; the instances
of planning artisans were too rare (for example, the plans used in
building medieval cathedrals certainly were not blueprints; they
were rough sketches indicating to the mason what he should do).
However, as technology progressed and abstract theoretical
considerations became increasingly relevant to all kinds of "making,"

[215] Cf. *ibid.* 19.

the link which the Middle Ages had established between ethics and politics, on the one hand, and technology, on the other hand, proved fateful.   As we shall see in the next chapters, it did not take long until politics and ethics turned from a practical knowledge, as Aristotle had conceived it, into the knowledge of a man who translates into practice abstract insights which *have* to work, since the politician *knows* the laws of society *like an architect knows the laws of mechanics and statics.*

7: "FRUITS AND WORKS"

> Of all signs there is none more certain or more noble than that taken from the fruits. For fruits and works are as it were sponsors and sureties for the truth of philosophies .... Human knowledge and power coincide, for ignorance of the cause deprives one of the effect. Nature to be commanded must be obeyed; and that which in contemplation is as the cause, in operation is as the rule .... In vain does one expect a great advancement of science from the superinducing of new things upon old; we must begin anew from the very foundations, unless we would want to revolve for ever in a circle with mean and contemptible progress ...[216]

These three well-known passages from Francis Bacon's *Novum Organum*, written about 1607 and published in 1620, strike a new note. In order to prove significant, knowledge has to bear palpable fruits, that is, lead to the making of useful things. The ultimate end of theoretical knowledge is power, that is, to obtain mastery over nature. And as until now science did not produce useful things and did not help man to command nature, one has to start from scratch, "anew from the very foundations."

It is important to note precisely the novelty of these ideas. No one ever denied that there exist some kinds of knowledge which have to be judged in terms of their fruits; Aristotle, for example, certainly would have argued that "productive knowledge" is worth only as much as an artisan is able to produce. Nor is the notion thoroughly new that there is some connection between knowledge and power; as we saw earlier, even the author of the pseudo-

---

[216] *Novum Organum*, ed. Th. Fowler (Oxford, 1889) 265, 192, and 209.

Aristotelian *Mechanics* dimly realized that an art helps one to prevail over nature only if it is based upon some adequate knowledge. But what neither the ancients nor the scholastics would have agreed with is Bacon's claim that *theoretical* knowledge has to prove itself by "fruits and works"; moreover, they probably would not even have understood Bacon's assertion that theoretical knowledge ought to be striven for *because* it has some fruits. In other words, even though thinkers of earlier ages occasionally may have realized that theoretical knowledge may in some vague sense be useful and even bear some palpable fruits, they hardly would have been able to appreciate Bacon's emphatic claim that scientific knowledge should be judged in terms of, and pursued for the sake of, its practical usefulness.

In fact, Bacon's insistence on this point is quite unique even as far as the seventeenth century is concerned. His notion that "truth is shown and proved by the evidence of works rather than by argument, or even sense,"[217] had little influence until it reappeared in the second half of the nineteenth century. In fact, one even may doubt whether Bacon himself was fully aware of the implications of the "pragmatism" which is ascribed to him today. Bacon was notoriously confused about the difference between experiments devised solely for the purpose of verifying or falsifying a scientific theory and "works" which, even though in some sense they may be said to verify a theory, certainly have not been performed with this purpose in mind. But even the notion that science should be

---

[217] *Cogitata et visa*: "Et quod in religione verissime requiritur, ut fidem quis ex operibus monstret; idem in naturali philosophia competere, ut scientia similiter ex operibus monstretur. Veritatem enim per operum indicationem magis quam ex argumentatione aut etiam ex sensu, et patefieri et probari"; cf. *The Works of Francis Bacon*, eds. J. Spedding, R. L. Ellis, and D. D. Heath (Boston, 1863) VII, 131. It should be added that Bacon's ideas on this subject somewhat changed in his later writings. In his earlier writings, especially the *Valerius Terminus* and the *Cogitata et Visa*, Bacon stresses the pragmatic nature of truth much more than in the *Novum Organum*, where he even writes (329) that "works are to be undertaken insofar as they are pledges of truth rather than insofar as they contribute to the comfort of life." For a detailed discussion, see F. H. Anderson, *The Philosophy of Francis Bacon* (Chicago, 1948) 32 ff.

pursued for the sake of its practical results is by no means typical
of the seventeenth century. Descartes, it is true, writes in a famous
passage toward the end of the *Discours de la méthode*[218] that the
"speculative philosophy taught in the schools" should be replaced
by a "practical philosophy by means of which ... we might render
ourselves the lords and possessors of Nature" and even suggests
that there is a significant similarity between the scientific knowledge
of nature and an artisan's knowledge of his artifacts. But those who
today quote this passage tend to overlook that there is only one
such passage in Descartes' numerous writings and that it would
be comparatively easy to show that Descartes' notion of science is
at least as little "pragmatic" as that of Aristotle, for example.
The same would seem to apply to founders of modern science such
as Galileo and later Newton; even though they treated with scorn
the scientific *method* of the Aristotelians, they adhered to the basic *spirit* of the Greeks in that they considered a theoretical discovery an end in itself which did not need to be justified by "useful"
results.

One reason why Francis Bacon is an embarrassing puzzle for
historians of philosophy, science, and scientific methodology is
that it has become customary to compare his ideas to those of
thinkers such as Galileo, Descartes, or even Newton. Seen from
this point of view (which implies that Bacon ought to be ranged
among the men who laid the methodological foundations of modern
science), the author of *The Great Instauration* is indeed a puzzle.
On the one hand, he seems to have anticipated a mentality and a
number of ideas which did not become common property until
several centuries later, so that modern pragmatists can hail him
as one of their precursors and even Marxists such as Benjamin
Farrington can compare him to "ideologists of modern industrial
society" such as Marx and Engels. On the other hand, recent
research has made it very questionable whether Bacon really understood the "new method" which brought about the so-called "scientific revolution"; philosophers of science have accused him of having
overlooked such an important point of the "new method" as the

[218] *Oeuvres de Descartes*, eds. Ch. Adams and P. Tannery (Paris, 1897) VI, 61 ff.

central role of hypotheses in scientific experimentation,[219] and
recently it has even been suggested that Bacon's whole methodology
is deeply indebted to that of Aristotle and significantly inferior
to it.[220]

Without pretending to be able to clarify completely this curious
ambivalence in Bacon's "new philosophy," we should like to suggest
here that at least a part of the puzzle may be due to the failure
to recognize Bacon as a thinker who systematized and raised to
a method the mentality characteristic of Renaissance artisans
and artisan-scientists. As we shall try to show, this pragmatic
mentality of Renaissance artisans which Bacon converted into a
system and program did *not* merge with the ideas of the founders
of the modern scientific mentality, and in fact, under the impact
of "Cartesian" rationalism all but completely disappeared during
the seventeenth and eighteenth centuries. In other words, what
we want to suggest is that the main reason why Bacon appears to
us an unusually "modern" mind, even though his philosophy of
science is radically inferior to that of Galileo and Newton, or even
Descartes, is that Bacon succeeded in articulating a mentality which
had existed *before* the break-through of modern science, but
which was overshadowed by the latter's "Cartesian" self-interpretation and did not re-emerge until this "Cartesian" spirit of modern
science entered a period of crisis in the nineteenth century.

In order to make this claim plausible, we might say a few words
on the development of technology since the end of antiquity and
the emergence of the belief in progress which is so characteristic
of Francis Bacon. One hundred years ago it still was a widespread
belief that the sole legacy of the Middle Ages consisted of abstract
and usually inconclusive debates and Gothic cathedrals. Only
during the last decades have we begun to realize that the more than

[219] Cf. M. R. Cohen, "Bacon and the Inductive Method," *Studies in Philosophy
and Science* (New York, 1949) 99 ff. For a different view see C. J. Ducasse,
"Francis Bacon's Philosophy of Science," *Structure, Method, and Meaning*
(New York, 1951) 139.

[220] R. E. Larsen, "The Aristotelianism of Bacon's *Novum Organum*," *Journal
of the History of Ideas* 23 (1962) 435-450.

one thousand years between the end of antiquity and the beginning
of the so-called "modern times" was also a period of significant
technological innovation which produced far-reaching social changes
and led to the emergence of a radically new attitude of Western
man both toward nature and toward his "world."

We have to restrict ourselves to essentials.[221] The first point to
be noted is the obvious relationship between the acceleration of
technological progress, the unearthing of iron resources in Northern
Europe, and the shift of the centers of occidental civilization from
the Mediterranean area to countries north of the Alps during the
second half of the first millenium. It would of course be an exaggeration to say that there was *no* technological progress in antiquity,
but on the whole the great mass of mankind seems to have lived in
the fifth or sixth century A.D. in a style which differed little
from that of a period several centuries before Christ. One reason
for this stagnation (we have in mind only technology, not "science"
and philosophy) was the fact that iron was so rare and costly that
it was used almost exclusively for arms and for cutting edges.
As L. White put it,[222] even so prosperous a Roman city as Pompei
was living more in a Bronze than in an Iron Age as late as the second
half of the first century A.D. For the main iron resources of the
European continent are north of the Alps. Accordingly, it was not
until the great mines of northern Europe were opened that this
metal became cheap enough to become available for common uses and
thus play a role in Western technology. Yet once technology
began to progress thanks to this new material, the centers of
European civilization quickly shifted from the Mediterranean area
to northern Europe. Until about 800 A.D. Italy was the unquestion-
ed cultural center of the occidental world; two centuries later no
one could, and in fact did, doubt that the center of European

---

[221] For the following paragraphs see, among others, L. White, *Medieval Techno-
logy and Social Change* (Oxford, 1962); *idem*, "What Accelerated Technological
Progress in the Western Middle Ages?", *Scientific Change*, ed. A. C. Crombie
(London, 1961) 272-291; A. C. Crombie, *Medieval and Early Modern Science*
(Harvard, 1963); *idem*, *Robert Grosseteste and the Origins of Experimental
Science, 1100-1700* (Oxford, 1963).
[222] *Medieval Technology* 40.

civilization was France and, to a lesser extent, Germany, the Low Countries, and England.

We may add that this last circumstance is quite essential for a correct appreciation of the Italian Renaissance. Precisely because European civilization had shifted to the north, Italy's active participation in most of the important aspects of medieval culture lagged far behind that of the northern countries prior to the thirteenth century. As P. O. Kristeller[223] has shown some years ago, this may be observed in architecture and music, in the religious drama as well as in Latin vernacular poetry in general, in scholastic philosophy and theology, and even in classical studies. When Italian Renaissance scholars and writers talked of a revival and rebirth and referred to the "Dark Ages," they mainly had in mind the past of their *own* country, which though it still shared in some aspects of the classical tradition of ancient Rome and moreover was exposed to Byzantine influence more than any other European country, stood outside the mainstream of technological, agricultural, economic, and, therefore, cultural development of the medieval world.

Just as the greater availability of iron sped up technological progress, so technological progress resulted in an entirely novel system of agriculture. In the sixth century the heavy plough was invented and quickly spread to all parts of Europe to permit a greater agricultural productivity than the scratch plough used in the Mediterranean area since antiquity. The emergence of the nailed horseshoe and the modern harness in the ninth century permitted the peasants a more consistent use of the horse, a quicker and more durable work animal than the ox, for ploughing and harvesting. The three-field system of rotation, known since the late eighth century and further improved in the eleventh century made possible an increase in the fertility of arable land by one-third and even as much as by fifty percent when later the fallow was ploughed twice. As these and other innovations coalesced into a new system of agriculture, more food was available for an ex-

---

[223] P. O. Kristeller, "Humanism and Scholasticism in the Italian Renaissance," *Byzantion* 17 (1944-45) 346-374, here 348 ff.

panding population. The greater speed of the horse enabled peasants to live farther from their fields, a condition which in turn contributed to the emergence and growth of agricultural villages with a type of life that was almost urban; and the new productivity and resulting wealth permitted more and more peasants to leave their land for cities, industry, and commerce.

Around the year 1000 A.D. Western man began systematically to use natural powers. Except for the few ingenious toys devised by the "engineers" of Alexandria, who occasionally used wind and even steam, the only natural power ever used by the ancients was water; yet even water power was never used for processes other than grinding grain before the beginning of the eleventh century. It was around this time that there emerged the first fulling mills, trip hammers, and water-driven mills cutting marble, treating hemp, and forging iron. One century later the first horizontal axle windmill was built.

Once invented, these machines quickly spread over all Europe. The Cistercian regulations of the early twelfth century, for example, already recommended that monasteries be built near rivers that could supply power, and the *vita* of St. Bernard contains an elaborate description of water wheels in the Abbey of Clairvaux which powered shops for grinding grain, for shaking the sieve which separated flour from bran, and for fulling and tanning.[224] And Clairvaux certainly was neither an exception nor a particularly advanced abbey; similar water wheels were found in the abbeys of Royaumont, of Vaux de Cernay, of Fontenay, and elsewhere. Nor did such machines exist only in France; towards the end of the twelfth century the Fountains Abbey in Yorkshire is reported to have harnessed an underground river to supply power for a brewery, a corn mill, and various workshops.[225] And windmills spread so quickly that in the fourteenth century they were already found over all northern Europe to serve a truly amazing variety of purposes: for tanning and laundering; for sawing; for crushing anything from olives to ore; for operating the bellows of blast furnaces, the hammers

[224] Cf. *PL* CLXXXV, 570 ff.
[225] Ch. Singer *et al.*, *A History of Technology* (Oxford, 1956) II, 650 ff.

of forges, or grindstones; for reducing pigment to paint, or pulp for paper, or mash for beer; and even for polishing diamonds and emeralds.[226]

This mechanization made possible production on a comparatively large scale and soon led to a significant refinement of techniques in general. It became possible to make instruments of precision such as the astrolabe, the compass, and the mechanical clock. New techniques were developed in a constantly increasing number of arts. In the eleventh century architects faced new problems of construction; the twelfth century witnessed innovations in glass and window making, and the thirteenth century, the first use of spectacles; in the fourteenth century the wood cuts and block printing known since the twelfth century were replaced by movable cast-metal type, thus making possible the printing of the entire books.

Beginning with the thirteenth century, this technological development tended to result in a new interest in methods for solving practical problems better than the age-old method of trial and error. Intellectuals, not only artisans, began to be interested in "practical problems" and techniques. Early in the twelfth century Adelard of Bath edited an eighth-century treatise on the preparation of pigments, the *Mappae Clavicula*, which contains the earliest-known account of the preparation of alcohol; about the middle of the same century a German artisan-monk writing under the pseudonym Theophilus Presbyter discussed in his *De diversis artibus* (which later excited Lessing and his contemporaries) all conceivable techniques in painting, glass making, and metal work, including sophisticated methods of casting bell chimes for playing in tune; at the end of the twelfth century Roger of Salerno published his *Practica chirurgica*,[227] the first great Western treatise on surgery; in the thirteenth century Peter of Saint Omer wrote his *Liber de coloribus faciendibus*, an elaborate study on the preparation of pigments which anticipated fifteenth-century treatises

---

[226] Cf. L. White, "What accelerated, etc." 283.

[227] In late medieval Latin emerged the uggly expressions 'practico' or even 'practizo' which often are used in connection with medicine ('practizo chirurgiam' = 'I practice surgery').

such as Cennini's *Libro dell'arte*; Walter of Henley and Peter of
Crescenzi wrote on agriculture; Giles of Rome on the "art of war."
The thirteenth-century encyclopedias of Albert the Great, Alexander
Neckham, and Roger Bacon contained numerous and quite exact
information about the compass, chemistry, agriculture, and other
technological matters. Robert Grosseteste's studies of optics led
to significant reflections on what later became known as the scientific
experimental method; toward the end of the thirteenth century
Dietrich of Freiberg's treatise on the rainbow, *De iride et radialibus
impressionibus*, already involved an intricate combination of geometry and experimental approach, in addition to methodological tenets
developed already by Grosseteste and his school, such as the principle of experimental falsification, or the *lex parsimoniae* (later
known as "Ockham's razor"), according to which an explanation
was the better the less unobservable entities it postulated and
the less assumptions it entailed.

It cannot be our task to further elaborate on this gradual but
increasingly powerful maturing of technology and science. But
we may add a few remarks on the emergence of the notion of
progress, which, it would seem, is closely connected with the de
facto progress just described and is essential for understanding
the attitude of men such as Francis Bacon. The notion of progress
in the wisdom and moral perfection of individuals is of course
very old; the Stoics discussed it repeatedly[228] and to Christian
thinkers it was a commonplace. But it is something quite different
to maintain that each generation builds upon the achievements
of previous generations and perfects them still further.

Earlier we quoted a few passages in Seneca which suggest that
even this kind of progress was not thoroughly unknown to the
ancients. In any case, *some* thinkers of antiquity knew of the
possibility of a progress of "scientific" knowledge and recognized
its value. However, one immediately will have to add that Seneca
certainly did not see the value of such a progress in any advantage
which it might bring to mankind in general. First of all, to all
thinkers of antiquity the value of a knowledge of nature and its

---

[228] Cf. *Stoicorum Vet. Fragm.* I, 234; III, 530-543.

progress lay in the contemplative activity itself and possibly in
the moral impact which this activity involved, but certainly
not in some improvement of mankind's lot which might result
from the progress in question. Secondly, this progress concerned
not mankind as a whole but only a few chosen individuals—the
philosophers who delivered themselves from the misery of this
world by transcending it in terms of a contemplative knowledge of
the eternal.[229]

In fact, it was Christianity, not antiquity, that prepared the
ground for the modern notion of progress. For it was Christianity
that definitively did away with the notion that the course of history
was cyclic, that is, consisted of a virtually infinite series of comparatively brief ages, each of which reiterated the preceding
one. Christianity for the first time made man aware of the fact
that history is a unique event which never had occurred before
and never would occur again. Moreover, it ascribed to history
as a whole (as opposed to the history of a tribe or a nation) a definite directional meaning. There was a prehistorical beginning,
the Paradise, and a posthistorical end, the New Jerusalem; and
if one viewed the Fall, not creation or the Paradise, as the beginning,
the movement of history quite clearly lead from a corrupt to a
perfect state—at least since Christ had come to save man and had
promised to return in glory.

Of course, this historical progress suggested by Christianity did
not first concern *visible* man and his world. St. Augustine's *City
of God* certainly to some extent entails the idea that there is progress
in history, indeed that the course of history as a whole is progressive.
But the progress which St. Augustine had in mind was neither
visible to the human eye nor, in particular, due to man's own
deeds; it went on behind the scene and was essentially a progress in
the order of grace and supernatural salvation. Nothing indicates that
St. Augustine ever had in mind an improvement of man's lot on
this earth; on the contrary, his theology of history was an attempt
to make sense of what most of his contemporaries considered a
perfectly unintelligible catastrophy, the fall of Rome in 410 A.D.

---

[229] Cf. J. B. Bury, *The Idea of Progress* (London, 1920) 14, cf. 51.

In medieval thinkers such as Hugh of St. Victor or Robert Kilwardby, on the contrary, one already notices some awareness of the fact that past ages had known less and that mankind had "progressed." This, in particular, is suggested by their great interest in the "origin of sciences." Hugh of St. Victor, for example, described arts and sciences as man's historical response to the wretchedness introduced by original sin. Banished from the paradise, man realized that he knew nothing, desired evil, and, last but not least, was infirm, naked, and mortal:

> Therefore he began with all might to struggle for liberation in order to overcome evil and become good. This is the origin of the quest for wisdom which one calls philosophy. It is sought in order that ignorance be illuminated by a knowledge of truth, evil concupiscence extinguished by the love of virtue, and bodily infirmity reduced by the discovery of useful things.[230]

One hundred years later Robert Kilwardby advanced a similar idea by arguing that mechanical arts arose because of man's bodily needs, for which nature had not provided (as in the case of plants and animals), because man had been given reason to use in clothing, feeding, housing, and defending himself.[231]

In the thirteenth and fourteenth centuries, it is true, such insights were somewhat overshadowed by the rediscovery of the wisdom of the ancients. Thinkers such as Albert the Great, Aquinas, or even Roger Bacon felt that Aristotle, despite a few shortcomings resulting from his paganism, had been a better philosopher than all the Fathers of the Church, including St. Augustine; the translation of Euclid's *Elementa* in 1254 made mathematicians aware of the fact that while they certainly had been able to use the conclusions of Greek geometry for practical purposes and even had advanced beyond the Greeks as far as "practical geometry" was

---

[230] *Epitome Dindimi in philosophiam*, ed. R. Baron, *Traditio* 11 (1955) 151 ff.: "Et idcirco [homo] coepit obniti et exire, qua potuit virtute, in liberationem suam ut evaderet mala sua et bona obtineret. Hinc profecta est quam dicunt philosophiam studium sapientiae quaerendam ut ignorantiam agnitio veritatis illuminaret, concupiscentiam pravam amor virtutis extingueret, infirmitatem vero studium quaerendi commodi temperaret."

[231] Cf. D. E. Sharp, art. cit. 18.

concerned, they still had to learn from the ancients how to dem-
onstrate their conclusions; scholars interested in medicine and
physiology realized that their knowledge of these fields fell far
short of that attained by Galen; etc. As a result, during this period,
to learn more and to progress in knowledge often meant to recover
and to rethink a wisdom of the past, not to make radically new
discoveries.

It would of course be an exaggeration to say that thinkers of the
thirteenth century, for example, had no inkling of progress at all.
Even a perfectly ahistorical thinker like Aquinas was aware of
the fact that theoretical knowledge had increased in the course of
the centuries and that something analogous applied even to the
realm of the *operabilia* useful to human society.[232] In fact, there
even existed thinkers who felt challenged by the fact that pagans
of the past had known more than contemporary Christians. Thus
Roger Bacon once argued that Christians ought to "complete the
paths of unbelieving philosophers, not only because we are of a later
age and ought to add to their work, but that we may compel the
widsom of the [pagan] philosophers to serve zealously our own."[233]

Yet it cannot be denied that the thirteenth century was much
less aware of progress than, for example, the twelfth or even the
eleventh century. This certainly was not due to a greater "otherworldliness" of the thirteenth century. Hugh of St. Victor, for
example, certainly was much more otherworldly minded than
Aquinas or Albert the Great; at the same time, however, he seems
to have been much more interested in the technological and quasi-
technological phenomena of his time than either of the two great
theologians of the thirteenth century—and significantly more aware
of the fact that man develops and progresses. What seems to
have happened here is that the rediscovery of the ancients, especially
of Aristotle, drew the attention of the best minds of the thirteenth
century to highly formal and abstract problems, an area in which
the Middle Ages, despite the great technological progress mentioned
above, were still lagging behind the insights of the ancients.

[232] *S.Th.* II-II, 1, 7 ob. 2; I-II, 97, 1.
[233] *Opus Majus* II, 14, ed. J. H. Bridges (Oxford, 1897) I, 57.

In a sense one might even argue that the thirteenth century was aware of a connection between the advancement of knowledge and man's fate in this world less than the two preceding centuries. Roger Bacon, it is true, occasionally argues that "practical" sciences such as "practical alchemy" should be valued higher than theoretical sciences because they grant a power over nature useful to man. But it would be wrong, as some authors do,[234] to ascribe to Bacon the belief in progress characteristic of his namesake, Francis. On the whole, Roger Bacon's image of the future of Christianity and mankind was quite pessimistic: he anticipated that the Mohammedans would overrun Europe, expected the Antichrist to come any moment, and was convinced that the world would end soon. In any case, when he wrote urging the pope to reform higher education, he did not have in mind either an improvement of mankind's lot or a satisfaction of man's more secular needs. He was simply interested in theoretical, scientific problems; and the "utility" which he expected from the various sciences consisted mainly in that they would enable Christians to understand better the Holy Scripture and be armed against the Antichrist. Thus he considered astronomy important because it helped to verify biblical geography and determine the dates of biblical events such as the deluge or even creation; or geography because it permitted one to predict the location of the Antichrist's birth; or his famous "experimental science" because it permitted the construction of wondrous instruments that could be used to convert the enemies of faith "who should be destroyed by the discoveries of science rather than by the warlike arms of combatants"[235]; and, in general, all scientific knowledge because it contributed to mankind's salvation (*ad salutem humani generis*) by helping Christians to grasp things which one had to know in order to reach the happiness of afterlife.[236]

Contrary to what one might expect, the Renaissance at first was even less concerned with progress than the thirteenth century and certainly much less aware of a progress achieved in the past

---

[234] A. C. Crombie, *Medieval and Early Modern Science* II, 54 ff.
[235] *Opus Majus*, ed. Bridges, II, 221.
[236] *Ibid.* II, 366.

than twelfth-century encyclopedists such as Hugh of St. Victor. This applies in particular to the humanists, to whom antiquity was the perfect age to an extent which Aquinas or Albert would have considered preposterous; the major and often only concern of the humanists was the study and imitation of classical Greek and Latin literature. This is not to deny that in some fields the humanists achieved a de facto progress, as, for example, when they tried to identify animals, plants, and minerals mentioned by the ancients and to their distress had to discover that the Greeks and Romans had not known everything. But in most instances this did not prevent them from considering the classical authors unsurpassable.

It is of course true that Renaissance writers constantly talked of a revival and rebirth; in fact talked about it more consistently than the men of any other period in European history. But they completely lacked the notion that their studies might be a contribution to mankind's knowledge and skills. Imitating their classical heroes, they felt that the main goal of literary activities was fame. Thus, for example, as late as 1621 the French humanist Bachet introduced his edition of Diophantus' *Arithmetic* by recounting that he became a mathematician because in mathematics "the subtlety of one's intellect especially comes to light" and that his publications would show whether he, Bachet, "deserved fame beyond the ordinary mathematicians."[237] In order to do justice to Bachet and other humanists, one of course will have to add that their yearning for fame was not simply an expression of personal vanity; it was based upon the classical notion that "immortality" through rememberance by future generation was the ultimate purpose of poetry and literature. But their striving for fame obviously made them blind to the possibility that their literary efforts might further science or the arts. In fact, as they constantly strove for fame, the literary and scholarly careers of the humanists were full of rivalries, quarrels, and personal intrigues. It certainly is not by chance that even though thinkers such as Ficino occasionally speculated

[237] Quoted by E. Zilsel, "The Genesis of the Concept of Scientific Progress," *Journal of the History of Ideas* 6 (1945) 325-349, here 330.

about human solidarity in a way unknown to previous ages, the humanists did not produce a single encyclopedia or dictionary composed by several authors in collaboration.

On the other hand, it was the humanists who in the last decades of the sixteenth century began to formulate the modern notion of progress. As historical information accumulated, scholars became official historiographers at various courts and historiography began to be a distinctive branch of learning. Humanists began to write treatises concerned with historiographical methodology—and at that point realized that their predecessors had been wrong in assuming that antiquity had been a golden age, after which only silver and iron ages could possibly follow. Thus in a treatise on the method of historiography first published in 1566 the French humanist and lawyer Jean Bodin argued that if one compared the so-called golden age to the present, one might well describe the former as an iron age:

> Here you have your golden and silver age: men were dispersed in the open country and the woods like animals and had only as much as they could obtain through violence and crime— until step by step they found their way from that savage and barbarian life to the civilized customs and the ordered society which we witness today.[238]

A contemporary of Bodin, Louis Le Roy, who gained a reputation among humanists by translating Aristotle and Plato into French, was even more explicit. Unlike Bodin, who was mainly interested in legal and political problems, Le Roy was struck by "the many discoveries of the past hundred years." In his *Considérations sur l'histoire universelle* he enumerates the "discoveries" which struck him most: "new seas, new lands, new kinds of men, customs, laws, practices, new herbs, trees, minerals," as well as "recently made inventions such as printing, artillery, and the use of the needle and magnet in navigation." A few years later, in his *De la vicissitude des choses en l'univers*, which was translated into English as early as 1594, Le Roy advanced what might be called the first modern articulation of the notion and ideal of historical progress:

---

[238] *Methodus ad facilem historiarum cognitionem* VII; J. Bodin, *Oeuvres Philosophiques* (Paris, 1951) V, 3, 226 b, line 39 ff.

The beginnings of the Artes have bin small, and the greatest
difficultie, was in the first inventing of them; then by the in-
dustrie of the learned, they were by little and little augmented;
correcting such things as were evill observed, and supplying
such as were omitted; but yet, without making any thing entirely absolute; whereunto there might nothing be added....
Almost all the Artes have bin invented by Use and Experience;
and after wardes gathered and made by observation and reason;
and then consequently reduced into the better forme and more
certain ... by general precepts and rules drawen from nature,
nor from opinion, and tending to the same ende: not by staying
and resting on that which men had formerly done, said or written;
nor by only imitating of them, after the manner of slouthfull,
and cowardly persons: but by the adding of somewhat of their
owne, by some that came after, according as the matters from
time to time discovered, and cleared themselves; the honour
commonly remayning to the last commers, as the most exquisite,
and accomplished. By whose example we ought to travaile
courageously, with hope to make ourselves better than them;
aspiring continually to perfection, which as yet is not seene any
where: considering that there remayne more thinges to be
sought out, then are alreadie invented and founde. And let
us not be so simple, as to attribute so much unto the Ancients,
that we believe that they have knowen all, and said all....[239]

Where did this sudden awareness of and enthusiasm for progress
come from? At first sight it might seem that it was due mainly
to new scientific discoveries. But in reality the sixteenth century
was *not* a period of great scientific discoveries, notwithstanding the
fact that the "scientific revolution" of the seventeenth century
would have been impossible without ideas developed at that time.
In fact, the only "discoveries" explicitly mentioned by writers of this
period are the three "inventions" made famous by Francis Bacon:
printing, the compass, and gunpowder. But these certainly were
not inventions of the sixteenth or even the fifteenth century.
Printing had gradually developed since the end of the twelfth century, the compass had been known at least since the beginning of
the thirteenth century, and the gunpowder formula was known

---

[239] Quoted by H. Weisinger, "Ideas of History during the Renaissance,"
Journal of the History of Ideas 6 (1945) 415-435, here 418 ff., according to *Of the
Interchangeable Course, or Variety of Things*, tr. R. Ashley (London, 1594).

to Roger Bacon around 1250.[240] Moreover, neither of the three items mentioned can properly be described as a scientific discovery; they are technological innovations.

But neither would it be entirely correct to argue that the new enthusiasm for progress was mainly due to technological innovations. For even though occidental technology was constantly progressing, nothing indicates that the last decades of the sixteenth century were a period of a particularly striking progress in technology. In fact, reading the authors of that time, one gets the impression that what most contributed to the new enthusiasm for progress was, on the one hand, the discovery of "new seas, new lands, new kinds of men" and, on the other hand, and above all, the *great wealth* produced both by these discoveries and by the technological progress of the past centuries. Certainly it cannot be denied that during this period the humanists became increasingly aware that as the ancients had known only a comparatively small part of the world, there still existed *des choses ... entièrement ignorées des anciens* (as Le Roy put it), and a great period of discovery still lay ahead. For example, in his popular autobiography of 1575 Cardano mentions as the most extraordinary circumstance of his life, which certainly was far from ordinary, that he was born in a century "in which the whole world became known while the ancients were familiar with but little more than a third part of it." In addition, the geographical discoveries had in turn contributed to the wealth of many European countries—at least people believed so. Le Roy, for example, lists the many new things which came to be known as a result of the discovery of new lands—sugar, pearls, spices, herbs, trees, fruits, gold—and intimates that they had brought about an economy of abundance. Several decades before Le Roy the same point had been made even more forcefully by the much read *Historia de las Indias* of the Spaniard Francisco Lopez de Gomara.[241]

But this is not the whole picture. After all, America had been discovered at the end of the fifteenth century, almost a hundred

[240] Cf. W. R. Newbold, *The Cipher of Roger Bacon* (Philadelphia, 1928) 141 ff.
[241] Cf. the article by Weisinger.

years before authors like Bodin, Le Roy, or Cardano wrote the lines just quoted. One will have to add that there was at least one group in Renaissance society which had begun to be aware of "progress" as early as the beginning of the fifteenth century, a group which was in close touch with technology and technological progress and, last but not least, introduced into European culture the pragmatic tone which today strikes us so much in Francis Bacon — *the artisans.* With the dissolution of the medieval social order beginning around the second half of the thirteenth century, the situation and also the mentality of the European artisan had undergone a significant change. While in the Middle Ages he had been taught to honor the tradition of his workshop and guild more than wealth or social position, rising capitalism and economic competition literally forced him to be above all inventive; only an artisan who either invented something new or at least knew how to use the invention of another fellow could hope to share in the constantly increasing wealth of society as a whole. At the same time, however, the postmedieval artisan was not cynical enough to admit openly that his motives were no longer the honor of his trade or the glory of God and the saints. Nor could he well strive for literary fame like the humanists. His social position, in combination with his Christian mentality and the sense of cooperation characteristic of artisans of all times, directed him to more impersonal goals. In order to justify his work and to explain why he tried to invent new things he pointed to the public benefit which would result from his work as well as to the usefulness of his innovations either to fellows in the profession or to mankind in general.

As E. Zilsel[242] has shown in an interesting article published more than twenty years ago, such ideas are in fact found in the occasional publications of superior artisans such as painters, instrument makers, and gun makers from the beginning of the fifteenth century, and from about 1500 in the writings of artisan-scientists such as military engineers (Tartaglia, Stevinus) and surgeons (A. Paré). Many

---

[242] Cf. fn. 237. On this point see also A. R. Hall, *The Scientific Revolution 1500-1800* (Boston, 1966) 220 ff.; *idem,* "The Scholar and the Craftsman in the Scientific Revolution," *Critical Problems in the History of Science* (Madison, 1959).

decades before the humanists began to speak about progress, such men argued that whatever man does should "better wherever there is something to be bettered," develop the existing arts, and serve mankind.

It is this attitude toward knowledge which Francis Bacon articulated into a program for revolutionizing the whole of science. Even though he somewhat overstated his point, Benjamin Farrington certainly was right when he argued that the greatness of the philosophizing Lord Chancellor consists neither in his scientific discoveries, virtually nonexistent, nor in his philosophy of science, which in fact had virtually no impact upon the "scientific revolution." Rather his greatness consists in having made explicit the self-understanding of an emerging industrial and capitalist society, of having translated into an articulate, philosophical program the social aspirations and ideals which, underneath the abstract thinking of philosophers and forerunners of science, had gradually developed in the minds of common people since the end of the thirteenth century. Knowledge, instead of aiming at patterns which are as lofty as they are useless, ought to bear fruits in works; science ought to be "practical," that is, applicable to technological progress and to an industry serving mankind; and all men "ought to organize themselves as a sacred duty to improve and transform the conditions of life."[243]

[243] B. Farrington, *Francis Bacon* (London, 1951) 3.

8: THE RATIONALIST REACTION

It would of course be an oversimplification to claim that Francis Bacon's antitheoretical attitude, which tended to make theoretical knowledge subservient to technology, was nothing more than an articulation of the artisan, urban, and basically bourgeois mentality which between the thirteenth and sixteenth centuries gradually got the better of the medieval otherworldly conception.

One would have to add that the three centuries in question were also a period during which philosophers came to emphasize the basic uncertainty of all theories concerning the natural world. This was in part an outgrowth of the momentous condemnation of 1277 in which the bishop of Paris, Stephen Tempier, declared contrary to Catholic faith more than two hundred cosmological and metaphysical theses of Averroistic inspiration. It has been argued that this condemnation had a generally salutary effect as far as the history of science is concerned, since it freed medieval natural philosophy from the bondage of Aristotelianism and its ultrarealistic attitude.[244] More recently, however, it has been rightly pointed out that this condemnation also created an *atmosphere of scepticism* which first had to be overcome before modern science could enter what Kant later called the "sure path of science," for many of the condemned propositions seemed philosophically well founded, so that their condemnation by the Church threw suspicion upon the force of philosophical and "scientific" arguments in general.[245]

---

[244] Especially P. Duhem, *Études sur Léonard de Vinci* (Paris, 1906 ff.) II, 412 ff.

[245] Cf. E. Grant, "Late Medieval Thought, Copernicus, and the Scientific Revolution," *Journal of the History of Ideas* 23 (1962) 197-220.

That the latter view is more correct is evident among other things from the fact that most of the fourteenth-, fifteenth-, and six-teenth-century precursors of modern scientific thought considered their theories mere "hypotheses" which did not "picture" reality but were only convenient means for calculating and thus for "saving the phenomena." To astronomers, it is true, this nonrealistic understanding of scientific theories was familiar since antiquity. When Ptolemy succeeded in "saving" astronomical phenomena better than anyone before him, but succeeded in doing so only in terms of assumptions which contradicted Aristotle's physics, many Aristotelians resolved the resulting dilemma by arguing that Ptolemy's astronomy did not describe the real motions of heavenly bodies but was only a mathematical fiction permitting the calcula-tion of apparent motions. In fact, Ptolemy himself suggested this interpretation when in the first book of his *Almagest* he de-fended as "objectively true" a number of Aristotle's principles which were incompatible with his astronomical model.[246] In the fifth century this conception was revived by Proclus, and in the sixth century in a famous passage in his commentary on Aristotle's *De Caelo*, Simplicius explicitly argued that astronomers, unlike natural philosophers, accepted their theories only to save the phenomena without at all maintaining that an "actual tapestry (ποικιλία) in the heaven" corresponded to them.[247]

Simplicius' commentary was translated into Latin by William of Moerbeke in 1271. But even before that time this nonrealistic interpretation of astronomy had a wide following among medieval thinkers. Scholars as different as Moses Maimonides in the twelfth century, Aquinas in the thirteenth century, John Buridan, Nicholas of Oresme, Albert of Saxony, and Peter of Ailly in the fourteenth century adhered to it; in general, it prevailed until the end of the sixteenth century. The only exception were the Averroists (who after their condemnation at Paris remained active chiefly in Padua); as they subscribed to Eudoxus' astronomy of homocentric spheres

---

[246] *Syntaxis*, ed. Heidberg, 24, 14 ff.

[247] *In de caelo* III, 1, 253 a 40-42; ed. Heidberg, *Comment. in Arist. Graeca* VII, 565.

which had been sanctioned by Aristotle because it was compatible with his physics, they staunchly upheld a realistic interpretation.[248]

From the fourteenth century, however this nonrealistic interpretation gradually was extended from astronomy to natural philosophy in general. We cannot possibly speculate here on the probable reasons for this development. It may suffice to point out, first, that it certainly was not without significance that the condemnation of 1277 chiefly concerned the Averroists, that is, the school which on the one hand had carried deterministic natural philosophy further than any other and on the other hand was famous for its interpreting all theories realistically. One of the many curious propositions condemned by Bishop Tempier was the claim *quod ratio philosophi demonstrans motum celi esse aeternum non est sophistica*, that the philosophers' arguments demonstrating the eternity of heavenly motions are not "sophistical."[249] It is very unlikely that Tempier wished to condemn the Averroists for not admitting that their cosmological arguments were "deceptive" (instead of simply condemning them for upholding the conclusions). Accordingly, it would seem likely that the expression '*sophistica*' did not mean "deceptive" but rather something like "dialectical" and that consequently the bishop of Paris reprimanded Siger of Brabant and his followers for claiming that their cosmological theories were more than expedient assumptions useful for astronomical calculations. This is how William of Heytesbury uses the expression '*sophistice*' half a century later: *physice loquendo*, one follows experience and the principles of Aristotle's physics, while *sophistice loquendo*, one is free to introduce whatever distinctions and cases are imaginable and convenient.[250]

This leads us to a second point. Ockham's nominalist reductionism, together with his emphasis upon the fact that science is not about the things themselves but at most about mental contents

---

[248] Cf. R. M. Blake *et al.*, *Theories of Scientific Method* (Seattle, 1960) 22 ff.
[249] Cf. *Chartularium Universitatis Parisiensis*, ed. H. Denifle (Paris, 1889 ff.) I, 458, proposition 91.
[250] Cf. C. Wilson, *William Heytesbury: Medieval Logic and the Rise of Mathematical Physics* (Madison, 1959) 25.

standing for things,[251] produced the tendency to put aside the problem of "literal truth" and instead to look for scientific workableness
and logical consistency. Throughout the fourteenth century
nominalists liked to use the phrase '*secundum imaginationem*'
and to work in natural philosophy in terms of "imaginable cases"
which they were fully aware were physically impossible. In fact, as
C. Wilson has pointed out in his interesting study on the connection
between late medieval logic and the rise of mathematical physics,[252]
the nominalist reductionist tendency in no way operated as a
prescription against the construction of remote conceptual possibilities. On the contrary, even while the nominalists argued that entities
of which there was no immediate experience did not exist, they
readily multiplied *imaginabilia* which permitted one to calculate
the appearances, even though they did not apply to the real.

Nicholas of Oresme, for example, in his *De configurationibus
qualitatum* seems to have been fully aware of the fact that he was
using the astronomers' approach, even though he obviously was
speaking about the sublunar world. This work, written around
1360, marks the first systematic discussion in history of qualita-
tive changes (including velocity) in terms of geometical constructs.
It abounds in phrases such as '*imaginatur*' and '*mathematice
fingere*,' thus emphasizing the fact that the analyses in question
are figurative presentations of "hypothetical" quality changes
completely unrelated to any conceivable empirical investigation.[253]
Similarly, in his commentary to Aristotle's *Physics* John Buridan
suggests that his theory of impetus might make obsolete Aristotle's
doctrine that intelligences moved the heavenly bodies, but in the
end he adds that he speaks only tentatively to challenge the theologians to tell him how such things *really* take place.[254] In the fifteenth
century Nicolas of Cusa, no longer taking seriously Aristotle's
distinction between celestial and terrestrial matter, enlarges upon

[251] Cf. e.g. *In Phys.*, prologus; Ockham, *Philosophical Writings*, ed. Ph.
Boehner (New York, 1957) 12.

[252] *Op. cit.* 25, 174.

[253] Cf. the text quoted in M. Clagett, *The Science of Mechanics in the Middle
Ages* (Madison, 1961) 368 ff.

[254] Cf. *ibid.* 536. Cf. the article by Grant.

his basic conviction that *no* human science can reach the *true* causes and essences of material things but forever has to be satisfied with *fictitious* conceptions that allow one to rationalize phenomena.

We may do well to add that this method of "saving the appearances" by geometrical fictions had little if anything to do with the so-called "hypothetico-deductive method." The nominalists were not interested in whether their theories were true; in fact, contrary to what is often believed, they were very little interested in the empirical verification which alone would have permitted them to decide this kind of question. What interested them were constructs to which they knew nothing real corresponded but which nevertheless permitted one to calculate, and in a sense even rationalize, appearances more successfully than allegedly "true theories." Apart from that the nonrealistic interpretation of theories often simply reflected an attitude common to all nominalists, namely, their basic scepticism as to the force of natural reason with respect to all but purely logical and formal matters.

A striking case in point is Nicholas of Oresme's often-quoted criticism of traditional arguments againts the earth's rotation. After showing with elaborate detail that one cannot argue against the earth's rotation either by an appeal to experience or by a test of reason, and that in fact one even can adduce reasons for the support of this assumption, he concludes by saying: *et nientmoins touz tiennent et je cuide que il* [sc. *le ciel*] *est ainsi meü et la terre non ... nonobstant les raisons au contraire.*[255] In other words, far from wanting to show that Ptolemaic astronomy is wrong and heliocentrism right, Nicholas' laborious argument only aims at showing that both conceptions are "imaginable" and consequently equally uncertain. In an earlier writing, *Quaestiones de spera*, he is even more explicit: by making a number of assumptions (*pono imaginationes*) he shows that the appearances can be saved even if one assumes the earth's rotation (*ad salvandum apparentiam sufficit ...*), and he concludes that therefore the conception that the earth does not move *non potest demonstrari sed persuaderi ... et ideo est credita,*

---

[255] Maistre Nicole Oresme, *Le Livre du Ciel et du Monde*, eds. A. D. Menut and A. J. Denomy, *Medieval Studies* 4 (1942) 279.

cannot be demonstrated but only argued by persuasion and thus is a matter of mere belief.[256]

The founders of modern astronomy and physics, on the contrary, were deeply convinced of the truth of their theories. Copernicus, for example, quite obviously felt that his astronomy was more than just a set of "imaginations" making possible the calculation of the apparent motions of heavenly bodies. While Andreas Osiander, in his utterly misleading preface to the first edition (1543) of Copernicus' *De revolutionibus*, clearly followed the traditional conception by arguing that astronomical theories need not be true or even probable,[257] Copernicus himself explained that the deficiencies of Ptolemaic astronomers were a result of their not having followed *certa principia*, sure principles. "For if the hypotheses assumed by them were not false, everything which follows from these hypotheses would be verified beyond any doubt."[258] And the *certa principia* in question quite obviously were physical laws. For Copernicus' basic objection against Ptolemaic astronomy was not it did not succeed in satisfactorily saving the appearances; in fact, he even granted that Ptolemaic astronomy was consistent with the numerical data. What he objected to was the fact that Ptolemaic astronomy violated a physical law generally agreed to be true, for Ptolemy had arranged the planetary motions to be uniform only with reference to some point other than their own center and thus had violated the "axiom of uniformity." In the

---

[256] Cf. the text quoted by M. Clagett, *op. cit.* 608 ff. It should be noted, however, that Nicholas of Oresme discusses only the *diurnal* rotation of the earth, which is not incompatible with a geocentric system. The notion of an annual rotation is due to Copernicus.

[257] Nikolaus Kopernikus, *Gesamtausgabe* (Munich, 1949 ff.) II, 403: "Neque enim necesse est eas hypotheses esse veras, immo ne verisimiles quidem, sed sufficit hoc unum, si calculum observationibus congruentem exhibeant."

[258] *Ibid.* 6: "Nam si assumptae illorum hypotheses non essent fallaces, omnia quae ex illis sequuntur, verificarentur procul dubio." One might add that the defenders of a nonrealistic interpretation of astronomical theories were of course quite well aware of the fact that as their theories were not "true" they eventually would encounter difficulties. But quite characteristically, this was not understood either as an objection against the theory itself or as an objection against its nonrealistic interpretation.

Commentariolus one even finds a highly characteristic reversal of the traditional way of arguing: while the Aristotelians had argued that the earth's immobility was a physical fact and any theory assuming the earth's rotation could only be a "hypothesis" helping to save the appearances, Copernicus argued that all arguments for the earth's immobility rested on appearances and thus literally accused the Aristotelians of trying only to save the phenomena instead of *piercing through them to the real heart of the matter*. "*I* treat earth's immobility as due to an appearance."[259]

A similar attitude may be found in Kepler and Galileo. When in 1597 a defender of the nonrealistic interpretation, Reimarus Ursus, argued that astronomical hypotheses were physically false by definition, Kepler heatedly replied that *good* hypotheses could not possibly be mere fictions, since if one started with false assumptions, errors were bound to result in the long run.[260] Similarly, when in 1615 Cardinal Bellarmine warned Galileo that he ought to content himself with advancing the heliocentric conception *ex suppositione e non assolutamente*, as a mathematical fiction and not as physically true, Galileo replied that even though his own conception conceivably might be wrong, the Ptolemaic system was *indubitabilmente falso*, false beyond any doubt, thus unambiguously suggesting that astronomical hypotheses could claim to be true in the literal sense of the term.[261]

We cannot possibly discuss all the implications of this obviously far-reaching shift of emphasis. It must suffice to point out that just as Francis Bacon's basically antitheoretical and pragmatic attitude among other things was a last articulation of the scepticism which had pervaded philosophy and science after the thirteenth century, the new interest in a pure and realistic theory, which is characteristic of the seventeenth-century founders of modern astronomy and physics, was due to their rediscovery of "absolute

---

[259] Cf. *Three Copernican Treatises*, tr. and ed. E. Rosen (New York, 1939) 59.
[260] R. M. Blake *et al.*, *op. cit.* 39 ff.
[261] For Bellarmine's letter, cf. *Le Opere di Galileo Galilei* (Florence, 1929 ff.) XII, 171 ff.; for Galileo's draft of a reply which eventually he did not send, *ibid.* V, 367 ff., here 369, no. 7: "Quello è indubitabilmente falso, si come è chiaro che questo, che si accommoda benissimo, può essere vero."

truth" in the study of nature. But it immediately has to be added that it was a *re*discovery in name only. For the "absolute truth" which thinkers such as Copernicus, Kepler, and Galileo discovered radically differed from that of the midthirteenth-century philosophers of nature such as Aquinas or Albert the Great. Indeed, the new truths were *mathematical truths*. Precisely because the founders of modern science interpreted realistically the *kind of* theories which earlier astronomers and physicists such as Nicholas of Oresme considered mere "hypotheses"—that is, theories fundamentally geometrical in nature—mathematical and mathematicophysical entities became for men such as Copernicus and Galileo the *essence of the natural world*. As Galileo put it in a rightly famous passage in *The Assayer*, the "grand book of the universe" continually stands open to our gaze, but one cannot understand it unless one first learns to understand the language and to recognize the letters in which it is written: "It is written in mathematical language and its characters are triangles, circles, and other geometrical figures ... without which one wanders about in a dark labyrinth."[262]

And just as in Plotinus the discovery of a radically transcendent object of contemplation had for centuries resulted in a degradation of practical wisdom, so in the seventeenth century the discovery of the geometrical transparency of the natural world completely overshadowed both the practical wisdom rediscovered by the Middle Ages and the pragmatic conception of "fruits and works" developed by the Renaissance. This is not unambiguously clear in thinkers such as Galileo, it is true; in spite of his belief in the mathematical nature of the universe many of Galileo's statements recall the Renaissance mentality. But already with Descartes this pragmatic attitude is completely replaced by the notion that all reality accessible to man ought to be deduced from and in a sense even reduced to mathematics. As Descartes puts it in a letter to Mersenne, he would feel that he knew nothing about the world of nature if he knew only "how things *may* be without demonstrating that they cannot be otherwise." And proudly he adds:

[262] *Ibid.* VI, 232.

"Having reduced physics to mathematical laws, I know it is possible."[263]

Nothing illustrates the mentality characteristic of this new rationalism better than the three pages on the unity of knowledge in which Descartes comments on the first of his *Regulae ad directionem ingenii*.[264] Traditionally, philosophers had distinguished between various species and subspecies of knowledge: theoretical and practical, physics, mathematics, metaphysics, knowledge about doing and about making, etc.; and in each case they had tried to classify each according to the degree of intelligibility and certitude available and the specific method to be applied. But, argued Descartes, it was only owing to a confusion that such distinctions were introduced. For there is only one human wisdom, *quae semper una et eadem manet*, which always remains one and the same; it suffers no more differentiation from its application to different objects than the light of the sun is affected by the differences amongst the objects on which it shines. Indeed, the ancients had belabored their distinctions between various sciences only because they confused science with arts. Seeing that the acquisition of an art requires bodily skills which make one unsuited for other arts, they believed that something similar was the case with science; for example, they thought that the certainty of mathematics was unattainable in sciences concerned with concrete realities and that the method of each science should correspond and therefore vary with its objects. *In quo sane decepti sunt:* here they erred radically, both because they overlooked that all sciences are interconnected so that to learn them all at once is easier than to separate them from each other and because they did not realize that science does not involve special skills but rather remains the same in whatever field it is applied. In a word, there is *a single and identical method* to be applied to each and every field of knowledge—a method discovered hitherto only in mathematics but ultimately reflecting the very nature of human reason itself.

[263] *Oeuvres de Descartes* III, 39.
[264] *Ibid.* X, 359 ff. Cf. L. J. Beck, *The Method of Descartes* (Oxford, 1952) 14 ff.

One implication of this conception is immediately obvious: all propositions which are only probable have to be rejected from the realm of science, as Descartes' second rule explicitly states. And it is the kind of knowledge characteristic of mathematics which decides whether a proposition is certain or only probable. Gone is the Greek insight that practical knowledge is a knowledge in its own right, even though the degree of certainty characteristic of it is far less than that of theoretical sciences; gone is the insight that the transparence and evidence of mathematical knowledge is due to the extreme abstractness, indeed unreality, of its object.

Descartes himself clearly realized that his conception creates serious problems for politics and ethics. For must one not know what one ought to do prior to one's having reached *le plus haut degré de Sagesse*, the summit of Wisdom? Descartes' solution to this question is well known: as ethics is the "last degree of Wisdom" and thus presupposes "a thorough knowledge of the rest of the sciences"—in particular, of metaphysics, physics, medicine, and mechanics[265]—and as nevertheless one has to make moral decisions even before one has become truly wise, there must exist a *morale par provision*,[266] a provisional ethics *qu'on peut suivre par provision pendant qu'on n'en sçait point encore de meilleure*.[267] This entails, of course, that moral decisions of ordinary men, in fact (since he never succeeded in developing a *morale définitive*) even those of Descartes himself, are not based upon genuine knowledge; as far as lived life (as opposed to the contemplation of truth) is concerned, one cannot possibly wait for mathematical evidence and therefore has to proceed on the ground of mere probabilities.[268] In the end such prescientific moral (and one has to add, political) decisions are based upon a determination of the *bare will*; as one cannot live without acting and as action always involves choices, man constantly has to choose even though he does not *know* in any truly relevant sense of the term. This even leads Descartes to say that although without a scientific proof God's existence

---

[265] *Ibid.* IX, 15.
[266] *Ibid.* VI, 22.
[267] *Ibid.* IX, 14.
[268] Cf. *ibid.* VII, 149.

remains doubtful intellectually (*quantum ad intellectum*), man is not permitted to doubt it by his will (*quantum ad voluntatem*); for as this issue involves one's salvation, one has to commit oneself to God prior to, and in fact quite independently of, one's having reached Him through knowledge.[269]

Thus the Cartesian exaltation of mathematical theorizing is paralleled by a virtually unprecedented irrationalism and, to some extent, scepticism in the practical order. By reducing all knowledge to *one* kind Descartes commits himself to a radical irrationalism in those areas, most significantly ethics and politics, where mathematical knowledge is irrelevant. Of course, very few thinkers followed Descartes in his conception of a *morale par provision*, but instead they developed Descartes' idea that ethics and the whole realm of the practical are capable of strict mathematical demonstration. Malebranche still argues that in "ethics, politics, medicine, and all other sciences which are practical, one is forced to be satisfied with probability, not forever but for the present, *non parce qu'elle satisfait l'ésprit mais parce que le besoin presse.*"[270] But already Locke, even though he radically deviates from the Cartesian conception by denying certainty to physics, argues that moral and political ideas can be shown to be "as incontestible as those in mathematics" and held with as much certainty "as that a triangle has three angles equal to two right ones."[271] Spinoza's "geometrical ethics" is too well known to require any quotation. But even Leibniz, whose insight in these matters is often superior to that of his contemporaries, argues that *la science morale* is as innate and therefore self-evident as is arithmetics and even compares moral laws to those of mechanics.[272]

[269] *Ibid.* IV, 62. Cf. R. Descartes, *Discours de la méthode*, ed. E. Gilson (Paris, 1947) 232 ff.

[270] *Recherche de la vérité* I, III, § 2; Malebranche, *Oeuvres Complètes* (Paris, 1962) I, 63.

[271] *Essays* IV, 3, 18; Locke, *The Philosophical Works*, ed. J. A. Sr. John (London, 1892) II, 154. On the ambiguities of Locke's notions of ethics, that is, his trying to combine Descartes' rationalism with an Epicurean hedonism as suggested by Gassendi, cf. R. I. Aaron, *John Locke*, 2nd ed. (Oxford, 1963) 256 ff.

[272] *Nouveaux Essais* I, 2; *Leibnitii Opera Philosophica*, ed. J. E. Erdmann (Berlin, 1840) 215.

In fact, some passages in Leibniz would even seem to suggest that at times he considered ethics no practical science at all. Thus in a draft for an "Encyclopedia to be Written in Terms of the Method of Invention" of 1679 he mentions ethics (taken to include politics and law) side by side with purely theoretical sciences such as geometry and arithmetic, and then adds a special science called "Practica" which is supposed to apply the insights of all sciences, from grammar and logic through mathematics and mechanics to ethics, to problems of human happiness and action.[273] Here, ethics and politics have become sciences as theoretical as mathematics, and the problem of their application hardly differs from that of the application of mathematical laws to technological problems. A few years later his friend and disciple, Christian Wolff, eventually succeeded in carrying out the Cartesian plan of the "mathematical" *morale définitive*; although he defined practical philosophy quite traditionally as the science of "directing the appetitive faculty in choosing good and avoiding evil," his *De philosophia practica universali* of 1703 rigorously applied what Wolff himself described as "the mathematical method."[274]

Although it may sound somewhat surprising, there are good reasons to argue that even Kant was influenced by this conception. Contrary to the whole rationalist tradition, he was of course deeply convinced that the exactness of mathematics cannot possibly be achieved or immitated by the philosopher, indeed, that "in philosophy the geometrician can by this method build only so many houses of cards."[275] Moreover, his distinction between the theoretical and the practical leaves nothing to be desired, at least as far as emphasis goes: "We view something theoretically when we attend only to what belongs to the being of a thing, while we

---

[273] *Opuscules et fragments inédits de Leibniz*, ed. L. Couturat (Paris, 1903) 40. It should be added, however, that Leibniz (in this respect following Descartes) seems to think of "scientific ethics" primarily as a science *de animo ejusque motibus cognoscendis et regendis*, that is, a sort of psychologico-metaphysical foundation of "practical ethics." As for the latter see *ibid.* 526 ff.

[274] Cf. Ch. Wolff, *Preliminary Discourse on Philosophy in General*, tr. R. J. Blackwell (New York, 1963) 36 ff.

[275] *Critique of Pure Reason* A 727 - B 755.

view it practically whenever we look for what should belong to it *per libertatem*, in terms of freedom."[276] But when he comes to discussing the relationship beween ethical and political theory and practice, Kant develops a conception at least as rigorous as was that of his rationalist predecessors. Thus in a small treatise of 1793 concerned with the popular saying "This may be correct as far as theory goes but is worthless in practice," he argues that the value of ethical practice "entirely depends" on its correspondence with an ethical theory thoroughly independent of that practice and that therefore:

> everything is lost if the empirical and therefore accidental conditions of the realization (*Ausführung*) of a law are made a condition of the law itself and thus a practice geared to an outcome probable in terms of past experience is permitted to rule the theory, by itself independent.[277]

In other words, ethical and ethicopolitical theory have less to learn from experience than even mathematics, and even though ethical laws certainly are not mathematical in nature, they apply to human actions with the inexorability of self-evident propositions. To use Kant's own example, to claim that ethics holds true in theory but not in practice is as ridiculous as if an engineer would argue that even though its theoretical laws are well worked out, ballistics does not apply in practice, "since in practice experience yields results quite different from those of theory."[278]

Kant's example is badly chosen, of course. For the laws of ballistics apply to practice mainly because they are based upon observation and experience. Kant's ethics, on the contrary, is divorced from experience even more than Kantian mathematics; while mathematics can at least avail itself of intuition, ethics has to disregard completely both "the nature of man" (and thus all anthropology) and "the circumstances in the world" and be exclusively grounded "a priori ... in concepts of pure reason."[279] This means of course that there is in Kant nothing comparable to Aristotle's

[276] Kant, II, 412 n.
[277] *Ibid.* VI, 359.
[278] *Ibid.* 358.
[279] *Ibid.* IV, 244 ff.

ἐπιείκεια, in terms of which abstract laws could be modified
(Aristotle even says "rectified"[280]) so as to fit the ambiguity and
variety of lived life; for Kant the all-important "equity" of Aristotle's
ethics reduces itself to a trivial fact relevant only to a judge,
namely, that there exist rights which are not legally coercible and
to which one therefore has to appeal without expecting any recognition, like to a "mute divinity which cannot be heard."[281]

It is worth adding that Kant was well aware of the pseudo-
mathematical rigorism which this conception involves. When
Schiller objected that his moral philosophy might easily mislead
one to "seek moral perfection by way of a gloomy and monkish
asceticism,"[282] Kant politely but firmly replied that indeed it
was impossible to associate his ethics of duty with Schiller's aesthetic
notion of "charm (Anmut)," especially since the former involved
"unconditional coercion" which was wholly incompatible with
aesthetic categories.[283] "If something holds true in theory on
rational grounds (aus Vernunftgründen), it holds true for practice
as well."[284]

[280] ἐπανόρθωμα, Nic. Eth. 1137 b 12 ff.
[281] Kant, VII, 36.
[282] Schiller, XI, 218.
[283] Kant, VI, 161 n.
[284] Ibid. 398.

9: THE MYTH OF SELF-DETERMINATION

Kant's copious remarks on theoretical and practical philosophy cannot of course be reduced to the few remarks just made. In fact, while the period between the Renaissance and the Enlightenment has given us relatively few reflections on the problem of theory and practice, at least reflections both explicit and original, Kant's discussion of this subject is even more elaborate than that of scholastic thinkers and certainly original to the highest degree. Accordingly, I should like to devote this concluding chapter of the first part to the great philosopher of Königsberg, concentrating on the exact meaning of '*praktisch*' in his writings, on the one hand, and trying to throw some light on Kant's momentous identification of practice with freedom in the sense of self-determination, on the other hand.

The reason why Kant had so much to say about theory and practice, or rather about theoretical and practical philosophy, is that he was faced with the problem as to how to preserve the unlimited rights of modern science, its mathematical method, and the ensuing Cartesian spirit without surrendering genuine ethics. To admit the possibility of a theoretical metaphysics of the supersensible world—the kind of metaphysics conceived by Aristotle, developed by the scholastics, and basically still adhered to by thinkers such as Descartes or Leibniz—would have amounted to giving up the notion that the mathematical method alone can comprehend natural reality. In this respect Kant always remained faithful to the Cartesian heritage; in fact, he developed this attitude more consistently than even Descartes himself, who occasionally granted the possibility of a transmathematical metaphysics. On the other hand, to admit that everything can be exhausted by this mathematical method would have amounted to denying freedom and thus to giving up genuine ethics—an obvious danger which Kant could observe in Spinoza's *Ethics* and even in Leibniz' difficulties in meaningfully explaining the freedom of the will.

As artificial as it may look to the contemporary reader, Kant's way out of this dilemma undoubtedly is most ingenious. As Richard Kroner puts it, Kant "maintains the nonmetaphysical but theoretical *Geltung* of mathematical science and the nontheoretical but metaphysical *Geltung* of moral life."[285] In other words, he identifies theoretical knowledge with the Cartesian mathematical approach but at the same time restricts its application to mere appearances. Whatever can be analyzed theoretically can be approached in terms of mathematical science, but the object of theoretical knowledge is not the really real. This permits Kant to rule out all theories which are not mathematical in nature, while it does not force him to approach morality through mathematics. Since theory and appearance coincide, it becomes possible to say that the noumenal world has to be reached by a nontheoretical and therefore nonmathematical approach—and to add that moral life, together with supersensible realities such as God and the human soul belong to the realm of the *Ding-an-sich.*

Obviously, of course, this conception has a serious drawback. For it amounts to saying that the really real is beyond the reach of knowledge in the strong sense of the term. That Kant did not take this difficulty too tragically points to the fact that his "practical philosophy," and in the end even practice itself, has a cognitive value which transcends the limits of what traditionally was called "practical knowledge." In fact, it would hardly be an exaggeration to say that Kant limited the rights of theoretical knowledge in order to be able to ascribe to practical knowledge infinitely more rights than ever had been ascribed to it.

This leads us to the first point which we wish to make in this chapter, namely, that Kant's use of the expression 'practical' so radically differs from the traditional Greek and medieval use

---

[285] R. Kroner, *Kant's Weltanschauung,* tr. J. E. Smith (Chicago, 1956) 4.

that it is possible to argue that Kant's distinction between theoretical and practical philosophy corresponds to Aristotle's distinction between physics and metaphysics at least as much as, quite obviously, it reproduces the Aristotelian distinction between theoretical and practical knowledge. In any case Kant's ethics embraces what Aristotle called "first philosophy"; it is the critique of *practical* reason, not that of theoretical reason, which reaches and analyzes the transnatural substances upon whose existence and cognizance Aristotle had grounded his metaphysics.

To be more precise, Kant preserves the essence of the traditional meaning of the expression 'practical' with reference to what Aristotle called "art" and "productive knowledge." But he considers this use of 'practical' improper and gives to the proper use, which relates to ethics, a radically new connotation. This may be shown by saying a few words about the distinction between the "technically practical" and the "morally practical" which Kant introduces at the beginning of the *Critique of Judgement* and which, moreover, occurs more than twenty times in the first volume of the *Opus Posthumum*.

Kant readily agrees that philosophy ought to be divided into the theoretical and practical.[286] But he immediately cautions against what he calls "highly detrimental misunderstandings" concerning the notion of the practical, in general, and the question as to what ought to be included in practical philosophy, in particular. His point seems to be the following. Propositions and therefore sciences may be practical either in the sense that a theoretical proposition or science is *used* for a practical purpose or else in the sense that they are concerned with a subject matter which cannot at all be reached theoretically. In the first case one uses the expression 'practical' improperly, and sciences which are practical in this sense have nothing to do with practical philosophy; they simply are corollaries to theoretical philosophy. In the second case, on the contrary, one is concerned with the practical in the strict sense of the term.

---

[286] For the following see the introduction to the *Critique of Judgement*, both the first and the final version; cf. Kant, V, 177 ff., 238 ff. For the *Opus Posthumum* see Vol. XXI of the *Akademie-Ausgabe*.

In short, while the *technically practical* reduces itself to secondary *uses* of *theoretical* propositions (as Kant puts it: "the theory of what belongs to the nature of things used so as to make possible the production of things in accordance with some principle"[287]), the *morally practical* radically differs from everything theoretical in that it cannot be reached through any theoretical knowledge whatsoever. As Kant adds that consequently the technically practical is only a "practical part" of theoretical philosophy, while the morally practical is the ground for a distinct "practical philosophy," one at first may have the impression that this analysis is basically Aristotelian. After all, what could be more Aristotelian than to point out that moral life radically differs from the kind of objects which may be approached by theoretical knowledge and to add that the realm of production is practical, too, but nowadays has become grounded in theory?

However, if one looks closer, one soon discovers that Kant's analysis is far from being Aristotelian. First of all, there is the circumstance, at first sight highly curious, that Kant describes the technically practical as mere "precepts" and "rules of skill," while he takes the morally practical to involve "laws" in the strictest sense of the term. Considering the fact that the technically practical is rooted on theoretical knowledge and only the morally practical is truly practical, this certainly is a remarkable claim—at least from the Aristotelian point of view, which seems to entail that the more a field is practical the less strict *Gesetzmässigkeit* it involves. In fact, however, this claim is far from curious. For (and this is the second and main point) the ultimate reason why Kant excludes sciences such as political economy or dietetics from practical philosophy is precisely that they *are* practical (or rather productive) in Aristotle's sense. Indeed, Kant's main point is not that such sciences are based upon theoretical knowledge; rather it is that they are "practical" only in the limited sense that they *aim at an end other than* the contemplation of truth.

As Kant himself puts it, such sciences differ from theoretical sciences only in terms of the *Vorstellungsart* involved, that is,

[287] Kant, V, 180.

the way in which they are conceived and used, *not in terms of their content.*[288] In order to make the reader realize the weight of this distinction, we must briefly recapitulate what we said about Aristotle in an earlier chapter. Aristotle's distinction between theoretical, practical, and productive knowledge was based upon a distinction between the respective *ends*: while theoretical knowledge is an end in itself (just as πρᾶξις, incidentally), practical knowledge aims at ordering human action and productive knowledge, at producing a material thing. Of course, Aristotle himself did not succeed in carrying through this distinction without adding that, moreover, the *subject matter* of the knowledges in question had to correspond to their ends: theoretical knowledge deals only with realities which cannot be either done or made, while the subject matter of practical knowledge is the doable or practice, and the subject matter of productive knowledge is matter in so far as it can be moulded into an artifact.

As we have seen, the Arabs and other medieval thinkers such as Aquinas eventually proceeded to show that one and the same subject matter can be studied theoretically and practically, to introduce the additional notion that it is possible to have theoretical knowledge even of things doable and makable. However, it never occured to the Arabs or Aquinas that the distinction in terms of ends might be considered secondary as opposed to the distinction in terms of the subject matter. They realized, it is true, that in order to make the former distinction unambiguous, one had to add another distinction; but they never felt that one could meaningfully distinguish between theoretical and practical philosophy solely in terms of the subject matter involved. As a matter of fact, when Aquinas grants that it is possible to view human actions or artifacts theoretically, his point is precisely that the distinction in terms of the subject matter, as important as it may be, is *so secondary* as to make it possible to consider even practicable and producible matters in a purely contemplative way.

As opposed to this, Kant's distinction between theoretical and practical philosophy is based solely upon a distinction between

<hr />

[288] *Ibid.* Cf. VIII, 395 ff.

the ontological character of their respective subject matters. Thus in the unpublished first version of the introduction to the *Critique of Judgement* one reads that:

> all practical propositions which deduce a possible natural entity from human will as its cause without exception belong to theoretical philosophy or the cognition of nature; only those propositions which impose laws upon freedom really differ from theoretical propositions. Concerning the former, one therefore may say that they constitute the practical part of philosophy of nature; only the latter establish a distinct practical philosophy.[289]

The same point is made even more forcefully in the final version of the same introduction:

> A complex of practical precepts given by philosophy does not constitute a distinct part of philosophy opposed to theoretical philosophy, merely because these precepts are practical; for they might be that, even if their principles were derived entirely from the theoretical cognition of nature. ... A distinct branch of philosophy is constituted only if their principle, as it is not borrowed from the natural concept which is always sensuously conditioned, rests on the supersensible which only the concept of freedom makes cognizable by formal laws. This part of philosophy is then morally practical, that is, contains not only precepts and rules relating to this or that purpose.[290]

In other words, all technological and "productive" sciences, in fact even disciplines such as empirical politics and eudaemonistic ethics (Kant mentions the "universal doctrine of happiness"[291]), are not practical in the strong sense which would demand their inclusion into practical philosophy. The reason furnished by Kant is highly revealing: it is not that they in fact are rooted in theoretical knowledge; the crucial point is that if ever one would succeed in basing them upon theoretical knowledge, they would remain just what they are, namely, practical rules and precepts relating to the realm of nature and thus ultimately based upon some insight into the ontology of the natural world. As opposed to this, that

---

[289] Kant, V, 180.
[290] *Ibid.* 241.
[291] *Ibid.* The expression refers to the Wolffian "universal practical philosophy."

part of philosophy which is concerned with the supersensible is practical in the strictest sense of the term.

Thus, while the distinction between anthropology and medicine, for example, is merely a distinction between a theory and its practical use, the difference between physics and ethics is a difference concerning the basic principles of the possibility of the objects involved—an ontologically rooted difference. Nature has to be studied in terms of *Naturbegriffe*, natural concepts, and to be dealt with in terms of deterministic natural causality; morality, on the contrary, has to be analyzed in terms of the *Freiheitsbegriff*, the concept of freedom, and the causality involved is a totally different causality of free will, a causality of autodetermination.

But why and in which sense is Kant's practical philosophy "practical" at all? Why does not the distinction between philosophy of nature and ethics reduce itself to the distinction between the study of sensible phenomena and intelligible noumena? Once more in his introduction to the *Critique of Judgement* Kant gives the only possible answer. It amounts to saying that that part of philosophy which operates with the concept of freedom is practical only because *freedom is transphenomenal* and thus cannot be reached by Kantian theory, which is restricted to appearances by its mathematical method:

> There are only two kinds of concepts, namely, *natural concepts* and the *concepts of freedom*, and these admit as many distinct principles of the possibility of their objects. The former render possible *theoretical* cognition according to principles *a priori*; the latter, in respect to this theoretical cognition, supplies by itself only a negative principle (that of mere contrast) but on the other hand furnishes synthetic (*erweiternde*) principles of the determination of the will, principles which therefore are called practical.[292]

In other words, even though the *distinction* between theoretical and practical philosophy is based upon the ontological difference among the respective objects (nature and freedom, appearance and noumena), Kant's practical philosophy is by no means "practical" only because it is concerned with the will and its freedom. Rather,

[292] *Ibid.* 239.

it is "practical" because the will and freedom in question do
not appear and therefore cannot be reached theoretically. One
might want to object that, after all, the Kantian distinction between
physics and ethics is based upon the distinction between that
which *is* and that which *ought to be*. But this is the case only because
the subject matter of physics "appears," while the subject matter
of ethics does not "appear." Only because freedom is not among
the objects of intuition and thus does not belong to the world of
appearances does Kant categorize physics and ethics as theoretical
philosophy and practical philosophy, respectively, rather than as
a theoretical philosophy of the sensible and a theoretical philosophy of the supersensible or intelligible (that is, as physics and
metaphysics).

In fact, if it could be shown that a genuine theoretical knowledge
of intelligible realities *is* possible, Kant's practical philosophy
would dissolve into nothing and a disciple of Kant could restrict
himself to a simple study of what is. This is exactly what would
happen in Hegel, where the distinction between sensible and intelligible realities no longer is a distinction between mere *Erscheinung* and an inaccessible *Ding-an-sich*. With Hegel's claim to have
transcended the limits of theoretical reason as delineated by Kant,
practical philosophy simply ceases to be a meaningful undertaking.
The Kantian *ought* disappears when the noumenal realm becomes
accessible; consequently, Hegel's "practical" philosophy, the *Philosophy of Right*, will be theoretical through and through.

All in all, then, Kant's whole practical philosophy is nothing but
an ontology of supersensible reality—an ontology which is "practical"
only because and to the extent that its subject matter cannot be
met anywhere in actual experience and therefore takes on the
character of an *ideal*, of something which ought to be, although
it is not. Kant himself says this in so many words in the paragraph
76 of the *Critique of Judgement*. Just as the distinction between
the possible and the actual has no foundation in the things themselves but is due only to the fact that the human intellect cannot
intuit and therefore grasps as a possible object whatever sense
intuition represents as actual — but not an object — so

it is owing to the subjective constitution of our practical faculty that the moral laws must be represented as commands and the actions conforming to them as duties, and that reason represents this necessity not by an *is* (as an actual event) but by an *ought-to-be*. This would not be the case were reason considered as in its causality independent of sensibility and so as cause in an intelligible world entirely in agreement with the moral law. For in such a world there would be no distinction between ought and does, between a practical law of that which is possible through us and the theoretical law of that which is actual through us.[293]

In other words, the subject matter of Kant's practical philosophy is altogether "theoretical" as far as its inner ontological constitution is concerned. Even though it is governed by a causality and thus by laws radically different from those of natural entities, it involves laws which *by themselves* entail nothing resembling an *ought*. Only because man's theoretical reason is ruled by the iron hand of the mathematical method and therefore relates solely to sensuous appearances do we have to approach this subject matter "practically." That practical philosophy is "practical," or that there is a practical philosophy at all, is due merely to the "subjective constitution" of our mind. By itself the moral law is man's own "necessary willing as a member of an intelligible world"; it is an *ought* only because man at the same time is a member of the world of sense.[294]

This conception is quite clearly reflected in Kant's notion of *Praxis*. In his precritical *Lectures on Ethics*[295] Kant's analysis still is fairly traditional. Practice is described here as the "conduct of beings possessed of a free will," and accordingly practical philosophy is defined as that part of philosophy "which provides rules for the proper use of our freedom." But even in these early lectures it is striking how strongly Kant emphasizes the fact that practical philosophy has to advance its rules "irrespective of particular application."

[293] *Ibid.* 482.
[294] Kant, IV, 315: "Das moralische Sollen ist also eigenes notwendiges Wollen als Gliedes einer intelligiblen Welt und wird nur sofern von ihm als Sollen gedacht, als er sich zugleich wie ein Glied der Sinnenwelt betrachtet."
[295] Cf. Kant, *Lectures on Ethics*, tr. L. Infield (London, 1930) 1 ff.

Aristotle would have argued the same, it is true; but he would have explained it by saying that ethical precepts are abstract and therefore cannot reach down to the concretness of particulars and that, moreover, the element of choice in human actions makes impossible a scientific knowledge of ethics in the strict sense. Kant, on the contrary, explains the same point by arguing that ethics lays down objective rules as to what ought to occur, even though it never actually occurs and therefore cannot possibly be based on actual practice.

This obviously brings about a rather curious disproportion between practice and "practical philosophy." For practice is man's *actual* conduct, while practical philosophy relates to an *ideal* conduct which might never occur. The moral *ought* has no obvious relationship to what man actually does, and ethics would be just what it is if in practice no one even as much as *could* carry out what it prescribes. It was probably this ambiguity which induced Kant in his later writings to describe practice almost as if it were theory. Thus he once defines it as an *Inbegriff von unbedingt gebietenden Gesetzen*, as a complex of unconditionally commanding laws;[296] in another passage he claims that "not each and every manipulation (*Hantierung*)" deserves to be called practice but only "that realization of an aim which ... is obeying definite principles of conduct."[297] Thus practice is either the moral law itself or else those human actions which are in thorough agreement with it.

In view of the fact that Kant's moral philosophy is concerned with the "*necessary* willing" of a "member of the intelligible order," this definition of practice would seem to fit well Kant's mature conception. Practice simply is the necessary happenings of the ideal order. On the other hand, this notion carries with it the obvious disadvantage that Kant's efforts to show that theory and practice cannot contradict each other result in a truism. Indeed, it clearly makes a pseudo problem of the whole issue of the relationship between theory and practice. For what problems could possibly

---

[296] Kant, VI, 456: "Praxis in objektiver Bedeutung, als Inbegriff von unbedingt gebietenden Gesetzen." Later, *Praxis* is opposed to mere *Praktik, ibid.* 460.

[297] *Ibid.* 357.

be involved in the relationship which obtains between laws and events which obey them necessarily, in fact, by definition?

In a sense, however, this precisely is the point which Kant wants to make. The relationship between the *ought* and the *is* is a pseudo relationship based upon the subjective constitution of our mind. Only the difference between the realm of sensuous appearances and the world of intelligible realities is based upon ontological differences. Thus, in the strict sense the task of ethical conduct is not so much to implement a moral *ought* but rather to bring to bear the laws of the intelligible world in which man participates.

This is particularly clear from Kant's analysis of his own claim that "nothing in the world, indeed nothing even beyond the world, can possibly be conceived which could be called good without qualification except a good will."[298] This statement usually is taken to mean that as far as ethical evaluation is concerned, only a man's intention counts, not his actual conduct. And there can be no doubt that Kant has this in mind, too. But when he explains what a good will is, it immediately becomes obvious that he feels moreover that the goodness of this pure intention consists in its *very ontological character*, namely, in its necessarily obeying laws of the intelligible order. The will is said to be good when it obeys the law, and the supreme ethical law is the will's fidelity to its own ontological nature.

> What kind of a law can that be, the representation of which must determine the will without reference to an expected result, in order that the will may be called absolutely good without qualification? Since I have robbed the will of all impulses which could come to it from the obedience to any law, nothing remains to serve as a principle of the will except the universal law of action as such (*die allgemeine Gesetzmässigkeit der Handlungen überhaupt*), that is: I should never act in such a way that I could not also will that my maxim should be a universal law.[299]

In other words, to have a good will is to obey the very nature of the will itself. For it is obvious that Kant cannot mean that although a good calculation of individual success does not suffice

[298] Kant, IV, 249.
[299] *Ibid.* 258.

to make a volition good, will without further ado becomes good
if the result at which it aims serves mankind as a whole. Even
though the concrete instances advanced by Kant occasionally may
seem to support such an interpretation, it is perfectly obvious that
Kant has in mind more than this. When he states that the "universal imperative of duty" amounts to saying: "Act as though the
maxim of your action were by your will to become a universal
law of nature,"[300] Kant actually argues that the supreme ethical
duty is to act so that, or at least as though, one's action could
succeed in making of the ontological laws governing the will itself
a law of "objective reality."

If one now goes further and asks what exactly this law of the
will is supposed to be, the answer is quite unambiguous: independence of everything exterior to the will itself, perfect autonomy,
self-determination. As Kant puts it, "autonomy of the will is
that property of it in terms of which it is a law to itself independently
of any property of objects of volition"; and this autonomy of the
will is the "supreme principle of morality." As the will is the
"faculty of determining itself to action in accordance with the
representation of definite laws,"[302] this amounts to saying that the
supreme principle of morality is the will's and freedom's fidelity
to itself, that is, the will's pure autodetermination. Or, as Kant
says in the *Critique of Pure Reason*, the moral *ought* is a "kind
of necessity and connection" which is found nowhere in nature and
which reason therefore has to, and is free to, "frame for itself with
perfect spontaneity."[303] It is not decisive *what* reason frames for
itself; truly "objective" grounds are lacking anyway. What counts
is that reason frames the intelligible order by acting and determining itself in "free spontaneity." The supreme law of ethical practice
is the spontaneity, self-reliance, and autonomy of practice itself.[304]

[300] *Ibid*. 279.

[301] Kant, IV, 299.

[302] *Ibid*. 285: "Der Wille wird als ein Vermögen gedacht, gemäss der
Vorstellung gewisser Gesetze sich selbst zum Handeln zu bestimmen."

[303] A 548 = B 576.

[304] For an interesting analysis of this subject see the article by J. Zelený in
Filosofický Časopis 12 (1964) 478 ff.

This brings us to the other aspect of Kant's thought which we want to touch upon in this chapter, namely, the identification of the practical with autonomy and autodetermination. The notion that freedom is self-determination is of course not Kant's invention. Already Aquinas defines the *liberum arbitrium* as a self-determination, more precisely, a moving oneself to a definite action through rational deliberation.[305] But there obviously is a great difference between this simple definition of free will which abstracts from practical implications and the more radical modern claim that it is man's very nature to be free to define for himself his position in the universe, so that in the end all except strictly physical laws are imposed upon man *by himself*.

The earliest expression of this modern conception is probably Pico della Mirandola's *Oratio de dignitate hominis*, a speech written as an introduction to a disputation held at Rome in 1487. In this "oration" Pico recounts that when God came to the point of creating man, he already had distributed all his gifts among other creatures and therefore

> decided that this being to which He could give nothing of his own should share in everything which belonged individually to each and every creature. He placed man, this product of a vague image, in the middle of the world and spoke thus to him: I have given thee, oh Adam, neither a fixed seat, nor a face of thy own, nor a gift peculiar to thee, in order that thou mayest have and possess by thine own wish and decision whatever seat, or face, or gift, thou consciously choosest. The determinate nature of other things is bound by the laws which I have imposed upon them. Thou art confined by no bonds except the free judgement in whose hands I placed thee so that thou mayest determine thy nature for thyself. ... Thou art the moulder and maker of thyself.[306]

Jacob Burkhardt has called this passage "one of the noblest bequests of this cultural epoch,"[307] the Renaissance; Ernst Cassirer more soberly described it as a summary of the "whole intent of

---

[305] E.g., *De ver.* XXIV, 1.

[306] *Dignità dell'uomo*, ed. (with Italian translation) B. Cicognani (Florence, 1943) 6 ff.

[307] Burkhardt, V, 255.

the Renaissance."[308]   In fact, it clearly reflects the end of the
medieval conception of man and points toward countless modern
ideas, such as Heidegger's claim that man is delivered over to
his own freedom and consequently possibility ranks higher than
actuality as far as human existence goes. The medieval conception
was governed by Pseudo-Dionysius' image of a hierarchical order
in which each being was assigned a definite place. The place occupied in this hierarchy by man was privileged, it is true; he was the
only being of the sublunar realm which had an intellect and thus
(in terms of Aquinas' principle *ubicumque est intellectus, est liberum
arbitrium*[309]) was free. Still man's place in the universe was only
one among many other places, and, assuming that he could leave
it at all, he certainly could not leave it without bringing disorder
into the universe. This is the notion which Pico rebelled against,
although, like most Renaissance Neoplatonists, he still basically
adhered to the hierarchical view of the cosmos. Man proudly
stands in the center of the universe rather than being lost somewhere
in the hierarchy between God and prime matter; in fact, being
both indeterminate and capable of becoming whatever he chooses,
he is almost the focal point of creation. And his dignity consists
precisely in that from his indeterminate central position he can
freely move to higher and lower levels and define his final position
at will. "Thou canst grow downward into the lower natures which
are brutes. Thou canst again grow upward ... into the higher
natures which are divine."[310]

Even though somewhat less eloquently, Marsilio Ficino expressed
the same idea when he wrote in his treatment of the soul's immortality, the *Theologia Platonica* (1474), that man is related to
and has share in all parts of the universe. While other beings are
always isolated and single, the human soul is *omnia simul*, everything at once, and thus mediates between the intelligible and the
corporeal order; indeed "it rightly may be called the center of the
universe, the middle term of all things, the series of the world, the

[308] E. Cassirer, *The Individual and the Cosmos in Renaissance Philosophy*,
(New York, 1963) 86.
[309] *S. Th.* I, 59, 3.
[310] *Dignità dell'uomo* 8.

face of everything, the bond and the juncture of the universe."[311]
Thirty years before Ficino, Nicholas of Cusa developed the same
idea by arguing that within the confines of the *potentia humanitatis*
everything in the universe is found: man can become a human
God, a human angel, a human animal, a human lion or bear, *aut
aliud quodcumque*. In fact, according to Nicholas of Cusa the
potentiality of human existence so radically embraces all dimensions
of the universe that when He created man, God had no intention
other than to unfold man's nature itself. *Non ergo activae creationis
humanitatis alius extat finis quam humanitas;* the meaning of man,
his doing and history, is man himself.[312] And more than two hundred
years later Giambattista Vico, the last great heir to the ideas of
Renaissance Neoplatonism, defined man as a *posse*, an indefinite
nature able and thus also forced to determine himself.[313]

It should be noted, however, that prior to the nineteenth century
this exaltation of man's capacity of determining himself usually
was not paralleled by any significant enthusiasm as to man's
capacity to grasp the theoretical secrets of the universe or even
his power to master nature by his inventions. In fact, it usually
was linked with a basic scepticism as to the force of theoretical
reason. In rationalists such as Descartes or Leibniz the notion
of self-determination plays a very minor role if any. On the other
hand, Nicholas of Cusa, even though he already believed that
nihil certi habemus in nostra scientia nisi nostram mathematicam,
nothing is really certain in our knowledge except mathematics,
certainly was not a precursor of Descartes, who believed that the
real secrets of the universe may be decoded through the mathe-

[311] Quoted by P. O. Kristeller, *Studies in Renaissance Thought and Letters*
(Rome, 1956) 268: "Hoc [sc. anima] maximum est in natura miraculorum.
Reliqua enim sub Deo unum quiddam in se singula sunt, haec omnia simul ...
ut merito dici possit centrum naturae, universorum medium, mundi series,
vultus omnium nodusque et copula mundi."

[312] *De Conjecturis* II, 14; cf. *Nicolai Cusae Cardinalis Opera* (Paris, 1514);
photo reprint (Frankfurt, 1962) I, fol. LX a. Cf. E. Cassirer, *op. cit.* 87; also
K. Kosík, *Dialektika konkrétniho*, 3rd ed. (Prague, 1966) 164.

[313] Cf. A. R. Caponigri, *Time and Idea, The Theory of History in G. V.* (London,
1953) 75.

matical approach. On the contrary, for Nicholas of Cusa the only
reason why mathematics was certain was that its objects "are
known by us as in their source, as our or reason's artifacts."[314]
Pico della Mirandola's criticism of astrology, which always puzzles
Renaissance scholars, probably has to be seen in the same perspective. For this criticism, which clearly is advanced in the name
of Pico's views on human freedom,[315] ultimately amounts to saying
that as astronomy is purely operational, a device to calculate
apparent motions, it cannot have any bearing on events *in rerum
natura*. Similarly, Vico's identification of the *certum* with the
factum,[316] of the theoretically certain with human artifacts, from
mathematical objects through language to history, is rooted in and
expressive of a deep-seated distrust of the trans-subjective bearing
of theoretical knowledge.

One may object that there is a great gap between these Renaissance ideas and Kant's notion of a "causality thoroughly determined
by itself,"[317] since Kant's notion of self-determination has an ontological connotation, while the corresponding Renaissance ideas
are but an exalted expression of the common sense view that man
is free to choose his way of life. To some extent this is correct.
Still, it cannot be denied that the Renaissance conception is grounded
in an ontological conception of man's nature and that Kant's
notion of self-determination is in one sense the expression of a
self-awareness of freedom which since the Renaissance had more or
less acquired the status of a common sense view. Just as Kant
links the notion of human self-determination with a *Leere der
Schöpfung in Ansehung ihres Zwecks*,[318] an emptiness of creation

---

[314] "Dialogus de possest," *Nic. Cusae Card. Opera* I, CLXXX a: "In mathe-
maticis ... quae sicut in suo principio per nos ut nostra seu rationis entia sciuntur
... Si igitur recte consideravimus, nihil certi habemus in nostra scientia nisi
nostram mathematicam et illa est aenigma ad venationem operum Dei" ("a
mirror for understanding creature"—since mathematical entities are "created"
by us just as real things are created by God).

[315] Cf. E. Cassirer, *op. cit.* 115.

[316] A. R. Caponigri, *op. cit.* 148 ff.

[317] Kant, V, 54 ff.

[318] *Ibid.* IV, 156. This notion is essential for Kant's claim that "nature has

with respect to its end, the Renaissance Neoplatonists always stressed that man is an *opus imaginis indiscretae,* the product of an indetermined exemplar idea (Pico), a *posse* (Vico). And just as the Renaissance thinkers mainly had in mind the fact that man is capable of shaping his fate himself (to the extent that during this period the old image of Fortune with a wheel seizing men and draging them along gives way to the image of a sailboat which man himself steers, and the classical Prometheus myth is reinterpreted so as to convey the idea of a rebirth and a regeneration), Kant's whole philosophy aims at "narrowing assertions of materialism, of naturalism and of fatalism, and thus to afford scope for the moral ideas beyond the field of speculation."[319]

This is not to suggest that Kant was a belated heir to the Renaissance. But it is to suggest that Kant's philosophy, later that of German Idealism, and, last but not least, the ideas of the young Marx are the last outcome of the peculiar self-confidence and the "new practical humanism" so admirably formulated in Pico's oration, a summary of the whole Renaissance intent and, in fact, an expression of the basic intent of postmedieval man. Of course, prior to Kant this notion of a human self-determination which is both meaningful and rightful, indeed the last end of man's life and of the whole creation, extended only to the ethicopolitical aspects of human existence, to which Kant himself added a gnoseological self-determination. It was not until Hegel and Marx that philosophers began to realize that the same notion could be extended beyond the realm of "doing" to the realm of "making," from the realm of ethics and politics to that of economics and technology. As far as I can tell, no one before Hegel, and in a sense no one before Marx, ever claimed that man can transform himself by transforming the *material* world. But as soon as this idea emerges, the role traditionally played by practice, in the sense of ethicopolitical doing, will decrease until in Marx it completely gives way to the notion of a *homo faber creans seipsum.*

willed that everything that goes beyond the mechanical ordering of his animal existence man should produce by himself," *ibid.* 153.
    [319] *Ibid.* 118.

Part II:

From Hegel to Moses Hess

There are two cardinal sins from which all other sins derive: impatience and indolence. Because of impatience they were expelled from Paradise; because of indolence they do not return. In fact, perhaps there is only one cardinal sin: impatience. Because of impatience they were expelled; because of impatience they do not return.

Franz Kafka, Considerations on Sin, Suffering, Hope, and the True Path.

10: HEGEL: *VERNUNFT* VERSUS *SOLLEN*

In Hegel there are only about five or six passages explicitly concerned with the relation between theory and practice.[1] This might mislead one into believing that Hegel ascribed little importance to this problem. Actually, however, this very problem is one of the cardinal points on which Hegel's whole philosophy turns. Hegel only treats it under a somewhat unexpected heading, namely, in terms of the opposition between that which ought to be and that which is.

This becomes most obvious if one considers the *Weltanschauung* against which Hegel is fighting throughout his writing or, rather, is trying to overcome—the "poetic and prophetic, but always longing, tendencies and excrescences" resulting from Fichte's romantic rationalism and ultimately from Kant's critique of theoretical reason. Hegel himself refers to this *Weltanschauung* as that of a "philosophy of *Sollen*." The expression '*Sollen*' which refers to Kant's ethics of duty has a somewhat unusual meaning here. It does not, at least not primarily, refer to moral obligation. Rather, it refers to ideals—both theoretical and practical—which are postulated in spite of the fact that they never can be exhibited in experience and which, accordingly, man can only strive for but never reach. Such ideals, Hegel claims, cannot be of any

---

[1] Literature concerning Hegel's notion of practice is relatively scarce. In fact, apart from the interesting article by W. R. Beyer[2] that discusses Hegel's notion of practice from a Marxist-Leninist point of view, there is only Heiss[1] and Heiss[2], 86 ff., which discusses certain developments of Hegel's ideas on the relation between theory and action, and the highly technical article by Röttcher, who concentrates on paragraphs 213 ff. of the *Encyclopaedia*.

value. As he puts it in the *Phenomenology of Mind*: "What is universally valid is also universally effective; *what ought to be*, as a matter of fact, *is* too; what merely *should* be, and is *not*, has no truth."[2]

In order to understand what this means, we have to consider how Hegel views Kant. Kant for Hegel is the theoretical counterpart to the French Revolution. What the French have achieved in terms of action, Kant has achieved in terms of theory—an ultimate autonomy of man. "The standpoint of Kantian philosophy is that, by its reasoning, thought has reached the point of grasping itself as absolute and concrete, as free and ultimate. It grasped itself as that which is everything in all things. It accepts no exterior authority; no authority except that of thought is of any value. Accordingly, thought determines itself and thus is concrete." At the same time, however, Kantian philosophy views this thoroughly autonomous thought as something merely subjective. "All knowledge remains within subjectivity; and beyond this subjectivity, as something exterior to it, is the thing-in-itself."[3]

Hegel is far from opposing Kant's claim that human thought is autonomous, i.e., determined by nothing except by itself and therefore accountable only to itself. What he opposes is Kant's conviction that such autonomous thought can be concerned only with appearances as opposed to things-in-themselves and is therefore subjective. In short, Hegel wants to keep the autonomy of reason discovered by Kant without giving up the claim to objectivity characteristic of pre-Kantian philosophy. Kant's mistake, according to Hegel, consisted in believing that human thought is finite. For if it is infinite, if there is no limit to its capacities, then its being autonomous cannot contradict its objectivity. The opposition between appearances and things-in-themselves was unbridgeable in Kant only because he was not bold enough to admit that autonomous thought is necessarily boundless, that there cannot be anything beyond its reach. If thought is infinite, it is both thoroughly autonomous and perfectly objective; the opposition between "phe-

---

[2] Hegel₂, II, 197; tr. Baillie, 289.

[3] Hegel₂, XIX, 552, 572; tr. Haldane-Simson, III, 424, 443. Cf. Hegel₂, I, 291, 324, etc.; IV, 41 ff., tr. Johnston-Struthers, I, 57.

nomena" and "noumena" restricts itself to that between what already is known and what still is waiting to be known.

It may be useful to add a few words as to how Hegel understands the expression 'thing-in-itself.' For he plays on the slightly ambiguous meaning which this expression already had in Kant. On the one hand, he takes it as referring to everything beyond the scope of possible human experience. For example, in the section of the *Encyclopaedia* devoted to Kant he explicitly points out that God is a thing-in-itself too. On the other hand, however, Hegel retains the original meaning of this expression: "that which things are of which we only know appearances." Accordingly, when he claims that there are no unknowable things-in-themselves, he claims at the same time that there is absolutely nothing beyond the reach of human thought. Instead of merely recovering the thing-in-itself relegated by Kant to the realm of the unknown, Hegel arrogates everything hitherto believed to transcend the possibilities of human experience. He even will go as far as to say that the "supersensual" (meaning both "tables-in-themselves," "cows-in-themselves," and immaterial realities such as God) *is* the sensual "taken as in truth it is"; objects of the senses, instead of being phenomena *opposed* to a noumenal world, as in Kant, become appearances *of* whatever transcends immediate experience, appearances whose very truth it is to lead us to what lies behind them.[4]

In short, Hegel argues that if there is no unknown thing-in-itself, then there is nothing at all which is unknowable. By tearing down the subjectivist barrier built up by Kant he claims to have conquered for human reason everything which man ever believed to lie beyond his cognitive abilities. Even God. For the claim that God cannot be known as he is in himself must be just as false as Kant's claim that there are unknowable things-in-themselves.

We may understand better now what Hegel has in mind when he criticizes the "philosophy of *Sollen*." In spite of the fact that Kant had excluded all things-in-themselves from the scope of

---

[4] Hegel$_2$, II, 119, cf. XVI, 234; tr. Baillie, 193; cf. tr. Speirs-Sanderson, III, 19.

theoretical knowledge—claiming that the "faculty of the Absolute," reason, is unsuited for theoretical purposes—he had argued that certain things-in-themselves such as God and human freedom have to be postulated as existing. As far as theoretical knowledge is concerned, we cannot possibly know whether they are or are not. But for practical purposes we have to assume that they are; we even have to assume that they have quite definite attributes. For if they are not, binding ethics cannot be justified.

Hegel's answer is unambiguous: "the instinct of reason is entirely within its rights when it stands firm on this point and refuses to be led astray by mere inventions (*Gedankendinge*) which merely *ought* to be and, qua *ought*, should be allowed to have truth though they are to be met nowhere in experience."[5] This, of course, does not mean that Hegel denies existence to that which Kant had described as "ideas of reason," above all to God and freedom. On the contrary, he claims to be able to lead them home to where they rightly belong, to the realm of theoretical thought.

In Fichte the Kantian *ought* became infinite striving; an ultimate rational explanation of reality is just as impossible as it is inevitably striven for, and the progress of humanity points toward a future without conceivable end.[6] In both cases, in Fichte as well as in Kant, man's desire for theoretical and practical completion points toward a *perennierendes Jenseits*, a perennial beyond, which entails a *perennierendes Sollen*, a perennial ought.[7] As Hegel puts it, ultimate perfection both of thought and of the will always remains abstract, never materializes, and therefore "evaporates into something completely powerless, into which I may introduce any and every content, while the subjectivity of mind becomes just as worthless because it lacks any objective significance."[8]

However, Hegel's *main* antagonists are his romanticist contemporaries rather than their forefathers, Kant and Fichte. For in them the ultimate consequence of Kant's philosophy of the *ought* has become obvious. Of that which in Kant was still a

[5] Hegel₂, II, 197; tr. Baillie, 289; cf. VIII, 48 ff., 118; etc.
[6] Cf. Hegel₂, XII, 103 ff.
[7] Cf. Hegel₂, II, 197; VIII, 444 ff.; XV, 238; etc.
[8] Hegel₂, VII, 224; tr. Knox, 258.

grim necessity, namely, that true being is beyond man's reach, they make a vain virtue. The ego now finds in subjectivism "its greatest vanity, indeed its religion." Instead of longing for objectivity they revel in their subjectivism. Fichte's eternal striving for perfection becomes an end in itself; longing itself becomes the only thing which is divine. Instead of looking for truth, reason, and objective perfection they find their satisfaction in a mere longing for the unattainable. Instead of remaining sober sceptics like Kant they make of scepticism a fireworks of irony. Instead of striving for an unknown God they revel in their subjective feelings of worship.

At the end of his *History of Philosophy* Hegel enumerates some of the thinkers and poets whom he has is mind and whom, usually without mentioning their names, he criticizes throughout his writings: the theorist of the romanticists, Friedrich von Schlegel, whose "irony" takes nothing seriously and always remains a "play with all forms" questioning value after value; the poet Novalis, whose "longing of a beautiful soul" is a longing for longing's sake, an "extravagance of subjectivity" which often borders on madness; and romantic theologians such as Jacobi, who speak of a "religion of the heart" and, as Hegel ironically remarks, seem to be able to understand each other in terms of "handshakes and dumb feelings."[9]

It does not matter whether Hegel does justice to the romantics and whether he is right in tracing their ideas back to Kant and Fichte. As we shall see, he in fact overlooks other influences in terms of which he himself is an ally of the romantics, not their antagonist. What concerns us here is that Hegel rejects this philosophy of the *Sollen*—the romanticists' nostalgia and irony as well as Fichte's *ought*—because it is a "dread of staining the radiance of one's own inner being by action and existence."[10] It is the subjectivity of an adolescent unable to cope with the existing world, unable to pass from his abstract ideals to objective reality.

---

[9] Hegel$_2$, XIX, 642 ff.; tr. Haldane-Simson, III, 507 ff. On Jacobi see the aphorism in Rosenkranz, 546.

[10] Hegel$_2$, II, 504; tr. Baillie, 666. On the "unhappy consciousness" of the Romantics see Wahl, 62 ff.

Indeed, it is the attitude of a hypochondriac. "The later man is taken by it, the more serious are the symptoms. Weak characters may suffer from it their whole life. When suffering from this almost pathological frame of mind, man does not want to give up his subjectivity; he does not succeed in overcoming his aversion for reality and therefore displays a relative unfitness which easily turns into a real one."[11]

As opposed to this, Hegel defends the standpoint of the adult who recognizes the "necessity and rationality of a world already given and complete," who is prepared to stand the test of reality and to achieve a union of his subjectivity with "true presence and objective value." Yet it must be immediately pointed out that Hegel is far from calling for a sober resignation to a world finite and miserable. He is far from wanting to disappoint the romantics. On the contrary, his whole tremendous speculative effort aims at showing that reality, just as it is, excels everything the romantics were dreaming of and longing for. Similarly, when he rejects the Kantian *ought* as something which merely should be but is not, Hegel does not want to say that everything which Kant had relegated to the realm of the unknown ought to be abandoned and forgotten; on the contrary, he argues not only that it *is* but also that it is within the grasp of man's knowledge. To use Hegel's own example of adolescence and maturity, far from trying to disillusion the youth, he claims that their ideals are reality, even if the reality differs somewhat from what the youth expected. In short, he invites all philosophers of *Sollen* from Kant to the romantics to follow him in an intellectual effort which, he believes, succeeds in leading up to a vision which transfigures the whole of reality into an Absolute, satisfying all human aspirations.

This intellectual effort, which makes up the content of Hegel's *Phenomenology of Mind*, consists in an ascent to the standpoint from which it becomes obvious that reality is exactly as it ought to be, namely, "rational." However, it immediately has to be added that when he speaks of *Vernunft*, Hegel has more in mind than man's "capacity to reason." To begin with, since it is both the

---

[11] Hegel$_2$, X, 93 ff; cf. Hegel$_4$, I, 314; cf. also Novalis, II, 336; III, 165.

essence and the highest achievement of the human mind, *Vernunft*
embraces, and is, a synthesis of all spiritual capacities of man:
of feeling, will, and thought. Moreover, the expression ' *Vernunft*'
refers both to man's mind and to reality. "Everything actual
is only insofar as it contains in itself the Idea and expresses it.
The whole objective and subjective world not only *ought* to conform
to the Idea; it is the very conformity of concept and reality. Reality
which does not correspond to the concept is mere *appearance*,
something subjective, accidental, arbitrary, something without
truth."[12] As a feature of reality, reason is that character of being
which permits the mind to penetrate the whole of reality without
presupposing anything except itself. As a human capacity, it
is the mind's ability to recognize itself in whatever it approaches.
Finally, it is that which is common to all mind and to all reality,
the basic character of what is, "the substance and the infinite
power of all natural and spiritual life, which is its own infinite
material as well as the infinite form, the activity of its own content."[13] Perhaps the best way to describe Hegel's *Vernunft* would
be to say that it is both the transcendental character of being,
in terms of which it satisfies the infinite aspiration of the human
mind, and the essence as well as the ultimate achievement of the
human mind itself. It is the thorough connaturality of the whole
of being to the human mind, which eventually reaches its completion in man's achievement of an "Absolute Knowledge."

In short, Hegel attempts to overcome all *ought* by transfiguring
reality into an Absolute, the knowledge of which satisfies all human
aspirations. We are using the expression 'transfiguration' in
order to indicate the point at which most of the problems of Hegel's
disciples will arise: instead of either *predicting* that the world
will become perfect through and through or trying to *transform*
the world in order to make it perfect, Hegel simply *describes* it
as perfect. His disciples soon will discover that Hegel overcame
the *ought* only at the level of speculative thought, leaving reality

---

[12] Hegel₂, V, 238; tr. Johnston-Struthers, II, 396. Cf. XX, 309: "An odd
error of our time consists in isolating the intellectual power from its natural
connection with our feeling and acting nature."

[13] Hegel₂, XI, 35; tr. Sibree, 9.

itself unchanged; and the romantic philosophy of *Sollen* will re-
emerge, though in a quite different form. But it is important to
see that Hegel himself did not conceive of his own philosophy
as an effort which takes place in man's subjective mind alone.
On the one hand, he is too much of an intellectualist to conceive
of an intellectual effort as "merely mental"; the ascent described
in the *Phenomenology* affects man's whole existence. To reach
Absolute Knowledge is more than to have a new idea, a new outlook;
it is a transformation of the whole of man's being. On the other
hand, Hegel views his philosophy as the conceptual expression
of something which has happened in reality, of an ultimate level
reached by history. The transfiguring ascent developed in the
Phenomenology takes up only the course of history which, if adequately understood, proves that man has reached the ultimate completion
of his being.

Later we shall try to show some of the reasons which led Hegel
to this belief. At this point, however, we shall consider the few
texts in which Hegel speaks of the relation between theory and
practice. As we shall see, they are little more than a corollary
to the ideas just considered.

At first sight, Hegel's treatment of theory and practice appears
fairly traditional. All of the texts in question treat of this distinction in a context which today we would describe as psychological and which Hegel explicitly qualifies as such. Moreover,
most of the texts are found in sections introducing or leading
to the analysis of "objective spirit," containing what remains
in Hegel of normative disciplines after the reduction of all *ought*
to being.[14]

In one respect, however, these texts are far from traditional.
They all reduce practice to theory, or rather, as Hegel treats of
this distinction in psychological terms, will to thought. Perhaps
the most explicit passage of this kind is found in the supplement
(*Zusatz*) to paragraph 4 of the *Philosophy of Right*:

> Spirit[15] is in principle thought, and man is distinguished from
> beast in virtue of thought. But it must not be imagined that

[14] Cf. Hegel$_2$, III, 25 ff., 215 ff.; V, 327 ff.; VII, 50 ff.; X, 302 ff.; etc.
[15] Whenever '*Geist*' has a connotation other than perfectly neutral, we

man is half thought and half will, and that he keeps thought in one pocket and will in another, for this would be an empty idea. The distinction between thought and will is only that between the theoretical attitude and the practical. These, however, are surely not two faculties; the will is rather a special mode of thought (*eine besondere Weise des Denkens*), thought translating itself into existence, thought as the urge to give itself existence.[16]

The first point to notice in this passage is that it explicitly rejects a distinction between thought and will in terms of "faculties." Spirit *is* thought and *is* will according to whether it maintains a theoretical or practical attitude. Instead of explicitly stressing this point, usually Hegel simply says: "*qua* will spirit is, etc."[17]

Taken by itself, this point would not seem overly important. Following a suggestion in St. Augustine, a number of medieval thinkers had maintained that expressions such as 'thought' and 'will' have the same referent, namely, the human soul, to which they refer according to whether it is conceived as thinking or as willing. In Hegel, however, there is a close connection between the claim that thought and will are not two distinct faculties and the statement that will is only a special mode of thought. Of course, he does not want to say that since spirit is essentially thought, and will is not a faculty distinct from thought, will must be a mode of thought. Rather, his argument goes the other way around: since will is a mode of thought, it cannot be a faculty distinct from thought.

Why, then, is will a "special mode of thought?" In the *Philosophy of Right* Hegel advances the following rather complex argument. In thinking an object, he argues, I deprive it of its sensibility, I make it into thought and thus into something which is "essentially and immediately mine." For to understand an object is to transfix it so as to make it cease standing over against me. Whenever I truly understand something, "I have taken away from it the charac-

have translated it by 'spirit.' For the expression 'mind,' which we have used only when no misunderstanding is possible, lacks the reference, e.g., to the "Holy Spirit," which is so characteristic of Hegel's notion of *Geist*.

[16] Hegel$_2$, VII, 50 ff.; tr. Knox, 226.

[17] E.g., Hegel$_2$, III, 25; VIII, 55; X, 365; etc.

ter of its own which it had in opposition to me." As Hegel puts it in the *Encyclopaedia*, it is the very essence of the theoretical attitude to be concerned with the rational and to posit it as mine, i.e., to free it from all presupposition different from myself.[18]

But all objects of will are "mine" in this very sense. After all, the difference between mere desire and will consists in the fact that the objects of will are intellectually known. Of course, will also introduces an element of alienation. As Hegel says, it "establishes a separation" and "posits a difference." For although it may be true that objects of will are mine as far as thought is concerned, they obviously are not mine as far as the proper intention of will goes. On the contrary, volitions by necessity aim at something which is not mine to the extent to which it is willed. But this separation is overcome by the action in terms of which I put my will into effect. Action, therefore, is the satisfaction of thought's urge to give itself external existence, and will is nothing but this very urge.[19]

This analysis remains unintelligible as long as one does not realize that Hegel uses the expression 'will' in a quite peculiar way. In everyday language we call "will" any human desire or appetite which the intellect approves of, or at least acknowledges as genuinely ours. Hegel, on the contrary, restricts this expression to the desire to impose upon reality a form which makes it conform to reason. In other words, he implies that any truly human desire, as well as any truly human action, aims at transforming the irrational into something rational. As Hegel says in one of his earlier writings, this can be expressed in two ways. One can say that will is the urge to give external existence to an internal determination, i.e., to thought. But one also can say that will aims at the abolition of a given externality, i.e., aims at "making it conform to the interior determination."[20]

---

[18] Hegel₂, X, 302. Cf. XI, 415: "Cognition (*Erkennen*) is to annihilate whatever is exterior and alien to consciousness and thus the return of subjectivity unto itself. Conceived of as the effective self-consciousness of the world, cognition is the world's reconciliation with itself," tr. Sibree, 323.

[19] Hegel₂, VII, 51 ff.; tr. Knox, 226.

[20] Hegel₂, III, 26.

Will, then, is an implement of thought; it aims at the assimila-
tion of what mere thought does not succeed in assimilating. In
this sense Hegel sometimes describes knowledge and will as com-
plementary appetites (*Triebe*) which aim at assimilating reality
to reason. Knowledge follows these appetites by discovering
rationality wherever it goes and by transforming its objects into
thought. But knowledge does not succeed in assimilating everything. In particular, the rationality available to it is always universal; the particular escapes it just as everything irrational escapes
it. Therefore there emerges another appetite: the urge to make
reality rational by acting upon it. This is will, which results in
actions transforming material and social realities, imposing upon
them the mark of rationality.[21]

Thus will is the urge resulting from an *ought* of thought. However, it is not only in the superficial sense that will results from
the thought that something ought to be, for example, that I ought
to have a good dinner. What Hegel means is that will is the urge
to actualize a rationality expressed in thought. It is an urge of
knowledge, of a knowledge not satisfied with what it discovers,
not the urge of a biological entity endowed with reason. It is the
urge of a being which, instead of being in need of the world, desires
that the world be rational.

Three implications are immediately obvious. First, the aim of
all will and action is a satisfaction of thought, of rational knowledge.
For how could man's actions upon the world satisfy his urge for
rationality if he were not able to contemplate the rationality
achieved? In terms of theory and practice this amounts to saying
that practice, taken as any action transforming a reality outside
thought, is for the sake of theory. It exists for the sake of theory,
not only because of it. Practice is for the sake of contemplation.

Secondly, the importance of will and action decreases as history
progresses. For the more man acts upon reality, the more he
succeeds in making it conform to the norms of reason; and the
more he makes it conform to reason, the more he transforms it
into a world to be contemplated rather than to be acted upon.

[21] For references see Grégoire, 10.

Fichte had claimed that man's knowledge is finite, but his will infinite; there always remains an *ought*. Hegel claims just the opposite. Knowledge is potentially infinite, and will is finite.[22] There is no conceivable limit to contemplation, since its object is the infinite; but there is a limit to will and action, namely, contemplation. When man succeeds in transforming the universe into a perfect embodiment of reason, will and action lose their function. Or to put in another way, both knowledge and will cease to be a *Trieb*, a desire; they become a thoroughly contemplative acceptance of the whole of reality.

The third implication, and probably the most important, is somewhat more complex. It leads us back to Hegel's criticism of the *ought*. Confronted with a reality which fails to satisfy the norms of reason, man can maintain two quite different attitudes. On the one hand, he can dream of another reality, long for a more perfect world, or call for action and eventually proceed to transform the reality in question. On the other hand, he may become suspicious of his own judgement, and instead of trying to transcend it he may look at the given reality long enough and close enough to discover its hidden rationality. Someone who does not understand, who is intellectually blind, will feel that there always remains something to be done. He never will be satisfied; his life will be an endless longing for improvement. In the end he will urge change for the sake of change alone. In opposition to this attitude the wise man will realize at a certain moment that all longing for another world and all calling for action are due to a lack of knowledge. He will realize that it is no longer his task to teach the world how it ought to be, but rather to show the world its own rationality.

In short, Hegel's criticism of the "philosophy of *Sollen*" as well as his treatment of the relation between thought and will—between the theoretical and the practical attitude—implies that there exists a point of time at which the task of philosophy consists in a "justification" of existing reality and in a "reconciliation" of man with the given world. History, as Hegel views it, is the process of the embodiment of Reason both in the external world and in man's

---

[22] E.g., Hegel₂, VII, 65; tr. Knox, 26.

mind. The whole history of humanity is nothing else than the gradual emergence and the eventual definitive break-through of reason. It is not very important at the moment whether this process is viewed as the doing of an anonymous Reason with a capital 'R' —which, using humanity as its tool, gradually gets a grip on and incorporates itself into reality—or whether it is viewed as the doing of man himself unfolding his potentialities while transforming the face of the earth. It is almost impossible to decide which of these two possibilities or its numerous variants Hegel had in mind.[23] The famous introduction of the *Philosophy of History*, for example, quite clearly argues for the first alternative, whereas a number of passages in the *Phenomenology of Mind* suggest the second alternative. What is important here is that Hegel believes that such an end of history has come. This is particularly obvious from the *Phenomenology of Mind*.

The *Phenomenology* has often been described as an introduction to the "system." But it is a very peculiar introduction. For even if we disregard the fact that during the execution of the work Hegel incorporated into his "introduction" large parts of the "system" itself, it is obvious that the *Phenomenology* aims at far more than simply making the reader familiar with Hegel's basic ideas. In a sense it is a justification of rather than an introduction to Hegel's system. For what Hegel tries to show is that the system— whose exposition, in 1807, was still a long time coming—would be written from the standpoint of "Absolute Knowledge," i.e., would unfold absolute, all-embracing truth perfectly conscious of itself. And he shows this by indicating, on the one hand, that the present (in 1807 the Napoleonic Empire) is the ultimate unfolding of all integral elements of reason in the real order and, on the other hand, that in his own philosophy this unfolded reason becomes conscious of itself. After having analyzed in the first five chapters all elements of human experience from sense certainty through perception, understanding, and self-consciousness to reason, he sketches the sociopolitical development of humanity from the Greeks to Napoleon. At the same time he traces religious develop-

---

[23] For a detailed discussion of this question see Grégoire, 140 ff.

ment from natural religion to Christianity in its highest Protestant form until in the end he reaches "Absolute Knowledge," which in fact is nothing else than the adequate philosophical self-consciousness of the ultimate form of human society, on the one hand, and of the ultimate form of religion, on the other hand.

In a sense the first seven chapters of the *Phenomenology* are an exposition of both the integral and historical elements of man's striving for wisdom and perfection. They are concerned with philosophy in the traditional sense of "love of wisdom." The last chapter, however, is no longer concerned with philosophy in this sense. In this eighth chapter, Hegel fulfils the promise made in the preface: he reaches the point at which human thought can "lay aside the name of *love* of knowledge, and be *actual Knowledge*,"[24] Knowledge *tout court*, or Wisdom. But it immediately has to be stressed that this claim does not entail the almost pathological presumptuousness of which Hegel sometimes is accused. For he is far from claiming that he has reached this "Absolute Knowledge" because he is a genius or because God has chosen him. It is of course true that Hegel, implicitly at least, views himself "as the particular man in whom God ... finally achieves full actualization."[25] But God achieves full actualization in Hegel only because it is God's very essence to unfold himself in history and because, quite incidentally, Hegel is the man who first saw that history had reached its completion and in whose philosophy this completed history became conscious of itself, thus reaching its ultimate perfection. Hegel is the first man who can call himself a "sage." But his contribution to Wisdom, though highly significant, is far from being superhuman. He did no more than to take the ripe fruit of the whole of history and make it conscious of itself. As Hegel himself often stresses, both contemporary human society and Protestant Christianity are ultimate with respect to their content. What Hegel adds is no more than the adequate self-

[24] Hegel₂, II, 14; tr. Baillie, 70. For Hegel's concept of Wisdom see Kojève, 271 ff.; for a brief comparison between Hegel's concept of Knowledge and Plato's concept of philosophy see Gebhardt₁, 39 ff.

[25] Cf. Tucker, 43.

consciousness of these historical results; he adds the scientific form of conceptual thought.

Though far less intricate, and less expressive as well, the *Philosophy of History* basically reaches the same conclusion. It culminates in an analysis of "our world" which, since modern constitutional monarchy has unfolded all essential aspects of rational freedom, is the "last stage of history."[26] In the concluding passage of the *History of Philosophy* which is concerned with "the final result"— with Hegel's philosophy—and which stresses that the history of philosophy is the "world's history in its innermost significance," Hegel describes his own achievement as that of the spirit's bursting "asunder the crust of earth which divided it from the sun, its concept, so that the earth crumbles away." "Previous philosophy is to be reverenced as necessary and as a link in this sacred chain, but all the same nothing more than a link. The present is the highest stage reached."[27] Indeed, it is the final stage:

> Spirit produces itself as Nature, as the State. The former is its unconscious deed in which it appears to itself another, and not spirit. But in the State, in the deeds and life of History, as also of Art, it brings itself to pass with consciousness; it knows very various modes of its reality, yet they are only modes. In knowledge alone it knows itself as absolute spirit; and this knowledge, or spirit, is its only true existence. This then is the standpoint of the present day, and the series of spiritual forms is with it for the present concluded.[28]

Again, it is obvious what all this means as far as theory and practice are concerned. "The ultimate aim and business of philosophy is to reconcile thought with reality,"[29] not to tell the world how it ought to be, not to try to reform it or to revolutionize it. And as philosophy is man's highest and most sacred achievement, as the philosopher is the ultimate man, reconciliation is man's most perfect deed. Reconciliation, not resignation. Hegel's pupils will accuse their master of accommodating himself and his philosophy to such existing realities as traditional Christianity or the

---

[26] Hegel₂, XI, 552; tr. Sibree, 442.
[27] Hegel₂, XIX, 690; tr. Haldane-Simson, III, 552.
[28] *Ibid.*
[29] Hegel₂, XIX, 684; tr. Haldane-Simson, III, 545.

Prussian Kingdom. In a sense, however, Hegel anticipated all their criticism and objections. His defence is an accusation: they do not understand, they do not know, they shun the "effort of the concept." "The easiest thing of all is to pass judgements on what has content and solidity. It is more difficult to grasp it. And it is most of all difficult at one and the same time to do both and to produce a systematic exposition of it."[30]

[30] Hegel$_2$, II, 13; tr. Baillie, 69 ff.

11: THE "KINGDOM OF GOD"

In the preceding chapter we were concerned with what might be described as the nucleus of original Hegelianism, indeed, as the basic intuition and the leitmotif of Hegel's whole thought: that the subjectivism characteristic of German Idealism can be overcome only by declaring human subjectivity as infinite and therefore objective; that this declaration is credible only if man can reach what up to now was reserved to God, namely, Absolute Knowledge; and that such an Absolute Knowledge, in turn, can be attributed to man only if it is described as the consciousness adequate to a history which, having unfolded all of its potentialities, essentially has completed its course.

In the present section we shall discuss some of the roots of this conception which are significant to an understanding of the development of German thought after Hegel's death. First, we shall try to place the ideas just outlined in the intellectual atmosphere of Germany around 1800. Secondly, we shall discuss some aspects of the theme around which the earliest arguments about Hegel's philosophy have flared up, namely, Hegel's interpretation of Christianity.

We may link these two subjects by proceeding from a circumstance which at first sight would seem to be only anecdotal. During his student years at Tübingen, Hegel and his two intimates, Schelling and Hölderlin, seem to have used a somewhat unusual password: "May the Kingdom of God come." A few months after they left the seminary, Hölderlin reminds Hegel that this was their farewell greeting, claiming that by it they would recognize each other "after any metamorphosis." Some months later Hegel himself writes in a letter to Schelling: "May the Kingdom of God come and our hands not remain idle," and adds: "Reason and Freedom remain our password; and our point of union, the Invisible Church."[31]

It is hardly necessary to stress that these words indicate that Hegel was not always the personification of detached philosophical Wisdom which, "weary of the stir of the immediate passions of reality, departs for contemplation."[32] Not until about ten years later did Hegel's antagonism toward all *Sollen* emerge. As a student he was as enthusiastic about the French Revolution and its aftermaths as his less prosaic[33] friends were; as far as we know, their discussion turned around the freedom to be gained and the tyrants to be fought. At the age of twenty-five, when he was already a private tutor in Berne, he still believed that a further development of Kantian philosophy might lead to a "revolution." How far he was from being "reconciled" with the world at that time is suggested by a well-known sentence contained in a letter to Schelling in 1795 : "With the dissemination of ideas as to how things ought to be, the indolence of those sedate people who eternally take everything just as it is will disappear."[34]

What is more important is that the password "Kingdom of God" gives expression to a feeling common to most German men of letters born between 1750 and 1800: that the consummation of history was imminent, that the "little while" which separates man from a restoration of his original harmony (and thus, by implication, from the "Kingdom of God") would be over within a measurable space of time. And yet, far from being an invitation to idle hopes, this prospect challenges all of man's forces and talents. "Humanity would not be humantiy if the millennium did not neces-

---

[31] Hegel₄, I, 9, 18. A brief analysis of the origin and the meaning of the expression 'Kingdom of God' is found in Hoffmeister₂, 222.

[32] Hegel₂, XI, 569; tr. Sibree, 457.

[33] Schelling often accuses Hegel of being "prosaic." Whereas Schelling aims at being engulfed by the Absolute, Hegel always remains conceptual and thus, to use Schellings words, in a "nonintuitive prosiness." Cf. Benz₄, 33.

[34] Hegel₄, I, 34. This passage is often referred to as illustrating the difference between Hegel's youthful enthusiasm and his later rejection of all philosophy of *Sollen*, e.g., Hyppolite₃, 47 ff.

sarily arrive."[35] As H. Popitz has shown in his brilliant study, this
distinctly eschatological mentality was a common theme, far
into the nineteenth century, of numerous German poets and thinkers
widely differing in most other respects. Herder, Schiller, Fichte,
Humboldt, Arndt, the young Hegel, Hölderlin, Novalis, Schelling,
Eichendorf, even Heine, to mention only the most important
names, revolve around this theme of a near restoration of man
which is often accompanied by overtones unmistakably religious.

The immediate origin of this attitude was of course the then
overwhelming experience of the French Revolution. It must be
noticed, however, that this experience entailed more than simply
the insight that man, after having passed a long period of immaturity
during which he had been engulfed by overwhelming natural and
social forces, had eventually become the "autonomous subject
of his own development."[36] The *Erlebnis* ot liberation was pre-
eminent, it is true. But at the same time, especially after the first
exaggerated enthusiasm began to slacken, it was accompanied
by an increasing bewilderment over a collapse of all hitherto
familiar frames of reference.

Reading the authors in question, one is often reminded of men
who, after having learned of their imminent rescue, realize for the
first time just how bad their state really is. Kant described only
one side of what the French Revolution meant to the Germans
when he wrote that the revolution of 1789 revealed talents and
powers in man's nature which no politician ever would have been
able to invent by looking at the previous course of history.[37] Kant
was still too much under the spell of the *Aufklärung* to see the
other side, which is best described by Novalis' image of serpents
clasping the cradle of the new human race, of dark powers of anarchy
and chaos wanting to take away the use of humanity's limbs just
gained.[38] To overlook this gloomy aspect of the French Revolution
amounts to making virtually incomprehensible why in Germany
the seemingly liberating effect of this event resulted in a kind of

[35] Novalis, III, 154.
[36] Marcuse$_4$, 3 ff.
[37] Kant, VII, 401.
[38] Novalis, I 296. Cf. Popitz, 24 ff.

flight from the present into the future—in a series of eschatological conceptions which combined hopes of a radiant future with strangely severe criticisms of the past as well as of the present.

The *Aufklärer* had believed that by a slow, yet continuous, progress human nature and also all sociopolitical settings would gradually become more and more perfect, a conception which obviously was based on a naive reliance upon a fundamentally untainted human nature. With Herder, Schiller, and Fichte this optimism loses its naïveté. For it is balanced by the painful awareness that up to now man has constantly fallen away from an originally perfect state rather that approached an ultimane perfection. Therefore, they repeatedly refer to a "suffering humanity" which in the course of history has lost more and more of its original dignity. Herder, for example, argues that if it were impossible to repair what superstition and barbarism have destroyed in the past, it would be better for Europe to perish; Schiller speaks of a Europe which falters between subtle perversion and barbarous brutality, between superstition and unbelief; and in a famous passage Fichte even goes so far as to claim that the present era is that of accomplished "sinfulness."[39]

Thus the *Aufklärung*'s idea that a better future will develop rectilinearly out of the present—that is, that it will be nothing else than a still more perfect present—quickly loses its meaning. Instead, history from now on will be described increasingly in terms of a trichotomy, the formal structure of which soon becomes the basic scheme of all philosophical thought up to Marx. The first period is always described as that of a spontaneous yet unreflective and naïve harmony, the model of which is Rousseau's idyllic child of nature (Fichte), the Greeks (Herder, Schiller, Humboldt, Hölderlin), or an idealized medieval Christianity (Novalis). There follows a period of dissolution and "alienation" in which man falls away from his original harmony; usually this second period is described as that of an uncontrolled and therefore chaotic growth of human potentialities, and all contemporary tensions and confusion are traced back to this stage. Finally there will come a period of restora-

[39] Cf. Popitz, 15.

tion of the original harmony in which at a higher, indeed at an ultimate, level all human talents and values will be reincorporated into an order which leaves nothing to be desired.[40]

This trichotomy obviously originates in the desire to make sense of the disappointing and terrifying outcome of the French Revolution. It is an attempt to preserve the cultural optimism of the *Aufklärung* in spite of the fact that "the attempt of the French nation to install itself in its sacred human rights and to gain political freedom ... has thrown a great part of Europe, and a whole century back into barbarism and servitude."[41] By interpreting all contemporary grievances as a sign of, and as a necessary step toward, the ultimate restoration of man, the trichotomy points toward a future which grants new hopes to the fate of humanity.

Though we shall take up this subject more explicitly in a moment, we may point out now that this conception quite unmistakably echoes the prophecy contained in the twenty-third chapter of the Gospel according to St. Luke: the advent of the Kingdom of God will be announced by a last crescendo of the machinations of the powers of darkness. As we shall see, this is more than the afterthought of a historian. Most of the men about whom we are speaking were originally theologians, and all of them were perfectly familiar with the Bible. Their whole attitude becomes intelligible only if one realizes that they view their time in terms of this prophecy, whether they are believing Christians or not.

But before we take up this subject, it may be useful to add that the millenarianism of Herder, Schiller, and the romantics significantly differs both from that of Hegel's followers and from that of the French Utopian socialists such as Babeuf, Saint-Simon, and Fourier,

---

[40] Contrary to what is often believed, this trichotomy does not originate with Hegel; cf. Mueller. The first to apply this scheme to history seems to have been Schiller; cf. XII, 363. Fichte uses it extensively in the *Wissenschaftslehre* (his scheme for history, however, being a pentadic partition). Hegel was the first to use it in such a way that history no longer is considered as a *unique* triple act. Cottier has suggested that this trichotomy originates in what he calls a "romanticist vitalism"; cf. Cottier$_1$, 26, Cottier$_2$, 13 ff. This "romanticist vitalism," in turn, probably goes back to the theologians of Swabian Pietism, e.g., to Oetinger's *Theologia ex idea vitae deducta.*

[41] Cf. *Schillers Persönlichkeit. Urtheile der Zeitgenossen* (Weimar, 1908) II, 284.

in spite of the fact that the latter were Herder's and Schiller's
contemporaries. For it is a thoroughly apolitical millenarianism.
Indeed it is quite consciously antirevolutionary. The political
revolution had failed because "the instant, though it was a most
propitious one, met a depraved generation which did not deserve
it and was unable to appreciate and to use it" (Schiller); thus
the only meaningful reform seemed to be a "revolution of convictions and of the way of looking at things" (Hölderlin). As
Schiller puts it: "All lasting reform has to start from the way
of thinking (*Denkungsart*)." In short, the restoration of humanity
which these men envisage is a cultural, ethical, and aesthetic restoration, not a political or social one.

This becomes particularly obvious if one looks at the topics
which make up their complaints about past and present history.
None of these men complains about economic or social grievances,
and only a few of them touch upon political problems in the proper
sense of the term. They are aware of the sociopolitical problems
of their time, it is true. But unlike the generation of Marx, they
had witnessed firsthand the chaos following the French Revolution;
and unlike the French, they did not have, to use a favorite phrase
of Hegel, *la tête près du bonnet*.[42] As a result, they almost instinctively shrank back from the dangers involved in political revolutions. Schiller once explained this reserve by an impressive met-
aphor: when a watchmaker repairs a clock, he simply stops the
wheels; but the "living clockwork of the state has to be repaired
while it strikes and the problem is to seize the turning wheel in
its very revolution."[43]

Man has to change, and then society and states will change as
though by themselves. And the change required of man consists
in becoming a true and whole man. "Be human beings and the
human rights will fall to your share."[44] This is also the sense of
Hölderlin's pathetic lamentation: "You see artisans, but no men;
thinkers, but no men; priests, but no men; masters and slaves,

---

[42] Cf. Hegel$_2$, XIX, 553; Haldane-Simson, III, 425. In the *Philosophy of
History* Hegel translates this phrase by "the French are hotheads"; cf. XI, 554.
[43] Schiller, XII, 9.
[44] Novalis, II, 416.

but no men. Does it not remind you of a battlefield on which there
are scattered about hands and arms and limbs while the spilled
blood of life runs out in the sand?"[45]

To some extent Hegel's lifelong opposition to all "revolutions,"
which after his death brought him under the suspicion of having been
an archconservative, is rooted in the very same attitude. As
early as 1796, when he was still far from opposing the Kantian
ought, he stresses that the great revolutions which strike the eye,
in order to be fruitful, had to have been preceded by a "still and
secret" revolution in the order of human attitudes and ideas.[46]
And his relation to the French Revolution always remained as
ambivalent as that of Schiller or Novalis, for example. He hails
it as a "glorious spiritual dawn," it is true; and he never forgets
the awe with which this event originally had inspired him, "as
if the effectual reconciliation of the divine with the world eventually
were achieved."[47] But at the same time he was well aware that
this revolution was not the final break-through of reason.

It is not by chance that the section of the *Phenomenology* devoted
to the French Revolution is entitled "Absolute Freedom and
Terror." Here the events of 1789 are described as a self-enthrone-
ment of the "undivided substance of absolute freedom." But
this new autonomy, as it shared in no objectivity, was according
to Hegel self-destructive. Its only deed, Hegel argues, was death—
a death without depth and meaning—"the most cold-blooded
and meaningless death of all, with no more significance than cleaving
a head of cabbage or swallowing a draught of water."[48] Similarly
in the *Philosophy of History* he describes the Revolution as the
reign both of virtue and of terror, for "subjective virtue, reigning
from the standpoint of mere personal sentiment (*Gesinnung*) brings
along the most dreadful of tyrannies."[49]

[45] Hölderlin, *Sämtliche Werke,* ed. F. Beissner (Stuttgart, 1944 ff.), III, 160.
[46] Nohl, 220; tr. Knox-Kroner, 152. Cf. Hegel[2], XI, 564; tr. Sibree, 453.
[47] Hegel[2], XI, 557 ff.; tr. Sibree, 447.
[48] Hegel[2], II, 450 ff.; tr. Baillie, 601 ff. For a more detailed analysis see Hyppolite[3], 70 ff., and Ritter[2].
[49] Hegel[2], XI, 561; tr. Sibree, 450.

However, contrary to all his contemporaries, Hegel was convinced from about 1803 that all this already belonged to the past, indeed that the "little while" separating humanity from the "Kingdom of God" already was over. He views his own time as a period of fermentation in which, "with a jerk," spirit has definitively transcended all its previous forms: "the whole mass of hitherto valid representations, indeed the bonds of the world, have dissolved and fall to the ground like a vision."[50] The new age is an ultimate synthesis of what Hegel in the *Phenomenology* calls "presence" and "essence," that is, of the secular order of facts and the beyond, both the supersensual and the ideal. The concluding passage of the *Philosophy of Right* states well what this synthesis amounts to:

> Presence (*die Gegenwart*) has discarded its barbarity and unrighteous caprice, while Truth has abandoned its beyond and its arbitrary force so that the true reconciliation which discloses the state as the image of actuality and reason has become objective. In the state, self-consciousness finds in an organic development the actuality of its substantive knowing and willing; in religion, it finds the feeling and the representation of this its own truth as an ideal essentiality; while in Philosophy (*Wissenschaft*) it finds the free comprehension of this truth as one and the same in its mutually complementary manifestations, i.e., in the state, in nature, and in the ideal world.[51]

Obviously it would be wrong to say that Hegel's thought is no longer eschatological—that he transformed the eschatological enthusiasm of his contemporaries into a resignation to the present. If anything, Hegel is *more* eschatologically minded than any of the romanticists. However, his eschatology no longer points toward the future.

Hegel has often been accused of a "presumptuous anticipation of the World Plan."[52] If this means that he made predictions about the future, nothing could be more false. For if one looks for passages in Hegel concerned with future events, one looks in vain. (At one time he does pride himself on having predicted

[50] Cf. Hoffmeister$_1$, 352.
[51] Hegel$_2$, VII, 456; tr. Knox, 222 ff.
[52] E.g., Burkhardt, VII, 2.

Napoleon's downfall,[53] it is true, but this hardly justifies the above accusation.) However, it must be noticed that Hegel's silence about the future is not due to the fact that he is in no way interested in it, or that he does not know the laws according to which the World Spirit advances. As the well-known letter to Niethammer in 1816 indicates, he knew that the World Spirit "gave to time the word of command to advance"; and as Hegel adds, "such an order one obeys; like an ironclad and compact phalanx, this being advances irresistibly in spite of all obstacles, with movements as imperceptible as those of the sun."[54] He also knew the laws according to which this "advancing ogre" proceeds; after all, his whole philosophy is nothing else than an exposition of these laws. If he does not predict, if he claims that the owl of Minerva spreads its wings only with the falling of the dusk, that philosophy paints its "grey in grey" only when a shape of life has become old, it is because he has nothing to expect from the future.

In short, Hegel's lack of interest in the future is parallel to, indeed rooted in, his overcoming of every *ought*. Every *ought* and every beyond has been brought home, both through real history and through Hegel's philosophic reconciliation. There is no more beyond, as far as present man is concerned; "there is no longer anything secret in God."[55] Accordingly, the future can be of no interest; there is nothing new which it can bring. Longing for another and better future is due to lack of insight alone; it amounts to letting oneself become entangled in the "soft element" of opinions where anything one pleases may be built. As the preface to the *Philosophy of Right* puts it: "To recognize reason as the rose in the cross of the present and thereby to enjoy the present, this is the rational insight which reconciles us to the actual, the reconciliation which philosophy affords."[56]

---

[53] Hegel$_4$, II, 28 ff.
[54] *Ibid.* 86 ff.
[55] Hegel$_2$, XV, 100; tr. Speirs-Sanderson, I, 85.
[56] Hegel$_2$, VII, 35; tr. Knox, 12. Cf. Hegel$_2$, XV, 293, tr. Speirs-Sanderson, I, 285; and for an almost cynical remark, XX, 448 ff. On the image of the rose and the cross see Löwith$_3$, 28 ff.

However, there is another sense in which the accusation of a presumptuous anticipation of the World Plan obviously holds true. For as we have said, Hegel shows no interest in the future because *it* cannot bring anything new, not because *we* cannot know anything about it. But it is somewhat difficult to decide whether, and to what extent, this conviction is "presumptuous" in the usual sense of the term. For it originates from a religious background, the knowledge of which considerably alters our image of Hegel and, in particular, of Hegel's *"apologia* for pride." It is well known that German romanticists and idealists, especially Schelling, Hegel, and F. von Baader, rescued from oblivion and incorporated into their thought the underground stream of German speculative mysticism.[57] As we cannot enter here into all details, it must suffice to mention the main representatives of this current, which was as much opposed by the authorities both of the Catholic and of the Lutheran churches, as its influence was widespread and persistent.

First, there is Meister Eckhardt (†1328) together with his immediate followers, Johannes Tauler (†1361) and Heinrich Suso (†1366), and other men influenced by him, for example, the Dutch mystic, Jan van Ruysbroeck (†1381). They were rediscovered at the beginning of the nineteenth century by F. von Baader, who beside Schelling was the one most interested in all kinds of mysticism, theosophy, and speculative *Naturphilosophie*. In 1824, on the occasion of his visit in Berlin, Baader seems to have read to Hegel a number of excerpts from Eckhardt, and Hegel was so enthusiastic that the next day he devoted a whole lecture to this subject.[58]

Far more important, however, is the influence of the *Philosophus Teutonicus*, Jacob Böhme (†1624). As he himself had predicted, his influence upon German thought was mediated by foreigners. In the seventeenth century his ideas came back to Germany from

[57] Cf. Benz$_2$, where further references are given. It is worth noticing that Hegel states several times that what he calls "speculative" is a continuation and expansion of what in earlier times was called "mystical," e.g., Hegel$_2$, VIII, 197 ff.; XIX, 91 fn.; tr. Haldane-Simson, II, 448.

[58] Cf. Benz$_2$, 283.

his pupils in England, the Philadelphian sect; in the eighteenth century, through the influence of the French thinker L. C. de Saint-Martin (†1803). Again, it was Baader who rediscovered Böhme for German philosophic thought. But, unlike Eckhardt, Böhme was known to the man in the street a long time before Baader became interested in him. In particular, two Swabian Lutheran theologians were influenced by him: Johann Albrecht Bengel (†1752) and Friedrich Christian Oetinger (†1782). Oetinger, in turn, familiarized the German public with the visionary mysticism of Swedenborg (†1772), which around 1760 became so influential in Germany that even a man like Kant felt impelled to devote to him a critical study of almost 130 pages.[59] Finally, Böhme's ideas, as interpreted by Bengel and Oetinger, were popularized by Johann Michael Hahn (†1819). He wrote no less than fifteen volumes of exegesis of the Bible in Böhme's spirit, which seems to have reached virtually every Swabian household.[60]

We have to restrict ourvelses to discussing one of the aspects of this mystic tradition's influence upon Hegel: its concept of, or rather theology of, history. Before we proceed, however, a word of caution may be in place. As E. Benz' studies show, it is comparatively easy to prove that Schelling was engrossed by the thought of such men as Böhme, Bengel, and Oetinger. Though he almost never reveals his sources and often even uses passages from the Bible as if they were his own words, we know from Schelling's letters that he tried to procure for himself as many books by these men as he could find. This is not the case with Hegel. He was well acquainted with Böhme, it is true, though he did not truly study his writings until after 1811.[61] But one looks in vain for references to Bengel and Oetinger either in Hegel's writings or in his letters. Possibly he read some of their writings as a student. Moreover, it is very likely that Schelling (whose grandfather and father, both parsons, adhered to Bengel's theology[62]) passed on considerable information to Hegel while they studied together at Tübingen.

[59] Cf. Benz₁, 237 ff.
[60] Cf. Schulze, 212 ff.
[61] Cf. Hegel's letter to van Ghert, Hegel₄, I, 381.
[62] Cf. Benz₄, 271 ff.

In any case, Bengel's and Oetinger's ideas were to a large extent
common knowledge in Swabia. Still, as Hegel never explicitly
mentions either Bengel, or Oetinger, or Hahn, much of what we
say will have to remain mere conjecture.

It was Bengel who inaugurated in Swabian Pietism the eschatological mentality which began to trickle into German poetry and
philosophy a few years after his death.[63] Personal experiences
had induced Bengel to view almost everything as "signs of the
time" announcing the imminent end of history. In his youth he
had seen his native town invaded by the armies of Louis XIV
time and again. Later he witnessed seeming catastrophies in
the spiritual realm: a new intensity of the antireformatory attack
against Protestantism, the steady advance of rationalism, the
emergence of materialistic and atheist philosophies as well as
their increasing influence, and the appearance of absolutist princes
who did not distinguish between good and evil. Eventually he began
to view the Bible as a "stock book of the Christian communion
from the beginning of the world to its end, in which there is written
what the origin, the course, and the end of mankind is," and he
tried to determine at which point of this predestinate development
his own time stood.

Not entirely new was Bengel's belief that the Bible, far from being
the relic of a revelation given once for all, contained the message about God's intentions concerning the world; that it permitted
one to view history as a progressive realization of a definite divine
plan which progressively revealed itself as history advanced; that
actual history was the unfolding of a truth revealed to the apostles,
of a truth which dawned, not at once, but rather step by step,
from one age of the Church to the other. The Dutch theologian
Johann Coccejus (†1669) had described the history of salvation
as consisting of a succession of covenants which progressively
reveal God's salvific will, and Coccejus, in turn, had resumed an
old tradition ultimately originating with St. Augustine. What
was new was Bengel's belief that this development had reached the

[63] Cf. Rohrmoser, 189 ff., who convincingly shows that the theology of
Bengel and Oetinger has to be viewed in connection with rather than in opposition to the *Aufklärung*.

point at which it became meaningful to look for a definite chronology. In 1724, while preparing a sermon, he suddenly reached the conclusion that the millennium would arrive 666 years after the rejection of the temporal power of the pope by the "Roman Commune" in 1143, that is, in 1809.

Later, after having reviewed his calculations, Bengel corrected this date to 1836. But it must not be imagined that Bengel was a silly enthusiast. On the contrary, he was a theologian of high caliber who published the first critical edition of the Greek text of the New Testament, and much of whose exegesis is still taken seriously by Protestant scholars. All the more effective were his eschatological calculations. In the minds of Swabian Pietists eschatological expectation quickly replaced naive faith in an indefinite progress. This expectation also seems to have been the immediate cause of the intense interest in history which about that time spreads over all Germany. For from then on everybody would pay attention to "signs of the time"; one would look for the Antichrist and his prophets; especially in Württemberg everybody would focus his attention on the imminent "Kingdom of God" (Bengel), on the "golden time" to come (Oetinger). As Bengel himself remarked: "Old people like to draw up inventories, and the world begins to be old. This is why the study of history is becoming so important."[64]

But there is still another element of this eschatological theology which is relevant to the appreciation of German Idealism. The predicted millenium, as described by Bengel and Oetinger, bears a striking resemblance to the ultimate unfolding of spirit which Schelling and Hegel describe as *Wissenschaft*. Bengel himself, it is true, was still too genuine a theologian to be unduly interested in what the "Kingdom of God" would be like; he simply expected the final coming of Christ and a universal descent of the Holy Spirit. Oetinger already was different. He was a careful student of Böhme and well familiar with the cabalistic tradition (the interest in which, incidentally, he owed to Leibniz), and his studies of

---

[64] Cf. Benz$_3$, here 540. Incidentally, around 1797, Novalis mentions a study based on a "treatment of history as if it were gospel"; cf. Novalis, I, 550.

Swedenborg's visionary writings only served to develop further his keen interest in a detailed knowledge of the "other world."

In particular, Oetinger's *Treatise Concerning the Last Things*, published in 1759, contains quite an elaborate account of the "golden time." His analysis would be far from original if, like Christianity in general, Oetinger were speaking about heaven. In fact, however, he speaks of a development within this world, of a development which is supposed to take place in about seventy-five years. Still, it is not a Utopian account in the proper sense of the term. For Oetinger is a theologian, not a social critic. Even though he describes the future society as democratic (for in Christ nobody is either master or slave, Greek or Roman), predicts the abolition of private property, argues that law will be replaced by love, still he is most interested in showing the meaning of the idea that God will effuse his Spirit over all flesh.

It is in this context that Oetinger describes what human knowledge will be like in the "golden time." There will be only one science, a "basic wisdom." Intuitively man will be able to grasp the majesty of God in its various forms. But Oetinger does not simply think of a contemplation of God alone. What he means is that the fragmentary knowledge of man will merge in a vision which will be the ultimate completion of the history of human thought. This "beatific vision" is no longer an event beyond the world and outside history; it is within the world which it embraces and completes the history of which it is the outcome. The following passage may serve as an illustration:

> Spirit has everything in itself, and reason transforms it into conceptual thought, though it adds only a little. In the golden time, it will be deemed exceedingly true ... that real knowledge (*wahre Wissenschaft*) is an embodying expression (*Inbegriff*) of divine things, an embodiment which has its seat in spirit and therefrom descends to reason. God has planted this knowledge in the spirit. By the help of God, the teacher has to bring it toward reason (*in die Vernunft*). Reason has to be reconciled with spirit and thereby spirit has to unite with God.[65]

---

[65] Cf. Benz$_3$, 547.

This passage quite unambiguously anticipates Hegel's idea that history is a process in which the Absolute unfolds its potentialities and eventually becomes conscious of itself in reason, that is, ultimately in man's mind. Oetinger still distinguishes between God and the spirit, a distinction which in Hegel will all but disappear. But it is significant that in Oetinger, too, it does not become clear whether 'spirit' refers to the third Divine Person and thus to God himself, or whether it refers to a sort of cabalistic *sephirot*, to a "force" emanating from God and penetrating history. Still, Oetinger says that the "teacher," that is, the divine, reconciles spirit with reason "by God's help." But from another passage it is obvious that Oetinger believes that the union of spirit with reason, and of spirit with God, is achieved in man, though it is for God's sake: "Since the creation of the world, it was God's intention in Christ to let pass many courses of time, or eternities, from the beginning to the end, from α to ω until eventually man becomes suited for God's being in him all in all." God fulfills his self-glorification in man. This is the classic *topos* of all (pseudo) mysticism from Eckhardt through Böhme and Angelus Silesius up to R. M. Rilke's *Stundenbuch*: God needs man to reach his ultimate completion, and by uniting with God, man comes to stand so close to the First Cause that he almost becomes a *causa sui*.[66] One has to forget Oetinger's expression "by the help of God" only for a brief moment to reach Hegel's claim that God develops, and ultimately exists, only insofar as man knows of him. As Hegel puts it in the *Encyclopaedia*: "God only is God if he knows himself; furthermore, his knowing himself is his self-consciousness in man and man's knowledge *of God* which leads to man's knowledge of himself *in God*."[67]

[66] For quotations from Eckhardt see Benz[2], 291 ff.
[67] Hegel[2], X, 454. Cf. XX, 292: "If, as the gospel teaches, God really is in his creatures, then God's knowledge is in them as well. And this knowledge of God's in man is precisely universal reason—not my reason, not a common or universal faculty, but Being itself, the identity of Being and Knowledge." However, it should be noticed that, following C. F. Göschel, Hegel explicitly denies that this amounts to identifying God with man. In particular, he argues that though God's knowledge is identical with God's being, and though God's knowledge of himself is identical with man's knowledge of God, it does not follow that because he knows God, man is identical with God. Moreover,

All this, no doubt, is highly presumptuous. But it is a quite peculiar kind of presumptuousness. For it is not the presumptuousness of a secular mind which rejects God's supremacy in terms of a self-proclaimed autonomy. Rather, it is the boldness of a thinker who knows by revelation that God has become man and who views Incarnation in terms of St. Paul's statement that God has "emptied himself to take on the form of a servant"; who professes to know that actual history has to be viewed as the palpable rendering of God's progressive taking possession of the world and thus as a sort of continued Incarnation; who professes to know from Holy Scripture that history, as it empirically is given, represents the story of God's ever-progressing glorification within the universe in terms of a transfiguration of this universe itself; and who, finally, on the strength of a heterodox understanding of the Bible, is convinced that the millenium with everything appertaining thereto finally has come.

However, this last point is more significant than it might seem at first. Not because it convincingly proves Hegel's presumptuousness after all; one must never forget that Hegel wrote his first mature work in 1807 and died in 1831, and that Bengel had predicted the final coming of Christ for 1809 or 1836. But Hegel's belief that the millennium already is present considerably changes the whole image; there is an almost inevitable shift of Bengel's and Oetinger's eschatological vision to a radically secularized version of it. For even if Bengel and Oetinger, and with them most Swabian Pietists, had believed that the "Kingdom of God" was imminent, for them it still was in the future; and thus it could retain the otherworldly character proper to the themes of Christian eschatology. It is true that all millennarian thinking as such is already sort of an "imminentization" of the other world; it expects the eschatological events to happen at a definite time and at a definite place (within this world at least), and it believes them describable in empirical

when he says that God's knowledge of himself is man's knowledge of God, Hegel quite obviously puts the accent upon God's self-knowledge. In other words, that man knows God as well as all development of man's knowledge of God is due to the presence of God's self-knowledge in man's mind. Cf. XX, 295 ff.

terms to some extent at least. But as long as the millennium still is considered a future event, its fundamental "otherworldliness" remains preserved. This inevitably must change as soon as the millennium is believed present. For now it no longer is possible to describe the second coming of Christ in terms of ideals transcending man's actual experience. Now the hard and unyielding facts of the real world have to be reinterpreted so as to yield the image of a New Jerusalem.

Hegel achieves this in two ways which complement each other. On the one hand, he glorifies and transfigures the present and with it the whole of history. We already have mentioned this point and need only note that often this glorification of the actually existing world bears a distinctly religious character. For example, the difference between the meaning of ' *Vernunft*' in Hegel and in the *Aufklärung* can to a large extent be explained in terms of the fact that Hegel quite explicitly views man's spiritual life as a participation in God.[68] Kant, for example, considered philosophy mainly as human thought aware of its limits. Hegel, on the contrary, views it as "divine worship," for it is concerned with "eternal truth in its very objectivity, with God and nothing but God and the explication of God."[69] Everywhere Hegel tries to show that man has reached the point at which he participates in God's eternal life. He has reached absolute knowledge; the modern state is "God become effective" and man must venerate it *wie ein Irdisch-Göttliches*, as if it were the deity on earth;[70] the whole of history is nothing but the "recollection and the Golgotha (*Schä-*

[68] Cf. Hegel₂, XI, 64; tr. Sibree, 34. In XV, 50, tr. Speirs-Sanderson, I, 30, Hegel explicitly describes man's reason as that which is "divine in man" and argues that there cannot be two reasons or two spirits. God's reason and man's reason, God's spirit and man's mind, cannot be *schlechthin verschieden*, totally different from each other. On the various connotations of "divine" in Hegel see Grégoire, 331 ff.

[69] Hegels₂, XV, 37; tr. Speirs-Sanderson, I, 20.

[70] Cf. Hegel₂, VII, 370; tr. Knox, 285. Knox's reference to Kant's description of nation states as *Erden-Götter* is somewhat misleading; for it is obvious from the context that Kant, contrary to Hegel, uses the expression ironically, cf. Kant, VI, 398.

delstätte) of Absolute Spirit, the reality, the truth, the certainty of its throne."[71]

On the other hand, Hegel quite obviously secularizes the symbols of Christian eschatology, and with it the whole of Christianity, in order to make it applicable to secular events. Often it is almost impossible to decide where the glorification of reality ends and the secularization of Christian symbols begins; both are closely connected. Hegel's tendency to secularize Christian ideas has often been noticed; usually, however, one simply traces it back to the persisting influence of the *Aufklärung* and, more generally, to the ever-increasing secularization of religious thought in modern philosophy since the Renaissance. But Hegel criticizes the *Aufklärung* too often, and too explicitly, to leave it at that. He accuses it of having emptied religion of all content and of having reduced the freedom of thought to a merely formal freedom "to fill out freedom at pleasure and according to mere opinions."[72] At the end of the *Philosophy of Religion* he argues that through the *Aufklärung* Christians, the salt of the earth, have become dull; Christianity has become "persistence in finitude, arrogant baldness, lack of content, scepticism."[73] In the same work he accuses liberal theologians of no longer trying to understand the particularly Christian sense of their dogmas, of reducing theology either to mere devotionalism or to trivial generalities.[74]

In short, Hegel's secularization of Christian ideas cannot be understood only in terms of the shallow watering down of the whole of revelation to a few basic "truths of reason" which was so characteristic of the *Aufklärung*. Though Hegel secularizes Christianity in a way significantly more radical than the *Aufklärung*, his interpretation is rooted in a quite different attitude. Of course, Hegel was "sicklied o'er" with the rationalist mentality, too. But the driving spirit of his interpretation of Christianity was different. One hardly can doubt that Hegel aimed at reinstating Christian faith in the minds of his contemporaries. He wanted to show that

[71] Hegel$_2$, II, 620; tr. Baillie, 808.
[72] Hegel$_2$, VIII, 29.
[73] Hegel$_1$, XIV, 230; cf. Hegel$_2$, VIII, 17 ff.
[74] Hegel$_2$, XV, 55 ff.; tr. Speirs-Sanderson, I, 38 ff.

a genuine Christian theology, as opposed to the Kantian "religion within the limits of reason," was compatible with the secular self-confidence which had been the motive power of history since the Renaissance. And though he constantly falls short of his intentions, it is obvious, too, that he aimed at elevating reason to the level of the mysteries of Christian faith rather than at tearing the Christian doctrines down to the profane level of human understanding. But in spite of his gigantic speculative effort, Hegel did not, and could not, become the Protestant counterpart to St. Thomas[75] because his understanding both of the Holy Scripture and of history constantly forced him to dissolve Christian ideas into symbols referring to real history, to secular events, to the actual world.

To illustrate this, it may be useful to say a few words about Hegel's implicit identification of the philosopher, or rather of the sage, with Christ.[76] Reading Hegel, one always is astonished at how central a figure Christ was for him. Not that there are many passages concerned with Christ in Hegel. But the few passages in question suffice to show that Hegel was far from viewing Christ merely as an excellent man. As the *Philosophy of History* states, Christ is the axis[77] on which the history of the world turns: "Christ has appeared—a Man who is God— God who is man; and thereby peace and reconciliation have accrued to the world."[78] In the

[75] Cf. Barth, 348.

[76] This point has been developed by Gebhardt$_1$, 37 ff.; cf. also Cottier$_1$, 28 ff.

[77] Cf. Hegel$_2$, XX, 321.

[78] Hegel$_2$, XI, 416; tr. Sibree, 324. Cf. XVI, 286. Of course, one might ask what the statement that God became man can possibly mean to Hegel; after all, in Hegel's philosophy, there is no God who "first" is and "then" incarnates himself. Cf. IX, 48; "Qua separated from the world (*als ein Abstraktum*) God is not the true God. He is truly God only as the living process of positing the other, the world which—taken in its divine form—is God's son." In the end, it could be argued that Hegel's Christ is simply the man in whom the emergence of man's divinity occurs for the first time. Through incarnation, God in no longer a "dark and dull (*verdumpftes*) being; he manifests himself, opens himself, posits a difference and is for another. In its highest expression this difference is the Son," XV, 338; tr. Speirs-Sanderson, I, 331. On the other hand, however, Hegel explicitly opposes the idea that Christ is merely a teacher of humanity, a martyr of truth, or an individual without sin; cf. XVI, 287, XI, 417, etc.

introduction to the third edition of the *Encyclopaedia*, written
one year before Hegel's death, it is even intimated that only those
who believe in Christ can ever reach truth.

However, when he says this, Hegel does not have in mind the
"temporal, sensibly present person of Christ" whom the disciples
were able to see and whom, "according to the same content,"
all later Christians possess in imagination. As far as this Christ
is concerned, Hegel shows little interest. For insofar as he still
is not transfigured (*verklärt*), Christ is only the beginning, a "con-
ditioning foundation" of a further development. Commenting upon
a well-known passage in St. John (7:37 ff.), Hegel even criticizes
those who cling to the sensible person of Christ; for this Christ
still has to be transfigured into spirit, and the faith in this Christ
still has to undergo a "spiritual expansion." The "rivers of living
water" which were promised to those believing in Christ flow
from the Paraclete, that is, from Christ the Glorified, not from
Christ who walked on earth.[79]

In his early writings Hegel once speaks of a "speculative Good
Friday." In his mature works he repeatedly takes up this subject
again. Christ has to die in order to overcome his individual existence,
in order to give way to the Holy Spirit who transfigures him into
something "universal."[80] In this sense Christ's death, which would
seem at first to be a trivial "nonbeing of this individual," becomes
something of world-historical significance: it results in a transfiguration of Christ into the "universality of Spirit who lives in
his congregation and daily dies and rises from the dead."[81]

It has been argued that Hegel's conception of the Trinity is very
similar to the so-called Sabellian heresy.[82] God the Father and
God the Son merely are "phases" of an Absolute which according
to its very nature is Spirit; according to "its immediate significance"
the incarnated Logos in Christ is only a "transitional phase" of

[79] Cf. Hegel₂, VIII, 28 ff. In XX, 291, Hegel speaks of a "living and experienced pentecostal faith," which develops out of and thus presupposes
an "obedience toward the dogma."
[80] E.g., Hegel₂, II, 580; tr. Baillie, 762.
[81] *Ibid.*, 597; tr. Baillie, 780.
[82] E.g., Balthasar, 616.

Spirit which has to dissolve into a higher form, the Holy Spirit. Yet there is an important difference between the heretic Sabellius and Hegel—a difference which to some extent would seem to explain how Hegel, though opposing the "baldness" of orthodox piety, can consider his philosophy a legitimate "expansion" of Christian trinitarian theology.[83] Whereas Sabellius, and with him all pre-Hegelian heretics who tried to reduce the Trinity to a single Divine Person, were in the end forced to admit that 'Father,' 'Son,' and 'Holy Spirit' are only three different *names* imputed to one and the *same* Divine Person (according to whether it is creator, savior, or sanctifier), Hegel's historicist dynamism permits him to speak of three somehow consecutive and thus different "phases" of the Absolute. To use Hegel's own examples, just as the blossom belies the bud to be in turn disowned by the fruit,[84] or just as the embryo has to disappear to give way to the child,[85] so the "Empire of the Father" has to give way to the "Empire of the Son," which in turn is replaced by the "Empire of the Spirit."[86] But just as bud, blossom, and fruit are three integral phases of the life of the plant; and as the child, and later the adult, are the embryo's "truth," that is, the embryo itself stripped of its limitations, so each phase of the Absolute is as necessary as the other, and the last phase is the "truth" of them all. The abstract idea of God is replaced by the sensuous presence of God in Christ, and Christ in turn dies and is replaced by God's spiritual presence to all men, the Holy Spirit. Far from contradicting Christ, the Holy Spirit is Christ's truth. In fact, he is Christ himself, stripped of his sensibility and finitude—Christ the Glorified.

Thus Hegel's Christ has to die in order to survive as Holy Spirit. But he does not survive to regain his abstract state in heaven. For the Holy Spirit no longer is an Absolute beyond the world, nor is he the Absolute united with one man alone, as in Christ. He is the living spirit of the *Gemeinde*, of the community of Christians.

---

[83] Hegel$_2$, VIII, 26 ff.

[84] Hegel$_2$, II, 12; tr. Baillie, 68.

[85] *Ibid.* 25; tr. Baillie, 83.

[86] See the structure of the third part of the *Philosophy of Religion*; for a brief summary see Hegel$_2$, XVI, 221 ff.; tr. Speirs-Sanderson, III, 1 ff.

In short, Christ dies in order to complete the work of Incarnation in order to be among his faithful as their spirit, as their spiritual life. It is not by chance that in the *Philosophy of Religion* Hegel describes this spiritual life of the Christian communion as the "Kingdom of God."[87] For the life of the Christian communion *is* the second coming of Christ, the coming of Christ the Glorified to those who believe in him, Christ's transfigured presence among all men.

But this spiritual life in turn "expands." Religious thought, theology, develops. The descent of the Holy Spirit, the transfiguration of Christ, grows in history, in the history of human thought. In fact, the whole of history is nothing but the growing of the One Truth which Christ has sown, which began to sprout at Pentecost, and then matures in man's theological thought. And Hegelianism is the ultimate expansion and fruit of Christian faith; it is faith transfigured into rational thought, faith transfigured into philosophy.[88] Thus, in the end Hegelianism is the ultimate transfiguration of Christ, the ultimate descent of Spirit, the completed presence of the glorified Christ among men.

Thus, what the philosopher does in fact is to complete the work of the Incarnation. And as for Hegel salvation is essentially Incarnation, the philosopher is also the one who completes Christ's work of salvation. Hegelianism is the ultimate expansion and realization of Christ's coming which "heals the pain and inward suffering of man."[89]

Again it has to be pointed out that Hegel sees no reason to boast about all this. He does not think of himself as savior. He is even too much of an intellectual to think explicitly of himself as the particular man in whom God finally achieves full actualization. He only gave to truth its proper and ultimate form. "Philosophy is not required in order to bring forth the substantial truth. Nor did humanity have to wait for philosophy to receive the awareness of truth." Philosophy does nothing more than to add

[87] E.g., Hegel₂, XVI, 308 ff.; tr. Speirs-Sanderson, III, 108 ff. Cf. XI, 425; tr. Sibree, 332.

[88] Cf. Hegel₂, XVI, 316; tr. Speirs-Sanderson, III, 325.

[89] Hegel₂, XI, 416; tr. Sibree, 324.

to the truth already present the "determination of the form."
It translates religion's symbolism into rational thought.[90] For
"thought is the absolute judge in the presence of which all content
has to stand the test and to prove good."[91]

> The true form in which truth exists can only be a System
> of knowledge. To help to bring philosophy nearer to the form
> of systematic knowledge—that goal where it can lay aside the
> name of *love* of knowledge and be *Actual Knowledge*—that
> is what I have set before me.[92]

Precisely by transforming faith into philosophy and philosophy
into Knowledge Hegel has achieved the ultimate act of salvation.
The Absolute, God, Christ, and the Spirit have become perfect
self-transparence in the hand of man; the wonder of Pentecost has
ceased to be infused knowledge and has become Knowledge which
man owns. Neither Christ nor the Holy Spirit is a true dispenser
of the "rivers of living water." From now on the water of life is
administered by the one who knows, by the philosopher whose "spiritual life" has become one with the life of the Logos, by the sage
whose thought is Christ himself in his ultimate glorification.[93]

[90] Hegel₂, XV, 166; tr. Speirs-Sanderson, II, 154 ff.
[91] Hegel₂, XVI, 353; tr. Speirs-Sanderson, III, 148.
[92] Hegel₂, II, 14; tr. Baillie, 70.
[93] In the *Philosophy of History*, when discussing the Neoplatonic "discovery"
that the Absolute is concrete and triune, Hegel writes: "This is not a private
idea of philosophy; it is an abrupt forward advance of the human spirit (*Men-
schengeist*), of the world, of the World-Spirit (*Weltgeist*).... These are deeds of
the World-Spirit and therefore of destiny, gentlemen. And philosophers are
closer to the Lord than those who feed on the scraps of spirit; they read, or
write, the original copy of the order in council. They are bound to write it.
Philosophers are the Initiated Ones who have attended to the World-Spirit's
forward advance in the innermost shrine," Hegel₂, XIX, 95 ff.; tr. Haldane-
Simson, II, 452 ff.

12: RICHTER AND STRAUSS:
ABSOLUTE KNOWLEDGE
VERSUS CHRISTIANITY

At first sight Hegel's queer "theology," as sketched in the preceding section, would seem to have little to do with the problem of theory and practice with which the present study is concerned. In fact, however, in combination with the changes on the political scene which we shall discuss later, it is the hidden determinant of the feverish development of the Hegelian school after the master's death in 1831. Moreover, it forever remains one of the major, though implicit, premises of all post-Hegelian ideas concerning "practice."

This is not only because the underground current of German millenarian thought in German Idealism had come to the surface and reached the consciousness of philosophers. As we have seen, millenarianism had invaded the minds of German intellectuals before Hegel. In fact, Hegel's whole philosophy aims at overcoming millenarianism, at least as far as it pointed either toward the future or to a beyond fundamentally different from this world. Moreover, at least after 1842 the details of the millenarianism of Hegel's followers, though obviously bearing the traces of Hegel's thought, have their sources in French and English social millenarianism rather than in the eschatological theology of Bengel and Oetinger.

Rather, what we have in mind is the quasi-religious connotation of Hegel's claim that man has become capable of Knowledge in the most far-reaching and daring sense, that is, of an Absolute Knowledge ascribed by Christianity to God alone. In spite of all their criticism and rejection of Hegelian tenets, most of Hegel's followers would never be able to forget that their master had transcended

183

all limits of human knowledge, or rather shown the boundlessness of man's cognitive capacities. Of course, as we shall see in a moment, his disciples soon discovered that Hegel's great reconciliation was an ideal rather than a fact. From about 1836 they only considered as a Knowledge of the world as it *ought to be* what Hegel had conceived as Absolute Knowledge of the world *as it is*. From about 1842 most productive Hegelians already agreed that Hegel's philosophy was not even an ideal image of the world; they accused their master of having reached his reconciliation in terms of accommodations to such passing and reactionary realities as the established Lutheran Church and the Prussian state. But what remained was the conviction that the completion of the incarnation of the Logos had already taken place. As much as their ideas differed in most other respects, they all agreed that the time had come when man could be, and the philosopher was, in possession of a Knowledge both certain and all-embracing, rather than being forced to grope his way through the twilight of fragmentary insights intermingled with ignorance or even error; that as far as knowledge was concerned, man had succeeded in taking the seat on the right hand of the Father.

This becomes most obvious if one compares the eschatological attitude of the romanticists with that of the post-Hegelian generation. At first sight it would seem that the post-Hegelians, having seen that Hegel's reconciliation had not succeeded, simply reverted to the philosophy of *Sollen*. But though it is true that in them the *ought* re-emerged with doubled force, the post-Hegelian differed from the romanticists in that they considered the *cognitive* aspect of the *ought* as completed. Of course they would argue that *this* ought to happen and *that* ought to be done; they would admit that as far as history and human deeds were concerned, there was still a true future; but they knew of no *ought* and of no future as far as knowledge was concerned. This was not necessarily in the sense that they considered Hegel's original philosophy as the last thought-deed of man. Though for the most part they did agree that Hegel was the last philosopher in the traditional sense of the term, they usually considered their own development of Hegelianism, rather than Hegel's philosophy as such, as the ultimate completion of Absolute Knowledge. But they no longer considered themselves as men who had to fathom reality by way of trial and error within the limited framework of a finite human mind. Even though they no longer believed that the millennium was already present, though their zeal was rooted in the conviction that man's ultimate completion still had to be brought about, they were convinced that *as far as theory went*, everything was essentially achieved . In short, they all shared Hegel's conviction that the Absolute had achieved full consciousness in them—even if they noisily proclaimed that they no longer believed in an Absolute different from man.

This outlook accounts for the almost insane presumption which many of Hegel's pupils displayed whenever they explained what "ought to be done." Since they were absolute knowers, their critical, "transformatory," or revolutionary, deeds could no longer be considered a mere groping in the complex universe of things, values, and ideals. They were salvific acts paving the way for a New Jerusalem already present at the level of thought. 'Practice' from now on would always have a salvific connotation. It becomes the activity of men who, having anticipated their salvation at the speculative level, now proceed to redeem the real world. This, incidentally, would also seem to be the reason why most post-Hegelians seem to have forgotten the unpretentious, but fundamental, virtue of prudence which the romanticists, in spite of all their millenarianism, were still aware of. For if one *knows*, one obviously can act as if past experiences would not count. One knows better than any experience can teach him. The malicious story sometimes told about Hegel came true in his pupils. When confronted with facts contradicting their explanations or predictions, they always felt entitled to say, *umso trauriger für die Tatsachen*, "so much the worse for the poor facts." For facts could be no real challenge to those who knew; they could always be reinterpreted or changed. But we are anticipating. At present we have to say a few words about the impact of Hegel's thought upon his disciples and about the problems with which the Hegelians had to struggle after their master's death.

The impact of Hegelianism is best illustrated by a passage
from a letter which a young student of Hegel wrote to his father
in 1830:

> Hegelian philosophy has reached a priori what Christianity
> and World History teach a posteriori.... Now I behold the
> Eternal Being just as it is, with thorough certainty, and all
> my longing is quenched. You will believe me mad if I say
> that I behold God face to face, and yet it is true. The other
> world has become this world; man is a luminous focus within
> the Eternal Light; and equal beholds equal. Since I am all
> being, I behold all being. And as I rest upon God's heart, I
> am blissful already now ....[94]

Though one may doubt whether the youthful writer of these words
really understood what Hegel meant, the passage well illustrates
the impact of Hegel's "transfiguration of the world" upon his
followers. Man had become one with the Absolute, he was able
to comprehend the whole of reality from the lofty standpoint
of God, and he recognized that reality, as it was, was good. The
"Kingdom of God" was present; the secret of history was obvious
and the meaning of history achieved; man had reached here and
now, within this world, the everlasting bliss promised by Christianity.

Of course not all of Hegel's disciples were as blindly enthusiastic as
the young student just quoted. But all of them shared in a pseudoreligious *Erlebnis* which seems to be without parallel as far as the
history of philosophy proper is concerned. They regarded the
world with the eyes of blessed ones. They knew, of course, that
there still were imperfections in this world. But their experience
of sharing in everlasting life and Absolute Knowledge was so
intense as to induce them to brush aside all such imperfections
as a "framework (*Folie*) permitting one to behold perfect infinity
in its proper luminous splendor."[95] Sometimes they were even
prepared to admit that Hegelianism did not fulfil the hopes raised

---

[94] W. Vatke, since 1837 professor of theology at Berlin, to his father; quoted
by Gebhardt$_1$, 53, from H. Bennecke, *Wilhelm Vatke in seinem Leben und seinen
Schriften* (Bonn, 1883) 47 ff.

[95] C. L. Michelet, quoted by Kühne, 3.

by Christian eschatology, but they hastened to add that the bliss offered by Hegelianism exceeded everything which man reasonably could expect. As Bruno Bauer put it in 1840, nine years after the master's death: "Like the blessed gods, the disciples dwelled with patriarchal peace in the Empire of the Idea which their master had bequeathed them for contemplation. All the dreams of millenarians concerning the fullness of time seemed to have come true."[96]

But this enthusiastic self-deception obviously could not last forever. The inevitable process of disenchantment began soon after Hegel's death. And it is highly characteristic of the way in which Hegel's thought acted upon his contemporaries that this disenchantment was initiated by discussions about the value of Christian eschatological symbols. For obviously it was not possible to "immanentize" Christian eschatology without either stopping the secularization halfway or else coming into conflict with genuine, if millenarian, Christian thought.

In 1833 a certain Friedrich Richter published a treatise on the Last Things which accused the Hegelians of being inconsistent and ambiguous in their treatment of Christian eschatology.[97] Richter took it for granted that Hegel had done away with Christianity by dissolving it into a philosophic thought referring only to inner-worldly events. What was still missing according to Richter was an explicit criticism of Christian ideas about the Last Things. Instead of frankly admitting that heaven or the last judgment, for example, did not exist, the Hegelians tried to fit such Christian dogmas into their philosophy by reinterpreting them; they would say that the Spirit's presence in man's consciousness was heaven and that the immanent court of world history was a continuous last judgment. In opposition to this view Richter explicitly undertook to discredit all philosophic and theological arguments both for an afterlife and for a transhistorical end of the world.

Richter's little-known treatise is important for several reasons. First, it was the starting signal for a discussion which eventually

[96] Bauer$_1$, 2 ff.

[97] Notice that the term 'eschatology,' as used by the early Hegelians, embraces both events usually connected with the "second coming of Christ" and events associated with after-life (personal immortality, heaven, hell, etc.).

resulted in the split of the Hegenlian school into a conservative Right and a radical Left. Secondly, it indicates that this split was rooted in two different attitudes toward Hegel's interpretation of Christianity. As we have seen, Hegel aimed at a "spiritual expansion" of Christian faith rather than at a criticism of Christianity. Those among his pupils who had been mature and well-balanced Christians before coming under the spell of Hegelianism always were aware of Hegel's original intentions; they thought of Hegel's philosophy as making possible a modern Christian theology.

This applied in particular to the leading spokesman for Hegelianism after the master's death, C.F. Göschel, whose *Aphorisms on Ignorance and Absolute Knowledge* had been highly praised by Hegel; and to the later editor of Hegel's *Philosophy of Religion*, P. F. K. Marheineke, whose *Christian Dogmatics* Richter had in mind when he accused the Hegelians of not being consistent. But there were others who, instead of viewing Hegelianism as an "expansion" trying to justify Christianity before the court of the modern mind, only saw that Hegel had *aufgehoben* Christian ideas into philosophy, and who soon discovered that Hegel had not gone far enough to permit a critique of Christianity which would not also entail a criticism of original Hegelianism. It is almost pathetic to see how many of the Hegelians began with a criticism of orthodox Lutheran faith and theology in the name of their master's philosophy of religion, gradually discovered that Hegel's deeply religious thought did not lend itself to their evermore radical critique, and eventually turned against Hegel himself, usually after having distinguished between a reactionary exterior and a progressive kernel in Hegel's philosophy.[98] As we shall see, after 1840 an analogous development took place with respect to Hegel's political thought.

It has to be emphasized, however, that the point at issue was the adequacy of Christian symbols, especially of eschatological symbols, to the level of Knowledge reached by Hegel's philosophy, not the validity of Christian doctrine as such. Even conservative Hegelians were aware that Hegel's Absolute Knowledge had "transcended" common Christian faith and theology. What divided

---

[98] First in Heine, IV, 148 ff. ; see also Ruge, IV, 563.

them from their more radical colleagues is the claim that this "transcending" was an expansion, rather than a renunciation, of Christian faith, and that it was therefore legitimate to interpret the content of Absolute Knowledge in terms of its premises, that is, of Christian doctrine. The others, on the contrary, viewed all Christian symbols still present in Hegelianism as a residue of a "finiteness" to be overcome by and in the name of Absolute Knowledge.

This point is of some importance for the appreciation and evaluation of D. F. Strauss' famous *Life of Jesus*, whose publication in 1835 was the immediate cause of the split in the Hegelian school. Usually, the *Life of Jesus* is considered only as an attack upon the credibility of the New Testament as a historical document. Yet though this quite obviously was Strauss' prime concern, one must not mistake his book for a simple continuation of the *Aufklärung*'s undermining of faith in the Gospel. It is Strauss' motive that counts here. By interpreting the Gospel as the result of a myth-making consciousness of a Christian community reared in the tradition of the Old Testament, and by reducing the person of Christ to a quasi-historical symbol of the universal deification of man, Strauss aimed at depriving conservative Hegelianism of its foundation. For if the Gospel was a myth rather than a valid historical document, then obviously Christian faith and theology no longer could be of any value if compared to Absolute Knowledge.[99] Instead of remaining a God-sent, "spiritual expansion" of

---

[99] This is well put by Bockmühl, 30 : "Strauss verstand die logische Aufeinanderfolge von Religion und Philosophie bei Hegel geschichtlich, dergestalt, dass er es für nunmehr an der Zeit hielt, die Wahrheiten des Glaubens in die ihnen eigentlich angemesseneren Formen des Wissens zu bringen. Er begann diese an und für sich absoluten Wahrheiten von der inadäquaten Form einer noch materiell gebundenen Vorstellung zu lösen, indem er die Heilsbotschaft, die evangelische Geschichte, in ihren 'materiellen' Bestandteilen, also ihrer Historizität nach, 'kritisch vernichtete.'" See also Gebhardt₁, 83-96. Strauss himself, it is true, advances the same idea in a somewhat more positive form: "Christ's supranatural birth, his miracles, his resurrection and ascension, remain eternal truths even though their actuality as historical facts is in doubt," Strauss, I, p. vii. Thus Strauss can claim that he does not touch the "inner kernel of Christian faith."

the historical event of Christ's incarnation, Hegel's Absolute Knowledge thus became the overcoming and the implicit destruction of a myth. The abyss which separates Strauss from Hegel is most obvious from the difference in their attitude toward Christ. Christ for Hegel was still the axis on which the history of the world turned; all spiritual expansions, including Hegel's own philosophy, were rooted in the person of Christ as their living principle. For Strauss, on the contrary, Christ was no more than a mythological instance of the universal divinity of man. Strauss' famous phrase, "Is not an incarnation of God from eternity a truer one than an incarnation limited to a particular point of time?"[100], as deeply as it may be rooted in Hegelian ideas, indicates that the personal relation to Christ's person, which still somehow determined Hegel's thinking, had disappeared. Hegel was a believing Christian, though admittedly a very unorthodox one. Thinkers such as Richter and Strauss were philosophers who had cast off all remnants of Christianity as misleading ornamentations.

But Richter's treatise is important for yet another reason. It is motivated by a thought which soon became the main determinant of the development of Hegelianism. It may sound odd, but Richter criticized Christianity because the bliss offered by Hegelianism was limited to philosophic thought, not the lived life of real man. By destroying the Christian element still present in Hegelianism, Richter hoped to do away with the speculative otherworldliness of Hegel's philosophy and to make Absolute Knowledge fruitful for practice. In short, Richter was the first to point out that the "salvation" proclaimed by Hegelianism had occurred in a world and in a man which were exactly as they had been before Hegel. Thought had changed; reality had remained the same. Accordingly, the whole transfiguration was meaningful only to the intellectual existence of philosophers, not to the real existence of living men. In this sense Richter accused his fellow Hegelians of an esoteric indifference to the salvation of the masses. The bliss allegedly offered by Hegelianism had its limits at the very point at which true bliss began. It did not reach man's pretheoretical

---

[100] Strauss, II, 734.

(or rather, as we shall see, posttheoretical) existence, that is, his practical life, or "practice."[101]

The connection between this argument and the tendency to "demythologize" Christianity is obvious. As long as Hegelianism had a Christian connotation, the speculative otherworldliness of Hegelianism was in a sense justifiable. The Christian whose real treasures are in another world is accustomed to solutions which are no solutions as far as his everyday existence is concerned. Hegel had cut short the temporal otherworldliness of the Christian reconciliation; man's reconciliation was to be sought neither in the future nor in an afterlife. But his reconciliation had remained "otherworldly" in that it concerned only man's intellectual existence. Accordingly, as soon as the otherworldliness of Christianity came under fire, this peculiar "otherworldliness" of Hegelianism became visible, too; the radical "immanentization" of Christian ideas entailed the demand for an "actualization," "materialization," of Hegelianism. On the other hand, it was not possible to make Hegel's speculative salvation fruitful for real life—for "practice"— without depriving it of its remaining otherworldliness; and the remnants of Christianity were the prop of this Hegelian other-worldliness.

In this respect, too, Strauss continued what Richter had begun. By accusing the Gospel of being only a myth, he definitively brought Hegel's millenarianism down to the level of this world.[102] Richter had criticized Christian eschatology in order to challenge man "to try to see in the total night of Christianity's unworldly naught and to recognize how many magnificent things remain."[103] Strauss,

---

[101] Cf. Gebhardt₁, 71 ff. Unfortunately, I was not able to obtain a copy of Richter's book (it will soon be reprinted by the Fromann Verlag, Stuttgart); my analysis depends upon that by Gebhardt, the only recent treatment of Richter known to me.

[102] Cf. Straus, II, 737: "Luther has already minimized the relevance of bodily miracles as opposed to the spiritual ones, which to him are the truly great miracles; yet we should be more interested in the cures at Galilee than in the miracles of world history, in the power of man over nature which is becoming incredible, in the irresistible power of ideas which even the greatest masses of men without ideas (des Ideenlosen) cannot oppose?"

[103] Cf. Gebhardt₁, 73.

after having shattered belief even in an approximately literal meaning of the Gospel, stated that man's victory over nature was far more valuable than all "overpowering of nature by the mere word of a thaumaturgist."[104]

The critical reference to Hegel is unmistakable. Incidentally, this quotation from Strauss also indicates why so many of the Hegelians, including Strauss himself, eventually ended in a dull faith in material progress characteristic of the "scientific" positivism of the second half of the nineteenth century. The increasingly radical criticism of Christianity, a criticism which had started in the name of Hegel's "spiritual expansion," of Absolute Knowledge, resulted in a criticism of Hegel's speculative solutions and eventually in a general estrangement from metaphysics. And it was no mere chance that those thinkers who were most infatuated with Absolute Knowledge eventually became the most radical antimetaphysicians. Richter's demand to "refute the beyond" in order to build on its ruins the *höhere Welt des Diesseits*, the "higher order of this world,"[105] though advanced in the name of Absolute Knowledge, was in fact an early sign of the withering away of metaphysics, a dying away which the last great trend of occidental metaphysics, German Idealism, had expedited both by its "immanentization" of Christianity and by its all too daring solutions.

[104] D. F. Strauss, *Streitschriften zur Verteidigung meiner Schrift über das Leben Jesu und zur Charakteristik der gegenwärtigen Theologie* (Tübingen, 1838) I/3, 116 ; cf. Gebhardt₁, 127.

[105] Cf. Gebhardt₁, 72.

13: CIESZKOWSKI:
ABSOLUTE KNOWLEDGE AND *PRAXIS*

It is well known that Strauss' *Life of Jesus* occasioned the final split in the Hegelian school. Surveying in 1837 the various reactions to his book, and alluding to the division of political parties in France, Strauss was able to point out that there already existed a Right wing, a Left wing, and a mediating Center. Though this split originated in disagreements about the value of Hegel's interpretation of Christianity, it was very soon aggravated by disagreements as to whether Hegel's great reconciliation was all-embracing or "only speculative." About 1838 most Hegelians of the Left wing and of the Center already agreed that Hegel's philosophy was unilateral in that it reconciled Spirit with reality only at the level of speculation. Thus, for example, C. L. Michelet wrote in his *History of the Last Systems of Philosophy in Germany*:

> As far as thought is concerned, the reconciliation is completed. It only remains for reality to elevate itself from all sides toward rationality, too .... Therefore, it is the task of future history to make Knowledge universally accepted, and more and more permeating all aspects of human life .... Thought thus ceases to be the last stage of the World Spirit's development. As is proper to the self-possession of old age, it becomes a first principle helping us consciously to climb to a higher stage. The world emerges from thought and is developed further by it. As philosophy teaches us, truth, in order to become ours, has to become our own activity; and by means of truth transformed into activity, we shall reach freedom.[106]

This is no longer a romantic hope of and a longing for completion. It is the determination of a man who knows what has to be done.

[106] Michelet, II, 799 ff.

Absolute Knowledge has been reached; as far as Knowledge is concerned, man is the master of the universe. Accordingly he must proceed to transform the world. Up to now the World Spirit had developed and dragged man along. Since the World Spirit was conscious of itself in man's mind, man would now hold in his hands the fate of the world. He would no longer be pushed around by the World Spirit; he could climb to a higher stage consciously and at will. He would be able to steer the future course of history. In this respect, incidentally, the difference between the Hegelian Right and the Left was one of emphasis only. The Left Hegelians believed that this steering of history entailed the destruction of the existing order which did not comply with the development of Knowledge. To the Right Hegelians the existing order was essentially sound; it only had to be taken in possession and guided toward further development.

At this point we have to devote a few pages to a small book which, at least as far as the notion of *praxis* is concerned, is the most brilliant and the most important single text published between Hegel's death in 1831 and the *Philosophic and Economic Manuscripts* of Marx: the *Prolegomena zur Historiosophie* by Polish Count August (von) Cieszkowski, published in Berlin in 1838.

As far as English literature on Hegelianism and on Marx is concerned, Cieszkowski is almost completely ignored.[107] Born in 1814, the son of a wealthy Polish aristocrat, he participated in the Polish revolution of 1830, then studied for a year at the University of Cracow, and in 1832 went to Berlin, where he made friends with Michelet. In 1838 he published the *Prolegomena* and at the same

[107] Neither Hook nor Tucker, for example, mentions Cieszkowski; the only recent English contribution to this subject would seem to be B. Hepner, "History and the Future: The Vision of August Cieszkowski," *Review of Politics* 15 (1953) 328-349. However, even German literature is comparatively scarce. The most comprehensive study is that by Kühne, a shortened version of which is found in Tschiževskij, 43-73. Excellent discussions are found in Gebhardt$_1$, 130-152, and Stuke, 85-122. Two doctoral dissertations submitted to the University of Fribourg, Switzerland, A. Żółtowski, *Graf August Cieszkowskis "Philosophie der Tat"* (Poznań, 1904); A. Wojtczak, *Philosophie der Freiheit bei Graf August Cieszkowski* (Fribourg, 1933), completely disregard C.'s relations to other Hegelians.

time submitted to the University of Heidelberg a doctoral dissertation on Ionian philosophy. The following year Cieszkowski, now
living in Paris, gained a reputation as an economist by publishing
a treatise in French on credit and money circulation. In 1842,
in a book with the curious title *God and the Palingenesis*, he defended
the orthodox Christian view of God being a person as well as the
doctrine of the immortality of the human soul, which had come
under criticism by his friend Michelet and other Left and Leftist
Hegelians. The same year he bought a manor in Poznań, and
from that time on he devoted himself, on the one hand, to the
composition of various treatises on political, social, and historical
questions, and, on the other hand, to the political struggle for
Polish rights in the grand duchy of Posnania. In Poland he is
mainly remembered for a study on contemporary social problems
modeled on the seven supplications of the Lord's prayer, the first
volume of which was published five years after his death, in 1899.
But his spiritual homeland was Germany; the majority of his friends
were Hegelians, especially those of the Right and of the Center.[108]
We may add that Cieszkowski was also one of the co-founders of
the "Philosophical Society of Berlin"; in 1891 he was even invited
to edit the *Festschrift* commemorating the ninetieth birthday of
Michelet, an invitation which he refused because of his advanced
age.

Here, however, we are interested only in Cieszkowski's first
work, the *Prolegomena*. As the title (*Foreword to a Wisdom of
History*) indicates, Cieszkowski aimed at rethinking Hegel's philosophy of history. In Hegel, he argued, philosophy had ceased to
be mere love of wisdom; it had become σοφία, Wisdom in the most
proper sense of the term. However, Cieszkowski continued, Hegel
did not succeed in elevating the philosophical consideration of

---

[108] Cornu$_3$, I, 142 ff., describes Cieszkowski as a Left Hegelian and as an
idealist precursor of Marx. This is only partially true. For C. explicitly describes himself as a "conservative in the fullest and most progressive sense of the
term," Cieszkowski$_2$, 11. The transformation of philosophy into practice which
C. envisages has nothing to do with a revolution; C. speaks of the necessity
of a "conservative progress" as opposed to a "radical overthrow"—of an "evolutionary, not revolutionary" development of Hegelianism, *ibid*. 96 ff.

history to the level of the absolute standard to which he had elevated logic, for example. For instead of consistently carrying through the trichotomy required by dialectics, Hegel had accommodated his interpretation to what he believed to be the real course of previous history; he had divided history into four main periods instead of three. According to Cieszkowski this accommodation was due to the fact that Hegel believed only in a retrospective interpretation of history; believing that Absolute Knowledge is the ultimate reconciliation, he had concluded that history was drawing to a close in his own philosophy. In opposition to this outlook Cieszkowski agreed with Hegelians influenced by Richter and Strauss that Absolute Knowledge could not be the ἔσχατον of man's salvation. The reconciliation at the level of thought had to be completed by a reconciliation at the level of man's real life. But this meant that the future was far more important than Hegel had believed.

It has been argued that Cieszkowski's interest in the future was actually a relapse to the pre-Hegelian way of thinking, indeed, a return to Fichte.[109] However, as we have already pointed out, there is one striking difference between Fichte and the romanticists, on the one hand, and Hegelians such as Cieszkowski, on the other hand. Fichte believed himself capable of guessing what the future course of history would be. Cieszkowski clamied to know it. He considered it his task to transform all previous philosophy of history into Wisdom of History, just as Hegel had transformed philosophy in general into "Wisdom par excellence."[110] Thus the first step of the "historiosopher" consisted in "vindicating for speculation the knowledge of the essence of the future."[111] The task no longer was to prophesy. Rather, the future had to be anticipated and "scientifically" predicted by being incorporated into Absolute Knowledge.

Cieszkowski, it is true, was well aware that this demand would sound "presumptuous and paradoxical." Actually, as he pointed out himself, it is no more presumptuous than the whole of Hegel's

[109] For example, Lukács₂, 6 ff., and, more cautiously, Stuke, 117 ff.
[110] Cieszkowski₁, 44.
[111] *Ibid.* 8.

great victory over "critical philosophy." For if reason was able to conquer the three absolutes relegated by Kant to the realm of the unknown (God, freedom, and immortality), why should it not be able to grasp the essence of the future? If man participated in Absolute Knowledge, why should he be unable to transcend the limits of time?[112] It is obvious that this argument only continues Hegel's implicit claim that a reconquest of the Kantian *Ding-an-sich* entails a conquest of everything normally believed to be beyond the reach of human experience.

But Cieszkowski did not leave it at that. He advanced a sort of empirical argument for the knowability of the future, an argument based upon the romantic "biologism of history" which goes back to the idea of Oetinger, Bengel, and ultimately St. Augustine, that history is an organic process gradually realizing God's intentions. If, Cieszkowski argued, a paleontologist is able to construct from a single fang the whole organism of an antediluvian animal, why should not the "historiosopher" be able to "construct from the already past section of the whole process of history its ideal totality and, in particular, its still missing future section"? Why should he not be able to view the past deeds of humanity as fossils from which he could "construct the universal character of the life of humanity"?[113]

Having said this, Cieszkowski proceeded to explain that the future can be known in three ways: by imagination, by thought, and by action. And though he always opposed Hegel's identification of the speculative order with the historical, he immediately projected this trichotomy on the screen of real history. Pre-Hegelian thought determined the future by imagination; philosophers of history before Hegel were "seers and prophets." The Hegelian is able to determine the future by thought—by thought which is related to imagination, just as St. Paul's "knowledge in part" is related to the distinct knowledge of the blessed (I Cor. 13:9 ff.). The post-Hegelians would determine the future by action; according

[112] *Ibid.* 10.
[113] *Ibid.* 13. Stuke, 90 ff., argues that in this respect Cieszkowski depends upon Condorcet and Saint-Simon.

to Cieszkowski this is the "new direction of the future," the ultimate "objective and real actualization of Truth."[114]

"That which imagination foreboded and which thought has recognized now has to be actualized by Absolute Will."[115] In short, history has to be subjugated to man's will. Since man has reached Absolute Knowledge, history can be planned and executed like any other human deed. In this respect Hegel's philosophy was the "turning point" at which practice, which up to now preceded consciousness, and in relation to which consciousness had always arrived too late, turned into "posttheoretical practice" which according to Cieszkowski is the "real substantial synthesis of Being and Thought."[116] For after man had reached Absolute Knowledge, he no longer was a "blind instrument either of chance or of necessity"; he was the "conscious master builder (*Werkmeister*) of his own freedom":

> After humanity has reached true self-consciousness, it must accomplish its very own deeds according to all rules of the art, that is, according to the Idea. This does not mean that Providence ought to abandon history to its fate. Rather, it means that humanity has become mature enough to make its own determinations perfectly identical with the Divine Plan of Providence.[117]

It even had become unnecessary to ask Providence to abdicate. Man now was an accomplice of the Absolute; he could fulfill the aims of Providence simply by acting according to reason, according to his *own* reason.

Cieszkowski was well aware that this conception meant that the only way to go beyond, and thus to overcome, Hegel consisted in overcoming theoretical philosophy, in *abandoning theory for practice*. Just as Aristotle had been the end of the beginning of philosophy, Hegel was the beginning of its end. For the only theoretical endeavor which still remained was to lay out the plan of future history. "Presently, philosophy has reached so classical

---

[114] Cieszkowski$_1$, 15 ff.
[115] *Ibid.* 29.
[116] *Ibid.* 18 ff.
[117] *Ibid.* 20.

a point that it has to transcend itself and thus to yield up the Universal Empire to another."[118] This "other" is "practical, social, life."[119]

Cieszkowski is still a historiosopher, however, not an "executor (*Vollführer*) of history," as he calls the man of the future. Accordingly, instead of abandoning theory for action he develops a highly complex justification of the alleged superiority of "post-theoretical practice" over theory, even in its supreme Hegelian form.

Cieszkowski's problem obviously consisted in showing that Hegel's synthesis was one-sided, that is, that it was not the ultimate synthesis. He solved it by reshuffling Hegel's tripartite division of Absolute Spirit. Whereas Hegel divided this ultimate realm into art, religion, and philosophy, Cieszkowski (who always remained faithful to Catholicism) claimed that religion embraces the whole realm of Absolute Spirit [120] and advanced a new tripartition: art, philosophy, and *praxis*. Art is the first and lowest reconciliation of Spirit with Nature, of Thought with Being; it is the simple *sensuous existence* of the identity of being and thought. *Qua* philosophical standpoint, it corresponds to classical antiquity. But its spontaneous harmony cannot persist forever; it reflects upon itself and passes into a *thought* synthesis of being and thought. Classical antiquity was a world of art and immediate beauty; the modern era up to the present was a world of thought, of consciousness, and of philosophy. It was introduced by Aristotle's "thinking of thinking" and culminated in Hegel's "thinking of the identity of thought and being."[121] Yet though art is the "product of being multiplied by thought" and philosophy is the "product of thought multiplied by being," that is, though both art and philosophy are syntheses of the highest order, they are opposed to each other and therefore have to be capped by a still higher synthesis. "The

[118] *Ibid.* 101.

[119] *Ibid.* 110 ff.

[120] *Ibid.* 100. C. explicitly refers to Richter who, he argues, has shown that "religion is the whole absolute sphere of spirit of which art, philosophy, etc., are only specific degrees."

[121] *Ibid.* 98.

synthesis has to be made still more synthetic."[122] This ultimate
synthesis of being and thought, a synthesis in which there no
longer is an emphasis either on being (as in art) or on thought
(as in philosophy), is action:

> From now on, the absolutely practical, that is, social action
> and life within the state ... will be the Ultimate. Art and
> philosophy which up to now were considered the highest identities
> turn into abstract premises of the life within the state (*Staats-
> leben*). Being and thought have to perish in action, art and
> philosophy in social life, in order to re-emerge and to unfold
> in the ultimate form of social life.[123]

Unfortunately we must refrain from further developing Cieszkowski's complicated speculations, which are hard to comment upon
without presupposing a detailed knowledge of Hegelianism. Yet
there is one point we still have to dwell upon: Cieszkowski's notion
of *praxis*.

In the beginning of the *Prolegomena* Cieszkowski introduced a
seemingly innocuous distinction between *facts* and *acts*. According
to his initial definition facts are all events which precede consciousness, that is, all those events which human consciousness can
only "explain and transfigure," but not determine. Acts are all
events which, having first been "reflected upon," are carried out
consciously; they are "active events (*Begebenheiten*) which are
thoroughly ours, no longer alien, conscious already before they
were actualized."[124]

As the later development of the *Prolegomena* shows, this distinction has little if anything to do with the traditional distinction
between preconscious acts which happen in man (*actus hominis*)
and truly human actions for which man is responsible (*actus humani*).
For Cieszkowski was concerned with history, not ethics; and he
was interested only in the salvation of humanity as a whole, not
in the salvation of the individual's soul. When he spoke of a consciousness preceding or following human deeds, he had in mind
the level of consciousness attained by post-Hegelian and pre-

[122] *Ibid.* 106.
[123] *Ibid.* 112.
[124] *Ibid.* 17 ff.

Hegelian man, respectively. "Facts," then, are humanity's deeds previous to the Hegelian *prise de conscience*; "acts," on the contrary, are the deeds of those who already have reached Absolute Knowledge. The difference between these two types of human deeds is obvious. What humanity did before Hegel happened "in a natural and as if incidental way"; after Hegel, however, man is no longer bound to register Divine Providence *post factum*. He knows it in advance and acts as its accomplice. Hegel, and with him the historiosopher Cieszkowski, stands "in the middle between the divination and execution of history, at the turning point at which mere facts turn into acts. This turning point is the Theory and Absolute Knowledge of History, Wisdom of World History."[125]

In short, there are two kinds of practice. Pre-Hegelian practice is little else than simple being, a material which consciousness explains and transfigures. On the contrary, post-Hegelian—or, as Cieszkowski calls it, "posttheoretical"—practice is the highest conceivable synthesis of being and thought, the ultimate reconciliation of spirit with nature. It is the world-governing activity of a humanity which has become one with God and which, therefore, has already reached salvation at the theoretical level.

Moreover, this second kind of practice is "posttheoretical" only in the sense that it is mediated by and outstrips Hegel's Absolute Knowledge. It is not posttheoretical in the sense in which human activities might be described as being beyond and outside human consciousness. Cieszkowski was well aware of the danger that his conception might be misunderstood as a relapse into pre-Hegelian philosophies which isolated theory from practice. When Hegel described will as a specific mode of thought, his point was precisely that nothing outside consciousness could be superior to consciousness; that will, if it follows and completes thought, must itself be a modality of thought. But if one claimed that action is superior to thought, did one not question the infinity of consciousness and thus relapse into the pre-Hegelian way of thinking which, though claiming for man absolute autonomy, got stuck in an even more radical finiteness of man's capacities?

[125] *Ibid*. 44.

Cieszkowski made the best of this bad job by declaring that posttheoretical practice was "thought which again has become being,"[126] that is, incarnated Absolute Knowledge, Ultimate Wisdom become real life. Whereas Hegel reduced will and action to thought, Cieszkowski reduced thought to action. But as the theory which he reduced to practice was Absolute Knowledge, the result was no longer an action outside the realm of consciousness. Rather, it was an action conscious of itself through and through, the action of the Absolute Knower.

It has to be emphasized, however, that Cieszkowski remained a philosopher, not a revolutionary seeking to solve philosophical problems by political action. As far as specific analyses of practice were concerned, his treatment remained very vague. His only illustration of "social practice" was a bashful reference to the "system of Fourier," which he commended to the "attention of speculative thinkers."[127] Apart from this, he only dilated upon his conviction that from now on philosophy would have to "descend from the heights of theory to the open country of *praxis*."[128]

Still, the *Prolegomena* is the crucial link between the theological problems of the early Hegelians and the political radicalism of thinkers such as Hess and Marx. For Cieszkowski succeeded in formulating a program which permitted Hegel's pupils to over-come their nervous anxiety that after Hegel it had become impossible to philosophize, at least in the highly original and creative way which was characteristic of German philosophy after Kant. As Hegel seemed to have penetrated all secrets of the Absolute and thus to have said the last word in philosophy, his pupils seemed to be condemned to elaborate in detail that which their master had sketched in bold outlines. Cieszkowski was well aware of this general uneasiness among the Hegelians; he explicitly referred to the embarrassment of those who "cannot decide what, in philosophy, still remains to be done."[129] His solution to this difficulty was soon to become epoch-making: philosophy has to put up with

[126] *Ibid.* 120.
[127] *Ibid.* 146.
[128] *Ibid.* 129.
[129] *Ibid.* 100 ff.

being applied. The future fate of philosophy is the "development of truth into concrete activity." Absolute Knowledge has to become the intrinsic principle of "life and social conditions."[130]

In fact, Cieszkowski succeeded in killing two birds with one stone. On the one hand, he indicated to the Hegelians a way in which they could avoid being either gravediggers or monument builders of Hegelianism, as the deadlock of Hegelianism was described by K. Rosenkranz in 1844. On the other hand, he found the obvious solution to the problem which occupied the Hegelians, namely, how to relieve the tension between the salvific character of Absolute Knowledge and the obviously bad condition of the real world. One simply had to apply Hegelianism to political and social action, to put the lever of Absolute Knowledge into effect. This of course entailed that Hegelianism had to become the ideology of the masses. Cieszkowski did not shrink from spelling this out in one passage of the *Prolegomena*. From now on, he argued, philosophy has to be serviceable; it has to be brought down to the level of the masses; it has to be *verflacht in die Tiefe*, to be laid flat, until by spreading out among all men it has reached the "depth" proper to it.[131]

I should like to conclude this section by saying a few words about the impact of the *Prolegomena* insofar as one can actually trace it. Curiously enough it is difficult to show that the *Prolegomena* was a widely read and successful book. As far as I can see, it was reviewed only twice.[132] And of the two reviews only that by Michelet in the organ of the Right Hegelians, the *Jahrbücher für wissenschaftliche Kritik*, can be said to have done justice to Cieszkowski. F. Frauenstädt, who reviewed the *Prolegomena* for the organ of the Left Hegelians, the *Hallische Jahrbücher für deutsche Wissenschaft und Kunst*, seems to have overlooked completely the fact that Cieszkowski was advancing a philosophy of action; in any case, he dwelled only upon the tripartition of history into past, present, and future. That there were no more reviews probably is due, on

[130] *Ibid.* 129 ff.
[131] *Ibid.* 131.
[132] C. L. Michelet in *Jahrbücher für wissenschaftliche Kritik* (1838) cols. 785-792, 793-797; J. Frauenstädt in *Hallische Jahrbücher* (1839) cols. 476-480, 487 ff.

the one hand, to the fact that the author of the *Prolegomena* was still a student preparing his doctorate and, on the other hand, to the fact that because Cieszkowski described himself as a conservative, the Left Hegelians, who were most likely to be interested in the subject of the book, had no reason to consider Cieszkowski one of their partisans.

In fact, at that early time the *Prolegomena* seems to have influenced directly only three thinkers, all of whom were somewhat outsiders to the Hegelian movement. In his *Europäische Triarchie* (1841) Moses Hess hailed Cieszkowski as the sole thinker besides himself who had found a "positive passage from German philosophy to action."[133] Similarly, Alexander Herzen, who planned to write a study on "Our century as the link between past and future," saw in the *Prolegomena* a corroboration of his activist understanding of Hegelianism.[134] Finally, Michael Bakunin gave to Cieszkowski's philosophy of action a distinctly radical twist in his famous article on the "Reaction in Germany," published under a French pseudonym in the *Hallische Jahrbücher* in 1842.[135]

As to Marx, there is no clear evidence that he ever read Cieszkowski's book.[136] The only time Marx mentioned Cieszkowski was in a letter to Engels dated January 12, 1882.[137] Marx wrote to him about an article by the Swiss Fourierist K. Bürkli, who wondered about the fact that Marx never mentioned Ciesz-

[133] Hess$_2$, 83, cf. 79, 89 ff.

[134] Cf. Scheibert, 107 ff.; R. Labry, 202 ff.; Tschiżewskij, 264, 287.

[135] Cf. Scheibert, 158 ff.; Tschiżewskij, 201 ff. An English translation of Bakunin's article can be found in *Russian Philosophy*, eds. J. K. Edie, J. P. Scanlan, and M.-B. Zeldin, with the collaboration of G. L. Kline (Chicago, 1965) I, 385-406.

[136] Lauth, 399-450, has argued for a dependence of Marx upon Cieszkowski by comparing Marx's dissertation to the *Prolegomena*. However, most of his arguments are based upon a rather complete ignorance of the terminology and problems common to all Left Hegelians; that which according to Lauth Marx had taken from C. could also have been taken from many other Hegelians. Lauth's main point consists in showing that, because of its dependence upon Cieszkowski, Marxism is certain to be of Slavic origin—and therefore succeeded in the East. This obviously is nonsense.

[137] *MEGA* III, 4, 521 ff.

kowski's study on credit money. Marx still remembered Ciesz-kowski, who, as he told Engels, had visited him in Paris around 1844; but, he ironically added, the Polish Count had so "bewitched" him that he never wanted to read any of his "sins." Nevertheless it is highly probable that Marx was at least familiar with the content of the *Prolegomena*. He came to know Moses Hess at about the time when Hess discovered Cieszkowski's book, and it would have been odd if Hess were not to tell him about his enthusiasm for the new "praxeology."

Actually, however, the importance of the *Prolegomena* is some-what independent of the question as to who, and how many, read it. For even if the direct influence of this book was as small as the scarcity of explicit references would seem to indicate, it remains a very important link in the sequence of *ideas*. It throws significant light upon the problem of how it was possible that Hegel's radically contemplative and almost quietist philosophy became the starting point for one of the most radical political ideologies. Of course one will have to add to the picture the changes on the political scene which we shall discuss in the next section.

Apart from that the *Prolegomena*, in spite of its obvious originality, was highly symptomatic of the problems which haunted most Hegelians around 1838. The passage by Michelet quoted at the beginning of this chapter suggests that Cieszkowski was far from being the only Hegelian who believed in the necessity of changing Hegelianism into a world-transforming weapon. And as to Ciesz-kowski's interest in the future, even so comparatively conservative a Hegelian as K. Rosenkranz granted in 1838 that the widespread, though odd, desire to transform Hegelianism into an instrument of prediction was justifiable. Of course it was preposterous to expect from a Hegelian a "detailed description" of the future course of history. But, Rosenkranz added, a Hegelian could well be expected to tell "what the future content of history will be." As far as this kind of general prediction went, he could rely upon Hegel.[138] Actually the *Prolegomena* had done nothing more. For even Cieszkowski took care to point out that a historiosopher can only

---

[138] Cf. *Hallische Jahrbücher* (1838) cols. 155 ff.

know the "essence of the future"; the particulars inevitably remain "arbitrary and thus unforeseeable in detail."[139]   Incidentally, Cieszkowski, too, was far from viewing his historiosophy as opposed to Hegel's basic insights; as he once put it, his "results" only corroborated Hegel's "new discoveries."[140]

[139] Cieszkowski$_1$, 7.
[140] *Ibid.* 10.

14: THE ERA OF POLITICS

Cieszkowski's demand for a translation of Absolute Knowledge into practice did not correspond to the Hegelian mentality alone. It also reflected the progressive "politicization" of all intellectual interests which began in Germany around 1813 and had its ultimate roots in the increasing desire for emancipation of the "third estate." As Ruge put it in 1842: "Our time is a political time and our politics desires the freedom of this world."[141]

Ruge's voice is here all the more important since he had participated in and suffered for the movement which most contributed to this infiltration of academic ranks by political problems—the so-called *Burschenschaften*, students' associations formed after the anti-Napoleonic wars of 1813. Having fought for "freedom and the nation" at the River Rhine, the students who had gathered for the defense of the fatherland were not willing to return quietly to their lecture rooms and to forget all the ideals for which they had shed their blood. Up to that time the life of a German student had been characterized by an odd mixture of crudeness and dandyism. Now, suddenly, the students were living for new ideals: for a

---

[141] *Hallische Jahrbücher* (1842) 755 ff. Ruge explicitly opposes his own era to that of Hegel: Hegel's time was "little favorable to politics," whereas Ruge's time is a political one. Cf. 761: "As a matter of fact, Hegel was not an enemy of political practice and of realistic thinking.... Yet his profession, namely, the work on a system of pure insight, makes him fall back upon a one-sided theoretical standpoint." Hess formulated a similar idea as early as 1840: Hegel was concerned with philosophy alone, his pupils, having transcended idealism and proceeded to practice, inevitably "criticize" more than Hegel did; cf. Hess$_1$, 8 ff.

general reform of morals, for a Germany which the war seemed to
have welded into one nation, and, above all, for "freedom."

For them the war against the French intruder had been a war
of independence within their own country, or, rather, a war of
revival. Misled by the patriotic proclamations of the monarchs and
of political writers committed to the governments in power, the
students at first believed that their increasing desire for a more
cultured and liberal system was shared by the sovereigns and
their officials. It was only after they discovered that as far as
their rulers were concerned, the patriotic proclamations were
little more than propaganda that they grew rebellious. From
about 1815 a general politicization of academic youth had set in.[142]
Where previously they argued about women, wine, and duels, they
now discussed politics; political problems became the topic of
poems, of literature in general, of journalistic efforts, of philosophy.
Soon the *Burschenschaften* became centers of liberal ideas which,
in view of the stubborn attitude of the governments, often took
on a subversive character. Attempts to curb this development
only poured oil on the flames. This was true in particular about
the so-called "resolutions of Karlsbad" of 1819, in which the representatives of most German-speaking countries ordered a severe
censorship of all publications, invited the universities to dismiss
all liberal professors, and banned the *Burschenschaften.*

However, it would be a mistake to attribute the "revolutionary"
attitude displayed by many Left Hegelians after about 1840 simply
to this over-all politicization of thought. For in most cases
this new political thinking insisted upon the necessity of reforms
rather than revolution in the proper sense of the term. Though,
for example, the revolution of 1830 generally was hailed as the
resolution of a number of problems which the revolution of 1789
had left undone, and though everybody agreed that still further
developments had to be pressed for and new forms of political
freedom had to be gained, there remained the basic uneasiness
about revolutions which we mentioned in connection with the

---

[142] For a more detailed analysis see Schnabel, II, 234 ff.; also Mayer₁, 2 ff.

romanticists. As a German historian has recently put it,[143] most German revolutionaries of the nineteenth century, with the exception of the Left Hegelians and the socialists influenced by them, were revolutionaries in spite of themselves. Throughout the whole nineteenth century for most representatives of the German bourgeoisie the idea of making revolutions remained loaded with the blemish of an infringement upon law, of terror, of a betrayal of freedom.

Up to 1848 the only exceptions were the Left Hegelians. In them the general politicization of thought had developed under the unlucky star of Absolute Knowledge. Whereas those who were outside the magic circle of Hegelianism always tended to shrink back from the anarchic character of revolutions, the Left Hegelians had fathomed the secrets of history too deeply to be bothered by historical experience. This was so especially because they lived in Berlin, a city which in their view was the self-consciousness of Europe, indeed the ultimate "self-revelation of the Lord's body,"[144] and which, on the other hand, was the capital of Prussia—since the early 1830's the symbol of reactionary politics.

When in 1818 Hegel was offered a chair in Berlin, Prussia was one of the most advanced states of its time.[145] It was distinctly more "progressive" than Metternich's Austria, France during the period of restoration, or England previous to the reforms of 1832. For after the Napoleonic warfare had spread the ideals of the French Revolution and undermined absolutism even outside France,

---

[143] Cf. Schieder, 235 ff.

[144] Thus K. F. F. Sietze, *Grundbegriff Preussischer Staats- und Rechtsgeschichte* (Berlin, 1829) 689 ff.; cf. Ritter$_2$, 49.

[145] Cf. Weil, 18 ff., 68 ff.; Ritter$_2$, 50 ff. Even Heine, who certainly was far from sympathizing with Hegel, acknowledges that Hegel lived in a state "which subscribed to the principle of progress at least in theory" and was member of a Church "which considers the principle of free research as its life element"— a statement that considerably attenuates Heine's accusation that Hegel "granted to the existing order in the state and in the Church a questionable justification," Heine IV, 287 ff. That even Frederick William IV was in no sense the despotic tyrant decried, for example, by S. Hook, but rather a romantic dreamer who made vain efforts to bring his people back to the faith of the fathers, is well shown by Mayer$_1$, 13 ff.

the Prussian government realized that only radical reforms could save the power of the state as well as the leading position of Prussia within Germany. It started a large-scale reform: it abolished villeinage, withdrew most of the privileges of the aristocracy, freed the peasants, granted autonomous administration to towns, and, last but not least, granted to universities academic liberties quite unusual at that time. This reform, it is true, never was completed as it originally was planned. In the 1820's the old feudal system began to reassert itself, and a reaction set in (a development which Hegel did not really notice). Still, when in his inaugural lecture at Berlin Hegel praised Prussia as the center of culture and knowledge, as a state in which the free empire of thought had been realized and whose metropolis sheltered a *Universität des Mittelpunktes*, a university toward which everything gravitated; or when in the *Philosophy of Right* he modeled his conception of a rational state on Prussian realities; or when at the end of the *Philosophy of History* he described "Germany," that is, Prussia, as the last completion of the World Spirit's path—his extolling of the Prussian Kingdom ought not to be taken as originating from a reactionary attitude or, even worse, from a fawning servility toward the government. Prussia as Hegel found it in 1818 differed radically from the *Polizeistaat* with which his followers were confronted around 1840. In fact, the Metternichian counter-revolutionary policy which all liberal-minded intellectuals were fighting was not installed in Prussia until after the revolution of 1830. As far as the Prussia with which Hegel was familiar is concerned, recent studies show that Hegel's judgment about it largely corresponds to that of today's historians.

We may add that Hegel never was the ideologist of the restoration (or even reaction) as anti-Hegelian critics from A. Ruge through R. Haym to K. R. Popper have described and still describe him. As we shall see, this legend originated among the Left Hegelians; that it became common conviction is due mainly to R. Haym's *Lectures on Hegel and his Time* (1857). In spite of his ambiguous attitude toward the French Revolution Hegel always considered the events of 1789, not the ensuing restoration and reaction, as the principle and the driving power of his time. Sometimes he may

have mistaken restorative attempts for fulfillments of the promises
of the French Revolution. But he clearly spelled out that he considered the restoration as a pendant to the "abstract freedom" of the
Jacobins. Whereas the French revolutionaries obstinately stuck
to the "extreme of abstract theory and idle talk," the restoration
simply was the other extreme of an "obstinate perseverance in
positive laws of past ages." Both extremes were equally "entrench-
ments of egotism" and therefore "sources of distress (*Unglück*)."[146]
When in 1817 he wrote these words, it is true that Hegel primarily
had in mind Southern Germany, where liberal ideas did not prevail
until after 1830, at a time when such ideas already were withering
away in Prussia. But there is no doubt that Hegel was convinced
that all attempts to restore a political system of the past was
only an antithesis to the "abstract" libertinism of the revolutionaries;
this conviction extended to all properly restorative tendencies and
persisted until Hegel's last years. In his very last writing, the
remarks on the English Reform Bill, Hegel explicitly took to task
the tendency of clinging to a faith in the excellence of institutions
"in spite of the fact that the corresponding realities (*Zustände*)
are thoroughly rotten."[147] In England, he argued, the contrast
between existing laws and social circumstances had becomes so
"shrill" that it could be described as a cancerous sore to which all
of England's difficulties could be traced. He even foresaw "an
opposition errected on a basis hitherto at variance with the stability
of Parliament and feeling itself no match for the other parties in
Parliament," an opposition which "could be led to look to the
people for its strength," thus bringing forth a revolution instead
of a reform.[148] Only an installation and application of rational

[146] Hegel$_2$, VI, 395.

[147] Hegel$_2$, XX, 477.

[148] *Ibid.* 518. I do not think Hegel's article on the English Reform Bill shows
that Hegel's philosophy ends in doubt and resignation, as Marcuse$_4$, 248,
following Rosenkranz, 413 ff., argues. Of course, Marcuse is right when he
claims that the old Hegel's belief in the stability of the "results" achieved
by political history was not as unflinching as it might seem at first sight. But
to say that Hegel ends in "doubt and resignation" is to overstate the point.
This impression is due to Marcuse's assumption that Hegel expected the solution
of all problems from the restoration. Moreover, though Hegel undoubtedly

principles to life could help here, not the clinging to past systems.

From the late 1830's, however, Hegel's followers lived in a
Prussia where the feudal reaction to all reformatory efforts already
had set in. France and England had undergone political development while the constitution which the Prussian king had promised
in 1808 was being postponed year after year. It took over thirty
years until this constitution eventually came to pass; and then,
even when it was almost too late for a really good constitution, it
was a fake. No wonder, then, that most intellectuals began to react
against the authoritarianism of the Prussian State; Prussia became
a symbol of everything reactionary.

In short, whereas for Hegel the "cross" of political problems
was never so burdensome as no longer to throw into relief the reconciling "rose of reason," Hegel's followers, confronted with a
Prussia become reactionary, increasingly felt obliged to fall back
upon the claim for an "actualization of the rational," that is,
upon the admission that, while present in political theory, reason
still was missing in political practice. This change, it is true,
cannot be explained in terms of changes on the political scene
alone. Hegel also had a much deeper insight into, and a much
higher opinion of, the reconciling and transfiguring power of rational
thought than his followers. Yet there is no doubt that the un-
favorable political circumstances contributed significantly to the
zeal for "actualization" among the Hegelians. In fact, one even
might argue that the criticism of Hegel's interpretation of Christianity turned into a frontal attack against religion only because the
religious problems were interconnected with political ones—the
Prussian Kingdom was officially committed to the Lutheran
Church, especially after Frederick William IV's ascent to the
throne. In any case, as we shall see in connection with the development of A. Ruge's *Hallische Jahrbücher*, the Left Hegelian critique
of religion in general and of Lutheranism in particular became

---

saw the danger of a revolution, he certainly did not believe that it is inevitable.
On the contrary, he quite obviously was convinced that reforms in terms of
an application of rational principles (*ibid.* 513) would succeed in solving the
"collisions, knots, and problems" of which he speaks at the end of the *Philosophy
of History* (XI, 563).

really violent only after the Left Hegelian criticism had turned against the Prussian Kingdom and after the question about the relation between State and Church had become topical.

There is another point which we may add. One may doubt whether the Left Hegelians ever would have become as radical as in fact they became if they had been permitted to participate in academic life. Richter's and Strauss' attack on Christianity had, quite contrary to their intentions, succeeded in uniting the various groups of Prussian Protestants who up to that time had been quarreling with each other. They were joined by romantic conservatives such as Radowitz and the brothers Gerlach. When in 1840 Frederick William IV, a romantic dreamer who believed himself able to curb the process of secularization by imposing Christianity through politics, succeeded to the throne, the Hegelians who had dominated Prussian universities for more than twenty years suddenly saw themselves pushed into the background. This applied, in particular, to all Hegelians critical of orthodox Lutheranism. Richter already had been reprimanded by Altenstein, the Prussian minister of education who had brought Hegel to Berlin and usually sympathized even with politically radical Hegelians such as E. Gans.[149] Strauss escaped such troubles only because he taught at the University of Tübingen in the more liberal Württemberg, but in 1839 even he considered it safer to leave Germany for Switzerland. In 1836 Feuerbach had to leave the University of Erlangen because of the offense given by his *Ideas on Death and Immortality* (1830); he spent the rest of his life in a small village, appearing in public only once more (in 1848, at the University of Heidelberg). Eichhorn, who succeeded Altenstein as minister of education in 1840, removed the few Left Hegelians still remaining. In 1841 Ruge lost his position at the University of Halle. One year later Bruno Bauer had to give up his meager *Privatdozentur* at the University of Bonn; Stirner, Marx, and others never had to give up

---

[149] On Altenstein's modeling of the University of Berlin see the first part of the second volume of the monumental study by Lenz; on the changes introduced by Eichhorn see Mayer$_1$, 15 ff.

an academic position, but only because they could not obtain one in the first place.[150]

Driven out of the universities, the Left Hegelians became journalists, a development which was furthered by a brief loosening of censorship during the year 1842. But even here they were fighting a battle lost in advance. Ruge's *Hallische Jahrbücher*, which had become the mouthpiece of Left Hegelianism, was suppressed by the Prussian government in 1841; two years later it was suppressed in Saxony as well, where Ruge tried to re-establish his magazine by publishing it under a different name. Marx's *Rheinische Zeitung* published its last issue on March 31, 1843, after having existed for exactly fifteen months. Another periodical influenced by Left Hegelians, the *Leipziger Allgemeine Zeitung*, was suppressed in 1843 after having published a letter by the political poet Herwegh considered offensive by the King; it had been suppressed in Bavaria the year before. Only the *Allgemeine Literaturzeitung*, a monthly edited by Bruno Bauer, was left to its fate; it withered away for lack of subscribers. Eventually the Left Hegelians could do nothing else than emigrate. The few who remained in the country, like Feuerbach and Bauer, were condemned to inactivity and ultimately to insignificance.

---

[150] Cf. Löwith₃, 81 ff. On Bauer's expulsion from the University of Bonn see Bezold, 373 ff., and Hertz-Eichenrode, 37 ff. On the impact of this expulsion on the Left Hegelians see Gebhardt₂, 209 ff.

15: *PRAXIS*: CRITIQUE OR ACTION?

We may add a few words about the three Left Hegelians who directly influenced Marx: Bruno Bauer, Arnold Ruge, and Moses Hess. Of these three men, it is true, only Bauer was a Left Hegelian properly speaking, as he was also by far the most brilliant thinker. Though his *Hallische Jahrbücher* became the literary exercise ground of all Left Hegelians, Ruge came into contact with Hegelianism at a comparatively late age and always remained a journalist, thinking in terms of the liberal nationalism of the 1810's rather than becoming a true Hegelian. As for Hess, he was a Left Hegelian only because, and insofar as, Hegelianism seemed to corroborate his own ideas which were rooted, on the one hand, in French socialism, and, on the other hand, in a sort of secularized Jewish messianism. Still, between 1839 and 1843 they all were occupied with the same problem: what it meant to translate absolute theory into practice.

Yet before going on, a word of caution may be in order. Some studies concerned with the origins of Marxism, especially those written by authors who are Marxists themselves, tend to overrate the over-all significance of the Left Hegelian movement in the Germany of 1840. The Left Hegelians surely were not the leading representatives of an increasingly powerful liberal movement.[151] It would not be correct even to describe them as a radical wing

---

[151] On the distinction "liberal-radical" see Mayer₁, 19. Liberals (southern Germany and Königsberg) were mainly interested in practical problems; they based themselves upon Kant and upon the ideas of the Prussian Reform; the radicals were mainly interested in political theory and took their ideals from Rousseau, the French Revolution, and Hegel.

of the movement of independence which since the revolution of
1830 had been gathering momentum in Germany. In fact, they
were nothing more than a small group of eccentrics with an oddly
exaggerated self-confidence, somewhat comparable to the "pro-
gressives" in France after 1945. Though it would be an exaggeration
to say that their ideas met with no approval among Germans, their
ideas usually passed more or less unnoticed. Like all cranks with
an interest in politics, they were a nuisance both to the government
and to prudent reformers opposing restoration; but they were far
from being a real threat or a nucleus of revolutionaries. Were it
not for the fact that the father of "scientific communism," who
later was able to depend on a powerful social trend, was one of their
numbers, the Left Hegelian movement would have remained an
interesting, but hardly important, curiosity in the arsenal of philosophical radicalism in European thought. In short, one must
take care not to confuse the situation of 1840 with that of the
1870's, for example, when there already existed a powerful movement consciously opposing the existing social order. All in all,
the Left Hegelian movement consisted of thirty persons at the
most who had virtually no support in the German nation and who
were noticed by the public only because they were constantly
harassed by the government in power. We may add that even
the *Communist Manifesto*, when considered only as an event of
1848—that is, independently of the later successes of Marxism—
was little more than a pamphlet by an eccentric.

All the more striking is the overweening opinion which most
Left Hegelians had of themselves. They were all convinced that
their thoughts, their publications, and their actions, the latter virtually nonexistent, were a powerful lever pushing history toward
the eschatological stage intimated by Hegel's philosophy. Imbued
by Absolute Knowledge, they were little short of being perfectly
blind to real events. As we shall see, this applies most to Bauer
and least to Ruge. But even Ruge, and with him the young Marx,
always tended to consider as destroyed whatever they had destroyed in thought, even if the object in question was still in the
best of health. They saw no difference between killing an enemy
on paper and in reality. For as they shared in Absolute Knowl-

edge, they were always inclined to believe that each step forward in their thought was representative of progress in reality.[152]

Above all this is true of Bruno Bauer.[153] Born in 1809, he began to study in Berlin three years before Hegel's death and became lecturer in 1834. Originally a representative of the Right Wing, indeed close to the orthodox Protestant theologians represented in Berlin by E. W. Hengstenberg, his criticism of Strauss' *Life of Jesus* gradually persuaded him of the correctness of his opponent's standpoint and eventually led him to a criticism of Christianity far more radical than that of Strauss.

But it is not Bauer's critique of religion (which, incidentally, had some influence on Nietzsche[154]) that interests us here. We have to restrict ourselves to a few intimations about Bauer's notion of *critique* which, together with the ideas advanced by Cieszkowski, and even more than them, would seem to be the most important link between Hegel's Absolute Knowledge and Marx's revolutionary *praxis*. Unfortunately there still does not exist a comprehensive study about Bauer's philosophical ideas. Among other things this is due to the fact that Bauer himself, being forced to live almost exclusively on his publications, never had the leisure to develop systematically the fundamentals of his thought. One has to gather his conceptions from relatively few remarks scattered throughout his writings, most of which are concerned with analyses of the Gospel and, after about 1843, with political problems.

---

[152] Cf. Gebhardt₂, 208 ff. On Bauer see also Mayer₁, 46 ff. A side-effect of this odd attitude was the unusual practice of replying to critical reviews by a "criticism of the criticism." As Beyer₁, 19 ff., points out, it was Hegel himself who started this practice; cf. Hegel₂, XX, 314-393.

[153] A thorough study of Bauer's philosophical ideas does not yet exist. Stuke, 125-187, though excellent, is incomplete; and the biography by Hertz-Eichenrode ends with the year 1848 and contains only a few analyses of Bauer's ideas. For a brief but highly informative summary see E. Barnikol's article, "B. Bauer," in the third edition of *Die Religion in Geschichte und Gegenwart. Handwörterbuch für Theologie und Religionswissenschaft* (Tübingen, 1957). The best summary of the development of Bauer's political ideas still is Mayer₁, 46 ff.; also Mayer₂, especially 430.

[154] Cf. Benz₅, 104 ff.

Perhaps the best way to throw light upon the Bauerian notion of *critique* is to compare it to Cieszkowski's notion of *praxis*. As Cieszkowski describes it, practice is the perfectly sovereign activity of a humanity which has reached Absolute Knowledge. It is the world-governing, and world-saving, activity of a humanity which has reached salvation in theory and now proceeds to organize society according to its absolute insights. However, Cieszkowski's practice is far from being revolutionary. Cieszkowski does not oppose society as it exists. He still shares Hegel's conviction that reality develops alongside knowledge. In fact, he opposes Hegel only in one respect: he no longer conceives knowledge as a *prise de conscience* of that which *has* developed and *already exists* but claims that knowledge has hurried on ahead of reality, thus giving the Absolute Knower the chance henceforth to organize history according to his absolute insights.

In short, Cieszkowski's *praxis* is not "critical." This is why Cieszkowski, though discussing a topic which would seem to be meaningful only in a Left Hegelian context, can claim to believe in "conservative progress" as opposed to a "radical overthrow," that he can argue for an "evolutionary, as opposed to a revolutionary, development" of Hegelianism.[155] Ultimately Cieszkowski's conservativism probably is due to the fact that he still believes that Absolute Knowledge, historiosophy, and the future "execution of history" are developments rather than an overcoming and abandoning of Christianity.

Bauer's starting point, on the contrary, was his critical studies of Strauss' *Life of Jesus*. Though at first inclined to defend the conservative standpoint according to which Hegelianism was only a rational expression of Christian faith, he increasingly became aware that the reason why Strauss had described the Gospel as a myth was that if Christianity was truth, Hegelianism had its ultimate justification outside itself and therefore Knowledge, by its very essence, was afflicted with finiteness. If the historical Christ was a necessary premise which Hegelianism only expanded without truly overcoming and negating it, then it was impossible

---

[155] Cieszkowski$_2$, 96 ff.; cf. Stuke, 85 ff.

to speak of Absolute Knowledge. In order to decide this question, Bauer proceeded to a critical analysis of Christianity's historical authenticity which step by step turned into one of the most destructive criticisms of the Gospel ever written. First, Bauer showed that the Fourth Gospel is only a work of art, not a historical document. Of the remaining three Gospels, that of Matthew was an elaboration of the Gospel according to Luke, which, in turn, was dependent upon Mark's Gospel. In short, there existed no evangelical tradition, but only one original author of the Gospels. But how could one possibly prove that the Gospel according to Mark was the literary expression of an already existing Christian tradition rather than being its starting point? In fact, only the second alternative was plausible. For, as Bauer tried to show by lengthy analyses, Mark's Gospel was too inconsistent to be acceptable as a historical document. In the end, then, a Jesus claiming to be the Messiah never existed. The whole of Christian theology was nothing but a "tissue of lies of an infernal sophistry." To the critic who, like Bauer, had succeeded in dissolving the wisdom of theology into nothing there only remained a tremendous disdain, a contempt which was the critic's "last duty and a prophecy of happier times when no one will want to hear anything of theological arguments."[156]

Bauer's first deed, then, was the critical destruction of Christianity—a destruction which aimed at actualizing the salvific stage of Absolute Knowledge by overcoming its last elements of finiteness. However, Bauer soon had to discover that there still were other aspects of finiteness: the social and political situation of the present time. Accordingly he proceeded to make further critical destructions. Everything opposed to Absolute Knowledge had to be destroyed, and the means of destruction in terms of which the universe was to reach its completion was the "critique," a literary criticism unmasking the irrationality of things which had to disappear before the world could enter the age of salvation. As Bauer once put it in a letter to Marx, probably with reference to Cieszkowski, true practice precisely is critical theory. For it is

[156] For a summary of Bauer's arguments see Schweitzer, 141-161. According to Schweitzer, Bauer's treatment of the problem is the "most ingenious and thorough repertoire" of the problems concerning the "life of Jesus," 161.

the critique which leads to the "ultimate actualization of the system" and thus has to be considered the "last deed" of Hegelianism.[157]

In short, both Cieszkowski and Bauer were aware that Absolute Knowledge as described by Hegel could not be the end of the affair; there still existed too many things which did not harmonize with the New Jerusalem. But whereas Cieszkowski sought the ultimate completion beyond knowledge, in an action translating the divine insight into a reorganization of social reality, Bauer saw it in a development of Absolute Knowledge in terms of criticisms, in the critical destruction of all finiteness still obscuring Absolute Knowledge itself.

In the *Holy Family* and in the *German Ideology* Marx and Engels have so well succeeded in ridiculing Bauer's "critical critique" that today we have to make an effort to take Bauer seriously at all. In fact, however, Bauer's conception is no more absurd than that of Hegel. For like Hegel, Bauer obviously did not view Absolute Knowledge as something which happens only in man's mind. Following Hegel, he was so deeply convinced of the basic rationality of being that he believed it sufficient to unmask the irrationality of an appearance in order to destroy it. If it were true that only the rational was truly actual, then irrationality could exist only insofar as, and only as long as, it did not become conscious of itself. As soon as it became conscious of itself, and be it only in the mind of the philosopher, its days were numbered. The "critique" was the lever which the *Weltgeist* (or, as Bauer called it, the *Selbstbewusstsein*) used in order to overcome its last elements of finiteness. In the end the only reason why Bauer's ideas sound perfectly ridiculous, while Hegel's ideas do not, is that Hegel was *justifying* existing reality, whereas Bauer was trying to *destroy* it. Both conceptions were based upon the same self-conceited illusion, namely, that human ideas can do something to reality. But whereas it was possible to deceive oneself about the fact that Hegel's glorifying transfiguration left the world as imperfect as it always was, the things which Bauer "critically destroyed" continued to thrive,

[157] Bauer$_2$, XXI. Cf. *MEGA* I, 1/2, 250.

making the whole Bauerian endeavor look perfectly ridiculous. It is simply easier to make the imperfect look perfect than to make the imperfect disappear. But if thought is supposed to change reality, the basic difficulty remains the same: neither glorification nor criticism would seem to have an immediate impact upon reality.

As time went on, Bauer was increasingly inclined to consider each of his rapidly changing convictions as world-shaking developments of "self-consciousness," which according to him was the only power of the world and of history. "History has no other meaning than the becoming and development of self-consciousness"[158]; and the only way in which this Bauerian counterpart of Hegel's *Weltgeist*[159] developed was through critical reflection, a critique which was occurring presently in Bauer's own mind. Again it is hard to accuse Bauer of presumptuousness in the ordinary sense of the term. As G. Mayer once put it, his whole conception was far too intellectual to fit the usual image of vanity. "As long as the critique is a fighting power," Bauer's brother, Edgar, writes, "it is irrelevant which person is at its service. The critics consider themselves important only insofar as they permit the critique to labor in them."[160] The question of who is the receptacle of the critique was far less important than the fact that nothing which did not pass through the "critical fire" was ever able to enter "the new world which is approaching."[161] For the critique was the magic focus through which the world had to squeeze to reach final salvation. It was the ultimate and only authentic lever of salvation. "As soon as the critique has cleared our heart and made it free and ethical, the new world will not be far away. What more does one want? Thereafter, what do we need beside the free development of self-consciousness?"[162] After man had been

---

[158] Cf. Hertz-Eichenrode, 41 ff.

[159] Cf. Stuke, 133 ff.

[160] Quoted by Mayer₁, 46 ff. Cf. Marx's letter to Feuerbach, dated August 11, 1844: "They consider themselves critics who quite accidentally have the bad luck of being men," *MEW* XXVII, 427.

[161] Bauer₃, 2 ff.

[162] Bauer₂, XXIV.

freed of all finiteness and made "absolute," the beatific vision, an ever-progressing bliss, could take place.

Accordingly, I cannot agree with S. Hook's claim that Bauer is teaching a quietism based upon a cosmic idealism.[163] If this description fits any Left Hegelian at all, it is Feuerbach, as we shall see in the next chapters. As to Bauer, there hardly ever existed a thinker so feverishly active for humanity's salvation, active in all realms, from philosophy through art to politics. Unfortunately his activity produced nothing except ink stains on paper. That Bauer was comparatively little interested in political action in the proper sense of the term is due solely to his belief that the critique was the only form of action adequate to the level of "self-consciousness" reached by Hegel, not to his subscribing to an inactive "cosmic idealism."

Inasmuch as he understood that the world was not willing to change in response to words alone, Bauer was unable to follow Marx, who concluded that critical activity had to materialize as political action. Instead he fell back upon an evermore radical interpretation of his own endeavor. After he had destroyed both the Old and New Testament, he turned against the State, which until 1842 he hoped to convert by reminding it of its own principles. Since he did not succeed, he began to publish his *Allgemeine Literaturzeitung*, in which he criticized the "idle talk, the self-deception, and the emptiness of the masses" which had failed to respond to his ideas. Even the Left Hegelians were not exempt now; the critique unmasked them as spokesmen of the "masses." Contrary to Ruge and Marx, who urged a spreading of Hegelianism among the masses, Bauer eventually retired into a splendid isolation of scorn and contempt from which he opposed everybody and everything.

Of course, Bauer was in a way aware that his critique did not succeed in changing anything, that his ideas were opposed to those of everybody else, and that even his former friends ceased to notice them. But instead of leaving his ivory tower of aristocratic scorn he praised all this as a sign of the critique's fidelity to itself.

[163] Hook, 109.

The world was condemned to perish; only the critique and its author would survive. If the masses did not collaborate, all the better; after all, history showed that all great actions failed because the masses took interest in and became enthused over them. When his *Allgemeine Literaturzeitung* disappeared because nobody subscribed to it, Bauer even went so far as to claim that the magazine had attained its goal by meeting no public approval.[164] And when Marx and Engels publicly ridiculed Bauer in *The Holy Family* for replacing concrete man with a chimerical "self-conscious critic," he replied in the most straightforward way that only by the act of criticism could man become free.[165]

Curiously enough, in spite of all his idealistic arrogance Bauer's predictions about the concrete political future of Germany turned out to be far sounder than those of Marx and Engels. His deep-rooted pessimism as to the chances of the existing world simply came closer to reality than Marx and Engels' optimistic faith in the arrival of the "proletarian revolution." Bauer had already developed before Marx the odd symbolism of the "bourgeois" world which to this day belongs to the stock of Communist ideas. It is the picture of a through-and-through immature and rotten German society which had refused critical salvation.[166] In Germany both intellectual life and the universities were stagnant, religion and the Christian way of life were deteriorating without being replaced by anything new, political parties and public opinion were dominated by empty slogans, and nowhere was there a politician worth following. How then should a truly human revolution, a revolution bringing about the age of salvation, succeed? The whole era was good for nothing; there was no group in German society able to restore the world.

---

[164] Cf. Hertz-Eichenrode, 104.

[165] Bauer's little known reply to Marx's and Engels' criticism, entitled "Charakteristik Ludwig Feuerbachs," was published in *Wigands Vierteljahresschrift* 3 (1845) 86 ff. Interestingly enough, Bauer here criticizes Feuerbach for making of the human species a new idol (a criticism which Marx and Engels were to take over in the *German Ideology*): "The species is a new God or God anew," *ibid.* 110.

[166] Cf. Gebhardt$_2$, 210.

Accordingly Bauer expected nothing from the revolution of 1848, which from its first symptoms up to its end Marx and Engels believed to be "their" revolution. After the revolution had passed, instead of recanting previous statements Bauer was able to repeat his gloomy prognosis: "This whole revolution was an illusion. Originating in the general pauperism, it merely was a bloody inter-mezzo in the smooth, passive dissolution in which the whole hitherto existing culture withers away and passes into decay."[167]

A more realistic notion of *critique* is found in the writings of Arnold Ruge, who of all Left Hegelians with the possible exception of Marx seems to have had the most genuine political sense. Per-haps this is because he had been engaged in political action a long time before he came into contact with Hegel's eccentric pupils; all in all, he was and always remained a premature herald of de-mocracy rather than a true Left Hegelian. Born in 1802, he studied classical philology, first in Halle, then at Jena, and in 1824 went to prison for almost six years for participating in prohibited students' associations. It was not until about 1834 that he learned to know Hegelianism; meanwhile he had become *Privatdozent* at the Uni-versity of Halle. In 1838, together with Th. Echtermayer, he founded the *Hallische Jahrbücher für deutsche Wissenschaft und Kunst* in order mainly to recommend himself to Altenstein as a representative of Hegelianism and thus to obtain a professorship.

Already at that early time Ruge conceived of the *Hallische Jahrbücher* as a sort of liberal counterpart to the *Jahrbücher für wissenschaftliche Kritik*, which Hegel had started in 1829 and which after his death had become the mouthpiece of Right Hegelianism. As early as 1837, though granting the "truly scientific" character of this influential periodical, Ruge had opposed what he termed its "sublime Brahmanism." It was always a great exception, he claimed, if a Hegelian (he mentions Feuerbach) condescended to transpose the monotonous death mask of Hegelian abstractions into a "character of life." In opposition to this the *Jahrbücher* which Ruge was preparing at that time were supposed to present "scientific critical journalism," that is, publish articles bearing

---

[167] Quoted by Hertz-Eichenrode, 111.

on problems of pressing importance which elucidated their subject "scientifically," that is, in terms of Hegelian philosophy.[168]

Moreover, from the very beginning the editors of the *Jahrbücher* strove to contribute to historical development instead of merely commenting upon it. As Ruge put it later: "We declared progress our principle. We wanted to live together with, and contribute to, the begetting of history. Both stimulating and challenging, the *Jahrbücher* thus became the *praxis* of historical dialectics."[169] In short, like Bauer, but earlier, Ruge aimed at pushing history forward through literary criticism. However, as we have already indicated, Ruge's claim that instead of only accompanying development his *Jahrbücher* were "directly the development of the spirit of the age, both of the philosophical and of the general,"[170] was considerably less pretentious than Bauer's analogous claim that his own extremely academic and cerebral "critique" was the lever of history. For the *Jahrbücher* very quickly became the mouthpiece of almost all Left Hegelians. As far as the development of the Left Wing of Hegel's school was concerned, it took place almost exclusively in Ruge's magazine; and as the *Jahrbücher* were a sort of newspaper rather than a scholarly journal (they were published six times a week), they actually had some impact even outside philosophical circles.

In any case, it is in the *Jahrbücher* that the passage from academic Left Hegelianism to a political "movement" is best exemplified.[171] It started at a time when the topic of the day was the fiery discussion on mixed marriage between the hierarchy of the Catholic Church and the Prussian government, which culminated in the arrest of the Archbishop of Cologne in November, 1837. In 1838 the Catholic political and theological writer J. J. Görres published his *Athanasius*, a vigorous criticism of the Prussian "abstract bureaucratic state" and, more generally, of the modern idea of a "sovereign state" as defended by Hegel. When, trying to refute Görres'

---

[168] Cf. Ruge, IV, 460 ff. Later, Ruge accused the Old Hegelians of "theoretical laziness," *Hallische Jahrbücher* (1840) col. 417; cf. Beyer$_1$, 240.

[169] Ruge, IV, 472.

[170] *Ibid.* 466.

[171] Cf. Neher, 32 ff.; Hook, 128 ff.

criticism, which he felt was an attack on Protestantism, the romantic Protestant historian H. Leo admitted that the Prussian state was vitiated by its commitment to Hegelianism, the *Jahrbücher* felt obliged to set themselves up as defenders of what they considered the only true spirit of Protestant Prussia. Ruge accused Leo of being a representative of the "impertinent exclusiveness characteristic of the little band of the pious."[172] Leo returned the accusation by claiming that the Left Hegelian enthusiasm for Prussia was rooted in the desire for a social revolution rather than in a true commitment to the Lutheran faith. And a weekly paper closely connected with the romantic crown prince concurred with him: "We have to expect a revolution, we have to expect a Prussian revolution, we have to expect a Prussian revolution from the Young Hegelian gang."[173] Ruge replied by speaking of "denunciation" and published a pamphlet on *Prussia and the Reaction.*

All this time Ruge and his collaborators still believed that they were defending the true nature both of Protestantism and of Prussia. Of course they knew their own identity; they were "Hegelian Christians" and "Hegelian Prussians."[174] But so, they believed, were all true representatives of Prussia. Was not the cultural policy in the hands of Altenstein, who represented Hegelianism at the governmental level? When Ruge went to Berlin for a visit and Altenstein told him that in spite of the urging of the crown prince he had refused to suppress the *Jahrbücher,* Ruge was convinced that his magazine was the true voice of Prussia.

Soon, however, he began to realize that he represented only a "party" in Prussia, not Prussia as such. Altenstein deferred his appointment as professor; when Ruge applied for an "honorable recognition" of his academic activities, Altenstein flatly refused.[175] Moreover, it became increasingly obvious that the heir apparent had no sympathies either with the Protestantism of the Hegelians or with their idea of a rational state. Prussia did not want to go

---

[172] Cf. Neher, 43.

[173] *Ibid.* 45. The expression 'gang' (*Rotte*) was introduced by H. Leo in 1839; cf. Beyer$_1$, 236; it does not mean much more than 'religious sect.'

[174] Ruge, IV, 487.

[175] Cf. Neher, 53.

the way of salvation; Prussia's true self-consciousness, as represented by Ruge and his magazine, more and more threatened to become an "opposition party."

As if still hoping to be able to prevent this development, the *Jahrbücher* started a large-scale critique of romanticism. They described it as Hegel had done: as the persistence in an ego unable to reach universality and objectivity, as a "self-satisfied, exclusive, aristocratic insolence, a studied lasciviousness, a self-enjoyment of an ingenious being."[176] Romanticism was the persistence in a past stage of history, the most outspoken apostasy from spiritual progress, and an attempt to restore pre-Hegelian Christianity in all realms: in culture, in education, in poetry, even in philosophy. At first, the *Jahrbücher* attacked only poets and thinkers such as Novalis, Schlegel, or Schelling. But as romanticism as a literary movement already belonged to the past, they soon extended their critique to political romanticism. It is at that point that Ruge and his collaborators, on the one hand, began to criticize official Prussian politics and, on the other hand, began to accuse Hegel of being its ideologist. In 1838 Ruge had spoken of a reaction in Prussia; now in 1840 he began to speak of a Prussia which itself was reactionary. In 1838 he only opposed the conservative "Brahmanism" of the Right Hegelians; now he began to criticize the master himself.

Whereas before 1842 Richter, Strauss, Feuerbach, and Bauer were almost exclusively interested in theological problems, and whereas Cieszkowski had concentrated on problems raised by Hegel's philosophy of history, Ruge seems to have been the first Left Hegelian who explicitly reflected on Hegel's political doctrine. In 1840, on the occasion of a review of the second edition of the *Philosophy of Right*, he explicitly contrasted Hegel's accommodation to the existing order with the fundamentally progressive Hegelian method. The distinction between the content of, and the dialectical method of, Hegel's philosophy had been familiar to all Hegelians since about 1836. What was new was its application to Hegel's political doctrine: Prussia, as Hegel had described it, could be as

[176] Ruge, IV, 482.

little the end of the affair as Christ was the completion of religion, as Goethe was the completion of poetry—and Hegel himself was the completion of philosophy. "They all are so little the end of Spirit as to be the beginning of a new development."[177] A few months later Ruge took up the subject once more and claimed that Hegel's philosophy had been "courtly," that is, committed to the existing Prussian state. Accordingly, he argued, it could no longer be meaningful to speak of a simple translation of Hegelianism into practice. Hegelianism had first to be freed from all reactionary elements; only then could it be translated into reality. In short, the *praxis* of the Hegelians had to be both negative and positive: negative with respect to reactionary elements both in reality and in Hegelianism; positive with respect to the progressive elements of Hegel's thought.[178]

But Ruge still was far from criticizing Hegelianism as a whole; he only opposed its accommodation to reactionary realities. In this sense he introduced a distinction which is reminiscent of that of Cieszkowski between pretheoretical and posttheoretical practice. Reviewing Baron von Gagern's *Kritik des Völkerrechts*, he accused the author of not being in possession of a true—that is, Hegelian—political doctrine; though granting that the author was familiar with philosophy up to Leibniz, he argued that von Gagern's pre-Hegelian political philosophy could only lead to a practice which is no more than "clairvoyance." As opposed to this kind of political theory, which he termed *resultatisch*, Ruge stressed the importance of a "developmental" theory, that is, a theory rooted in Hegel's Absolute Knowledge after it had been freed of all reactionary elements.[179]

Yet even now Ruge was defending the "essence of Prussia." Of course Prussia's present "existence" could not possibly be defended as against its essence, for this existence was "faulty and untrue." Still Ruge continued to believe that "the essence of Prussia, that is, Protestantism together with its rational implica-

---

[177] *Hallische Jahrbücher* (1840) col. 1217.
[178] *Ibid.* 2331.
[179] *Ibid.* 1202.

tions," was "the Truth."[180] He even shared in the hopes of most Left Hegelians that the new king who succeeded his father in the summer of 1840 would embrace the "modern" political conception. When another Left Hegelian and friend of Marx, C. F. Köppen, published a booklet in which he hailed the new king as a successor of the "hero of the *Aufklärung,*" Frederick the Great, Ruge joined in the general cheerful expectation.[181] The definitive breach with Prussia came only with the suppression of the *Jahrbücher* in July, 1841. Ruge had to leave for Saxony and publish his magazine under a different name. From that time on the *Jahrbücher* openly criticized the Prussian state, decrying it as an embodiment of reaction. But as the editors of the *Jahrbücher* began to extend their criticism to Germany as a whole, and as Ruge began to argue for a "republican monarchy" and eventually for "democracy," the government of Saxony also soon suppressed the new version of the *Jahrbücher.* Ruge went to France, the dream country of all radicals and democrats.

Ruge's final breach with Hegel's political philosophy—which at one blow transformed him from a critical journalist-philosopher into a radical bent on action—was of course connected with his disappointment in "Europe's self-consciousness," Prussia. In 1842 he published an article entitled "Hegelian Philosophy of Right and Contemporary Politics," which at the level of political theory had an impact comparable only to that which Strauss' *Life of Jesus* had at the level of theology. Hegel's illusion, Ruge now argued, consisted in that he had believed that man could be free "theoretically" without being free politically.[182] Hegel's whole philosophy had aimed at man's insight and reason, not at his will. Considering everything from the point of view of reason, Hegel had been unable to discover anything which "ought to be done." But as soon as one turned away from abstract reason and instead looked at the "unreasonableness of existence," Ruge argued,

[180] Ruge, IV, 490.
[181] *Hallische Jahrbücher* (June 30, 1840). Köppen's book was dedicated to "my friend Karl Heinrich Marx of Trier."
[182] Ruge, IV, 567.

there emerges unrest, dissatisfaction ... and the nasty *ought* of
praxis. Now something *has* to be done. Reason has to come
into its own even at the level of this kind of existence; it has
to return to itself. The theoretical standpoint is abandoned,
the word of the critique addresses itself to man's will. Just
as pure insight is the starting point of thought, the decision to
subject reality to this insight is its final point. Only will (based
upon rational insight, of course) is realistic thinking.[183]

Hegel's mistake was to want to actualize theory as such, that is,
merely *qua* theoretical wisdom. But this was not possible. No
longer was it meaningful to "transfigure" reality; it had to be
changed. As soon as insight was reached and critically opposed
to reality, the practical enthusiasm no longer could be "repressed."[184]

It has been argued that this "new idealism" which Ruge began
to proclaim after his magazine was expelled from Prussia—an
idealism which stresses Fichte's "will" more than Hegel's "knowledge" and thus, paradoxically, tries to overcome Hegel in term
of what Hegel himself had overcome—was due to Bauer's influence.
Bauer joined the *Jahrbücher* at just about the time of its first
suppression. And the disappearance of any positive relationship
to an existing state must have left a vacuum in the *Jahrbücher*,
whose central aim had always been to make Prussia "rational and
free"—a vacuum which Bauer's "critique" filled out.[185] However,
though it cannot be denied that Bauer had considerable influence
upon the *Jahrbücher* during the last two years of its existence,
there remains a basic difference between Ruge and Bauer. Bauer's
critique aimed at transforming the world exclusively in terms of
knowledge. In Ruge, on the contrary, there already was the idea
that critical knowledge is a *principle of action*. Cieszkowski thought
of an action beyond knowledge which was constructive rather than
critical; Bauer believed in critical action in terms of knowledge;
Ruge, of all the Left Hegelians, comes closest to Marx in that he
argued for action rooted in critical knowledge, an action which
would destroy what knowledge had recognized as inadequate to

[183] *Ibid.* 569.
[184] *Ibid.* 583.
[185] Cf. Neher, 79.

reason. Of course, contrary to Marx, Ruge never was able to draw the last practical conclusions. After a brief collaboration with Marx he shrank back both from his friend's revolutionary radicalism and from his illiberal intolerance. Though he actively participated in the revolution of 1848, Ruge ended (like Bauer, incidentally) as a supporter of Bismarck, who in 1877 even allowed him a yearly honorarium of 3000 Marks for his journalistic services to Prussia.

Before we come to discuss the notion of *praxis* in the young Marx, we have to take into consideration one more thinker who, though he was a Left Hegelian even less than Ruge, gave to Left Hegelianism that special "socialist" twist which is characteristic of Marx: Moses Hess, known to his contemporaries as the "Communist rabbi" and as the "father of German socialism." Born in 1812, he received his first education from his grandfather, a deeply religious Jew who bequeathed to him the belief in a divine mission and the eventual glory of God's Chosen People. During the early thirties Hess went to Holland and France, where he came into contact with German emigrant circles which at that time were already beginning to discuss the ideas of French socialists, of Babeuf, Saint-Simon, and Fourier. After he came back to Germany, he attended the University of Bonn for a few months[186] without, however, completing his studies. In 1837 he published his first book, *The Sacred History of Mankind*, an odd mixture of secularized Jewish messianism and French socialism which anticipated a number of ideas contained in Cieszkowski's *Prolegomena* (though it is quite unlikely that Cieszkowski ever read this elaboration).

Hess, like Cieszkowski, viewed history as a sort of organism which develops in three stages, the last of which may be reconstructed on the grounds of the past and the present. In the first period, symbolized by Adam, we find Spirit and Nature harmoniously but unconsciously united; there reigned a sort of natural communism. In the second period, symbolized by Christ, this harmony dissolved. Precisely because Christ brought the first conscious awareness of the union of Spirit and Nature, the order of the ideal and that of the real fell apart. On the one hand, Christianity

---

[186] Recently, E. Silberner has questioned the truth of this statement, generally accepted by historians up to that time; cf. Hess$_3$, 51.

cultivated the highest spiritual values; on the other hand, politics
and society were ruled by brute force and lawless strife. In particular, private property and inheritance, the symbols of all evil,
opened the door to "chance and despotism, to superstition and
blind obedience, to injustice and slavery."[187] In the last period,
which began with Spinoza, the mysticism of the Middle Ages is
being replaced by reason and social harmony; now man becomes
able to "adjust his thinking and acting to recognized laws"[188]
and to actualize his ideals. This last period still is in the making.
Accordingly, whereas the first part of Hess' book treated of the
past, the "ground of that which will happen," its second part
treats of future events, of the "consequences of that which has
happened."

Hess, contrary to Cieszkowski, made no effort to prove that a
knowledge of the future was possible. He was convinced that
history would develop along the same lines which it had followed
until now. "World history is no liar."[189] Whether the last stage of
history would emerge organically or in terms of a revolution still
was not certain. A revolution, a blind struggle of uncontrolled
passions, was conceivable; but a revolution could possibly be
avoided by "peaceful arbitration based on mutual comprehen-
sion."[190] In any case the future would consist in perfect social
equality. Because moneyed aristocracy concentrates all forces
of society on its side while the other side is "covered with out-
rage and slavery," life eventually will almost come to a close.
But at the moment when the opposition between wealth and
misery will have reached a climax there will emerge a process of
equalization in the course of which private property and the laws
of inheritance will be abolished and the social equality of the
age of Adam reinstated. In the end there will emerge a universal
religion based on love. The Church will become superfluous,
and the state, too, will retain only an administrative function.
"The whole country will be a great garden. In it everybody will

[187] Hess₂, 8.
[188] *Ibid.* 35.
[189] *Ibid.* 47.
[190] *Ibid.* 44 ff.

be diligent and happy. Everybody will enjoy life as befits man. One will look for misery in order to remedy it. Yet one will find little of it. Distress will have left man."[191]

Though strangely confused, and very little noticed, Hess' *Sacred History of Mankind* is a landmark in the history of German thought. It contains very little of German influence. The influence of the French socialists is all the more obvious. The idea of social harmony, together with the criticism of contemporary society, comes from Fourier; the claim that the state will turn into a purely administrative body is from Saint-Simon; the claim that social harmony can only be reached in terms of perfect social and economic equality is from Babeuf. This last idea in particular was completely foreign to German Idealism. Kant, Fichte, Schelling, and Hegel only aspired to "rational freedom." And even revolutionary minded Germans such as the poet Börne, who lived in voluntary exile in Paris, fought only against "despots and tyrants," not against the "moneyed aristocracy." The only prominent German writer who had mentioned social equality before Hess was Heinrich Heine, and he had mentioned it only to reject it with disgust.

Contrary to Cornu,[192] I cannot find in Hess' first book any attempt to elaborate a philosophy of action. Hess was too sure that social inequality would disappear to be interested in a doctrine of *Tat*. This idea only emerged in Hess' second book, *The European Triarchy* (1841). Meanwhile he had studied the writings of Fichte, Schelling, and Hegel, and, most important of all, Cieszkowski's *Prolegomena*. Thus he now could translate his ideas into a philosophical language. Elaborating on the Left Hegelian notion of an actualization of Absolute Knowledge, he declared that Hegel was the "keystone of the foundation of a philosophy of action." Hegel's philosophy of spirit, being based upon Schelling's philosophy of nature and, ultimately, upon Spinozism, had achieved everything which pure philosophy could accomplish. "If it entails deficiencies," Hess quoted Cieszkowski, "then these are due to philosophy itself, to the narrow-mindedness of the philosophical sphere."[193]

[191] *Ibid.* 66.
[192] Cf. Cornu$_1$, 12.
[193] Hess$_2$, 78. Cf. Cieszkowski$_1$, 124 ff.

In the end Hess took over Cieszkowski's whole "philosophy of *praxis*" and only articulated it more than Cieszkowski had done. Thus, for example, he linked the problem of the knowableness of the future with the problem of the existence of "true" freedom. If, he argued, only those actions are truly free which are preceded by consciousness, then such actions and also the whole future must be knowable. Thus freedom, knowableness, and Absolute Knowledge again became synonymous just as in Hegel; only they were ordered toward *salvific action*. Similarly, Hess reproduced Cieszkowski's distinction between "facts" and "acts" as a distinction between "profane facts" and "sacred acts."[194] All actions committed by man who still did not share in Absolute Knowledge, who had not reached "consciousness," who were not at the height of "theory," were "profane acts"; they were not even truly free. Only those actions mediated by "reason which is conscious of itself as of the whole of being"[195] were "sacred." "If one does not consider free, human, self-conscious action incompatible with God's providence and universal empire—if, on the contrary, one believes that humanity shares in divine spirit—then only by a very odd confusion of the mind can one deny that the future is knowable. For, as the author of the *Prolegomena* correctly remarks, consciousness succeeds only to unfree acts. As to free acts, it precedes them."[196]

Pursuing this idea, Hess concluded that since Hegel was interested only in the past, he was inevitably bogged down in necessity. For everything belonging to the past, as it did not proceed from man, happened by necessity. Only that which happened through those sharing in Absolute Knowledge was truly "free." The future was the only place where true freedom reigned. Accordingly, in order to reach freedom, humanity had to project itself toward the future through "self-conscious action." Action, then, being a synthesis of self-consciousness and the future, was the ultimate realization of freedom. "From now on the positive has to be sought in another realm than in that of $\theta\varepsilon\omega\varrho\acute{\iota}\alpha$."[197]

[194] Hess₂, 87.
[195] *Ibid.* 79. Cf. Hegel₂, VI, 22.
[196] Hess₂, 83.
[197] *Ibid.* 89.

Compared to these oddly confused but obviously highly explosive ideas, the actual content of Hess' *European Triarchy* is of little relevance to our study. It was a detailed and perfectly fantastic analysis of what Germany, France, and England had to do in order to realize social equality and perfect freedom. Even the often-mentioned article "Philosophy of Action" which Hess published in G. Herwegh's collection *Einundzwanzig Bogen aus der Schweiz* (1843), added little to the introductory chapter of the *European Triarchy*. It merely repeated that "action, as opposed to being, is the first and the last."

> The task of the philosophy of spirit now consists in becoming a philosophy of action. The whole of human action, not only thought, has to be elevated to the standpoint at which all contradiction disappears.[198]

Thus the development of activist Hegelianism which was introduced by Cieszkowski's *Prolegomena* culminated in a "philosophy of action" which included socialist ideas in addition to Hegel's Absolute Knowledge and the mystical *praxis* of the Left Hegelians. There had yet been no mention made of the proletariat; this point emerged only when Marx, sharing Bauer's views on the apathy and total incapacity of the German bourgeois "philistines," began to look for a mystical agent adequate to the mystical act of *praxis* supposed to propel humanity toward final salvation. But Marx did not need to go far: Hess had reduced the "not-being-redeemed" of the present to "the social question"; Bauer had opposed the merely "bourgeois" revolution to the final revolution emancipating humanity.[199] Marx had only to look for the social potentialities of his time. Incidentally, as early as the summer of 1843 Bauer's brother Edgar had pointed out that it might be the "poor, working, and laboring classes of humanity" which were destined to "destroy the present condition of the world" and to "establish a new form of life."[200]

[198] *Ibid.* 321; cf. 309.
[199] Cf. Gebhardt$_2$, 210.
[200] E. Bauer, *Der Streit der Kritik mit Kirche und Staat* (Bern, 1844) 276 ff., quoted by Stuke, 173. The book was written in the summer of 1843.

Part III:

Marx

The first sign of beginning wisdom is the wish to die. This life seems unbearable, another unattainable. One no longer is ashamed to want to die. One asks to be brought from the old prison, which one hates, to the new one, which one still will learn to hate. A remnant of faith contributes to this decision. One hopes that during the transfer the Lord by chance would pass through the corridor, look at the prisoner, and say: "This one should not go into the prison again. He comes to me."

.   .   .   .

The crows claim that a single crow can destroy heaven. This certainly is true. But it does not prove anything against heaven, for heaven precisely means: the impossibility of crows.

Franz Kafka, Considerations on Sin, Suffering, Hope, and the True Path.

16: PHILOSOPHY AND REALITY

Marx's first philosophical utterances, above all his doctoral dissertation which was begun in the winter of 1838-1839 and completed in the early spring of 1841, indicate that he too was captivated by the two basic issues with which the Left Hegelians were struggling about 1840: on the one hand, the problem of reconciling the still unchanged world with the salvific heights of Absolute Knowledge; and, on the other hand, the more "existential" issue as to how one could be an original and creative philosopher in view of the "last philosopher," Hegel. However, whereas most other Left Hegelians were almost exclusively occupied with the first problem and touched upon the second only occasionally, Marx seems to have felt that in order to determine the relation between philosophy and reality, he had to first determine what the philosopher's task could be after Hegel's all-embracing synthesis.

Marx came to Berlin in the fall of 1836. Sometime in 1837 he joined the *Doktorklub*, a loose group of young Hegelians among whom only Bruno Bauer was already teaching at the university. Under the influence of his new friends Marx soon began to abandon both the study of law imposed upon him by his father and what he considered to be his vocation, poetry. Though first frightened off by the "grotesque rock melody" of Hegel's philosophy, he soon threw himself into the arms of the "treacherous siren." During a brief illness he studied "Hegel from the beginning to the end, together with most of his pupils." Soon, as he writes to his father on November 10, 1837, he felt himself definitively "chained to the present World Philosophy."[1]

[1] *MEGA* I, 1/2, 220.

His doctoral dissertation, although claiming to be an objective historical study, presents eloquent evidence of Marx's state of mind around that time. Originally Marx had planned a comprehensive study of Epicurean, Stoic, and sceptical philosophy, and although eventually he restricted himself to an analysis of the difference between the Democritean and the Epicurean philosophy oi nature, the general subject is significant enough to deserve a brief remark.

At first sight it seems that Marx simply wanted to close a lacuna left open by Hegel's *History of Philosophy*. For although Hegel had discussed the "universal characteristics" of the philosophical systems in question, he did not enter into details. Moreover, Marx claimed that Hegel was too much interested in what he considered as "par excellence speculative" to be able to do justice to post-Aristotelian philosophy.[2]

Yet this implicit criticism of Hegel indicates that Marx chose the eclecticism of late antiquity as the subject for his dissertation for yet another reason. Aristotle had completed Greek philosophy in a way similar to Hegel's completion of German philosophy. Marx therefore expected to find clues to the understanding of his own situation by studying the mentality of Aristotle's spiritual heirs. "To Greek philosophy seems to happen what should not happen to a good tragedy, namely, that it has a weak conclusion. With the Alexander the Great of Greek philosophy, Aristotle, philosophy's objective history seems to come to a close in Greece, and even the bold and manly Stoics seem to have been unable to do what the Spartans did in their temples, namely, to prevent Athena from escaping by fettering her to Hercules."[3] It is not difficult to translate this description into modern terms: the post-Hegelians seemed to be an epilogue to the magnificent scene of Hegel's original synthesis, an epilogue which followed and could not measure up to the preceding climax.[4]

---

[2] *MEGA* I, 1/1, 9.

[3] *Ibid.* 13.

[4] As Friedrich, 31 ff., points out, all Left Hegelians were very much interested in the philosophy of late antiquity.

One therefore is not surprised to find among the drafts for the thesis a passage which takes up this very problem. Instead of admitting that both the post-Aristotelians and the post-Hegelians are delayed births condemned to being inferior followers, Marx translates the Young Hegelian claim to originality into a "historical law." In the history of philosophy, he argues, there are "key points" during which philosophy becomes universal and all-embracing, thus interrupting its own "linear progress." In the after-times philosophy abandons its purely theoretical attitude and appears on the historical scene as a "practical person (*praktische Person*) hatching intrigues with the world." In short, after philosophy has reached a definite degree of universality, it ceases to be contemplative and becomes active. The spectator becomes himself an actor.[5]

But the philosopher does not become an actor only because the door to further theoretical developments is slammed. Philosophy throws its eyes away "because its heart has become strong enough to create a world."[6] As Marx puts it in another passage, once spirit has reached a definite level of universality, and thus also of freedom, it turns into "energy." It becomes *will* which turns on a reality still deprived of spirit.[7]

Though it is well put, all this is not as original as some students of Marx want us to believe. After all, Marx does nothing other than translate into a "law" what all Left Hegelians already were striving for. Moreover, this "law" is based almost exclusively upon Marx's desperate wish to prove that in spite of Hegel one can continue to philosophize. "If one denies this historical necessity, one has to deny that after a universal philosophy men can continue to live,"[8] that is, to be creative philosophers.

A footnote to the fourth chapter of the thesis' second part, however, indicates that Marx has more to say than that. Unfortunately it is no longer possible to determine from what context this footnote arose; the corresponding chapter is not preserved. Moreover it

[5] *MEGA* I, 1/1, 131 ff.
[6] *Ibid.* 131.
[7] *Ibid.* 64.
[8] *Ibid.* 132.

combines several heterogeneous ideas and accordingly is somewhat confused. Yet the basic idea is clear. Marx takes to task those Hegelians who tried to explain "morally" Hegel's occasional accommodations to the existing world, that is, by accusing Hegel of insincerity or cowardice. This kind of accusation, Marx argues, misses the point. For even if it was true that Hegel accommodated to the Lutheran Church or to the Prussian state out of cowardice, for example, the crucial point consists in discovering what made Hegel believe that such accommodations were compatible with his philosophy. "In this way, what appears as a progress of conscience," namely, a condemnation of Hegel in ethical terms, "actually will be a progress of knowledge," a step beyond Hegel. In short, that Hegel was a coward is only of biographical interest; that he was able to justify his accommodations theoretically throws significant light on his system as a whole.[9]

At the same time Marx tries to degrade Hegel's philosophy to a stage of the development of spirit as described by Hegel himself. One has to separate Hegel's private consciousness *about* his system from the objective consciousness expressing itself *in* his system. This, of course, does not mean that Marx takes Hegelianism to be one philosophy among many. Except for Feuerbach[10] all Left Hegelians at that time agreed that Hegelianism was *the* philosophy. Their problem was to separate it from its interpretation in Hegel himself and in his conservative followers, not to find another philosophy. Marx expresses this in terms of a distinction between "exoteric" and "esoteric": whereas Hegel's interpretation of his system is "chatty and exoteric," the system itself is the highest expression of the "constantly digging mole of true philosophical knowledge."[11]

---

[9] *Ibid.* 63 ff.

[10] Cf. Nüdling, 38 ff.

[11] *MEGA* I, 1/1, 143. The "digging mole" refers to the end of the *History of Philosophy* where Hegel (having varied Vergil's *Tantae molis erat Romanam condere gentem* into *Tantae molis erat se ipsam cognoscere mentem*) quotes Hamlet's "mole" ("Well said, old mole! canst work in the ground so fast?"; tr. Tieck: "Brav gearbeitet, wackerer Maulwurf!") to illustrate the *Weltgeist*'s activity; cf. Hegel$_2$, XIX, 685; tr. Haldane-Simson, III, 547.

This, in turn, implies that original Hegelianism cannot critically turn against the world without first passing through the fire of criticism itself. As we have seen, Ruge formulated this idea before Marx. However, Marx's analysis goes deeper than that of Ruge. Ruge simply believed that after Hegelianism has been freed from its reactionary elements, one can proceed to is actualization without further ado. Marx, on the contrary, realized that the very essence of Hegelianism consisted in its "totality character," that is, in its claim that it is absolutely all-embracing. Accordingly he concluded, contrary to Ruge, that all attempts to translate Hegelianism into practice are "essentially afflicted with contradiction."

For a "total philosophy" inevitably ceases to be a "totality" as soon as it assumes a critical attitude. To criticize involves conceding that not everything is as it ought to be. A philosophical critique of the world entails that the world is "unphilosophical." And an "unphilosophical" world is *outside* philosophy. Thus, by turning against, and by opposing itself to, the world Hegelianism ceases to be "total." Before philosophy was critical, it was full of "self-satisfaction and roundness"; with the critical attitude this self-satisfaction is "broken" and Hegelian philosophy is degraded to a "one-sided totality." But this, in turn, means that all attempts to actualize a "total" philosophy must fail. Either one wants to preserve its "totality character," and then one cannot want to go beyond it, to actualize it; or else one wants to actualize it, and then one has to sacrifice its "totality character."

Marx no longer is able to take the first alternative seriously after Richter, Strauss, Cieszkowski, and Bauer. It is already obvious to him that Hegelianism is only an "abstract," merely theoretical, "totality"; that it stands over and against an unphilosophical, and therefore unredeemed, world. But Marx, contrary to all other Left Hegelians, considers the second alternative highly problematic, too. For he has to admit

> that in the extent to which the world becomes philosophical, philosophy becomes worldly; that the actualization of philosophy simultaneously is its loss. What philosophy fights outside actually is its own inner shortcoming. It succumbs to the

> defects which it fights; indeed, it cannot abolish these defects
> except by succumbing to them.[12]

This well-known passage alludes to a problem of which, as far as I
can see, no Left Hegelian besides Marx was ever really aware,
and the solution of which was to carry Marx farther away from
Hegel than any of his friends. This problem may be expressed as
follows. Granted that Absolute Knowledge alone cannot be the
final salvation. Granted, too, that the actualization of Hegel's
Absolute Knowledge entails a double-edged criticism; the critique
has to turn both on the world and against Hegel. There remains
the problem that the salvific character of Cieszkowski's "practice"
as well as of Bauer's "critique" depends upon their *being effluences*
of Absolute Knowledge. "Social life" à la Cieszkowski or Bauer's
"critical critique" were salvific activities only because they were
carried out by men who already shared in speculative salvation
and now had to translate it into a more realistic one. But (and
this is the problem raised by Marx) a salvation which still has to be
actualized is no actual salvation at all. If true salvation has to be
sought in the actualization of Absolute Knowledge, then Absolute
Knowledge, taken by itself, is not salvific. But the "practice"
and the "critique" had their salvific halo from being the consequence
of a salvific Knowledge. In short, by trying to convert Hegel's
speculative salvation into a practical one the Left Hegelians had
abandoned the premise upon which the salvific character of their
endeavor depended.

This, of course, does not mean that Marx argues against the
salvific character of *praxis* as advocated by all Left Hegelians.
It only means that at this early time he is aware of the need to
justify it in terms of more than Absolute Knowledge alone. Of
course he only sees the problem, and even this only vaguely; he
still has no answer. At this time he is far from thinking of political
or social action in the proper sense of the term. In this respect
he is still under the spell of Bauer's notion of *critique*. He even
falls short of Cieszkowski's vague allusions to "social life." He
is convinced that "the *praxis* of philosophy is itself *theoretical*.

[12] *MEGA* I, 1/1, 64 ff.

It is the *critique* which measures individual existence against the essence, particular reality against the Idea."[13]

Originally Marx had hoped to follow Bauer to the University of Bonn and to become *Privatdozent*. But when in the spring of 1842 Bauer was expelled from his university, Marx had to abandon this ambitious project. In the summer of the same year he joined the editorial staff of the *Rheinische Zeitung* at Cologne; soon afterwards he became editor in chief. In March, 1843, the *Rheinische Zeitung* was suppressed and Marx moved to Kreuznach at the Swiss-German border, where he began to compose his *Critique of the Hegelian Philosophy of the State*.[14]

During the years 1839-1842 his intellectual development roughly corresponds to that of the *Hallische Jahrbücher*: he began by criticizing religion and ended by criticizing the whole political setting of Germany. While still at Berlin he wrote to Bauer that when he came to Bonn, he would lecture on Hermesianism, a heterodox Catholic theology based on Kantianism which the Prussian government supported in its fight against the Catholic Church;[15] also he edited a memorandum by his father defending the attitude of the Prussian king in his struggle with the archbishop of Cologne.[16] During a stay at Bonn in 1841 he helped Bauer to compose a pamphlet entitled *The Trumpet of the Last Judgment over Hegel the Atheist and Antichrist (An Ultimatum)*, in which Bauer, affecting the standpoint of an orthodox Lutheran, tried to prove that Hegel had been an atheist and that the atheism of the Left Hegelians was a logical consequence of original Hegelianism. Also he worked with Bauer on another pamphlet, *Hegel's Teaching on Religion and Art, Judged from the Standpoint of Faith*, which eventually was published in 1842.[17]

When he joined the *Rheinische Zeitung*, it already was clear to him that no salvation was to be expected from Prussia; it was a year after

---

[13] *Ibid.* 64.

[14] On the exact date of composition there is some disagreement; cf. Friedrich, 56.

[15] Cf. *MEGA* I, 1/2, 239 ff.

[16] *Ibid.* 231 ff.; cf. Wackenheim, 81 ff.

[17] For a summary see Wackenheim, 84.

the *Hallische Jahrbücher* had been suppressed by the Prussian government. For fifteen months he was engrossed almost exclusively in political problems of the day: with the freedom of the press, with laws concerning the theft of timber, with protective tariffs, and so on. In spite of the Leninist legend that at that time Marx was already beginning to pass from idealism to materialism and from "revolutionary democratism" to communism, his articles contain little more than brilliantly written and extremely sarcastic criticisms of the policies of the Prussian government.

Only once did Marx touch upon the hot iron of "communism." When in September, 1842, the *Rheinische Zeitung* called the attention of their readers to certain abuses in Berlin tenements, the *Allgemeine Zeitung*, a conservative and anti-Prussian paper published in Augsburg, accused its counterpart in Cologne of being a "Prussian Communist" newspaper. In his reply Marx claimed that as it does not grant to contemporary communist ideas even as much as "theoretical reality," the *Rheinische Zeitung* cannot possibly support their "practical realization." How far Marx was then from his later notion of "revolutionary practice" is shown by the following passage:

> We are firmly convinced that the theoretical realization (*Ausführung*) of communist ideas, not practical experiments, are the proper danger. To practical experiments, even mass experiments, one can answer with guns. Ideas, however, which conquer our intelligence, which subdue our mind, to which reason forges our conscience, these are fetters from which one cannot rescue oneself without tearing one's heart into pieces; these are demons which man can conquer only by submitting himself to them.[18]

At that time Marx knew only one man who defended communist or socialist ideas: Moses Hess. And it seems that Hess was far more impressed by Marx than Marx by Hess.[19] In any case, in spite of a number of friendly encounters it does not seem that Hess succeeded in convincing Marx. Only Engels, who met Hess in Cologne at the end of October, 1842, allowed himself to be con-

---

[18] *MEW* I, 108.
[19] See Hess' letter in *MEGA* I, 1/2, 260 ff.

vinced that socialism is the logical consequence of German Idealism.[20]
Marx's relation to Engels at that time was still rather cool; he
was at the point of breaking off relations with his Left Hegelian
friends at Berlin and therefore regarded Engels, who had just
arrived from Berlin, with some suspicion.

[20] Cf. Hess₃, 103; also Mayer₃, I, 103, 107.

17: FEUERBACH

In spite of its subject the first great work which Marx wrote after his dissertation, the *Critique of Hegel's Philosophy of the State*, reveals little progress as far as Marx's notion of *praxis* is concerned. However, it contains a number of ideas which are highly relevant to an understanding of the general development of Marx's thought. In particular it signalizes a twofold progress: a progress in Marx's critical attitude toward Hegel and a renunciation of his faith in the importance of politics. As we shall see, the last point is crucial for an understanding of Marx's eventual conversion to communism.

Again it would seem quite understandable that Marx chose precisely the *Philosophy of Right* as the starting point of his critical disengagement from Hegel. Since Ruge's famous article in the *Hallische Jahrbücher* it was Hegel's political philosophy rather than his "theology" which occupied the minds of the Left Hegelians. Marx's keen sense for topical problems made him feel that by analyzing Hegel's political doctrine he would both touch upon a crucial problem of the day and discover the most palpable limits of his master.

Of course, compared to all later works, Marx's critique of Hegel's philosophy of state was somewhat schoolboylike. Commenting upon Hegel's text paragraph by paragraph, and sometimes word by word, more often than not he became lost in a thicket of verbal arguments instead of trying to survey Hegel's political philosophy as a whole. Still this piecemeal procedure brought forth some remarkable results. In any case it was far more appropriate to a critique of Hegel than to the criticism of Bauer and other Left Hegelians which Marx developed two years later in the *Holy*

Family. The same procedure which proved fruitful against the giant, Hegel, turned out to be a pedantic and highly unjust gibe when applied to Bauer and Stirner.

Marx's disengagement from Hegel was largely based upon ideas developed by Feuerbach in an article entitled "Preliminary Theses for a Reform of Philosophy" and published in Ruge's collection *Anecdotes Concerning Recent Philosophy and Journalism* (1843), which also contained one of Marx's first opuscules in prose.[21] In the preceding chapter we did not mention Feuerbach because he seems to have contributed to Marx's notion of *praxis* only indirectly. For reasons to be discussed shortly, Feuerbach was comparatively little interested in the post-Hegelian notion of *praxis* and even less in political problems. In his earlier writings he refers to politics only once, in an article which was not published until after his death.[22] Apart from that Feuerbach was and always remained an outsider to the Left Hegelian movement. Though he was the first Hegelian explicitly to attack orthodox Christian eschatology (his *Ideas on Death and Immortality* having been published one year before Hegel's death and almost three years earlier than Richter's study on the Last Things), his earlier writings were little noticed by the Right or by the Left Wing of the Hegelian school. In fact, the Left Hegelians began to notice him only after he had become a reviewer of the *Hallische Jahrbücher* and had published in 1839 his "Critique of Hegelian Philosophy," one of the first articles which took to task Hegel himself instead of only the Right Hegelians. And even then his claim that Hegelianism was an "inebriate philosophy"[23]—a "rational mysticism"[24] which suffered from the basic difficulty of all post-Cartesian philosophy, namely, the overlooking of sense perception and therefore an "unmediated presupposing of philosophy"[25]—was not thoroughly

---

[21] Though the *Anecdota* were published in February, 1843, Marx's two articles were written in the spring of 1842, that is, before the articles in the *Rheinische Zeitung*.

[22] Feuerbach, II, 218.

[23] *Hallische Jahrbücher* (1838) col. 2340. Cf. *MEGA* I, 3, 301.

[24] *Hallische Jahrbücher* (1839) col. 1715.

[25] *Ibid*. 1700.

to the liking of the Left Hegelians still intoxicated with Absolute
Knowledge. In short, it was not until after 1842, when a general
disenchantment with Absolute Knowledge began to come to the
surface, that the Left Hegelians began to take Feuerbach's arguments seriously.

This may also be the place to say a few words about the influence of Feuerbach on Marx. To make a long story short, this
influence would seem to be far less than is generally believed.
The overestimation of Marx's dependence upon Feuerbach is due,
on the one hand, to the fact that for many decades the *Holy Family*
was the only known writing by the "early Marx," and, on the
other hand, to Engels' statement of 1895 that after the publication
of the *Essence of Christianity* (1841) they all were "for the present,
Feuerbachians."[26] Since the publication of Marx's literary remains
in the 1930's it has become increasingly more obvious that Marx's
enthusiasm for Feuerbach, if one can speak of enthusiasm at all,
was comparatively short-lived and that from the very beginning
it was not without critical overtones. Thus, for example, referring
to a prospective article on religious art, Marx wrote as early as 1842
that his own ideas concerning the nature of religion would conflict
with those of Feuerbach, though only as regards the form (*Fassung*)
and obviously not to the advantage of religion.[27] And a few days
before he left the *Rheinische Zeitung*, in March, 1843, he wrote
to Ruge that he disliked Feuerbach's insistence on nature to the
disadvantage of politics.[28]

Moreover, Marx seems to have been impressed by Feuerbach's
"transformative" criticism of Hegel far more than by his critique
of religion. There is nothing to indicate that he was particularly
impressed by the *Essence of Christianity*. He no doubt read it.
Everybody did. But the time of theological discussions was already over.

Comparing Feuerbach to Hegel, Marx will many years later
describe the former as "very poor indeed."[29] In point of fact, one

[26] *MEW* XXI, 272; tr. Moscow, II, 367.
[27] *MEGA* I, 1/2, 272.
[28] *Ibid.* 308.
[29] "Verglichen mit Hegel... durchaus arm," letter to Schweitzer of January

wonders today how Feuerbach's almost unbelievably primitive
criticism both of Christianity and of Hegelianism could have been
such a success. Paradoxically enough, the secret of Feuerbach's
success consisted precisely in his almost disarming naïveté (Marx
once spoke of an "unpretentious simplicity"[30]). As he opposed to
Hegel's extremely complex and abstract system a few rough and
ready principles which permitted him to handle Hegel as though
he were a puppet, his ideas had an emotional effect which overshadowed the primitiveness of his arguments and thus significantly contributed to, indeed sealed, the final downfall of Hegelianism.

We have to restrict ourselves to Feuerbach's criticism of Hegel.
Feuerbach proceeds from the assumption that the "essence" of
theology is anthropology and that, in turn, the secret of speculative
philosophy from Spinoza to Hegel is theology. Theology originates
from a misstatement of the true relation between primary and
secondary aspects of human nature, while speculative philosophy
is only "theology brought to reason and made topical."[31] In regard
to Hegel, Feuerbach says that he describes as *abstract* and derived
entities whatever common sense recognizes as reality properly
speaking, and whatever common sense considers as *abstract* entities,
Hegel hypostatizes to realities par excellence. Still under the spell
of Hegel's logicism, Feuerbach puts this in logical terms: whatever is subject Hegel describes as if it were a predicate and vice
versa. For example, instead of admitting that reason is an attribute of humanity and of humanity alone, he separates it from
its true subject and hypostatizes it; and eventually this hypostatized
reason prevails over human reality and becomes its subject, to
degrade human nature to a mere predicate of reason. "Hegel
thinks all objects only as predicates of Thought which thinks itself."[32]
Marx was to echo this in his critique of Hegel's philosophy of the

---

1, 1865, contained in K. Marx—F. Engels, *Ausgewählte Briefe* (Berlin-Stutt-
gart, 1953) 181; quoted by Schmidt, 144.
[30] *MEGA* I, 3, 151; tr. Milligan, 145.
[31] Feuerbach, II, 225.
[32] *Ibid.* 239.

state: "Everywhere Hegel makes of the idea a subject and of the subject properly speaking ... a predicate."[33]

Obviously Feuerbach has more in mind than simply a question of logic. By inverting the relation between subject and predicate, he claims, Hegel succeeds in ascribing autonomous reality to what in fact are abstract predicates. The inversion of subject and predicate entails a reassessment of reality: autonomous reality becomes derived and vice versa. To this Feuerbach opposes his claim that the "real relation of thought to being is as follows: being is subject, thought is predicate. Thought proceeds from being, but being does not proceed from thought."[34]

This, of course, is a meaningful criticism of Hegel only if one identifies "thought" with individual human thought. But this precisely is what Feuerbach wants to say: all predicates attributed by Hegel to the Absolute in fact are predicates of man which were separated from their only legitimate subject and thereupon hypostatized. This hypostatizing separation produces the impression that pseudo entities such as thought and reason are autonomously active. Hegel writes as if thought and reason were developing and acting; in fact, however, all real events take place in the realm of Hegel's predicate (since they are the true subjects).[35]

To this Feuerbach adds another idea. He accuses Hegel of having alienated man from himself, that is, of having deprived him of his natural absoluteness. By positing man's essence outside man, in hypostatized predicates of man, both theology and speculative philosophy ascribe man's own perfections to a being different from man which does not even so much as exist. And the more they exalt the Absolute, the more they degrade man. As Feuerbach puts it in the *Essence of Christianity*, "to empty the real world and to enrich God is one and the same act."[36] Eventually, it is true, theology and speculative philosophy will try to reunite what they have separated. Theology, after it has ascribed all of man's perfections to God, will allow for a reunion

[33] *MEGA* I, 1/1, 410; cf. 407, 447, 473, 477, 537, etc.
[34] Feuerbach, II, 239.
[35] Cf. *MEGA* I, 1/1, 410.
[36] Feuerbach, VI, 89 ff.

in terms of grace, of mystical union, of beatific vision. Similarly, Hegel had reunited man with the Absolute in terms of a series of "mediations," both speculative and historical. But as the separation was artificial to begin with, the union never really succeeds. In the end what is lacking in Hegelianism is "immediate unity, immediate certainty, immediate truth."[37]

This insistence on immediacy reveals the ultimate roots of Feuerbach's difference from Hegel. Usually Feuerbach's atheism and materialism are viewed as a reaction against Hegel's extreme spiritualism. Exactly as German Idealism, it is argued, was rooted in a profound distrust of the immediately perceived and sensible (and, consequently, of the material world), Feuerbach's anti-idealism feeds on an even more profound mistrust of everything which can be grasped only by abstract thought. As if surfeited with abstractions and spiritual realities, Feuerbach (and after him Marx) enthusiastically turns toward the concrete, the immediately lived and experienced, the sensible, indeed the sensual.[38] It is pointed out that Feuerbach never got weary of repeating that only the objects of sense, of perception, are "indubitable and immediately certain."[39] In short, it is argued that because German Idealism still shared the conviction of classical philosophy that the "really real" is spirit, reason, idea—and indeed precisely because German Idealism had exaggerated this claim—the post-Hegelian generation looked for true reality in those realms in which spirituality and rationality appear only as epiphenomena: in the realm of matter, of the bodily sensible, of economy.[40]

It is true that Feuerbach constantly emphasizes that the "mystery of being" reveals itself only to life in being lived, to sensible perception, indeed to passion.[41] But if Feuerbach's "materialism" is viewed too exclusively as a mere antithesis to idealist "spiritualism," the centering of his interest around man, not around matter, becomes unintelligible. Both the French materialists of the eight-

[37] *Ibid.* II, 217.
[38] Cf. Löwith₃, 93.
[39] Feuerbach, II, 217.
[40] E.g., Löwith₃, 156 ff.; Gollwitzer in *Marxismusstudien* IV, 39.
[41] Feuerbach, II, 287 ff.; 297 ff.

eenth century (Lamettrie, Holbach, Helvetius, and so on) and the German materialists of the second half of the nineteenth century (Vogt, Moleschott, Büchner and Engels) were almost exclusively interested in matter. Feuerbach's "materialism," on the contrary, is little more than a corollary to his anthropology, and the same, though in a somewhat different way, is true of the young Marx. Some may want to argue that Feuerbach did not manage to free himself completely from the idealist heritage. But, then, who did? In this light it becomes perfectly unintelligible to say that Marx, who in a sense was a more radical materialist than Feuerbach, reverted from Feuerbach to Hegel—a claim often intimated by those defending the above interpretation.

The importance of Feuerbach's insistence on "immediacy" has to be seen in connection with Hegel's idea of history as a process both of the humanization of the Divine Being and of the deification of man. As Hegel saw it, the unity of God and man appeared for the first time in Christ; and history afterwards became the gradual expansion and universal realization of this fundamental "reconciliation that heals the pain and inward suffering of man." In this process, just as Christ died and was transfigured into "universal" spirit, and just as the originally individual Incarnation of the Logos is realized with ever-increasing universality, so God abandons his transcendence and man transcends his finiteness. God becomes man and man becomes God.

"But this unity must not be superficially conceived, as if God were only man, and man, without further condition, were God."[42] Though it may, and in fact has, become true that God is man and man is God, this unity never will be simple identity. It will always remain the dialectical unity of two totally different things. It will always remain a unity *achieved in terms of innumerable mediations*. The mediating steps, instead of dissolving into nothing, will forever remain an inextinguishable seal both of the humanity of God and of the divinity of man. To the revolutionary impatience of those who claim that man *is* God without further ado, Hegel opposes the patience of someone who knows the secret

---

[42] Hegel$_2$, XI, 416; tr. Sibree, 324.

both of the Absolute and of history: "impatience asks for the impossible, namely, the achievement of the end without the corresponding means .... Even the World Spirit had the patience to cross its form through the long extension of time."[43]

Feuerbach is no longer able to summon up this kind of patience. In this respect he differs from *all* Left Hegelians. In fact, in spite of his almost existentialist mentality he is an early herald of late nineteenth-century positivism. His criticism of Christianity and Hegelianism is an attempt to show that in order to reach divinity, man needs neither a speculative ascent nor a wearisome historical process. For he is divine by his very nature. Whereas all other Hegelians from Richter to Hess took it for granted that man cannot escape his finite condition except by reaching a new level, either in his speculative or in his material existence, Feuerbach simply denied Hegel's claim that the divinity of man, and thus also salvation, is different from natural man, that it is something to be achieved, that it is mediated by a lengthy and laborious process. Whereas Hegel had insisted that man is God only insofar as he "annuls the merely Natural and Limited in his Spirit and elevates himself to God,"[44] Feuerbach declared that he simply has to recover that which always was his—his own divine nature.

This, incidentally, is the reason why Feuerbach was so utterly ahistorical a thinker and why he was comparatively little interested in *praxis*. In order that the all-embracing reconciliation be achieved and final salvation be brought about, Hegel and all Hegelians needed history; Feuerbach only needed nature. And since his man is divine by his very essence, there is no need to "criticize" or to transform the world. As soon as he has realized that religion and Hegelianism are nothing but a belief in ghosts,[45] he recognizes himself as the rightful owner of all the perfections alienated from him. Thereafter man simply has to give way to his divinity.[46]

---

[43] Hegel$_2$, II, 31 ff.; tr. Baillie, 90. Cf. VII, 117, tr. Knox, 51, where Hegel speaks of the "length of time" which, in spite of all human "impatience of opining," the *Weltgeist* needs for its progress.

[44] Hegel$_2$, XI, 416; tr. Sibree, 324.

[45] Cf. Feuerbach, II, 227.

[46] Gollwitzer, in *Marxismusstudien* IV, 38, points to Feuerbach, II, 219,

In short, to claim that Feuerbach's philosophy "contains elements of a critique of pride," even though it dispenses with the notion of a transmundane God and sets up the human race as the supreme being,[47] is completely to misunderstand Feuerbach's intention. Far from initiating a "critique of pride," he is interested only in an *"ensarcosis* or incarnation of the Logos"[48] which would make possible the elimination of the complicated process of self-elevation and the achievement of the unity of God and man by a simple return to natural man. Hegel and his pupils may have been gnostics in the sense that they tried to break man's natural condition, but what Feuerbach is doing resembles a gnostic "short circuit." Instead of trying to transcend man's finite condition he simply declares man's finite condition infinite. The task of philosophy, then, consists in "putting the infinite into the finite,"[49] that is, in re-discovering the original infinity of natural finite man.

All in all Feuerbach's "empiricism" and "materialism" are far from simply being an antithetic reaction to Hegel's rationalism and "spiritualism." Feuerbach sought the "really real" in matter as opposed to spirit, in the senses as opposed to reason, in perception as opposed to abstraction, the living of life as opposed to philosophy, because he restricted Hegel's speculative reconciliation and deification of man to man's primitive, prespeculative nature. Hegel conceived the self-realization of man as a transcendence of the limited and natural biological level; Feuerbach, on the contrary, condemned all such transcendence as "alienation." In this sense he is a precursor of all "philosophies of life" from Nietzsche to Klages.

and argues that Feuerbach was not such an apolitical thinker after all. Of course, Feuerbach was well aware that, after has man overcome his state of alienation, he will be obliged to reorganize society, to build up a new kind of state, and so on. But here "politics" does not mean the building up of something radically new (as most Left Hegelians understood it); it simply means the organization of life according to the ever-present divinity of man.

[47] Cf. Tucker, 93 ff.

[48] Feuerbach's letter to Hegel; cf. Hegel₄, III, 245. On this letter see Löwith₃, 85 ff.; Stuke, 52 ff.

[49] Feuerbach, II, 230.

18: CIVIL SOCIETY

Marx never joined in Feuerbach's rather primitive idolatry of natural man. In his *Critique of the Hegelian Philosophy of the State*[50] he simply took over Feuerbach's scheme for criticizing Hegelianism. Again and again, by an almost microscopically close analysis, he tries to show that Hegel's political theory turns reality upside down. Instead of admitting that family, civil society, public opinion, sovereigns, and such are the natural "ground" of the state, Hegel describes them as if they were "a determination of, a result of, a product of, the Idea." Hegel does not "develop his thinking from the object"; he develops the object from a thought "which is perfectly satisfied with itself."[51] The *Logic*, instead of serving as a proof *of* the state, actually is proved *by* the state.[52]

However, as the analysis proceeds, instead of merely showing that man, family, civil society, and such are primary realities and the state only a secondary reality, Marx increasingly tends to say that the state is a hypostatized abstraction comparable to Feuerbach's God; indeed, that the whole realm of politics is a realm of "alienation" comparable to that discovered by Feuerbach in religion.

---

[50] Cf. Rubel$_2$, 55 ff.; Popitz, 68 ff.; Lewalter, 645 ff.; Derbolav, 271 ff.; cf. also J. Hyppolite, "La conception hégélienne de l'état et sa critique par Karl Marx," *Cahiers internationaux de sociologie* (1947) 142-161, and Sh. Avineri, "Marx's Critique of Hegel's 'Philosophy of Right' in its systematic setting," *Cahiers de l'ISEA* (August, 1966) 45-81.

[51] *MEGA* I, 1/1, 414.

[52] *Ibid.* 418.

This, of course, does not mean that Marx reduces the state to a compound of abstract predicates. He is enough of a realist to acknowledge that, unlike God, the state really exists. But the obvious analogy between Hegel's "theology" and his political philosophy increasingly suggests to him that political solutions are comparable to both theological and speculative solutions. Hegel's speculative salvation in fact saved nobody; it was only a "transfiguration," a self-delusion. But do political solutions save anybody? Are not the freedom and the equality granted by constitutions as illusory as Hegel's speculative salvation or the salvation promised by Christianity for the afterlife? Christians, though equal in heaven, are unequal on earth. May not men be equal in the heaven of their political conception, remaining perfectly unequal as far as the "earthly existence" of real society goes? In the end, is politics not "the religion of a nation's life, the heaven of its universality as opposed to the earthly existence of its reality"?[53] Must not the whole "political sphere" be reincorporated into real human society just as God has to be reincorporated in man, must it not still be translated into practice just as theoretical salvation has to be actualized?

It has seldom been noticed that this extension of Feuerbach's notion of alienation to politics is thoroughly incompatible with Feuerbach's original conception. For the Feuerbachian "alienation," being after all only a misguided evaluation of an otherwise sound reality, required merely an adjustment in knowledge. Though by his very nature divine, man has a wrong idea of himelf; as soon as this idea is corrected, his divinity will be restored. In fact, his underlying divinity never had been challenged.

But a reality such as the state cannot be abrogated by revealing its unsound character. Even if one admitted the efficacy of a "critique" such as that of Bauer, it still remained true that the *world* had to be changed, not only *ideas about* the world. But if the *real* world was to be transformed, if *reality*, not only human thought, needed to be corrected, then it could not be true that the humanity underlying political alienation was divine. In short,

[53] *Ibid.* 436.

almost without being aware of it Marx reverts from Feuerbach to Hegel even while he is using Feuerbach's "transformative criticism." By being a more radical realist than Feuerbach, by reducing thought alienation to real alienation, Marx is forced to admit that the divinity of man is still something to be achieved.

However, Marx for the time being is still interested in understanding more than in acting. Contrary to most other Left Hegelians, he does not really accuse Hegel of having identified Prussia with the rational state.[54] He is well aware that Hegel's "state" is a construction rather than an image of reality, a construction and an ideal in terms of which Hegel tried to overcome the individualistic dissipation of mankind in modern "civil society." But he indeed accuses Hegel of having modeled this ideal on the pattern of Prussia. Accordingly, he denounces Hegel's whole conception of the state as an "unfortunate hybrid" in which the form belies the content as much as the content belies the form.[55] "Hegel is not to blame for having depicted the essence of the modern state as in fact it is; but he indeed is to blame for pretending that the state as in fact it is, is the essence of the state."[56]

Whereas most other Hegelians accused Hegel either of accommodating his conception of state to the "existence" of the Prussian Kingdom or of justifying Prussia by transfiguring its reactionary existence into a progressive idea, Marx is prepared to admit that Hegel's philosophy of the state is an adequate picture of Prussia's existence and thus a significant contribution to knowledge. What he objects to is Hegel's mistaking Prussia's existence for an embodiment of the ideal state. We witness here the first emergence of Marx's later notion of *ideology*. For an ideology, as Marx understands this expression, is a picture or reflection of a "wrong" world which, though adequately depicting reality, does not reveal its wrongness. The ideological reflection is both true and false. It is true insofar as it depicts reality as it is; it is false insofar as it does not express the wrongness of this existing reality. Contrary to ideology, "science" has to depict reality as it is in such a way

[54] Cf. Weil, 105 ff.
[55] *MEGA* I, 1/1, 500 ff.
[56] *Ibid.*

as at the same time to make its "ontological wrongness" evident.

But what exactly is it that Hegel's philosophy of the state adequately depicts and of which nevertheless it does not reveal the wrongness, thus confusing actual existence with the Idea? Hegel describes the state as something above and beyond civil society; like most of his forerunners since Rousseau, he seeks to solve the problems of civil society in terms of a state separated from, and hovering above, society. Of course Hegel is right insofar as in modern times the state has detached itself from its natural ground, society. Nonetheless his solutions of the problems of civil society are no real solution. They are only the theoretical counterpart of a historical development in the course of which man increasingly was trying to solve his *real* problems in an *unreal* beyond. Just as religion tries to solve man's problems in terms of a realm which is outside man's reality, political philosophy tries to solve society's problems in a "political sphere" which is beyond society's real existence. Moreover, a political philosophy such as that of Hegel is only the theoretical counterpart of an alienation in the order of being, of real society, just as religion is the theoretical counterpart of man's ontological wretchedness.

To be more precise, Marx accuses Hegel of not having overcome the duality of *homme* and *citoyen* which since Rousseau's times had haunted all political philosophy. As Rousseau had pointed out, *l'homme de nos jours*, man in modern society, lives a sort of schizophrenic life in two heterogeneous realms: on the one hand, he is an independent individual with self-will and a private conscience; on the other hand, he is the member of a society which almost inevitably curtails his self-will and constantly threatens to violate his conscience. How can man give in both to his *penchants*, his individualistic inclinations, and to his *devoirs*, his social obligations? How can he both keep his individuality and be a sterling member of society?

The problem obviously consists in harmonizing everyone's self-will and conscience with the will of society as a whole, that is, ultimately, of the state. The solution advanced by Rousseau in his famous *Contrat Social* (1762) is well known. Each member of society has to give up all his rights to the whole community.

This total self-sacrifice makes emerge a *volonté générale*, a sovereign and infallible common will which grants to each individual a new harmonious freedom. In short, Rousseau tries to solve the "contradiction" between the individual and society by appealing to a sort of Absolute which, being rooted in a universal consent, grants a freedom compatible both with the self-willing individual (for it has given up its self-will) and with society (for the *volonté générale* consists of the consent of the majority of the members of a given community).

Hegel, it is true, criticizes Rousseau. But his criticism aims exclusively at Rousseau's appeal to an entity as arbitrary as a common consent, not to his appeal to a mystifying Absolute beyond both the individuals and society. Consent, he argues, being a form of individual will, lacks all objective universality; it is always revocable and, in general, is dependent upon the caprice of individuals. In the end the Absolute to which Rousseau appeals is nothing but a sort of common denominator of the self-will of a number of individuals (*das Gemeinschaftliche des Willens*). Rousseau should have appealed, not to consent, but to the rational core of will as such (*das an und für sich Vernünftige des Willens*).[57] In short, the only way of reconciling the individuals with society consists in transcending society toward a superstructure which is perfect and efficient rationality, the rational state.

For the state, as Hegel views it, is an organization whose very essence is "substantial will which thinks and knows itself and carries out whatever it knows and insofar as it knows it."[58] Of course, Hegel is aware that this state of his is an ideal. But it is not an ideal to be actualized in a dim future. Rather, it is an ideal comparable to Plato's "idea." Political philosophy, as Hegel understands it, is not concerned with particular states: "one has to consider the Idea, this true God, as it is in itself; not particular constitutions." All existing states have to be measured against this Idea; after all, they are parts of the real world and thus partake in the "caprice, chance, and error" characteristic of it. But if

---

[57] Hegel₂, VII, 330; tr. Knox, 156 ff.
[58] *Ibid.* 328; tr. Knox, 155.

an organization deserves the title of "state" at all, it partakes in, and therefore contains, the integral elements of the "idea of State." "The ugliest of men, or a criminal, or an invalid, or a cripple, is still always a living man. The affirmative, life, subsists despite its defects, and it is this affirmative with which we are concerned."[59]

We may add a few words about why Hegel considered it imperative to overcome natural society. It is seldom noticed that the first radical criticism of modern bourgeois society was raised by Hegel, not by Marx. Marx himself was the first to acknowledge it. He explicitly qualifies Hegel's analysis of modern society as "noteworthy" because it describes civil society as a *bellum omnium contra omnes*,[60] as a war of everyone against everybody. And this is indeed what Hegel has in mind. Civil society, as he sees it, is characterized by a radical "particularization" of mankind. It is an organization of egoists interrelated in such a way as to make the self-assertion and satisfaction of one dependent upon the self-assertion and satisfaction of another.

We cannot discuss here the difficult question as to whether Hegel's analysis of civil society only concerns "a mere abstraction, a one-sided dialectical phase which is superseded in the state,"[61] or whether it contains Hegel's view of modern society. One will probably have to grant both. In any case it is obvious that Hegel modeled his analysis of civil society on the social world as he knew it. And this he viewed as a world governed by economic rather than "ethical" laws.[62] Civil society is governed by an odd "mixture of physical necessity and caprice," not by reason.[63] Hegel, following Fichte, describes the political structure inherent in this society as based on want and necessity, as a mere "external state."[64] The members of this "state" live exclusively for the satisfaction of the wants, which in fact are "accidental caprice and subjective pleasure"

---

[59] *Ibid.* 336; tr. Knox, 279.
[60] *MEGA* I, 1/1, 450.
[61] Cf. Stace, 413 ff.
[62] Hegel$_2$, VII, 270 ff.; tr. Knox, 126 ff.
[63] *Ibid.* 262; tr. Knox, 122.
[64] *Ibid.* 263; tr. Knox, 123. Cf. *MEGA* I, 1/1, 595.

and lead to debauchery and misery and to the "physical and ethical corruption characteristic of both."[65]

Last but not least, this society generates poverty without being able to remedy it. For, on the one hand, it leads to an accumulation of riches; and, on the other hand, it leads to a "particularization and narrowing of specialized labor and thus to a dependence and misery of the class bound to it."[66] And there seems to be no adequate way of curbing this development. To help the poor by charities amounts to satisfying their needs without the mediation of labor, a solution which whould seem to be both "against the very principles of civil society and against the self-esteem and honor of individuals." Yet to help the poor by giving them adequate labor amounts to increasing production "in the excess of which the very evil consists." In the end, then, despite all its excess of wealth civil society is not rich enough "to check excessive poverty and the creation of a penurious rabble."[67]

Considering this gloomy picture, which undoubtedly redounds to the honor of Hegel's realism, and remembering that Hegel considers it his task to reconcile man with reality, one easily understands why Hegel describes civil society only as a "difference which intervenes between family and state"[68] and tries to transcend it toward a more rational order, the state. Of course Hegel's grandiose conception of the state solves all problems except the most pressing one, the problem of ever-increasing pauperization.

It is difficult to decide if when he wrote his critique of Hegel, Marx had already studied paragraphs 182-256 of the *Philosophy of Right* containing Hegel's analysis of modern society as just described.[69] We possess only Marx's commentary on paragraphs 261-313, and there is nothing to indicate that another commentary on earlier paragraphs ever existed. In fact, it would even seem that Marx never fully realized how close Hegel's criticism of the *bürgerliche Gesellschaft* came to his own conception of capitalist

---

[65] *Ibid.* 265; tr. Knox, 123.
[66] *Ibid.* 318; tr. Knox, 149.
[67] *Ibid.* 319; tr. Knox, 150.
[68] *Ibid.* 262; tr. Knox, 266.
[69] Cf. Heiss$_3$, 178.

society. This is not as amazing as it sounds. For when Marx began to develop his economic doctrine, he was already beyond the point of rereading Hegel. Moreover, Hegel's analysis was based upon the insights of modern economists; Hegel explicitly quotes Smith, Say, and Ricardo. Marx only had to read these writers with the eyes of a trained Hegelian to come to conclusions similar to those of Hegel. Finally, the criticism of bourgeois society was already a Left Hegelian shibboleth before Marx took it over; as we shall see, Marx's eventual commitment to what Hegel called the "penurious rabble" was prefigured by the Left Hegelian criticism of the "bourgeois philistines," which Marx only had to connect with the famous Master-Slave Dialectic of the *Phenomenology of Mind*.

For the moment we are concerned with Marx's criticism of Hegel's conception of the state. From what we have seen we may anticipate his reaction: this whole political synthesis is a "mystification." However, Marx opposes Hegel's conception of the state neither because it is Utopian nor because it does violence to the real individual. On the contrary, Marx agrees with Hegel that the only way to reconcile the individual with society consists in transcending the particularized social atoms toward something "universal," a path which at the same time would entail an ultimate development of man's very nature. What he opposes is Hegel's claim that such a "universal" must be different from society itself, from real man in his social interdependence.

Hegel insisted that civil society and the state differ, because he realized that prepolitical society is governed by economic laws and because he could not see how a society governed by economic laws instead of by reason might develop into something truly "universal." Only by transcending economic necessity, that is, by transcending the merely social level, could a true universality of man be achieved. When Marx argues against this conception, as in fact he does throughout his commentary, he does not mean to say that present civil society *is* the ideal which Hegel described as the state. Nor does he claim that the state should be dissolved into civil society as *presently* it is. Though he never says so explicitly, it is quite obvious that he argues with Hegel that present civil society has to be overcome. But he argues that present civil society has to be superseded by another kind of society, not vaulted over by a political abstraction. Which is to say that Marx translates Hegel's *logical* sequence of civil and ideal society into a *historical* one. To him the ideal which Hegel believed possible only in a realm of political superstructures is a potentiality and therefore the future of social man himself.

Two points are obvious: this idea is based upon Feuerbach's demand for "immediacy" and it inevitably leads to emphasizing the importance of economics. Just as man, according to Feuerbach, does not need an Absolute different from himself to achieve his ultimate completion, society does not need a superstructure to develop all its potentialities. The true locus of freedom and, in general, of man's ultimate completion is the level of social interdependence, not a religious or political "heaven." The infinite is the finite, at least potentially; man's and society's ultimate perfection is to be found in man and in society themselves. But Hegel had taught Marx that "society" is governed by economic laws. Accordingly, a few months after completing his critique of Hegel, Marx will turn to economic studies.

But at present he still does not fully realize the importance of economics. He knows only that politics has to be reduced to social problems. This is best illustrated by his concept of democracy.[70] When he praises democracy, Marx does not have in mind a republic as opposed to a monarchy. The dispute between monarchy and republic is one within the boundaries of the "abstract state." Marx is not interested in a republican constitution. What he is interested in is an organization of society which would succeed in absorbing the abstract state with all its accessories. As Marx describes it, democracy is a *society*, not a state; a social, not a political organization; a society performing all functions ascribed by Hegel to the state without at all entailing a political superstructure.

Of course Marx still did not have a very clear idea as to how such a democracy would look in detail. Therefore he restricted himself to

[70] Cf. *MEGA* I, 1/1, 434 ff.

applying the Feuerbachian scheme once more. Just as anthropology
is the "secret" of theology and man is the "secret" of God, so
democracy is the "secret" of all states. It is the "unraveled riddle
of all constitutions," a political organization which in fact is social
rather than political; all previous political elements are reduced
to their "real ground, to real man, to the real nation" and put
into effect as "their own enterprise."

How much at that point was Marx influenced by the French
socialists? He explicitly refers to "recent French authors" who
had claimed that true democracy would make the political state
disappear, and there can be no doubt that he has in mind Saint-
Simon and Proudhon. Still, the allusion is so vague as hardly
to suggest that Marx had yet read these authors.[71] Probably
he knew about their basic ideas through Hess. In any case, contrary to Rubel,[72] for example, I cannot believe that at that time
Marx was already thinking of "communism." No doubt he already
realized that all contemporary problems can be reduced to social
ones, but he still was not truly aware of the equation of "social"
and "economic." The expression 'communistic' appears only once,
and it is easy to show that, when using this expression, Marx did
not have in mind "communism" in the sense of Hess, for example.[73]

[71] That political problems needed to be replaced by social ones at that time
was seen by many. Thus, for example, V. Hugo, in his *Littérature et philosophie
mêlées* of 1834, spoke of the necessity of a "substitution of social questions
for political questions"; cf. Evans, 31. Insofar as this idea was also suggested
to Marx by L. Stein's book on French socialism and communism and, in particular, by Hess' review of Stein's book, see Hess₂, 198 ff. It might seem meaningful
to say that around this time Marx began to think as a "communist"; however,
see fn. 73.

[72] Rubel₂, 64. On the reference to "French authors" see *MEGA* I, 1/1, 435.

[73] *MEGA* I, 1/1, 496: "Die Atomistik, in die sich die bürgerliche Gesellschaft in ihrem *politischen Akt* stürzt, geht notwendig daraus hervor, dass das
Gemeinwesen, das kommunistische Wesen, worin der Einzelne existiert, die bürgerliche Gesellschaft getrennt vom Staat oder *der politische Staat eine Abstrak-
tion* von ihr ist." Instead of 'Gemeinwesen,' Marx first wrote 'Kommune.'
This suggests that the expression 'kommunistisches Wesen,' as added to
'Gemeinwesen,' is only supposed to emphasize that the expression 'Gemeinwesen' here does not have the usual sense of "public affairs." What Marx
wants to say is that, in contemporary society, political activity results in an

Marx's last utterance on democracy is somewhat puzzling: he calls it the genus of all political constitutions "as a specific constitution." Marx seems to be influenced here by Feuerbach's claim that man achieves his ultimate perfection by embracing the human species; until the *German Ideology* he is to adhere to this somewhat confused identification of "social" and "generic." Still his meaning is clear. Though, as Hegel has pointed out,[74] all constitutions are based upon, and rooted in, real men of a living society, they always remain idealizing constructions which make man forget his real situation. In democracy, on the contrary, the constitution will have ceased to be an abstract ideal. It will be the *intrinsic form* of a society which, then, is truly "ideal"; for it is the earthly actualization of what other societies only possess in the abstract heaven of political constitutions. "In democracy, the formal principle is, at the same time, the material principle."[75]

However, this democracy still lies in the future. In order to bring it about, present society has to be transformed. Accordingly, after having replaced Hegel's "state" by "democratic society," Marx sets about criticizing civil society. Generally this critique still follows that of Hegel. It aims at the contemporary particularization of mankind which Hegel had taken to be the basic character of civil society. "Contemporary civil society is the accomplished principle of individualism, individual existence is the ultimate end."[76]

However, for the first time there also crops up the idea which will be the leitmotif of the *Manuscripts of 1844*: by considering his activity, his labor, and his profession as mere means for the fulfilment of the ego, man becomes the servant of his own products. Thus, for example, in criticizing Hegel's doctrine on the political significance of primogeniture Marx writes that "compared to the brutal stupidity of independent private property, the insecurity of trade is elegiac, the mania of making money is pathetic (dramatic),

"atomism," rather than in socially relating people to one another, and that, consequently, contemporary society is split into two realms: an earthly, secular one (civil society) and a heavenly one (the state). Cf. Rubel$_2$, 74.

[74] Cf. Hegel$_2$, VII, 376; tr. Knox, 178 ff., 286 ff.

[75] *MEGA* I, 1/1, 435.

[76] *Ibid.* 498.

the variability of estates is a serious fate (tragic), and the dependence upon state property is even ethical."[77] For, as Marx explains, there may be injustice and suffering involved in the life of a trader, of a peasant, or of a civil servant. But their dependence still is a dependence of "men upon men." As opposed to this, the landowner is dependent upon a thing. In fact, the *Majoratsherr*, the owner of an entailed estate, is only an *accidens* of his property. Landed property "honors the first-born of the house as its own attribute. The thing is subject, man is predicate. Human will becomes a property of property."[78]

These passages, it is true, are primarily aimed at Hegel's defense of primogeniture and estates in general. But Marx opposes Hegel's defense because estates seem to degrade man to an attribute of the soil he owns, not because estates are based upon an unjust distribution of land. What is wrong with civil society, in the end, is that man is degraded to a predicate of his own products, that relations between men are mediated by things.

In this sense Marx even will go so far as to admit that Hegel's inversion of "subject" and "predicate" is an adequate picture of the real world. In civil society man in fact has become the predicate of entities different from man. He is no longer the genuine ground of the state. In a letter of May, 1843, to Ruge, after having stated that the only "idea of despotism" is "scorn for man or scorned man," he adds that "as compared to all other ideas, this one has the advantage of being a fact." In contemporary monarchy man really *is* dehumanized, deprived of his character of ultimate subject. Only because he is so dehumanized, the monarch does not, and cannot, treat him as an independent being, as the ultimate subject and end of politics. After all, if a monarch sees only men who "drown before his eyes, and for his sake, in the mud of ordinary life," how should he not adhere to the idealist notion that man is only a predicate of the state? "The king of Prussia will be the man of his time as long as the inverted world is the real one."[79]

[77] *Ibid.* 522.
[78] *Ibid.* 527.   Cf. Popitz, 84 ff.
[79] *Ibid.* 563.

19: HUMAN EMANCIPATION
AND THE PROLETARIAT

At the end of October, 1843, Marx left Kreuznach for Paris in order to edit together with Ruge the *Deutsch-Französische Jahrbücher*, a review which was supposed to promote a synthesis between French political reality and German philosophy.[80] However, all efforts to establish such a periodical proved unavailing; not a single French author was prepared to contribute and even Feuerbach declined to collaborate. The first and only issue was published in February, 1844. It contained three contributions by Marx: three letters to Ruge which, together with letters by Ruge, Feuerbach, and Bakunin, served as a sort of introduction; a lengthy review of two books by Bruno Bauer on the "Jewish Question"; and the famous introduction to the critique of the Hegelian philosophy of Right in which Marx for the first time owned up to his commitment to the "cause of the proletariat."

Apart from containing some rather important recapitulations of already familar ideas, these three contributions center around two new problems: the opposition between a merely political and a truly human emancipation and the idea of the "proletarian revolution."

As we have seen in the preceding section, his study of Hegel's political philosophy had helped Marx to free himself both from

---

[80] The idea of such a synthesis was rather common among the Left Hegelians. It was emphasized, for example, by Feuerbach (II, 236) and by Ruge in his preface to Bakunin's "Die Reaktion in Deutschland." Cf. *Hallische Jahrbücher* (1842) 985 ff., where Bakunin wrote under a French pseudonym. Even Rotteck's and Welcker's *Staatslexikon* speaks of a "ridiculous Gallomania" of the Left Hegelians; cf. Suppl. II, 755.

the overwhelming shadow of Hegel and from the political way
of thinking characteristic of most of his German contemporaries.
As regards his attitude toward Hegel, Marx has now reached a
temporarily final formula. Alluding to the backward political
situation in Germany as opposed to that in France, he claims that
Hegel's political philosophy is the only German reality corresponding
to the stage reached by the "official modern present." Because
of Hegel and his followers, Germany with all its hopeless backwardness still can claim to be "contemporary" after all. "Just
as old nations witnessed their prehistory in imagination, in *mythology*, we Germans have witnessed our posthistory in thought, in
philosophy. We are philosophical contemporaries of the present
without being its *historical* contemporaries. German philosophy
is the *ideal prolongation* of German history."[81]

This almost sounds as if Marx wanted to justify Hegel rather
than to criticize him. However, one must not forget that his
critique already attacked modern "bourgeois" society, of which
France for Marx was the most developed instance. What Marx
wants to say is that it no longer makes any sense to criticize German
political realities. They are hopelessly obsolete. And so are the
Left Hegelian critics attacking them. The only German "reality"
still worth criticizing is the "ideal prolongation of German history,"
Hegelianism. And Hegel's philosophy, in turn, has to be criticized
because even the historical reality to which it corresponds, namely,
contemporary French and Anglo-Saxon society, is going out of date.

In his doctoral dissertation Marx had claimed that the "immediate
actualization" of Hegelianism is afflicted with contradictions. Now
he advances a new justification of this claim, a justification referring to the relation between Hegelianism and the "real world" rather
than to the intrinsic structure of Absolute Knowledge. It is no longer the "totality character" of Hegelianism which prohibits its
"immediate actualization." What at present prohibits the putting
of Hegelianism into practice is the fact that even the social *reality*
which corresponds to Hegelianism is obsolete. The order of being,
of *real* history, is beginning to outstrip even the most advanced

---

[81] *MEGA* I, 1/1, 612; tr. Bottomore, 49.

outpost of thought. Still it remains true that Hegelianism is "the most consistent, the richest, and the ultimate" version of philosophic thought in the traditional sense of the term. To criticize Hegelianism, therefore, amounts to criticizing the *essential* backwardness of *all* theory, of philosophy as such.

Of course, to negate philosophy cannot mean to mutter a "few angry and banal phrases"; it cannot mean that one simply may turn one's back upon philosophy. Political practitioners who think that way (Marx seems to have in mind South German liberals) forget that up to now the living buds of the German nation have only proliferated in German minds, not in German practice. To overcome theoretical philosophy even in its highest form cannot mean that one ought to consider it as something which is beneath the political practice of contemporary Germany. It can mean only that one ought to transcend theory toward action. "You cannot abolish philosophy except by actualizing it."

On the other hand, however, to actualize philosophy does not mean to criticize the German world in terms of Hegelianism, as Bauer and his friends at Berlin did. For Hegelianism itself belongs to the world to be criticized. The demands and consequences of Hegelianism can be retained only in terms of a negation of Hegelianism. The only way of actualizing philosophy consists in abolishing it.[82]

This slogan about the correlation between an *Aufhebung* and a *Verwirklichung* of philosophy has often been hailed as one of the most original utterances of the young Marx. However, as it stands, it would seem to add very little to the ideas advanced by Cieszkowski, Bauer, and Ruge. In fact, around the same time Feuerbach had formulated almost exactly the same idea: *"True* Philosophy is the negation of philosophy—is *no* philosophy."[83] In the end it states no more than the necessity of overcoming original Hegelianism, that the only way of overcoming it consists in transcending it toward *praxis*, and that this *praxis* must take care to be post-Hegelian rather than pre-Hegelian, transcending Absolute Knowl-

[82] *Ibid.* 613; tr. Bottomore, 50 ff.
[83] Feuerbach, II, 409.

edge rather than falling back upon something beneath it. In 1843, with the possible exception of the small circle of purists that had formed around the Bauer brothers at Berlin, most Left Hegelians already agreed that the "critique" ought to have some palpable results instead of constantly going astray in the thicket of its own verbalism.

One may even go further and say that Marx in 1843 still had not reached Cieszkowski's notion of *praxis* as concrete social activity. *Praxis* to him still is "critique." He speaks of a "critique in a hand-to-hand fight," it is true. But if one reads the passage in question carefully, one has to admit that Marx is far from asking his fellow critics to go out in the streets and begin a brawl. He only means that the critic should cease to be nice to his object. Instead of showing consideration for the Germans he should take away from them the last chance of self-deception and resignation. "The actual pressure must be made still more pressing by adding to it a consciousness of the pressure; the shame must be made still more shameful by making it public."[84] The cynical lack of consideration for fellow men expressed in these words was nothing new either. As early as 1841 Bauer had written about a "terrorism of the true theory."[85]

One may object that, after all, Marx speaks of a "revolution." But at that time most radical Left Hegelians spoke about it. As early as 1841 Bruno Bauer had written: "Philosophy wants a revolution, a revolution against everything positive, including history." Based upon the "true theory" of man and history, philosophy had to give the signal for a *Sturz des Bestehenden*, for an overthrow of the existing order.[86] And in 1842 Bruno's brother Edgar wrote that now philosophy no longer restricts itself to sending to the front ideas against ideas; it sends men against men.[87]

[84] *MEGA* I, 1/1, 610; tr. Bottomore, 47.
[85] Cf. Bauer's letter to Marx, *MEGA* I, 1/2, 247. In *Die gute Sache der Freiheit und meine eigene Angelegenheit* (Zürich-Winterthur, 1842) 207, Bauer calls the true theory "reckless." Cf. Stuke, 159 ff.
[86] Cf. Stuke, 164.
[87] *Hallische Jahrbücher* (1842) col. 1187.

This is not to say that in 1843 Marx still embraced Bauer's idea of a purely theoretical critique. But it is important to see wherein the difference lies. Marx was neither more radical nor more revolutionary minded than his former friend. And he was more realistic only in one respect. He asked himself the crucial question, In what way can the critique become truly efficacious? This is what Marx means when he says that the "weapon of criticism" cannot replace a "criticism of weapons." He still adhered to the idea that the main weapon at the philosopher's disposal was criticism. In fact, as we shall see, he clung to this idea throughout his life; everything he wrote was a "critique." But in what way was the critique a weapon? How could it succeed in paving the way for salvation in the order of being, not only in that of thought? How could mere words transform the world?

Bauer was relatively uninterested in this question because he was convinced that the theoretical revolution had to be completed before the practical revolution could start. He always remained sceptical with regard to Marx's claim that the order of thought would change as soon as the order of being was transformed.[88] In this respect he still adhered to Hegel's conviction that the fetters of law and freedom cannot be stripped off without a preceding liberation of conscience, that a revolution has to be preceded by a reformation in order to be successful.[89] Marx, on the contrary, though admitting that confusion still reigned in the realm of thought, was already looking for a way to make the critique historically efficacious.

The critique had to do with "material forces": with the churches, with the state, with a "philistine" society. And material forces could only be overthrown by material forces. How was the critique to become a material force? By becoming the guiding consciousness of a social group which was a material force even before it embraced the theory. By "gripping the masses."

This seemingly insignificant step is of utmost importance. For it entails a shift in the meaning of '*praxis*' which will become

---

[88] Cf. Stuke, 174.
[89] Cf. Hegel$_2$, XI, 564; tr. Sibree, 453.

increasingly obvious as we follow Marx's struggle to come to grips with the problem in question.

Whereas even such realistic Hegelians as Ruge, not to speak of Cieszkowski and Bauer, always took *praxis* to be a salvific deed either of the philosopher himself or at least of men whom the philosopher gathered around his wisdom, Marx now suggests that it is the deed of an extraphilosophical humanity, or a part of it, *which meets the theory half-way* (later Marx even will feel that this humanity fulfils its task without at all needing theory). In short, whereas all other Left Hegelians considered *praxis* as an effluence of Absolute Knowledge, Marx discovered that it also might be an almost "ontological" development on the part of history. If present society contained a group powerful enough to transform the world, and if this group was to accept the critique as its program of action, then it was possible to argue that history had destined this group for being the world,s ultimate savior. In that case, however, *real history* rather than Knowledge was the true principle of salvation.

Already Cieszkowski had realized that Knowledge and Theory, however "absolute," cannot be the *locus* of salvation. But he as well as most other Left Hegelians was convinced that Knowledge is the prime lever, the *principle* of salvation. Salvation could be reached only in terms of a continuation and prolongation of Absolute Knowledge. Marx, on the contrary, discovered that the actualization of theory depended upon whether reality itself pressed for it. "It is not enough that thought urges for actualization. Reality itself has to force its way toward thought."[90] But this meant that reality and its potentialities, not Knowledge, were the ultimate source of man's emancipation, of salvation.

We must hasten to add that we have articulated Marx's ideas somewhat more expressly than he did himself in 1843. At that time he still was far from saying that theory and consciousness only are epiphenomena of a salvific path of history. Theory still was the active element. Still the idea that salvific *praxis* emerges

[90] *MEGA* I, 1/1, 616; tr. Bottomore, 54.

out of the mute course of history rather than being an efflux of Absolute Knowledge begins to take shape in Marx's mind.

It has been argued that by making *praxis* a deed of extra-philosophical humanity Marx in fact was more faithful to Hegel's basic insight than all other Left Hegelians.[91] And though it would seem that, apart from Feuerbach, Marx was the first Left Hegelian who managed to free himself from the opiate of Absolute Knowledge, there is some truth in this statement. For in a sense at least Marx is the only Left Hegelian who can claim not to have relapsed into the Fichtean *ought*. All others, from Cieszkowski to Hess, considered salvation dependent upon something to be done by philosophers and their adherents: upon deeds of "historiosophers" organizing social life, upon critical and journalistic activities, upon "sacred acts." In each case there was an *ought*: Absolute Knowledge ought to be actualized, it ought to be translated into practice, its still remaining finiteness ought to be "criticized away," and sacred actions ought to be carried out.

Of course in most cases the Left Hegelians connected their summons with predictions. One might even argue that it was a distinct trait of the Left Hegelian notion of *praxis*, first, that it pointed toward the future, and, second, that it entailed knowability of this future. On closer examination, however, one will have to admit that all predictions of the Left Hegelians were based upon their authors' private determination to go ahead and save the world, together with a vague though intense optimism as to the promise of this endeavor. Even Cieszkowski and Hess, who of all Left Hegelians were most interested in grounding their predictions, connected the predictability of future events with their being carried out by Absolute Knowers. But what if for one reason or another the Absolute Knowers were prevented from acting? As long as salvation rested upon the determination of individuals who willfully decided to act because they believed that their actions would bring about humanity's salvation; as long as salvation did not depend upon men who acted virtually by necessity, so much so that it would be possible to argue that they might have acted

[91] Lukács₂, 9.

even without knowing the salvific character of their deeds; in
short, as long as the actualization of salvific *praxis* was not governed
by laws independent of individual will, salvation was not certain,
not ineluctable.

When prediction is viewed from this angle, it appears rather
natural that Marx chanced upon the "proletariat."

Since about the sixteenth century in France the expression
'*le prolétaire*' referred to the lowest class of the people, to beggars,
vagrants, and, in general, the poor. Rousseau in his *Contrat Social*
and certain governmental decrees issued after the Revolution of
1789 still use the expression in this sense. From about the middle
of the seventeenth century the same applies to the English expression 'the proletarian.' In its modern meaning the expression
seems to have first been used by the French historian and economist
J. Ch. L. Sismondi. In his *Nouveaux principes d'économie politique*,
the first edition of which was published in 1819, Sismondi pointed
to the existence of a special *classe de prolétaires* "whose idea of
wealth simply is to exist and whose idea of poverty is to die of
hunger."[92] In 1829 the expression was taken up by the two Saint-
Simonists, St.-A. Bazard and B.-P. Enfantin, in their *Exposition
de la Doctrine de Saint-Simon*, in which they described the modern
industrial wage earner as a direct descendant of the slave and the
serf: "sa personne est libre, il n'est plus attaché à la glèbe, mais
c'est tout ce qu'il a conquis."[93]

That the Saint-Simonian doctrine had a considerable impact
upon German intellectuals is well known. The Hegelian Eduard
Gans, whose lectures on law Marx attended at Berlin and who,
incidentally, was the only old Hegelian ever respected by the Left
Hegelians, was familiar with Saint-Simonism from 1825 and thought
highly of it.[94] K. L. Michelet, the main representative of the
Center of the Hegelian school, came to know Saint-Simonism
during a stay in Paris in 1828; he seems to have been Hegel's
informant on the movement and in 1830 even lectured on it at

[92] Cf. the fn. in *Doctrine de Saint-Simon* 239; also Halévy, 48 ff.
[93] *Doctrine* 94. Cf. Ramm, 294.
[94] Cornu$_3$, I, 87 ff.

Berlin.[95] Another Hegelian, E. W Carové, reviewed the *Exposition* in the *Jahrbücher für wissenschaftliche Kritik* while Hegel was its editor; later he published a detailed criticism of the Saint-Simonian doctrine, which up to the publication of L. Stein's book remained one of the major German sources on Saint-Simonism.[96] In 1837 a critic of Hegelianism, H. M. Chalybäus, whose book on the development of speculative philosophy from Kant to Hegel was one of the best of its kind and is still worth reading, even went so far as to claim that Hegelianism is the philosophical theory of socialist systems such as that of Saint-Simon.[97]

Non-Hegelians as well showed considerable interest in Saint-Simonism in the late thirties. Romanticist theologians and historians such as E. W. Hengstenberg and H. Leo discussed Saint-Simonism as a sect propagating a *nouveau christianisme*. Heine entered into contact with Saint-Simonists almost immediatly after he left Germany for Paris in 1831; his *De l'Allemagne*, which among other things contained Heine's sarcastic argument with German Idealism, was dedicated to Enfantin.[98] The leader of the Young German literary movements, Karl Gutzkow, in whose *Telegraph für Deutschland* Engels published his first articles, was interested in Saint-Simonism the greater part of his life.[99] Even Goethe, who always had been interested in modern trends but seldom found the courage to side with them, regularly received and read one of the journals published by Saint-Simon's followers.[100]

We may add that Marx's native town, Trier, witnessed what probably was the first explicit defense of Saint-Simonian ideas on German grounds. In 1835, when Marx was seventeen, a certain Ludwig Gall, whom Brügel and Kautsky christened "the first German socialist," published a booklet entitled *Beleuchtung der*

[95] Cf. Stuke, 60.

[96] Cf. *Jahrbücher f. wissenschaftliche Kritik* (December, 1830) no^s. 115 ff.; and *Der Saint-Simonismus und die neuere französische Philosophie* (Leipzig, 1831).

[97] Cf. *Staatslexikon* Suppl. II, 779.

[98] Cf. Butler, 88 ff. On Heine's relation to Marx see Demetz, 106 ff.

[99] Cf. Butler, 258 ff. On Gutzkow and Engels see Demetz, 25 ff.

[100] Cf. Evans, 18.

Förster'schen Kritik der gerühmten Destillirgeräthe, a title which did not really match the subject discussed. Gall, a former functionary at Trier, had acquired an interest, prompted by the economic crisis following the Napoleonic wars, both in the development of agricultural implements and in Saint-Simonian ideas. He concluded from his studies that contemporary society was divided into two classes with diametrically opposed interests, the *Geldprivilegierte* and the laboring classes, and he argued for a "socialization (*Vergessellschaftung*) of the working classes," which he idealized somewhat along the lines of Fourier's profit-sharing associations, the "phalanxes."[101] It has even been argued that the suppression of the hub of Trier's social life, the *Literarische Kasino-Gesellschaft*, of which both Marx's father and the headmaster of his high school were members, was to some extent due to its connection with Gall.[102]

However, it would not seem that Marx's notion of proletariat stemmed from the Saint-Simonists. Bazard, Enfantin, and their friends were interested in the proletariat only marginally; their main interest centered around a general restoration of human society, a reorganization to be implemented by "social engineers" rather than by the proletariat. We therefore have to turn our attention to two German publications: a little-known pamphlet with an extremely long-winded title published in 1835 by Franz von Baader[103] and L. v. Stein's justly famous *Der Socialismus und Communismus des heutigen Frankreich*, first published in 1842.

Still using the loan-word '*der Proletair*' instead of '*der Proletarier*,' which later was common, Baader described the proletarian as a member of a social group which had emerged in connection with the modern "industrial system" and the "moneyed interest."

---

[101] Cf. *Der deutsche Sozialismus von Ludwig Gall bis Karl Marx*, eds. F. Brügel and B. Kautsky (Wien-Leipzig, 1931) 21 ff.

[102] Cf. Gurvitch, 575 ff., repeated by Evans, 19. However, it would seem that Gurvitch's claim is based upon a somewhat superficial reading of B. Nikolaievski-O. Maenchen-Helfen, *Karl Marx, Man and Fighter* 8 ff. For biographical data on Gall see Rubel$_2$, 22.

[103] *Über das dermalige Missverhältnis der Vermögenslosen oder Proletairs zu den Vermögen besitzenden Classen der Societät in Betreff ihres Auskommens sowohl in materieller als intellectueller Hinsicht aus dem Gesichtspunkt des Rechts betrachtet* (München, 1835); cf. Baader, VI, 125-144.

Among other things he explicitly pointed to the susceptibility of proletarians to demagogues and crackpots, and reduced the contemporary "revolutionability and inflammability of society" to the wretched conditions imposed upon this social group by recent developments. He argued for an enfranchisement of the proletariat and suggested that it be represented in the diet by priests, "to whom alone these men are likely to open their heart."

Lorenz von Stein was more realistic though less *engagé*. He was the first to realize clearly the difference between the poor, who existed in all states and nations from time immemorial, and the modern proletariat. Whereas the *plebs* of the Roman Empire, for example, were an "accumulation of ne'er-do-wells whose only life work was to enjoy life at the state's expense," the proletarian, though having no property, had labor energy and the will to apply it. "He wants to work, readily, well, and much; but in return for his labor he wants fair wages. It is the disproportion between his effort and his earnings which first stimulates his dissatisfaction and thus also causes his opposition to those who make great profits without much effort." A keen observer, Stein added that only France and some "Germanic nations" had a proletariat. Russia or China, for example, might have many poor who might even be willing to work. But these poor did not put forward claims in terms of an "estate" to which they belonged; they were not conscious of themselves as a special estate. According to Stein only France and England had a proletariat. Germany still only knew it by description; North America was too rich in resources and "too much wanting in peace"; Italy was too deeply enslaved; Spain too much divided. For as Stein pointed out, the emergence of the proletariat was ultimately connected with the French Revolution and its reverberations. Who indeed were the *tricoteuses* and the *aimables faubourgs* who had freed the National Assembly, conquered the Tuileries, brought Robespierre to power, and formed Hanriot's guard? No one else but the proletarians. During the fury of the Revolution they had learned two things: they became aware of themselves as a special estate and they realized the significance of all revolutions. "This is the result which the Republic handed down to imperial times and the Empire to the Restoration."[104]

There is no way of telling whether Marx ever read Baader's pamphlet. But it is virtually certain that he read, indeed carefully studied, Stein's book. It was reviewed in one of the last issues of the *Rheinische Zeitung*;[105] moreover, Hess reviewed it for the *Einundzwanzig Bogen aus der Schweiz*, which also contained Hess' article on the "Philosophy of Action."[106] In any case, from the very beginning Marx used the expression 'proletariat' in the technical sense first delineated by Stein. In addition, like Baader and Stein, he saw a close connection between proletariat and revolution.

After Babeuf's *conspiration pour l'égalité* had rather abruptly ended with the ringleader's execution in 1797,[107] the idea of a truly "revolutionary" transformation of society was somewhat alien to the theoreticians of French socialism. Between 1800 and 1840 several smaller proletarian uprisings took place in France, it is true, but most of the French socialists were not ideologists of the proletariat in the proper sense. They were either social engineers like Saint-Simon and, to a lesser extent, Fourier, who believed

---

[104] Stein, 8 ff.

[105] *Rheinische Zeitung* 75 (March 16, 1843) Beiblatt, 1. This review does not seem to be by Hess, contrary to Rubel$_2$, 64 (Hess refers to this review in *Einundzwanzig Bogen* 313). Hess used to sign his articles by ' $\div$ $\div$ ' while this article is signed by 'x.' Cf. Cornu's remark in Hess$_2$, 495, fn. 376.

[106] *Einundzwanzig Bogen* 74 ff. Tucker, 113, somewhat exaggerates when he says that the idea of the proletariat was "wholly absent from Hess' version" of communism. Still, it is true that at that time Hess' communism did not entail a *commitment* to the proletariat. Stein had opposed "socialism" (Saint-Simon, Fourier) to "communism" (Babeuf, Cabet) by describing the former as more theoretical and mainly interested in a reorganization of labor, and the latter as "immediately practical" and aiming at a radical transformation of society; cf. Stein, 349 ff. Moreover, he claimed that communism, as it is a radical rejection of the existing order, is possible only among proletarians (thus implying that communism is possible only if everybody is a proletarian); cf. 355. Hess, in *Einundzwanzig Bogen* 83 ff., criticizes this conception as "materialistic," since it reduces the equality aimed at by communism to an equality of *Genuss*. Cf. Stuke, 243.

[107] Cf. Ramm, 174 ff.

it possible to transform society in terms of new laws and a social reorganization; or else they were dreamers who wanted to convince humanity by peaceful experiments like that of Cabet, who eventually emigrated to the United States to build his *Icarie*.[108]

One may object that when speaking in 1843 of a "revolution," Marx did not have in mind a violent uprising. This is probably correct. We shall even see that "revolution" never unambiguously implied violence for Marx. Still there is no doubt that he had in mind a transformation far more radical than any of which his French colleagues ever dreamed. The usually very well informed *Staatslexikon* by Rotteck and Welcker indicates that his contemporaries were well aware of this difference between original French socialism and its Left Hegelian counterpart in Germany. As the author of the article "Communism," W. Schulz, put it in 1846, the "communist suckers sprouting on the tree of Hegelian school-wisdom" aimed at a "perfectly insipid denial of the whole existing world order" rather than at a reasonable reorganization of society. "They are no longer blisters on the surface of the seething life of the nation; they already are burst blisters, nothing but a wind."[109] Later this description turned out to be wrong as far as the impact of "Hegelian communism" was concerned. But it captures well the abstractness and unreality of the atmosphere out of which Marxism was born.

In fact, though it does not redound to his honor, it has to be emphasized that Marx chanced upon the proletariat because he wanted, and was convinced of the imminent coming of, the ultimate revolution; it was not because he pitied the suffering proletarians. He wanted, and knew of the coming of, a revolution; but he also knew that criticism alone could not bring it about. Accordingly, he looked about for a historical force to which the "dissolution of the hitherto existing world order" was the "secret of its own existence"; a force which, if critically enlightened about its "secret,"

---

[108] Cf. Evans, 56 ff.; Ramm, 473.

[109] *Staatslexikon* Suppl. II, 70. In his *Philosophy of Right*, first published in 1830, the conservative political scientist Julius Stahl writes, "Hegel's theory stands on the same grounds as the revolution." Cf. 4th ed. (Heidelberg, 1854) I, 473, quoted by Beyer₁, 89.

would become the "material weapon" of the critique by using it as its "spiritual weapon."[110]

That Marx chose the proletariat rather than liberal nationalists, for example, testifies to his acuteness and discernment as to the chances of the future balance of social power. But I cannot agree with M. Rubel, who claims that it testifies to *moral* indignation as the leitmotif of Marx's thought.[111] Although it would seem possible to argue that Marx's idea of revolution entailed some kind of moral indignation, even if the indignation in question were so eccentric as to make its "morality" somewhat doubtful, Marx's choice of the proletariat as the executor of this revolution clearly did not entail indignation over their plight. For he chose the proletariat in terms of two premises, neither of which had to do with the immorality of the fact that a part of humanity suffered while the rest thrived. We have already alluded to the first premise: Marx's conviction that the proletariat would become a major social force within the immediate future. The second premise is the salvific character of the revolution envisaged by Marx. For among other things Marx quite obviously committed himself to the "cause of the proletariat" because he envisaged a revolution which would raise Germany and with it the whole world "not only to the official level of the modern nations but to the heights of humanity," a *total salvific revolution*.[112] Such a revolution was conceivable only as a deed of a social group which transcended the existing world order almost in a "metaphysical" way. The savior had to be thoroughly free of all blemishes from which he was to deliver humanity. And he had to be in an "all-round antithesis" to the very premises of the existing order so as to make impossible all accommodation.[113] In short, he had to be an outcast of contemporary society.

[110] Cf. *MEGA* I, 1/1, 620; tr. Bottomore, 59.
[111] Cfr. Rubel$_2$, 100.
[112] Cf. *MEGA* I, 1/1, 614; tr. Bottomore, 52.
[113] Cf. Marx's "definition" of the proletariat, *ibid.* 619; tr. Bottomore, 58: "A class with *radical chains*, a class of civil society which is not a class of civil society, an estate which is the dissolution of all estates ... which can invoke no *historical* but only its human title, which does not stand in any one-sided antithesis to the consequences but in an all-round antithesis to the very premises

Ultimately Marx's passage to the proletarian cause is so perfectly "logical" as to make rather unconvincing the widespread
notion that by declaring himself for the proletariat Marx ceased
to be an *abstract Left-Hegelian revolutionary.* Apart from insinuating
the obvious untruth accepted even by many non-Marxists that
Marxism corresponded to objective needs on the side of the proletariat, this interpretation overlooks the fact that Marx's commitment to the proletariat was only a variant of Bruno Bauer's
stubborn adherence to the purity of his "critique." For just as
the mythical salvific character of Bauer's critique was inseparable
from the critique's total opposition to all aspects of the contemporary world, the salvific function ascribed by Marx to the proletariat
ultimately was rooted in the proletariat's being the embodied
negation of the existing social order. Both Bauer's and Marx's
levers of salvation were mythical realities which existed in the
midst of the world without forming a part of it. In both cases
the savior was an outcast, and he had to be one in order to guarantee
salvation from the world as it was. That the Marxist lever of
salvation was a social *reality*, whereas that of Bauer was a purely
intellectual affair, should not make us forget that the premises
of Marx's and Bauer's conception were equally mythical.

How little Marx was concerned with the empirical sufferings
of the real proletariat (which he came to know only *after* he had
conceived of the "proletarian revolution"[114]) becomes most obvious
if one analyzes his concept of *human versus political emancipation*,
which was the leading theme of his review of Bauer's book on the
"Jewish Question." It is seldom asked why Marx took the trouble
to write this oversized review at all. Nothing indicates that he
was particularly interested in the "Jewish Question" taken as
such, nor is it plausible that he intended to render a friendly service

---

of German statehood." What resembles moral indignation is in fact only a
sort of side-effect of Marx's desire to describe the proletariat as the total negation
of the existing order. "Germany, being the deficiency of the political present
constituted as a world of its own," 617, can only be overthrown by a class
that is the "embodiment of the general limitation" and of the "notorious crime"
of present society, 618.

[114] Cf. Tucker, 113.

to Bauer. If one studies it carefully, it soon becomes obvious that Marx wrote this review because Bauer, using the "Jewish Question" as a sort of symbol, had tried to articulate his ideas about the aims of salvific *praxis*, the "critique." Both Bauer and Marx used "the Jew" as a symbol of the "limited nature" of contemporary man which was to be replaced by a "universal human nature." "The Jew," for them, was the symbol of the "old world," just as "Man" was the symbol for the new age to come.[115]

That this is no artificial construction is obvious from the way in which Bauer argued. Viewed superficially, his book discusses the chances of Jewish emancipation within a Christian state such as Prussia. On closer examination, however, one discovers that Bauer does in no way intend to outline the possibility of a coexistence of Jews and Christians. Rather, rejecting all such coexistence as a "false peace" and adding that the whole Jewish question "is only a part of the great and universal question at whose solution our time labors,"[116] he tries to show that the only consistent solution to contemporary problems consists in casting off the old religious Adam and becoming Man. Within a Christian state the emancipation of Jews is consistent only if Jews are emancipated from Judaism and the state is emancipated from Christianity. Again this sounds as if Bauer wanted to solve a political problem of the day: if Jews were no longer embracing Judaism and the state were to cease to be Christian, the problem would disappear. However, Bauer has more on mind than merely a change of face on the side of both Jews and Christians. The change which he has in mind is almost an ontological one and, in any case, "existential." He expresses this by equating the Jew's "essence" with his Judaism, and the "essence" of the Christian state with its being Christian. The Jew is no "man"; he is a Jew; just as the Christian is no "man," but a Christian; and a Christian state is no "state," but a sort of embodied Christianity.[117] In short, the emancipation of which Bauer speaks is an emancipation of the Jew, the Christian, and the Christian state from the very nature and "essence" which

[115] Cf. Gebhardt₂, 217 ff.
[116] Bauer₃, 3.
[117] *Ibid.* 19 ff.

they *presently possess.* Both Jews and Christians have to give up that which presently they "existentially," almost ontologically, *are*; they have to put on the new Adam and become Men. For the "fire of the critique" cannot permit the old Adam, be he Jewish or Christian, to enter the age of salvation. And the new age, in turn, cannot descend before the old Adam is put away.

When Marx objects that Bauer identifies human emancipation with political emancipation, he somewhat misses the point of Bauer's argument. For Bauer obviously did not want to say that the change from a Christian to a "true" state consisted only in the state's giving up its Christian ideology. To Bauer the emancipation of the state from Christianity was as ontological as the emancipation of the Jew from Judaism and of the Christian from Christianity.[118] Still Marx is right when he claims that Bauer did not analyze the "relation between political emancipation and human emancipation."[119] For though Bauer's "emancipated state" obviously was more than merely a republic like the United States, he still saw the wickedness of the present era in its *particular* way of being political, not in its being political at all. In other words, whereas Bauer still saw the basic evil of the present in its being religious and imagined the aeon of salvation as areligious but political, Marx saw the evil in the present world order being political, and accordingly envisaged the salvific age as apolitical and social. For Marx the emancipation leading from "prehuman" stages of history to the Age of Man was no longer primarily an emancipation from man's religious essence; it was an emancipation from his political essence, which of course entailed an emancipation from the religious one.

However, Marx continued to use religion as a symbol of the evil of the existing world; even much later, when he no longer was interested in scholastic discussions with his Left Hegelian colleagues, he still liked to use this symbol. In order to illustrate his point, he would refer to the "North American Free States." In many of them *la constitution n'impose pas les croyances religieuses ...*

[118] Cf. Gebhardt₂, 226 ff.
[119] *MEGA* I, 1/1, 580; tr. Bottomore, 8.

comme condition des privilèges politiques, as Marx quotes from a
book by Beaumont de la Bonninière, a French political writer who
had visited the United States together with Tocqueville to study
its penitentiary system. These states already have reached complete political emancipation, but the symptom of all evil, religion,
persists. Thereby it is proven that

> the existence of religion does not contradict the completion
> of the state. But as the existence of religion is the existence of
> a defect, the source of this defect only can be sought in the
> very *essence* of the state. For us, religion no longer is the *cause*
> but only a *phenomenon* of the secular limitation (*Beschränktheit*).
> Therefore we explain the religious restraint (*Befangenheit*) of
> free citizens in terms of their secular restraint. We do not
> claim that they have to give up their religious restraint as soon
> as their secular limits are abolished. We do not transform
> secular questions into theological ones. We transform theolo-
> gical questions into secular ones.[120]

It is important to see the point of this criticism against Bauer.
The difference between Bauer and Marx is not that the former
still takes religion seriously, whereas the latter does not; that
Bauer is fighting ideological windmills, whereas Marx is attacking
"material" realities. Rather, the point at issue is what are the
criteria of ultimate emancipation; or, to put it in another way,
to decide what the "fire of the critique" has to burn to ashes and
what it may permit to pass into the universe of salvation. Both
Bauer and Marx discuss this problem in terms of the question as
to how the wretchedness of the present world order ought to be
described. Whereas Bauer describes this wretchedness in terms
of the laws of Judaism and its full development in Christianity,
Marx describes it in terms of the very structure of civil society,
which of course he understands as the ultimate foundation of
Judaism's and Christianity's negative qualities.[121] It would seem
possible to say, then, that Marx suspects Bauer of not being radical
enough in his rejection of the present world order, of granting too
much of the present age to the phoenix supposed to be resurrected

[120] *Ibid.* 581; Bottomore, 9 ff.
[121] Cf. Gebhardt₂, 226 ff.

from the critical holocaust. Bauer believes that an emancipation which replaces the laws of Judaism and Christianity by "human rights" is sufficient. On the contrary, Marx is not prepared to admit that it is the final step from the old to the new world, though he admits that "political" emancipation is the "last form of human emancipation *within* the present world order."[122]

We can refrain from elaborating on Marx's critique of the political sphere and of civil society. For he only repeats the arguments with which we already are familiar from his *Critique of the Hegelian Philosophy of the State*. Even the "completed political sphere" is only an abstract completion of man, a completion hovering above and outside man's "material life." In civil society man lives two lives: he is redeemed in the abstract heaven of politics, where he exists as a *Gemeinwesen*, but he remains unredeemed and atomic in civil society, where he is only a *Privatmensch*.[123] The individualistic limitations of the old Adam are overcome in civil society only as far as the heavenly abstractions of politics go, not within the "material" reality of civil society itself.

However, in the second part of the review under discussion, a part which must have been written several weeks after the first one,[124] there emerges a new idea. Marx continues to use the "Jew" as the symbol of evil, and he continues to say that the emancipation of the Jew can only consist in his emancipation from Judaism. But this time he proposes to discuss the "everyday Jew" rather than Bauer's theological "Sabbath Jew." As he says, the worldly ground of Judaism is self-interest; the Jew's worldly cult is haggling; and his worldly God is money. The Christian, in turn, is nothing but a theorizing Jew, just as the Jew is a practical Christian and the practical Christian a Jew.[125] Accordingly the

[122] *MEGA* I, 1/1, 585; tr. Bottomore, 15.

[123] *Ibid.* 584; tr. Bottomore, 13 ff.

[124] Judging by internal criteria, the first part of the review seems to be written immediately after the *Critique of the Hegelian Philosophy of State*; according to Rjazanov, the editor of *MEGA*, the *Critique* was written between March and August, 1843, while the review of Bauer's book was begun in August, 1843.

[125] *MEGA* I, 1/1, 605; cf. I, 3, 284. Cf. Hess₂, 334: "Christianity is the

emancipation from Judaism must be an emancipation from the antisocial and egoistic character of contemporary society. In the end Judaism is only the "Jewish limitation" of civil society.[126]

Here the criticism of both religion and the "political sphere" turns for the first time into a rather explicit criticism of civil society in *economico-ethical* terms. Accordingly there also emerges for the first time the theme of "economic alienation" around which the *Manuscripts of 1844* will revolve. As Marx puts it, "selling (*Veräusserung*) is the *praxis* of externalization (*Entäusserung*)," the "practical" counterpart of religious alienation:

> Just as man, so long as he is restrained by religion, can only objectify his essence by turning it into an *alien* fantastic creature, so under the domination of egoistic needs he can act in a practical way, create his objects practically, only by subordinating these products as well as his activity to the power of an alien being and bestowing upon them the significance of an alien being— money.[127]

Tucker[128] probably is correct in suggesting that this second part of the review under discussion was strongly influenced by an article which Hess submitted for publication in the *Deutsch-Französische Jahrbücher* in 1843 but which eventually was published in H. Püttmann's *Rheinische Jahrbücher zur gesellschaftlichen Reform* in 1845. Marx probably read this article while preparing the first and only issue of his magazine. In any case Hess' article anticipates a number of ideas contained both in the second part of the said review and in Marx's famous *Manuscripts*. Its German title, "Über das Geldwesen," literally means "on monetary matters." But whoever was familiar with Feuerbach's *Essence of Christianity* must have understood that Hess would speak of the "essence of money," reducing it to anthropological categories as Feuerbach had done with religion. Somehow, one was even reminded of book titles such as *Über das Unwesen der Preussischen Politik*, in which case one understood "on the mischief of money."

theory, the logic of egoism. The classical instance of egoistic *praxis*, however, is the modern Christian world of shopkeepers (*Krämerwelt*)."

[126] *MEGA loc. cit.*; cf. Hess$_2$, 335 ff.
[127] *MEGA loc. cit*; tr. Bottomore, 39.
[128] Tucker, 110 ff.

And in fact Hess' article intimated that the very essence of money was a "mischief." Developing an idea already advanced in his article "Philosophie der That," namely, that life is activity,[129] Hess now argued that "life is the exchange of productive life activity." As Hess explained, this meant that cooperation both in production and in consumption was the medium and life element in which human individuals reached their completion. Indeed, it was the "true essence" of individual men, so much so that the individual had to be understood as a means of the "species," and that any social order in which individuals used the "species" as a means for the satisfaction of their private needs had to be considered "perverse."[130] But this perverse world order was in fact the essence of all previous history. For up to now history had been nothing else than the history of the regulation and universalization of man's most primitive and perverted form of exchange, of robbery and slavery. Robbery and slavery were presently culminating in "cannibalism": "the point has been reached at which, without exception and at each moment, we all barter away our own activity, our productive force, our potentialities, ourselves."[131] It is hardly necessary to point out that each of these statements prefigures those of Marx's *Manuscripts*: labor is man's life activity, its socialization is man's "species-life" and thus his ultimate completion; but up to now history had led just to the opposite of such a socialization, to an atomism which presently reaches its culmination in that man has to barter away his very life-activity for the satisfaction of his most elementary biological needs.

But, Hess continued, if the individual does not live for the species but only for himself, using the species as a means, he inevitably creates for himself a "perverted world." At the level of theory, this perverted world is Christianity; at the level of practical life, money. "What *God* is for theoretical life, *money* is for the *practical* life of the perverted world—the exteriorized

[129] *Einundzwanzig Bogen* 309 ff. In this article activity is still described in Fichte's sense as a self-positing and a self-determination of the ego.
[130] Hess$_2$, 330.
[131] *Ibid*. 333. Throughout the whole article the expressions ' *Verkehr* ' and ' *Produktion* ' are used in a highly metaphorical way.

potentiality of man, life activity bartered away." According to political economists money is the universal medium of exchange and thus (in terms of Hess' concept of *life* as "exchange") the medium of life, *the* human potentiality, the treasure of humanity. In reality, however, it is only the "product of mutually alienated men, indeed externalized man."[132]

The eminent French sociologist E. Halévy once stated that Marx was a "powerfully systematic mind" rather than a "great creator of ideas."[133] Of Marx's early writings none corroborates this statement more convincingly than the *Economic and Philosophic Manuscripts*, which we now have to discuss. For what Marx does there is to articulate Hess' ideas just sketched, to enlarge them in terms of an economic analysis supplied by Engels, and to elevate them *à la hauteur des principes* in terms of a reinterpretation of Hegel's *Phenomenology of Mind*.

[132] *Ibid.* 334 ff.
[133] Halévy, 75.

20: ALIENATION I:
"THE LOST PRODUCTS OF FREEDOM"

Usually the importance of the *Manuscripts*, which were first published in 1932, is explained, first, by pointing to the fact that they afford a glance into Marx's thought at a time when, to use a phrase of Hegel, it still was not "a corpse which had left behind its living impulse"[134]; and, secondly, by arguing that the *Manuscripts* advance ideas which are "humanistic," indeed "existentialist," rather than materialist and naturalistic, and in the light of which Marx's later economic thought appears quite different from what Social Democrats such as Kautsky and Mehring, and Communists such as Lenin, believed it to be.

In a way Marx's *Manuscripts* are comparable to Hegel's "early theological writings," whose publication by Nohl in 1907 completely revolutionized the interpretation of Hegelianism. Up to 1907 Hegel was viewed almost exclusively from his mature systematic writings: the dogmatically precise *Logic*, the skeletal *Encyclopaedia*, the lofty *Philosophy of Right*. Then suddenly there emerged a Hegel who spoke of love, who tried to reconcile the immanentistic realism of the Greeks with the religious transcendentalism of Christianity, who tried to overcome the *Aufklärung* as much as he opposed the romanticists. The *Phenomenology* appeared in a new light too: instead of an unintelligible introduction it turned out to be the most important link between the still living and an already dogmatically hardened Hegel, a link in terms of which Hegel's rigid system had to be reinterpreted. Similarly with Marx:

[134] Hegel$_2$, II, 12; tr. Baillie, 69. Cf. Löwith$_2$, 205.

whereas Kautsky and Mehring had made of him a deterministic economist and Lenin's philosophical utterances seemed to suggest that Engels' materialism, positivistic rather than dialectical, was the foundation of Marxism, the *Manuscripts* revealed a Marx whose dialectic was as supple as that of the *Phenomenology*, who struggled with Hegel on properly speculative grounds instead of only turning him "upside down," and who made profound statements about the interrelation of economics and philosophy as well as about the "alienation" of human products from their originator, the worker. Rereading *Das Kapital*, one could see that behind the sober economic analyses there was hidden a highly speculative idea about the meaning of man and his universe. Rereading Marx's later definitions of his "historical materialism," one began to realize that they were congealed postscripts to an earlier "humanistic" philosophy.

The difficult question as to whether the *old* Marx was still thinking in terms of his earlier philosophical speculations or whether he had succumbed to the almost positivistic materialism exemplified in Engels' philosophy of nature we will have to discuss in another volume. In this section we want to restrict ourselves to an analysis of Marx's concept of *alienation* which, as we shall see in the following sections, can be correctly understood only if it is viewed against the background of Marx's notion of labor and, ultimately, of Marx's critique of Hegel.

If one surveys the list of books which Marx read and from which he often carefully took excerpts while writing the *Manuscripts*, one at first has the impression that Marx was tired of his "profession" as eschatological critic and wanted to change over to economics. Between November, 1843, and February, 1845, he devoured all the contemporary literature on economic problems on which he could get his hands. He had to restrict himself to books available in French and German; his English was still not very good. But even so he read more than ten thousand pages, a remarkable undertaking if one considers that during the same time he wrote the *Manuscripts* and spent more than two months composing the *Holy Family*. Among French authors he read Boisguillebert,

Buret, Pecqueur,[135] Say, Skarbek, possibly Sismondi, and very
probably Proudhon; among English authors, Lauderdale, Mac
Culloch, James Mill, Ricardo, and Smith; among German authors,
List, Schulz, and Schütz.[136]

Yet on closer examination one discovers that Marx was far from
wanting to desert the "critique." Rather, he had come to the
conclusion that the critique of the existing world order had to start
with that of political economy. The *Manuscripts* were drafts for
a book which Marx wanted to call *Critique of Politics and Political
Economy*. In February, 1845, he even signed a contract with
a publisher at Darmstadt, which eventually was cancelled in the
spring of 1847 when it became obvious that the book would never
be completed,[137] And though the *Manuscripts* criticize only political
economy, not politics, we know from Marx's draft for the preface
that he intended to publish further monographs criticizing the
state, law, morals, civil life, and so on.[138]

In short, Marx's sudden interest in economics was entirely a
result of his discovery that the economic order was the fundamental
sphere of wretchedness of the present world order. From about
1842 he knew that the problem of salvation consisted in freeing
man from the fetters of civil society without thereby escaping
into political abstractions. Hess had indicated to him that this
wretchedness had a theoretical side exemplified in religion and a
more basic practical side exemplified in economic matters such as
barter and money. But though Hegel already had taught him that
civil society was governed by economic laws, it was not until he
read Engels' "Outlines of a Critique of Political Economy" that
Marx realized that the social atomism of civil society was rooted
in its very economic structure. Though Engels himself later described his "Outlines" as "completely obsolete and full of inaccu-

[135] On Pecqueur's allegedly considerable influence upon Marx's economic
thought see Halévy, 51 ff.
[136] Cf. *MEGA* I, 3, 413, as well as the index to this volume of the *MEGA*.
[137] Cf. Marx's letter to his publisher, K. W. Leske, dated August 1, 1846,
MEW XXVII, 447 ff.; cf. also fn. 6, 364, in *MEW* XXVII.
[138] *MEGA* I, 3, 413 ff; tr. Milligan, 15.

racies,"[139] Marx still praised it as the "sketch of a genius" as late
as 1859.[140] For Engels' article suggested two things to him: first,
that the asocial character of the present originated from the division of labor into living and congealed labor, into labor and capital;
secondly, that all categories of the political economy had to be
reduced to anthropological ones, just as Feuerbach had done with
religion and Hess with money; and that when this was done,
classical political economy turned out to be a conscious or unconscious *apologia* of the wretchedness of the present world order.
Hess had given to Marx the idea that money ought to be treated
in terms of Feuerbach's concept of *alienation*. Engels' article,
in turn, suggested to Marx the idea of transferring this scheme
from monetary matters to the economically most important phenomenon of the time—the separation of labor and capital, which,
being the cause of society's division into capitalists and proletarians,
had to be the ultimate root of the "social atomism" of the present.

Reading the first forty pages of the *Manuscripts*,[141] one might
easily be misled into believing that out of moral indignation Marx
wishes to throw into relief the tragic situation of the proletariat.
Quoting and paraphrasing various books on political economy,
Marx describes how wages under the present system are always
as low as the bare preservation of the working class permits. The
worker has become a machine which has to be serviced like any
other machine; the laws of this servicing are those of rentability,
not human laws. The worker has become a commodity whose
treatment and wage is determined by laws completely extrinsic
to the human quality either of the worker himself or of his labor.
Society is dominated by a Moloch, capital, whose advantages
are always opposed to those of the working class and, finally, of
all men. Though the worker is the ultimate source of all wealth
of a nation, he in no way shares in it:

> It is true that labor produces for the rich wonderful things,
> but for the worker it produces privation. It produces palaces,
> but for the worker, hovels. It produces beauty, but for the

---

[139] Letter to Liebknecht, approximately April, 1871; cf. *MEGA* I, 2, LXXIII.
[140] Cf. *MEW* XIII, 10; tr. Moscow, I, 364.
[141] *MEGA* I, 3, 39-80; tr. Milligan, 20-65.

worker, deformity. It replaces labor by machines, but some of the workers it throws back to a barbarous type of labor, and the other workers it turns into machines. It produces intelligence, but for the worker idiocy, cretinism.[142]

This, as we shall see, is the "actual economic fact" on which Marx bases his theory of alienation. At present we only want to point out that Marx is interested neither in the sufferings of the proletariat taken as such nor in the injustice involved in the fact that the originators of a nation's wealth are not permitted to share in it. He is interested in something far more abstract and speculative. This is most obvious when one notices Marx's silent admiration for the capitalist. For him the "inactive, extravagant wealth given over wholly to pleasure" belongs to the past. The man whom he contrasts with the proletarian is the *"working, sober, economical, prosaic* industrialist,"[143] a man who serves the Moloch "capital" with the same grim asceticism[144] as does the worker. For example, an industrialist's vacation will always be calculated pleasure which in the end serves capital and nothing else. The industrialist debits the furlough to his capital's expense account, and whatever is squandered on his vacations must amount to no more than will be replaced with profit through the reproduction of capital. In this way the capitalist is as much under the sway of an "inhuman power" as is the proletarian, though of course on the whole the capitalist is much better off.[145] "The propertied class and the class of the proletariat present the same human self-alienation."[146] Why Marx nevertheless applied the scheme of alienation to the worker alone will become obvious when we discuss Marx's notion of labor.

In this section we shall restrict ourselves to a discussion of the origin and basic meaning of Marx's concept of *alienation*. Taken as such, this concept does not seem to be overly relevant to the Marxist notion of *praxis*. Yet certainly it is an important and

---

[142] *Ibid.* 85; tr. Milligan, 71.
[143] *Ibid.* 136 ff.; tr. Milligan, 127.
[144] *Ibid.* 130; tr. Milligan, 118.
[145] *Ibid.* 136; tr. Milligan, 126.
[146] *Ibid.* 206; tr. Dixon, 51.

rather fruitful idea in the young Marx's philosophy. Moreover, as S. Hook has pointed out in the new introduction to his *From Hegel to Marx*, such "an extraordinary amount of nonsense is being written these days" about this subject[147] that a discussion would not seem to be out of place here.

Unfortunately, however, we shall have to argue that Hook's own analysis has contributed to the said "extraordinary amount" rather than checking it. Hook mentions as an instance of the "nonsense" in question E. Fromm's claim that Marx's thought is closely related to that of Zen-Buddhism; without doubt Hook is correct in referring to this association as the "ultimate in absurdity." From his review of Tucker's *Philosophy and Myth in Karl Marx*[148] it would seem permissible to impute to Hook a basic readiness to extend the same criticism to Tucker's psychoanalysis of Marx. Again, one would basically have to agree with him, at least as far as Tucker's ultimate conclusions are concerned. However, Hook's own tendency to associate Marx with Dewey, especially with reference to his claim made in 1940 that Dewey is the most "outstanding" and legitimate heir of Marxism,[149] quite probably would have to be condemned in terms of the same criticism.

One of the reasons why Hook opposes the recent emphasis on Marx's theory of alienation is that he believes the concept of alienation to be "originally and primarily religious in nature." For according to Hook the idea underlying this concept is the "Hebraic-Christian tradition's" idea of a Fall from divine grace and the neo-Platonic idea of a Fall from ideal perfection, or the One. Now, I am far from denying that the ideas mentioned by Hook are of religious origin. However, I fail to see what they have to do either with the meaning of '*Entfremdung*,' in German, or with the use of the expression '*Entfremdung*' in German Idealism and in Marx. For neither the Greek language, nor classical Hebraic[150]

---

[147] Hook, 4 ff.

[148] Cf. the review in *Survey* 3 (1962) 552 ff.

[149] Cf. S. Hook, *Reason, Social Myth and Democracy* (New York, 1940) 132.

[150] With the possible exception of the Cabala. Thus, for example, the idea of Isaac Luria (1534-1572) that creation is made possible by a sort of "contraction" (*Zimzum*) within God himself, i.e., that God in himself makes room

and Christian theology, have ever used an expression such as 'alienation' to describe the Fall.

In Latin the expression '*alienatio*' had a legal and a medical sense, both of which, together with various secondary meanings, have been preserved in the French and English derivatives. In the first case, to use Seneca's words, it meant the "transferring of one's property and one's right in it to another"[151]; in the second case, it meant insanity, especially in the form '*mentis alienatio*' first used by Cornelius Celsus in his famous *De Medicina*.[152] The secondary meanings varied from desertion and defection (already used in Cicero[153]) through estrangement[154] to quasi-religious uses such as St. Augustine's use of the expression '*mentis alienatio*'[155] for the vision of St. Paul. As to the German expression '*Entfremdung*,' its vernacular use roughly corresponded to that of the English expression 'estrangement,' while the expression '*Entäusserung*' had a more legal connotation corresponding to 'renunciation' and 'abdication.'

for something to be created, prefigures some aspects of the notion of alienation. Cf. G. Scholem, *Die jüdische Mystik in ihren Hauptströmungen* (Frankfurt, 1957) 285 ff. It is well known that the Cabala, through Böhme and Oetinger, had an influence upon eighteenth- and nineteenth-century German thought. This applies also to the cabalistic idea of *Zimzum*. Schelling, for example, writes in 1812: "Alles Bewusstsein ist Konzentration, ist Sammlung, ist Zusammennehmen seiner selbst. Diese verneinende, auf es selbst zurückgehende Kraft eines Wesens ist die wahre Kraft der Persönlichkeit in ihm, die Kraft der Selbheit," VIII, 74; cf. Scholem, *op. cit.* 444. Unfortunately, there exists no satisfactory study on the influence of the Cabala upon German Idealism; for Böhme see W. Schulze, *Judaica* 11 (Zürich, 1955) 12-29; for Oetinger see Benz$_1$. See also Habermas$_2$, 120 ff.

[151] *De Beneficiis* 5, 10: "Venditio alienatio est et rei suae iurisque in ea ad alium translatio."

[152] IV, 2, 2.

[153] *Ad Quintum Fratrem* 1, 4, 4: "Multa convenerunt quae mentem exturbarent meam—subita defectio Pompei, alienatio consulum, etc."

[154] Cicero, *De amicitia* 21, 76: "Scipio ... propter dissensionem quae erat in re publica, alienatus est a collega nostro Metello."

[155] *MPL* XXXVII, col. 1359: "Facta est illi mentis alienatio quam Graeci ecstasin dicunt, id est aversa est mens eius a consuetudine corporali ... alienata a praesentibus."

However, neither of these etymological considerations contributes substantially to the understanding of the use of '*Entfremdung,*' or '*Selbstentfremdung,*' in Marx. For the expressions '*Entäusserung*' and '*Entfremdung*' as used in Marx are closely connected with the history of German Idealism. Accordingly, the best approach to an initial understanding of Marx's notion of alienation would seem to be a brief survey of the development of German philosophy from Fichte onwards.

One of the ideas underlying Fichte's *Wissenschaftslehre* was that if the coercive character of experience (or, to use Fichte's own words, the "system of representations accompanied by a sentiment of necessity") was to be explained in terms of man-independent things, then man could not be said to be truly free. Or, to put it in another and more precise way, those people whose image of themselves was only a reflection of their knowledge of things had not succeeded in elevating themselves to the "full sentiment of freedom and absolute autonomy." After all, whatever these people were, they had become in terms of the external world. As opposed to such "dogmatists," the "idealist"—that is, the man who was conscious of his "autonomy and independence of everything outside him"—was in no need of things to support his self. "The ego which the idealist owns and which interests him abolishes all faith in things; the idealist takes a fancy to his independence and embraces it out of emotion. His faith in himself is not a mediated one."[156]

However, this Jacobin protest against all necessity imposed from outside[157] could not possibly argue away the existence of

---

[156] Fichte, III, 18. We restrict ourselves to the last and most intelligible version of Fichte's *Wissenschaftslehre*.

[157] Cf. Gehlen, 339. This Jacobin attitude is most visible in a small pamphlet entitled "Zurückforderung der Denkfreiheit von den Fürsten Europens, die sie bisher unterdrückten. Eine Rede," which Fichte published in 1793. In this pamphlet, which he later described as the "dearest" of his writings, freedom of thought and speech is described as a human right that in past times man had delivered up to the princes and that now has to be regained. Cf. *J. G. Fichte-Gesamtausgabe*, eds. R. Lauth and H. Jacob (Stuttgart, 1964) Vol. I, 167-192. It may be added that this Jacobin attitude had its theoretical counterpart in the description of man as a being which determines itself, an idea that we

"representations accompanied by a sentiment of necessity." In spite of the fact that the only value which the idealist recognized was "freedom" and though he viewed all being only as freedom's "negation,"[158] these representations had to be explained. Fichte's "solution" consisted in saying that all necessity allegedly imposed upon the ego from the outside was in fact a series of laws imposed by the ego upon itself in free, creative activity. But this creative activity preceded consciousness. Therefore, when man became conscious of himself, he was already confronted with products of his "freedom" which he, or the "freedom," had produced "without distinct consciousness," *durch das Ungefähr*.[159] Still, these products were originating from him; they were *his*, although man did not experience them as such. Accordingly, it was the task of the *Wissenschaftslehre* to restore these "lost" products of man's freedom by reconstructing the preconscious "life story of consciousness," by developing the whole universe out of the ego as if "out of an onion."[160] The idealist philosopher had to be a *Nacherfinder des Bewusstseins*, a reconstructor of consciousness,[161] one who construed the universe out of the ego and thus showed that seemingly independent things are in fact products of the ego's freedom.

It is in this context that Fichte several times uses the expression '*entäussern*.' Thus the first version of his *Wissenschaftlehre*, published in 1794, contains a passage in which the ego's activity of positing objects is referred to as a *Tätigkeit des Entäusserns*, an activity in which the ego "externalizes" itself.[162] Similarly, in the *Wissenschaftslehre* of 1801, in an important passage which anticipates the use of the expression '*Vernunft*' in Hegel, Fichte describes the "object" as *entäusserte Vernunft*, "externalized"

---

touched upon earlier and that is well discussed by Zelený, *Filosofický Časopis* 4 (1964) 482 ff.

[158] Fichte, III, 83.

[159] *Ibid.* 571. Cf. 117: "Ohne unser Bewusstsein"; 109: "Ohne deutliches Bewusstsein."

[160] *Ibid.* 599; cf. 623: "Gnosogonie."

[161] *Ibid.* 582.

[162] Fichte, I, 360.

reason.[163] In both cases the primary connotation of '*entäussern*' would seem to be that of "externalization." But it also seems to have a connotation of "renunciation" and "abdication," which, incidentally, indicates the connection between the vernacular and the specifically idealistic use of '*Entäusserung.*' Thus, for example, when Fichte writes that in knowing itself knowledge *entäussert sich seiner selbst, und stellt sich hin vor sich selbst, um sich wiederum zu ergreifen,*[164] he obviously does not only want to say that the self-knowledge of knowledge is an "externalization" of knowledge. Rather, what he wants to say is that knowledge, in order to grasp itself, has to abdicate its very nature, to empty itself of itself, so as to be able to be confronted with itself and eventually to regain itself. That usually Fichte describes knowledge's knowledge of itself as "immediate" and that consequently the above sentence would have to be understood as conveying only an image is immaterial to our analysis.

Schelling tried to overcome Fichte's one-sided emphasis on the ego by reverting to and emphasizing the concept of *nature.* As he explains in the introduction of his *System of Transcendental Idealism* of 1800, Fichte's deduction of the "objective" from the "subjective" was only one of idealism's dimensions. It was also possible to start from a philosophy of nature which proved that nature had an inherent tendency to become "intelligent," that is, to grasp itself by becoming conscious of itself in man's mind.[165] But it is another aspect of Schelling's new interest in nature that is relevant to our study. Schelling argued against Fichte that the "system of representations accompanied by a sentiment of necessity" could not possibly be a product of the ego's freedom. If there was a production of necessary representations at all, it had to be rooted in the ego's very *nature.* For there were "too many things which the ego would like to change if it were true that external being depended upon its will."[166] If this were the case, however, then the recovery of a "lost freedom," which was the

---

[163] Fichte, IV, 73.
[164] *Ibid.* 8.
[165] Schelling, III, 340.
[166] Schelling, X, 92.

theme of Fichte's *Wissenschaftslehre*, had to be understood as the subject's "labor of coming to its senses," as a historical process through which the ego reached its completion rather than as an arbitrary act of an individual. Yet this, in turn, entailed the idea that the ego in question was an *Absolute* which reached its completion in and through man rather than man's *subjective existence*. In this way, as he himself stated in a lecture on the history of recent philosophy in 1827,[167] Schelling introduced the peculiar "tendency toward history" thereafter characteristic of German Idealism and its offshoots.

Somewhat later in the lecture just mentioned, Schelling tried to explain his belief that man was able to have an "immediate vision" of the world's emanation from God. The passage very well illustrates the cosmic idealism into which Schelling had transformed Fichte's idealistic voluntarism:

> What reaches itself and becomes conscious of itself in man is something which has traversed the whole of nature, supported everything and experienced everything, and which now has been brought back from self-alienation (*Selbst-Entfremdung*) to itself, to its essence. But as thus it is the regained beginning man's nature is again what it was at the beginning of creation. No longer similar to creation, it is again similar to the source of creation. Being the end of creation, human consciousness also is its beginning. To it, then, the whole movement from the beginning to the end ought to be transparent; human consciousness ought to be inborn *Wissenschaft*.[168]

---

[167] *Ibid.* 94.

[168] *Ibid.* 185. This passage might suggest that the notion of alienation is "religious" after all. However, three points must be noticed. First, contrary to what Hook believes, 'alienation' does not connote a fall from an ideal state, either in Schelling or in Hegel. This is most obvious from the way Schelling continues the passage just quoted; for he goes on to say that *in fact* man's mind is *not* inborn *Wissenschaft*, since man has fallen. Second, the idea of a "self-alienation" of the divine being seems to be foreign both to Greek philosophy (with the exception of the Gnostics who then influenced the Cabala) and to Christian theology. Neoplatonists sometimes used images of this kind, but Plotinus, for example, always took care to introduce such images by the expression οἷον, 'as if.' Finally, with respect to Marx's notion of alienation, one may add that even the "cosmic" dimension present in Schelling's and Hegel's thought has disappeared.

Anyone familiar with Hegel will admit that this passage might
well have been written by the author of the *Phenomenology of
Mind*. However, Hegel rarely uses the expression '*Entfremdung*';
he prefers the expression '*Entäusserung,*' with which he connects
an idea definitively articulating Fichte's original conception: to
be a thing or an object amounts to being an "externalization"
of the Mind. In fact, Hegel's whole philosophy may be reduced
to a constant reapplication and reinterpretation of the central
idea expressed in the *Phenomenology*:

> The Mind's immediate existence, consciousness, has two
> aspects—knowledge and the being-an-object (*Gegenständlichkeit*)
> negatively opposed to it. Since it is in the medium of conscious-
> ness that Mind develops and brings out its various moments,
> this opposition is found at each stage in the evolution of Mind
> and each of Mind's aspects appears as an expression (*Gestalt*)
> of consciousness.... Consciousness knows and comprehends
> nothing other than what falls within its experience, for what
> is found in experience is merely spiritual substance *qua* object
> of its own self. *Mind, however, becomes object, for it consists
> in the movement of becoming an other to itself, that is, an object
> for its own self, and in eventually transcending this otherness.*[169]

Thus, for example, in the often ridiculed paragraph 244 of the
Encyclopaedia Hegel describes Nature as an "externalization" of
the Mind's basic *Gestalt*, the Idea. The Idea "freely decides... to
discharge itself *qua* Nature," becomes another to itself, and then
gradually transcends this otherness until, by a complete return,
it becomes Spirit. However, Hegel's notion of *Entäusserung* expresses only one aspect of Fichte's idea of a "lost freedom" to be
regained. For Fichte's abstruse speculations also might be understood as a quite ingenious presentiment of a phenomenon known
only to modern times, namely, that human products may become
independent of their originators and then dominate them rather
than being dominated by them. To give a modern example familiar
to all sociologists: simply by reaching a certain size an industrial
undertaking may impose upon its originator obligations at which
he never had aimed; it extricates itself from its originator's hold

---

[169] Hegel₂, II, 36 (see 602 ff.); tr. Baillie, 96 (see 789 ff.). The italics are mine.

and develops laws of its own which deflect and restrict the ends originally envisaged.[170]

Though he never was able to isolate this psychologico-sociological phenomenon from the merely speculative "phenomenon" of *Entäusserung*, Hegel deserves the credit of having first described it in an articulate way. For the first parts of the famous section of the *Phenomenology* entitled "Spirit Alienated from Itself" are in fact an analysis of this very phenomenon. What Hegel tries here to describe is the gradual dissolution of unreflective life embedded in custom and tradition, a development which according to him took place between the end of the Middle Ages and the French Revolution. In antiquity and in the Middle Ages, Hegel intimates, man had accepted the existing intellectual, political, social, and economic order as an order of "being," as something utterly natural, upon which he saw no reason to reflect. With the emergence of modern individualism, in fact of "civil society," this naive harmony between man and his *Lebenswelt* (to use Husserl's term) began to dissolve. For man began to realize that all such order originated from himself. But if it was true that the whole organization of human society was his product, then all hardships and discomforts ʼimposed upon man by society were unnecessary. However, even though they were unnecessary, they did exist.

Thus, at the very moment at which man realized that the order of society was his deed, this very order began to appear as something different from and alien to man. It began to appear as an "alienation" of man from himself. As Hegel puts it in his awkward language: "the existence of the world was the work of self-consciousness, but likewise an actuality immediately present and alien to it, which had a peculiar being of its own and in which self-consciousness did not recognize itself." The whole man-made world formed itself into an order both oddly coherent and alien; it appeared as an "externalization and de-essentialization (*Entwesung*) of self-consciousness," as an *Entfremdung der Persönlichkeit*, an alienation of the human person from itself. Man's own intellectual, political, social, and economic life had become an "objective reality" existing

[170] Cf. Gehlen, 338 ff.; Marcuse$_2$, 274 ff.

independently on its own account. In the end, then, man's universe seemed to be divided into a "present" of the individual's private life and a "beyond" to which belonged all ideas, ideals, social patterns, and, more generally, the whole realm of human "culture." "The beyond is directly opposed to the present. The former is both the thinking and being thought of the latter and its alienated actuality."[171]

We cannot enter into a more detailed discussion of Hegel's analysis of "self-alienated spirit," which is both one of the most challenging and one of the most intricate passages of the whole *Phenomenology*. However, there is one aspect of this analysis which we still have to mention, namely, that it is in connection with this self-alienation of spirit that Hegel discusses the struggle of the *Aufklärung* with religion. According to Hegel the alienation of the world of culture from its originator, man, expresses itself in a "flight" of religion from the "real world."[172] Religion ceases to be a mastery of the present and turns into a sort of escapism seeking all solutions in the beyond; it turns into what Hegel calls "belief (*Glauben*)." The inevitable reaction to this degeneration of religion is the *Aufklärung*, which, though it is only another aspect of the general alienation, "upsets the household arrangements which spirit carries out in the house of belief, by bringing in the goods and furnishings belonging to the actual world, a world which spirit cannot refuse to accept as its own property, since its consciousness likewise belongs to that world."[173] In short, Hegel understands the *Aufklärung* as a protest against religion's artificial overcoming of alienation in terms of an escape from this world, an escape which in fact only perpetuates the general alienation.

Reading the subsection "The Struggle of Enlightenment with Superstition," one easily understands why many commentators have suggested that it was here that Feuerbach had dug up his idea that religion was an alienation.[174] But it is important to see

---

[171] Hegel$_2$, II, 372 ff.; tr. Baillie, 509 ff.

[172] *Ibid*. 376; tr. Baillie, 513.

[173] *Ibid*. 375; tr. Baillie, 512.

[174] Hyppolite$_1$, 422; Seeberger, 432 ff.; Gehlen, 343 ff. One may add that Hegel himself interprets Judaism in this way: for the Jew, God is outside man,

that Feuerbach, instead of taking over Hegel's analysis of the *Aufklärung* in its struggle with religion, took up the standpoint which Hegel had *ascribed to* the *Aufklärer*. For this circumstance throws a significant light upon the difference between Feuerbach's and Marx's interpretation of religion as well as upon the difference between Feuerbach's and Marx's understanding of the notion of *alienation*. By contracting the standpoint which Hegel had ascribed to the *Aufklärung*, Feuerbach always remained a figure on a scene set up by Hegel. Like Hegel's *Aufklärer*, Feuerbach mistook a perversion of religion for its true nature and fought religion as an isolated phenomenon instead of reducing it to a more basic kind of alienation.

That the claim that Feuerbach took up the standpoint of Hegel's *Aufklärer* (as opposed to Hegel's own standpoint) is far from being an artificial construction can easily be shown by comparing Feuerbach's antireligious critique with that of Hegel's *Aufklärer*. Both Feuerbach and the *Aufklärer*, as analyzed by Hegel, describe religion as a "tissue of superstition, prejudice, and error."[175] Both maintain in the face of belief that "the belief's Absolute Being is the essence of the believer's consciousness *qua* self, or that this Absolute Being is produced by consciousness."[176] Both "distort all aspects of belief, making them something quite different from what they are to the belief itself"[177] (one has only to think of Feuerbach's "transformative critique"). Both accuse religious consciousness of being "divided within itself in having both a beyond remote from actuality and an immediately present embodiment of that beyond,"[178] that is, of illegitimately "doubling" the real world into an earthly and a heavenly realm. Last but not least, both display in the face of religion the "vanity of witty criticisms"

and thus the essential character of consciousness is outside consciousness; cf. Hyppolite$_1$, 191.

[175] Hegel$_2$, II, 416; tr. Baillie, 561.
[176] *Ibid.* 436; tr. Baillie, 583.
[177] *Ibid.* 433 ff.; tr. Baillie, 581.
[178] *Ibid.* 437; tr. Baillie, 584.

and the arrogant "knowing better" which Hegel always decried as one of the most repellent traits of the *Aufklärung*.[179]

Marx, of course, understands religion in the same way as Feuerbach did. Like Hegel's *Aufklärer* and like Feuerbach he mistakes a historically conditioned form of religion for religion's true nature. But contrary to Feuerbach and together with Hegel he does not treat religious alienation as an independent phenomenon but reduces the escapism of "belief" to a more fundamental alienation. Thus, whereas Feuerbach remained a figure of a drama written by Hegel, Marx succeeded in truly rewriting Hegel's drama of the "spirit alienated from itself." This, incidentally, also indicates the fundamental difference between Feuerbach's and Marx's notion of *alienation*: Feuerbach's "alienation" ultimately is the self-delusion of an escapist which can be corrected in terms of "enlightenment"; Marx's "alienation," on the contrary, like that which Hegel had in mind, is an utterly real phenomenon, an alienation of man's whole existence, against which all "enlightenment" is impotent.

This already is obvious from the way in which Marx introduces his treatment of alienation. He points to an "*actual* economic fact" which classical political economy had discovered without being aware of its implications: "the worker becomes all the poorer the more wealth he produces, the more his production increases in power and range."[180] In other words, the intensity and quality of the worker's labor as well as the quantity and the quality of the products of his labor are inversely proportioned to the quantity and quality of the satisfaction of the worker's needs. The more the worker labors and the more wealth he produces, the greater his misery becomes. He produces his misery by his very labor. This, according to Marx, can only mean that the object which labor produces confronts the worker "as an *alien being*, as a *power independent* of the producer."[181] The two elements mentioned by Hegel as components of "alienation" are thus present: *B*,

179 *Ibid.* 415; tr. Baillie, 560.
180 *MEGA* I, 3, 82; tr. Milligan, 69.
181 *Ibid.* 83; tr. Milligan, *ibid.*

originating from A, is the proper and adequate result of A's very own activity; but at the same time B opposes A as an alien and independent being—instead of satisfying A's needs, it becomes the embodiment of A's constant frustration. Hence, "in the condition dealt with by political economy the actualization of labor appears as the worker's deactualization; the objectification of labor appears as loss of the object, indeed as object bondage; appropriation appears as alienation, as externalization."

Marx then proceeds to distinguish four different aspects of this alienation. First, there is the alienation of *products* to the producer which we have just described. Secondly, the very *act of labor* is alienated from the worker; it is something external to him, something in which he denies himself rather than affirming himself, an activity in terms of which he does not feel content but unhappy, "does not develop freely his physical and mental energy but mortifies his body and ruins his mind." This is most obvious from the fact that as soon as no compulsion, be it the master's whip or the worker's hunger, exists, "labor is shunned like the plague." Thirdly, man is alienated from the *"human species."* For as neither the products nor the very act of labor are truly his, man considers all collaboration and, in general, social life as a limitation rather than as a fulfilment of his humanity and uses his being social only as a means of satisfying his private needs. Finally, there is an alienation of man from man. For "every relationship in which man stands to himself ultimately is realized and expressed in the relationship in which man stands to other men." Indeed, if the product of his labor does not belong to the worker, it only can belong to a "man outside the worker"; if it does not satisfy the worker's needs, it necessarily satisfies the needs of another whom sooner or later the worker begins to hate. For in spite of all misery and alienation the worker undoubtedly produces, creates wealth.[182]

Of these four aspects of alienation Marx seems to consider that alienation inherent in the very act of labor as the most fundamental. In this way he succeeds in reducing all wretchedness of the present

---

[182] *Ibid.* 85 ff.; tr. Milligan, 72 ff.

world order to a basic anthropological datum. For if there is
alienation in man's fundamental productive activity, then everything which man produces must reflect this fundamental sickness,
from economic phenomena such as commodities and capital through
social, political, and legal settings to "products" of human consciousness such as philosophy and religion.

In the next section we shall try to show that this whole conception becomes truly intelligible only if one takes into consideration Marx's idea that labor is *the* activity of human self-actualization. At present we want to point out a basic difficulty in this
conception, a difficulty which may be the reason why Marx never
again explicitly took up the "theory of alienation" just described.
Marx's basic objection to classical political economy is that it
"proceeds from the fact of private property but does not explain
it to us."[183] In opposition to this, Marx claims that his own notion
of alienated labor succeeds in explaining both the existence of
private property and its nefarious effects which Proudhon had
expressed by the lapidary sentence: *la propriété, c'est le vol.* With
the analysis of the concept of alienated labor it becomes obvious,
according to Marx "that though private property appears to be
the source, the cause of alienated labor, it is really its consequence,
just as the gods *in the beginning* are not the cause but the effect
of man's intellectual confusion," and only much later does this
relationship become reciprocal.[184]

Obviously Marx argues this way because he wants to reduce
private property to a properly human phenomenon. But it is
equally obvious that if this is the meaning of the "theory of alienation," it inevitably results in an insuperable difficulty. For there
immediately arises the question, Why is labor alienated? As
long as one supposes that labor is alienated because the existing
economic conditions and, in particular, the unequal distribution
of social wealth forces the worker to barter away his own activity
of production, this problem obviously does not arise. However, as

[183] *Ibid.* 81; tr. Milligan, 67.
[184] *Ibid.* 91 ff.; tr. Milligan, 80.

he had inverted the causal relationship, Marx was confronted with the problem of defining the cause of labor's alienation.

One may even go further and say that if private property has to be viewed as an effect of the alienation of labor, the very notion of alienation completely loses its original realistic connotation. For if it is true that private property is generated by the alienation of labor, this alienation should be describable without reference to the labor's being owned by another, that is, without reference to private property. In that case, however, what remains of the phenomenon of alienation is merely a *psychological* fact which would seem to be socially relevant only in a very remote way, namely, the worker's uneasiness about and dissatisfaction with his labor. In spite of that, however, Marx could not possibly argue that private property was the cause of alienated labor. For in this case he would not have succeeded in actualizing his fundamental aim, namely, to reduce economic categories to human categories.

The only way out of this difficulty was a thorough reinterpretation of "alienation." Contrary to what is often believed, Marx continued to use the expression 'Entfremdung' even after 1844; in the first volume of *Das Kapital* it appears at least three times.[185] Nor is Hook right in claiming[186] that the only abiding sense in which Marx believed that human beings were "self-alienated" is expressed in the section on the "fetishism of commodities" in the first volume of *Das Kapital.* The Fichtean idea of a "lost freedom" to be regained always remained one of the implicit premises of Marx's thought. However, after the *German Ideology* Marx describes this idea in a way which, as opposed to the notion of *alienated labor* in the *Manuscripts*, is perfectly "nonmystical" (which, however, does not preclude that the *Aufhebung*, even of this more realistic kind of "alienation," remains both gnostic and Utopian).

The best description of this idea is found in the *German Ideology*; Marx speaks here of a "consolidation of what we ourselves produce

---

[185] Cf. *MEW* XXIII, 455, 596, 674; tr. Aveling-Moore, I, 432, 570, 645.
[186] Hook, 4.

into an objective power above us, growing out of control, thwarting
our expectations, bringing to naught our calculations,"[187] in short,
he speaks of the absence of a "control and conscious mastery"
of the socioeconomic powers which are born "of the actions of
men on one another."[188] In the *German Ideology* Marx still believed
that this "alienation" by which man limited himself instead of
becoming free was rooted in what he called the "subsumption of
individuals under the division of labor," that is, in the limitation
of human creativity imposed upon man through the division of
labor and in the ensuing congealment of human relations because
of their unconscious reduction to relations between objects of
barter. Toward the end of his life, however, Marx seems to have
realized that the realm of human creativity and freedom is limited
by man's very nature, by the "human condition" itself. As he
puts it in a famous passage in the third volume of *Das Kapital*,
a passage to which later we shall have to return:

> The realm of freedom actually begins only where labor which
> is determined by necessity and exterior purposiveness (*Zweck-
> mässigkeit*) ends; thus in the very nature of things it lies beyond
> the sphere of material production in the proper sense. Just
> as the savage must wrestle with Nature to satisfy his wants,
> to maintain and to reproduce his life, so must civilized man,
> and he must do so in all social formations and under all possible
> modes of production. With his development this realm of
> physical necessity expands, as do his wants; but at the same
> time the forces which satisfy these wants also increase. In
> this field, freedom can only consist in that socialized man,
> the associated producers, rationally regulate their metabolic
> interchange with nature, bringing it under their control instead
> of being ruled by it as by blind forces, and achieve this with
> the least expenditure of energy and under conditions most
> favourable to and worthy of their human nature. But it always
> will remain a realm of necessity. Beyond it begins the develop-
> ment of human energy which is considered an end in itself,
> the true empire of freedom, which, however, can blossom forth
> only with the realm of necessity as its basis.[189]

[187] *MEGA* I, 5, 22 ff.; tr. Pascal, 22 ff.
[188] *Ibid.* 27; tr. Pascal, 28.
[189] *MEW* XXV, 828; tr. Aveling-Moore, III, 799 ff.

21: ALIENATION II: *FELIX CULPA*

In the last section we saw Sidney Hook's opposition to the recent emphasis on Marx's theory of self-alienation on the ground that the notion of alienation is originally and primarily religious in nature (and thus, Hook implies, incompatible with the atheism characteristic of Marx's thought). But Hook has advanced still another and a more serious objection against the notion of alienation being genuinely Marxian in origin. To speak of man's nature as alienated, he argues, makes sense only when one assumes "either that there is an already agreed upon *ideal* or *norm* of what man's nature should be ... or that there *already* exists some ideal or norm ... which is identical with the *natural* essence of man and from which the forms of human behavior dubbed alienated are aberrant."[190]

With regard to the second assumption Hook is undoubtedly correct in claiming that the letter and above all the spirit of Marx's philosophy excludes a conception of human nature as a "constant and fixed character in history." However, the same may be said about German Idealism in general and about Hegel in particular. Marx is the first to acknowledge this. He explicitly praises Hegel's *Phenomenology* for having shown that the emergence of man's humanity is a process of human self-procreation[191] and that all previous history must be taken to be a history of man, not as a given subject, but as "man's act of *procreation*," the story of man's *coming* to be.[192] In *this* respect there would seem to be only two

---

[190] Cf. Hook, 6. For a more careful analysis see Habermas$_1$, 181 ff.
[191] *MEGA* I, 3, 156; tr. Milligan, 151.
[192] *Ibid.* 153; tr. Milligan, 146.

313

disagreements between Hegel and Marx: whereas Hegel's *Phenome-nology* views human self-procreation mainly as a *speculative act*, Marx views it as the result of "material" *labor*; and whereas Hegel views the *present* as the time of man's definitive emergence, for Marx this emergence still lies in the *future*. In connection with this last point Marx stresses the provisional character of all previous history more emphatically than Hegel. In his *Critique of the Hegelian Philosophy of the State*, for example, he describes the Middle Ages as the "animal history of humanity, its zoology,"[193] implying that in those times man still was not aware of himself as an individual and consequently was no "person" in the proper sense of the term. In the *Deutsch-Französische Jahrbücher* Marx even seems to extend this idea to contemporary bourgeois society by describing the "philistine" as a "political animal" on whose neck stands the only real "end of this whole society," the hereditary lord.[194] Finally, in the *Manuscripts* he explicitly states that all previous history was only "preparatory history," the prehistory of man's truly human needs and thus of man's full humanity.[195] In short, Marx unambiguously rejects the idea of an unchanging and transhistorical human nature; developing ideas found in Hegel's *Phenomenology*, he is even inclined to doubt whether the "animal" of the presalvific era deserves at all the title 'man.'

It is somewhat more difficult to decide whether and to what extent the notion of alienation, in order to be meaningfully appli-cable, presupposes an ideal or a norm of what man's nature *should* be. On the one hand, it would seem obvious that the notion of alienation, as developed by German Idealism and further articulated by Marx, implies that it is possible to measure actual history and, in general, reality against an "idea." For the basic connotation of 'alienation' is that something which is *his* opposes man as if it were an alien and independent being. For example, Marx's statement that under capitalism the products of man's labor are "alienated" from man presupposes the "idea" that man produces

---

[193] *MEGA* I, 1/1, 499.
[194] *Ibid.* 562.
[195] *MEGA* I, 3, 123; tr. Milligan, 111.

in order to satisfy his needs, and "the need of a thing is the most obvious and irrefutable proof of this thing's belonging to my essence, of its being for me ... of its being a proper characteristic (*Eigentüm-lichkeit*) of my essence."[196] The same, incidentally, would seem to apply to Marx's later analysis of the "fetishism of commodities." For when Marx says that the social character of man's labor appears to him as an objective and impersonal feature stamped upon the product of that labor, he quite obviously implies that under the capitalist mode of production a "human dimension" has separated itself from man, to whom it rightfully belongs. Marx never described the "fetishism of commodities" as if it were only a wrong *idea* which people have about reality; accordingly, even in this analysis he undoubtedly measures man's socioeconomic *existence* against an "ideal" or at least an "idea."

On the other hand, however, neither Hegel nor Marx measures man's "alienated state" either against a transhistorical human nature or against a "logically predetermined" future. Rather, they measure it against a human potentiality revealed by the very phenomenon of alienation—against a human potentiality which, though at first it emerges in an alienated state, allows one to envisage a previously unknown possibility of ultimate human self-actualization. This may be illustrated by referring once more to Hegel's analysis of "spirit alienated from itself." In the very first sentences of this section Hegel suggests that before man realized that the universe of culture was his own work, there was properly speaking no "alienation." The world of culture still did not have the connotation of something shut out from man; man viewed it as something belonging to the very order of "being"—like the laws of nature, for example. Eventually, however, man became aware of the fact that the world of culture was produced by him and thus was a part of himself. Yet in spite of this insight the world of cultural products remained as independent as ever; although man knew now that it was his work, he still had no hold on it. In fact, it was only now that man's own products appeared alien and inimical to him. He recognized them as being "his," and still

[196] *Ibid.* 537.

they were not "his." At the same time, however, man now could envisage a completion previously unknown to him—the possibility of identifying himself with his world, of recognizing himself in the surrounding world as in a mirror, of achieving his self-actualization beyond his limited ego in the whole universe.

It is extremely important to see this fundamental ambivalence of the notion of alienation both in German Idealism and in Marx. Both consistently view alienation as something negative, which, though it is highly undesirable taken by itself, is desirable as the only gate to ultimate completion. If alienation sometimes has the connotation of something wrong and perverse, of a "sin," it has at the same time the connotation of a *felix culpa*, of a sin which is glorious, not because it *talem ac tantum meruit habere redemptorem*—as Catholic liturgy, remembering that Adam's Fall was the occasion for Incarnation, sings on the eve of Easter—but rather because it is a necessary premise of man's ultimate *self*-completion.

As to *this* aspect of the notion of self-alienation, it is undoubtedly of pseudoreligious origin. This is obvious from the fact that it crops up each time German Idealists speak about the Fall and about evil in general. As in many other instances, the first to describe the Fall as a necessary step toward man's completion was Schiller. In an article published in 1790 in which he developed his ideas concerning "the first human society according to the Mosaic document," Schiller argued that the expulsion from Paradise, in which man was no more than the "happiest and most gifted of all animals," was necessary in order that man could become "free and ethical." Man had to lose his innocence in order to learn "to regain it by *his reason*, to return as a free and rational mind to the point from which he had started as a *plant* and a creature of instinct."[197] Somewhat later in the same article Schiller even formulated the basic idea underlying the notion of alienation: order can be reached only in terms of a recovery from disorder.

[197] Schiller, XIII, 25. Cf. Kant, IV, 153: "Nature desires that everything which is beyond the mere mechanical organization of his animal existence be produced by man out of himself through and through; and that man does not reach any happiness or perfection other than the one which, free of instincts, he has achieved by his own reason."

"Only lawlessness leads to law."[198] The same idea is present in
Fichte's famous lectures on the "fundamental characteristics of
the present age" which were delivered at Berlin in 1804-1805.
Fichte, like Schiller, described history as a gradual liberation
from instincts and their replacement by autonomous reason. In
the beginning, he argued, reason governed man through his instincts alone; the human race was living in a state of perfect innocence. But soon these instincts were codified and transformed into
an "exterior coercive authority"; the age of sin began. Eventually
there came the epoch of liberation from all authority—Fichte's
own time. Man had liberated himself from all instinct and authority,
but thereby also from all reason. This is the age of disorder, of
dissolution and dissoluteness, the "state of accomplished sinfulness." But at the same time this total disorder contains the
germs of a future superior order. Man will learn, and through
Fichte already learns, to love reason, thus to enter into an era
of justification. Eventually he will rebuild himself to a perfect
embodiment of reason, and history will culminate in an epoch of
"accomplished justification and sanctification."[199] We may add
that Fichte's description of the age of "accomplished sinfulness"
anticipates Hegel's (and Marx's) analysis of "civil society." Abandoned by his instincts and still not having reached Knowledge
(*Wissenschaft*), man is reduced to "mere naked individuality,"
and the species, "the only thing which truly exists," degenerates
into an empty abstraction.[200] With reason *qua* instinct having
withered away and autonomous self-conscious reason still not
being within man's reach, "there remains nothing but mere individual, personal life." No wonder, then, that the "present age"
knows only one virtue, "shrewdness (*Klugheit*) in pursuing one's
personal advantage."[201]

As far as historical analyses are concerned, Hegel's ideas about
this subject are much less naive. In any case the basic scheme
all but disappears behind the wealth of details, the interest in

[198] Schiller, XIII, 35.
[199] Fichte, IV, 403 ff.
[200] *Ibid.* 420.
[201] *Ibid.* 460.

which significantly distinguishes Hegel from other German Idealists.[202] But whenever Hegel discusses the Fall or the nature of
Evil, it immediately becomes obvious that he adheres to this
scheme after all. For example, he will say that the biblical story
of the Fall is a mythical description of the fact that spirit can
reach completion only in terms of an estrangement (*Entzweiung*).
Our sympathy for childlike innocence is meaningful only insofar
as this innocence reminds us of what ought to be produced autonomously by the spirit. "The harmony which, as something natural,
we contemplate in children has to become the result of the labor
and self-shaping (*Bildung*) of spirit. Christ says: if you do not
become like children, ... ; but this does not mean that we should
remain children."[203] The first men were prohibited from "knowing"
because the consciousness of being for oneself as against other
things, the separation of the subject from the object which is
characteristic of all knowing, is the very essence of evil. "To
be evil means to be abstract, to isolate oneself; evil is isolation, to
be separated from the universal which is the rational .... But
through this separation also emerges ... the universally spiritual."[204]
Only by being "sinfully opposed to truth, removed from it, alienated
from it," can man enter the *Intellectualwelt*, the "intellectual
world which opens to knowledge God's nature, his determinations
and ways of acting."[205] Of course, as Hegel says in the *Phenomenology*, the negative will turn into sheer vanity if man does not succeed
in grasping its positive dimension.[206] Nevertheless, it is this negativi-
ty, "evil," "sin," separation, and alienation which is the ultimate
principle of all true development. Even God's own life would de-
generate into a devotional insipidity if "the seriousness, the pain,
the patience, and the labor of the negative" were missing from it.[207]

[202] In a letter of 1816, Hegel explicitly opposes the view that wealth of factual
information is irrelevant or even opposed to philosophy and "beneath its dignity,"
Hegel₄, II, 98; cf. Hegel₂, III, 319.
[203] Hegel₂, VIII, 94.
[204] Hegel₂, XVI, 264; tr. Speirs-Sanderson, III, 53.
[205] Hegel₂, XV, 35; tr. Speirs-Sanderson, I, 17.
[206] Hegel₂, II, 55; tr. Baillie, 117 ff.
[207] *Ibid.* 23; tr. Baillie, 81.

All this indicates that alienation, as viewed by German Idealists and later by Marx, has little if anything to do with an "aberration of human behavior" from a norm either agreed upon or identical with man's natural essence. To some extent, this widespread misunderstanding may be due to the psychopathological connotation of the English expression 'alienation' which, however, is all but completely absent from the German '*Entfremdung*.' More fundamentally, this misunderstanding probably can be traced back to an overestimation of Feuerbach's influence upon Marx (particularly, if this overestimation is combined with a superficial knowledge of Hegel). For, contrary to both Hegel and Marx, Feuerbach did indeed use the expression '*Entfremdung*' to refer to an aberration of man's thought from his natural essence: viewing man's biological existence as the ever perfect and "divine" essence of man, Feuerbach always tended to describe religion as well as speculative philosophy as a sort of sick, aberrant self-awareness. But as we have already seen, neither Hegel nor Marx ever believed in the existence of such an ahistorical human nature. Or rather, they never considered man's prehistorical biological existence as the "true essence of man." Accordingly, what Hegel as well as Marx have in mind whenever they speak of alienation is not an aberration but rather a phase in the process of man's self-development which, on the one hand, is essential to the achievement of full "humanity," and, on the other hand, is experienced by man as a radical frustration of his aspirations for self-completion.

This amounts to saying that alienation must not be mistaken for a loss of something which either originally belonged to man or else always ought to have belonged to him because of his very nature. Rather, it has to be viewed as a stage in the development of man's potentialities during which man experiences as his what in fact still is not his. Fichte's "lost products of freedom," Hegel's "absence of a mastery over the world of culture," as well as Marx's "alienation of labor," are experienced by man as a sort of loss. But, strictly speaking, man did not lose anything; he has only reached a stage in which he realizes that something on which he has no hold and on which he never had a hold originates from himself and thus is something on which he *should* have a hold. If this

were not what German Idealists and Marx meant, their claims
that man can reach his completion only by passing through a state
of alienation and that this alienation itself is the germ of ultimate
completion would have to be considered as pure mythology and
a rather preposterous mythology at that. Only if one assumes that
alienation is a phase of human self-development in which man
realizes what an ultimate completion might amount to and nevertheless still cannot achieve it, does it become meaningful to say
that alienation is a fundamental premise of, and by itself leads
to, the ultimate emergence of the *homo vere humanus*.

22: ALIENATION III: ALIENATED LABOR

In the foregoing discussion of alienation we have focused attention on an idea common to Marx and the German Idealists. But Marx speaks not of alienation in general, but of an alienation of labor. Accordingly, we have to proceed to a discussion of Marx's notion of labor as developed in the *Philosophic and Economic Manuscripts*.

However, in order to be able to fathom Marx's conception of labor, we have once more to return to Hegel, and this for a very simple reason. Marx never hid his admiration for Hegel's analysis of labor. He explicitly acknowledges that "Hegel's standpoint is that of modern political economy," since Hegel grasps labor "as man's essence in the act of proving itself (*das sich bewährende Wesen des Menschen*)," and he hails the *Phenomenology* for having shown that man, "true because real," is the outcome of his own labor.[208] Yet his ensuing criticism of Hegel's "dialectic" conceals an important fact, namely, that almost everything which Marx says about labor can be traced back to Hegel. It has to be admitted that Marx never denied this. But the way in which he dissociates himself from Hegel easily misleads one into believing that Marx objects to Hegel's notion of labor, while in reality he only objects to Hegel's dialectic of self-consciousness.

For after having expressed his admiration for Hegel's emphasis upon labor, Marx immediately goes on to say that Hegel saw only the positive, not the negative, side of labor. And at this point his argument takes an unexpected turn. One would expect Marx

[208] *MEGA* I, 3, 156; tr. Milligan, 151.

to advance an analysis of Hegel's concept of labor and to indicate how it differs from his own. Instead, Marx advances an interpretation of the whole of Hegel's *Phenomenology* in arguing that it is a coded description of the development of humanity in terms of labor. This turn is so unexpected that most commentators have been mislead into retaining only one of Marx's statements—namely, that "the only labor which Hegel knows and recognizes is abstract mental labor"[209]—and into taking this statement to mean that Hegel restricted himself to a discussion of mental activities and, in any case, reduced labor activities to thought activities. But it is quite obvious that Marx must have known better than that. Though he had no way of knowing Hegel's early writings, which even contain passages anticipating the notion of alienated labor,[210] he was familiar with the cryptic discussion of labor in the *Phenomenology* as well as with the lengthy section on labor in the *Philosophy of Right*.

In short, Marx does not accuse Hegel of having treated labor as if it was a thought activity. Rather, he accuses him of having in the *Phenomenology* described human history in terms of a dialectic of consciousness, not in terms of dialectic of labor. When he says that the only labor which Hegel recognizes is abstract mental labor, he has in mind the structure of the *Phenomenology* and in fact of Hegel's whole philosophy, not the passages on labor in the *Phenomenology* and other writings by Hegel. For what Marx wants to say is that Hegel's description of the movement of self-consciousness is an adulterated description of the historical movement of laboring humanity. Hegel's *Phenomenology* assumes that consciousness grasps its true essence only by externalizing itself into a world of objects and then in turn transcending this externalization; externalization and transcendence of externalization are both the motive power and the fundamental scheme of consciousness' movement toward its ultimate completion, Absolute Knowledge. This according to Marx is a coded description of

[209] *Ibid*. 157; tr. Milligan, 152.
[210] See, for example, Hegel₁, XX, 217, where Hegel describes exchange as an *Entäusserung*. For a brief commentary see Friedrich, 127.

the real circumstance that the motive power as well as the fundamental scheme of humanity's history is man's self-alienation in and through labor and the eventual transcendence of this alienation.

Moreover, Marx claims that the very fact that Hegel translates the real dialectic of laboring humanity into a dialectic of a mentally laboring self-consciousness is itself a reflection of alienated labor. Just as in religion man believes his own mind to be a divine entity outside him because in real life he is alienated from the products of his life activity—that is labor—so Hegel's description of history as a movement of a mentally laboring self-consciousness is nothing but "the self-objectification ... of the alienated mind of the world thinking within its self-alienation."[211]

Later we shall see that this criticism of Hegel embodies Marx's desire to show that philosophy is essentially "the alienation of man in his knowing himself"—Marx's attempt to overcome theory for the sake of *praxis*. At present we have to focus our attention on those passages in which Hegel really discusses labor, for in spite of all his misleading criticism it is in Hegel that Marx found his basic ideas concerning the nature of labor. It should be added that this discussion of Hegel's concept of labor should not be understood as a search for "Marxist aspects of Hegel's concept of alienation."[212] For to approach Hegel's treatment from this angle amounts to assuming that Hegel's theories about the dialectical movement of self-consciousness are spurious discussions of labor which time and again boil down to discussions of labor proper. In short, it amounts to assuming that Marx's interpretation of Hegel is correct, an assumption which is far from obvious. As we shall see, only the *Phenomenology* seems to corroborate Marx's conception; and even in this case one has to view this masterpiece of Hegel's from a very particular angle.

Hegel's interest in the problem of labor seems to have two roots. The first and more obvious root is Hegel's interest in economic problems which quite obviously is connected with Hegel's desire to understand the structure of contemporary civil society. Thus,

---

[211] *MEGA* I, 3, 154; tr. Milligan, 148.
[212] Cf. Friedrich, 124 ff.

for example, during his years at Frankfurt (1797-1800) he regularly scrutinized newspapers for economic information, especially such concerning property relations in England, and even wrote a commentary to J. Steuart's *An Inquiry into the Principles of Political Economy*, which unfortunately has not been preserved. During his ensuing stay at Jena (1801-1807) and in fact through his whole life Hegel continued to gather as much information on economic matters as he could.

Though Hegel never attempted to write a separate treatise on economics but always incorporated the results of his studies into general analyses of civil society, his interest in economic problems significantly distinguishes him from other German Idealists. Kant seems to have known some writings by Adam Smith, it is true; and Fichte's treatise on the "Closed Trade State" indicates that he too was familiar with modern economic ideas, especially with those of the French physiocrats. But neither Kant nor Fichte ever succeeded in viewing man's actions within society from a point of view other than that of ethics and jurisprudence. Their studies of economics had virtually no impact upon their concept of man's practical activity and its social implications. In particular they had no use for the notion of labor. In his *Critique of Judgement*, for example, Kant was far more interested in the notion of play than in that of labor; his analysis of labor reduces itself to the banal statement that it is "an occupation by itself disagreeable which is enticing only in terms of its consequences (e.g., wages)."[213] Fichte had a somewaht higher opinion of labor, but though he made a number of rather preposterous suggestions as to how labor should be divided and how one should work and when, he never attempted to inquire into the very essence of labor. What comes closest to Hegel's and Marx's ideas is Kant's statement that nature has equipped man so poorly because it wanted him to achieve a completion rooted in self-esteem rather than in well-being,[214] that in society, for example, nature uses an "unsociable sociability" to force man to develop himself. "Man wants concord, but nature

[213] Kant, V, 378 ff.
[214] Kant, IV, 153 ff.

knows better what serves his species and wants discord."[215] The same idea, though translated into moralizing terms, is found in one of Fichte's earliest writings: "Need is not the source of vice; it is the stimulus for action and virtue. The source of vice is idleness."[216]

The second root of Hegel's interest in the problem of labor is probably his almost instinctive opposition to Schelling's artificial aestheticism. For Schelling, in one sense at least, had succeeded in overcoming Kant's and Fichte's narrowly moralist conception of human actions. While Kant had regarded all rules of "making" as a corollary to theoretical philosophy and therefore without more ado identified the practical realm with that of ethics, and Fichte discussed in his "practical philosophy" only the problem of infinite striving, Schelling concluded his *System of Transcendental Idealism* of 1800 with a philosophy of artistic production by which he claimed to be able to overcome the Kantian dichotomy of a theoretical philosophy concerned only with nature and a practical philosophy concerned with freedom. He argued somewhat as follows. Theoretical philosophy assumes that mind is determined by being; practical philosophy assumes that being is determined by the mind; in short, the assumptions of practical philosophy contradict those of theoretical philosophy and vice versa. "How can one maintain both that representations conform to objects and that objects conform to representations?"[217] The only way to overcome this dichotomy consisted in saying that nature originates from the same activity which produces works of art or that "what we call nature is a poem written in a secret and wondrous script."[21] Nature is produced by this activity at a preconscious level, and therefore human representations conform to it. Works of art are produced with consciousness and therefore conform to human representations. Accordingly, "the objective world is only the primitive and still unconscious poetry of the mind—and philos-

215 *Ibid.* 155.
216 Fichte, I, 271.
217 Schelling, III, 348.
218 *Ibid.* 628.

ophy of art is the universal organon of philosophy and the coping stone of its whole vault."[219]

It has to be admitted that by this philosophy of art Schelling had succeeded in extending the notion of human *praxis* to actions which had a somewhat more "realistic" connotation than mere ethical decisions or the performance of duty. But as these actions were aesthetic ones, Schelling was increasingly inclined to identify philosophy with art and eventually understood his whole philosophy as the beginning of a new poetic mythology. Though we know very little about the development of Hegel's disagreement with Schelling, it would seem quite probable that among other things it was Schelling's overemphasis of such aesthetic activities which led Hegel to study the more sober, but far more fundamental, activity of labor.

Hegel discusses the problem of labor at some length four times: in two of his early writings of which Marx did not know and in the *Phenomenology of Mind* and the *Philosophy of Right*. Though each of these writings puts the accent in a slightly different way, they all seem to agree as to four main characteristics of labor. First, labor is an activity in terms of which man appropriates nature, that is, destroys its irrational independence and thus asserts his own metaphysical right of a "subject" over a world of "objects." Secondly, labor mediates between man's needs and the corresponding means of satisfying them and thus is a prolongation and sublimation of biological functions such as eating and drinking. Thirdly, labor is an activity by which man extricates himself from his biological existence, thus gradually leaving the animal kingdom. Finally, labor is in a very fundamental sense social, that is, while it extricates man from his animal existence, it leads him into society, in which both man and his labor find their ultimate completion.

While the third aspect emerges most clearly in the *Phenomenology* and the fourth aspect is best developed in the *Philosophy of Right*, the first two aspects are one of the central themes of Hegel's early writings. Moreover, in his early writings Hegel

[219] *Ibid.* 349.

knits these two first aspects so closely together that the resulting notion of labor is rather paradoxical. This is most obvious in the *System of Morality* (1802), in which Hegel seems to describe labor as a prolongation and sublimation of vital activities such as eating and drinking, that is, vital activities by which an animal acquires the necessary means of subsistence and thereby maintains and reproduces its life. For though Hegel views labor in connection with such biological functions, he never stresses their properly biological aspect. Instead he emphasizes an aspect which no biologist would bother to mention, namely, that eating and drinking (and in the end also labor) "annihilate." In short, in his early writings Hegel is most interested in the fact that by labor man both satisfies his vital needs and destroys nature's brute "facticity," its being given in a "natural immediacy" (which in turn is closely connected with the third point, namely, that by labor man extricates and dissociates himself from nature).

Hegel's first biographer, K. Rosenkranz, once quotes Hegel as saying: *Arbeiten heisst die Welt vernichten oder fluchen*,[220] to labor is to annihilate the world or to curse. And in fact, especially in his early writings, Hegel tends to describe labor as a curse. Yet he is far from saying that labor is a curse imposed upon man, though in his later writings he occasionally does acknowledge this. Rather, he describes labor as if it were a curse which man hurls against the nature and life upon which he depends. He does not, of course, deny that man eats, drinks, and labors because of his dependence upon nature, that is, in order to satisfy his vital needs. But Hegel's description of need is very peculiar; he describes it as if it were the experience of the presence of realities which bar a "subject" from being self-contained. Thus, for example, in the *System of Morality* Hegel speaks of need as of a lack of "absolute identity." The object of this need is described as a sort of stubborn entity which obstructs the subject's self-enjoyment rather than something which the subject is lacking.[221] Accordingly he describes fundamental forms of satisfying needs such as eating and drinking

[220] Rosenkranz, 543.
[221] Hegel₁, VII, 418 ff.

as if their main function were to remove a nullity which bars the subject from being what it truly is. An echo of this idea is found in a famous passage at the beginning of the *Phenomenology* in which Hegel argues that animals know better than some philosophers how to handle things of sense: assured of the nothingness of such things, they reach out for them without more ado and eat them up. Here Hegel quite obviously wants to say more than that the proper thing to do with objects of sense is to satisfy one's needs by them. What he wants to say is that such things have to be treated as if they were nothing—that is, annihilated—and that hunger and thirst are an animal awareness of the reality or rather unreality of things of sense. The secret of an adequate handling of things of sense is an initiation into the "Eleusinian mysteries of Ceres and Bacchus," that is, eating and drinking.[222]

However, though Hegel views eating and drinking as a fundamental form of treating the unreality of nature, he immediately adds that this kind of annihilation is ineffective, since it is governed by the law of eternal recurrence. The animal has constantly to begin afresh and never achieves what it aims at, to annihilate nature. Man, on the contrary, annihilates nature by transforming it. "The object is annihilated ... by being replaced by another."[223] Instead of again and again making nature disappear, man gets it under control until eventually he lives in a nature which "remains while it is annihilated"[224] and is surrounded by a world which embodies his self-assertion *qua* "subject."

On the other hand, although Hegel never describes labor *as* something biological or quasi-biological, he views it so much *in connection with* biological functions that he takes a *tool* rather than, for example, a house or a garden to be the main instance of nature as transformed by labor. What Hegel has in mind might perhaps be described as follows. No longer satisfied with what brute nature offers, man labors in order to adapt it to his needs: he cultivates the soil, grows crops, tames animals, and so on.

[222] Hegel₂, II, 90 ff.; tr. Baillie, 159 ff. Cf. VII, 98 ff.; tr. Knox, 41 ff.; VIII, 57.
[223] Hegel₁, VII, 420.
[224] Hegel₁, XIX, 220.

But as long as he only transforms nature in order to consume it, his "annihilation" still moves at a level similar to that of animals. Only when he constructs a tool has he achieved an annihilation which does not annihilate itself as soon as it is carried out and therefore endlessly has to be repeated. "In the tool the subjectivity of labor is elevated to something universal."[225] Annihilation has become a lasting appropriation, for a tool is a piece of nature which man has snatched away from nature, which he has got under his control and now uses *against* nature. Ultimately man constructs machines which he only has to service, that is, he leaves the annihilation of nature to nature itself. He succeeded in out-witting and deceiving nature[226] by using its own laws against it.[227]

However, this complex "annihilation" of nature's immediacy has still another aspect. Hegel describes labor as an activity which, while it grows and develops, is accompanied by a gradual sublima-tion of man's original animal needs. It does not become per-fectly clear whether Hegel wants to say that the increasing sublima-tion of man's needs is due to the development of labor or whether, on the contrary, the development of labor—its becoming more complex and all-embracing—is caused by a development of man's needs. Occasionally he seems to mean that the annihilating trans-formation effected by labor concerns man's own nature too, not only nature outside man. In any case he repeatedly points out that when he labors, man checks his desire and postpones his satis-faction, and thus sublimates both.[228] Animal hunger cannot wait;

[225] Hegel$_1$, VII, 428.

[226] Hegel$_1$, XX, 198 ff. Cf. Dubský, 20 ff.

[227] *Ibid.* Contrary to his mature writings (e.g., Hegel$_2$, VII, 277; X, 402), Hegel's early writings sometimes dwell upon gloomy aspects of machines. Thus the *Jenenser Realphilosophie* describes how through machines human labor loses its value and becomes "dead," degrading the consciousness of a factory worker to "ultimate dullness," Hegel$_1$, 237 ff. However, it should be observed that in the beginning of the nineteenth century the notion of machine was not very well defined; even a more complex tool was likely to be described as a *Maschine*. Thus, in the *Staatslexikon* of 1834 (I, 653 ff.), the economist, F. List, cites as machines not only ships and steam engines, but also the plow, the mill, the axe, etc.—indeed, streets, bridges, and banks.

[228] Hegel$_1$, VII, 421; XIX, 220; Hegel$_2$, II, 156, etc. A similar idea is already

it accepts whatever nature offers. That man is prepared, for example, to grow crops instead of devouring whatever he can find indicates that he is prepared to check more primitive needs (hunger) for the sake of the satisfaction of more sophisticated ones (appetite). When he constructs a tool, he has already dissociated himself enough from nature, both within and outside himself, to be able to afford an activity whose results are not intended for immediate consumption. When he produces something in order to trade with other men, he must be able to "abstract" from his own needs and to adjust nature to the needs of others. Eventually there emerges a situation which Hegel calls "abstract-universal labor," when everybody's labor aims at the satisfaction of the needs of others and when nobody can satisfy his own needs without satisfying those of others. Labor has become the binding agent of society.

The idea that labor leads man beyond the animal kingdom is best exemplified in the famous Master-Slave Dialectic in the *Phenomenology*. The passage in question is found in a lengthy section in which Hegel describes how consciousness finds its way back to itself and eventually learns to understand itself as the ultimate essence of reality, that is, as reason. The previous sections had discussed consciousness as a knowledge of another, as a knowledge of the sensible world. But as consciousness found no "truth" in this other, it now returns to itself to search in itself for the truth of everything other than itself. Consciousness has become self-consciousness. But this self-consciousness is not the "motionless tautology" of Fichte's "I am I." Rather, it is "essentially a return from otherness," a "movement" opposing and therefore mediated by the "real" world which consciousness no longer respects. Taken as such, consciousness is "desire"; for, like the animals initiated into the Eleusinian mysteries mentioned above, its self-assertion depends upon an annihilation of everything outside it. But this self-consciousness is at the same time that of a living animal; by its very essence it is bound to that by whose annihilation it is

---

formulated in Marx's dissertation: "In order that man as man becomes his only real object, he must have broken his relative existence, the power of desire and of brute nature," *MEGA* I, 1/1, 31; cf. Schmidt, 118.

constituted, the sensible world. Consequently, in order to find "truth" in itself, consciousness tries to prove its independence from nature by risking that which most fundamentally binds it to nature: its life. It enters a life-and-death struggle with another who is equally interested in proving his independence from the world. "It is only by risking life that freedom is obtained; only thus is it tried and proved that the essential nature of self-consciousness ... is not merely an absorption in the expanse of life."[229]

However (and at this point Hegel's abstract analysis turns into a "story"), if neither of the two foes gives in, they will kill each other, thus altogether missing that at which they had aimed. Though their death may grant the certainty that both did risk their life, it obviously does not grant it to them; and "in this experience self-consciousness becomes aware that life is as essential to it as pure self-consciousness."[230] One of the foes gives in and becomes the slave of the other, the master. The master has shown his independence from life; he has shown that nothing except freedom and self-consciousness counts for him. The slave, on the contrary, remains bound to the world, as he was not able to "abstract" from life.[231] In fact, as Hegel indicates, it is mainly his submission to the laws of life and the world which makes him a slave. While the master is the "power controlling independent being, for he has shown in the struggle that he holds it to be merely something negative," the slave is kept in bondage by the master through his dependence upon the world. He is a half-human entity, which the master can interpose between himself and nature, to enjoy the latter without at all being bound to it.

However, if this situation is considered more closely, the master has not achieved what he had aimed at. In order to prove this point, Hegel had argued in an earlier passage that to be recognized *as* self-consciousness is an integral element of self-consciousness itself. Accordingly he now can argue that the master's being self-consciousness has no objectivity; his certainty of himself as self-consciousness is "without truth." For though his slave recogniz-

[229] Hegel₂, II, 151; tr. Baillie, 233.
[230] *Ibid.* 153; tr. Baillie, 234.
[231] Cf. Hegel₂, III, 110: "... the bondage which prefers life to freedom...."

es him as self-consciousness, this recognition is of no value, since the master does not recognize his slave in the same way. The master is recognized by someone whom he himself does not recognize. Thus the master finds himself in an "existential impasse"[232]: he has overcome the biological order, but as there is no equal to acknowledge it, he is stuck in his subjectivity. As he cannot possibly desire to become a slave in turn, he has reached the top of the ladder without having reached full objective humanity. Though he has not reached full satisfaction, there is nothing for which he possibly could strive. He has reached a dead end. As Kojève puts it, he is stuck in his being a master: "he cannot transcend himself, change, progress. He has to win and become a master ... or die. One can kill him, but one cannot transform him."[233]

The slave, on the contrary, has an ideal: to overcome his slavery. By his very nature he is dynamic, he strives for something higher. While the master represents a blind alley of man's history, the slave is its future. Of course the true end of the slave's dynamism cannot be his becoming master; this way he soon would find himself again in the impasse just described. Rather, it is his status as slave which is the germ of his being the ray of hope of humanity. For the master forces him to work, and by his *labor* (which the master never would have taken upon himself) the slave transforms nature instead of simply abstracting from it, or "annihilating" it:

> Desire has reserved to itself the pure negating of the object and thereby unalloyed feeling of self. This satisfaction, however, just for that reason is itself only a state of evanescence, for its lack of objectivity and subsistence. Labor, on the other hand, is desire restrained and checked, evanescence delayed and postponed—it shapes. The negative relation to the object becomes a form of the object and passes into something permanent, precisely because for the laborer the object has independence.... Thus laboring consciousness reaches an intuition of independent being as of itself.[234]

I am far from denying that even when retold in this way the Master-Slave Dialectic is rather puzzling. In particular it never

---

[232] Cf. Kojève, 25.
[233] *Ibid.* 27.
[234] Hegel$_2$, II, 156; tr. Baillie, 238.

becomes clear whether Hegel had in mind a historical process (for example, the gradual emergence of man in primitive society) or whether in genetic terms he is describing an essential structure of self-consciousness. Since in the following chapters he will discuss the Stoic's and the sceptic's way of transcending the world and suggest that these are superior types of "annihilation," it is difficult to accept Kojève's suggestion that Hegel had in mind the fundamental pattern of the history of man's becoming man. On the other hand, if the passage is nothing but a parable illustrating an aspect of the "logical" structure of self-consciousness, it is almost impossible to interpret it literally.

But be that as it may, the Master-Slave Dialectic points to two aspects of Hegel's philosophy of labor which quite obviously have influenced Marx. First, it suggests that labor is an activity in terms of which man succeeds in transcending his biological existence and thus in becoming man properly speaking. Before self-consciousness entered the life-and-death struggle, it was absorbed in the "expanse of life"; man was an animal with human potentialities, nothing more. As master, self-consciousness succeeded in extricating itself from life, but it ended in a blind alley. Only insofar as it was laboring, self-consciousness succeeded in doing away with the stubborn independence of nature and life. In order to assert himself as man, as a full-fledged human being, man has to transform the world so as to be able to recognize himself in something independent of himself. And this only labor can achieve.

However, and this is the second important lesson of the Master-Slave Dialectic, man would never labor if no one were to force him. Though eventually man will try to extricate himself from slavery, this slavery is a necessary prerequisite of his becoming man. As Hegel puts it,[235] both mortal fear and labor are necessary for the humanization of man. For without fear the shaping of the world would never be more than mere caprice. If his labor was not forced labor, man's labor would only nibble at reality. To put it in Marxist terms, man would never be more than a reformer. To revolutionize the world, to change the *condition humaine*,

---

[235] *Ibid.* 157; tr. Baillie, 239.

he has to experience the "mortal terror of his absolute master," be this master death, God, another man, or nature. It is hardly necessary to add that it is by reading this passage that Marx came to the conclusion that although both the capitalist and the proletarian, both the master and the slave, are in a stage of alienation, only the proletarian's alienation really counts.

Our analysis of Hegel's philosophy of labor would not be complete without a few words about Hegel's most sober analysis of labor in paragraphs 189 and following of the *Philosophy of Right*. These paragraphs take up a subject already alluded to, namely, labor as a constitutive element of civil society. Here Hegel explicitly refers to political economy by mentioning Smith, Say, and Ricardo. Political economy, as Hegel understands it, studies society precisely from the point of view from which Hegel discusses the problem of labor, namely, as a "system of wants" in which everybody satisfies his own needs by satisfying those of others. Interestingly enough, Hegel also points out that it is in this context and actually only in this context that his philosophy of right— that is, his moral, legal, and political philosophy—studies man *as man*, a statement anticipating Marx's claim that need, labor, and satisfaction as touched upon by political economy are the proper and indeed most fundamental human dimensions. "From the point of view of law the object is the *person*; from the point of view of morals, the *subject*; from the point of view of the family, the *member of the family*; in civil society, the citizen (*as bourgeois*). Here, from the point of view of needs, the object is ... that which one calls *man*."[236]

Accordingly, when discussing the system of wants, Hegel refers to a basic difference between man and animal. The needs of animals are as limited as the means and modes of satisfaction of which they dispose. Man, on the contrary, is a being whose needs constantly develop: they reproduce each other (*Vervielfältigung*), become more articulate and "abstract." What Hegel seems to

---

[236] Hegel$_2$, VII, 272; tr. Knox, 127. Marx refers to this paragraph when, in *Das Kapital*, he says that in civil society a general or banker plays a greater role than "man as such"; cf. *MEW* XXIII, 59; tr. Aveling-Moore, I, 57. Cf. Löwith$_2$, 206 ff.

imply is that a few primitive needs fan out into a number of more sophisticated ones: first, man simply wants to quench his thirst, later he wants cold water when he is hot and a hot drink when he is cold, a glass with which to drink, a pot in which to heat the liquid, and so on. At first man is satisfied with what nature offers. But while an animal never overcomes this primitive stage, human needs develop and thus force man to modify nature, to destroy its "natural immediacy." Man simply cannot have it as easy as an animal; indeed, "being a mind, he should not have it as easy."

It is this constant development of needs which leads man out of the animal kingdom. For it entails an inhibition and sublimation of his desires. And as the multiplication and diversification of needs entails and later is in turn furthered by a multiplication and diversification of the means of satisfaction, the general result is a constant refinement of man and his world. But this refinement brings with it a constantly increasing "socialization" of man. Though Hegel still does not use the expression ' *Vergesellschaftung*' ('socialization'), he undoubtedly has in mind the idea conveyed by this Marxian expression. *Alles Particulare wird ... ein Gesellschaft-liches*[237]: all individual desire, labor, and satisfaction become entangled in society. As Hegel puts it in the *Encyclopaedia*,[238] the more abstract labor becomes, the more unconditional is the individual's dependence upon the social context (*gesellschaftlicher Zusammenhang*). For the more refined a man's needs are, the less is he able to produce the means of satisfaction by himself. He has to acquire them from others, which entails that he has to subordinate his needs, his labor, and his satisfaction to the needs, the labor, and the satisfaction of many, and ultimately of all, other men. A man who needs only a few pieces of raw meat and some water, a cave in which to live and a hide with which to cover himself, is almost completely independent of other men. But if he needs a well-prepared meal three times a day along with a well-furnished house and sophisticated clothes, he depends upon a virtually infinite number of other men whose needs he has to

[237] Hegel$_2$, VII, 274; tr. Knox, 269.
[238] Hegel$_2$, X, 402.

respect in order to be able to satisfy his own needs. He has to adjust his labor to the needs and often to the opinions and whims of others; indeed he has to curb oversophisticated needs in order not to threaten the satisfaction of more fundamental and generally recognized ones (a practice which, as Hegel intimates, leads in many respects to a leveling of differences between men). In short, man has to give up all willful individualism; his whole human existence becomes social.

However Hegel is far from complaining about this development. He sees in it the self-assertion of rational universality as opposed to individual particularism. Although everybody aims only at the satisfaction of his own particular needs, the very nature of these needs makes it impossible to satisfy them without at the same time satisfying the needs of everyone else. Indeed Hegel even goes a step further: he explicitly describes the increasing "socialization" of modern man as a process of "liberation." To him the idea that primitive presocial man had more freedom than modern socialized man is simply false. For according to Hegel the alleged freedom of the presocial savage was in fact only a thorough dependence upon nature, both within and outside man, and thus an ultimately irrational arbitrariness characteristic of all "external necessity." Modern social man, it is true, is also bound by necessity. But it is a necessity imposed upon him by other men and thus ultimately *selbstgemachte Nothwendigkeit*, a self-imposed restraint which is only an aspect of true freedom.[239]

At this point, even though we have to interrupt the analysis of Hegel's ideas, we cannot refrain from pointing out that this argument of Hegel's is a sophism—a sophism characteristic of German Idealism since Fichte, which through Marx has become common property of all communists, Marxists, and pseudo-Marxists. It is not easy to decide whether modern man, *even though* "socialized" to a previously unknown degree, *nevertheless* is more free than man was in earlier times. But even if it were true that he is more free, the claim that his dependence upon society *is* freedom simply is false. One might argue that modern man could not possibly

---

[239] Hegel₂, VII, 275; tr. Knox, 128.

be as free as in fact he is if he were not "socialized." But even then restraints imposed upon him by society would be restraints, that is, the opposite of freedom. Hegel's sophism consists in his describing social restraints as restraints which man imposes upon himself. There is a certain truth in his statement when it is put in a general way, for social restraints undoubtedly differ from restraints imposed by nature in that they are due to man. But what Hegel (and after him Marx) overlooks is that it is not *I* who imposes these restraints upon myself but *other men* who impose them upon me. In short, Hegel confuses a mythical self-restraint of a Man with a capital 'M' with the fact that men impose restraints upon each other, that *other men* impose restraints upon *me*. Seen from this point of view, social restraints are as "external" to man as those imposed by nature and have as little to do with freedom as natural laws. After all, society is not a religious order into which one enters at will. Each of us, whether he likes it or not, is "thrown" into it—and thereby his freedom is curbed.

Hegel would of course reply that this restraint of willfulness is in fact an essential aspect of freedom. Freedom consists, not in doing whatever occurs to one's mind (or body), but in doing that which is rational. But even if this were true (which in a sense it is), there seems to be no reason to expect that restraints imposed by men are more "rational" than those imposed by nature. They *may* be more rational, it is true. But recent history seems to have demonstrated that they may just as well be far less rational.

Of course Hegel was well aware that the "liberation" entailed by the emergence of civil society is not perfect. In particular, as we have seen earlier, he was aware of the fact that in civil society the luxury and thus implicitly the freedom of the one is the misery and unfreedom of the other. But instead of arguing that in this world man's freedom cannot reach its ultimate perfection, that man always will remain restrained either by nature or by other men and in fact by both, and that the most which he can achieve is a precarious balance of freedom and restraint, Hegel idealized a perfect identity of reason, necessity, and freedom in the rational state, just as Marx later idealized the same identity for his communist society. To both of them it never seems to have occurred that in this world of ours necessity is never rational enough, and reason never necessary enough, to coincide with absolute freedom.

When this is said, there remains little to add about Hegel's notion of labor which is really relevant to our subject. The only point still worth stressing is that Hegel's view of the division of labor is far less nostalgic than that of Rousseau or Marx. For contrary both to the Romantics and to Marx, Hegel is too much of an intellectualist not to see that it is precisely the much decried division of labor which permits man to forget nature and to turn to higher and more important realms. He even hails the mechanization of labor: the fact that human labor is less and less aimed at the satisfaction of immediate needs "makes labor increasingly mechanical and thus eventually permits man to step aside and to let machines take over."[240] Similarly, Hegel does not seem to object to an unequal distribution of riches. He describes the inequality of private property as a "sphere of particularity which the universal incorporates into itself (*die sich das Allgemeine einbildet*)" and views it as an element of difference which "the reason immanent to the system of human wants ... organizes into an organic whole" of various estates.[241] This, of course, does not mean to say that Hegel favors a disproportioned accumulation of wealth in the hands of a few. But he is far from believing that the emergence of a pauper class should be prevented in terms of economic equality artificially introduced. As far as property is concerned, Hegel argues that the demand for equality is an abstract demand of "empty understanding ... which considers its *ought* as the real and rational."[242]

As we already have said, Marx's basic notion of labor differs little from that of Hegel. At first one might want to see a major difference in the fact that Marx describes labor as an activity by which not only man but also nature reaches its completion, while Hegel tended to describe it as an activity by which man

[240] *Ibid.* 277 ff.; tr. Knox, 129.
[241] *Ibid.* 279; tr. Knox, 130. It hardly is necessary to remind the reader of the fact that this "reason immanent to the system of human wants" is the Hegelian counterpart to the "invisible hand" of Adam Smith's *Wealth of Nations*.
[242] *Ibid.* Cf. 103.

outwits, overpowers, dissociates himself from, in short, "annihilates," nature. Thus, for example, Marx tends to describe labor as a historical deed by which nature becomes "human" as much as man becomes "naturelike (*natürlich*)," a deed by which man and nature and therefore also humanism and naturalism,[243] indeed idealism and materialism,[244] gradually become one until eventually human history is a part of natural history and vice versa.[245] One might add that, contrary to Hegel, Marx stresses the properly "natural" (biological) aspect of needs and, ultimately, labor. For example, instead of stressing the "annihilatory" character of needs he describes hunger as a "need of my body for an object existing outside it, indispensable to its integration and to the expression of its essential being."[246] Here need is no longer described as a "subject's" urge for self-identity, as self-consciousness' urge for intellectual self-integration aiming at the annihilation of everything extraneous to it. Rather it is described as a biological want of a sensuous and therefore bodily being which, far from being able to abolish nature, needs it as its means of subsistence.

However, viewed from precisely this angle, the difference between Hegel's and Marx's notion of labor is apparent rather than real. First of all, after the *Phenomenology* Hegel has seldom stressed the properly "nihilating" effect of labor; and even in the *Phenomenology* the liberating effect of labor is seen in the fact that by labor man reaches an "intuition of *independent* being as of himself." Secondly, it might be argued that even in his early writings Hegel describes labor as an activity by which nature, not only man, comes into its own; the proper thing to do with nature is to annihilate it because *qua brute* nature it is not what it ought to be, not because it ought not to be at all. Finally the "nihilating" aspect of labor is not completely absent in Marx either; it crops up at those points at which Marx discusses labor in its relation to "revolution," that is, *qua* "revolutionary *praxis*."

[243] *MEGA* I, 3, 114. Cf. 116, 160; tr. Milligan, 102, cf. 104, 155.
[244] *Ibid.* 121, 160; tr. Milligan, 109, 155.
[245] *Ibid.* 122 ff.; tr. Milligan, 110 ff.
[246] *Ibid.* 161; tr. Milligan, 156 ff.

This does not mean of course that there is no difference between Hegel's and Marx's treatment of labor. But the difference lies in the *role ascribed* to labor rather than in the very *notion* of labor; what at first looks like a disagreement as to how labor should be described may be reduced to, or at least can be understood in terms of, a disagreement about the role of labor within the whole of man's potentialities. In other words, what Hegel and Marx disagree about is the relation between the speculative and the "bodily" mastering of the world, between speculative transfiguration and "material" transformation, between contemplation and labor, not the notion of labor taken as such. More precisely the difference consists in Hegel viewing the transformation effected by bodily labor as a premise and a subordinate form of the ultimate, reconciling transfiguration achieved by speculative thought, while Marx is and increasingly will be inclined to see in all theoretical activities only an epiphenomenon of labor and practice in general.

In short, what is at stake here is the relation between theory and *praxis*. However, one has to be careful not to oversimplify the issue by saying that Hegel's ultimate aim is to understand the universe, while Marx's aim is to transform it. Indeed, one has to be mindful of a very fundamental kinship of Hegel's contemplative philosophy to Marx's philosophy, or rather nonphilosophy, of action, a kinship which becomes most obvious if one compares Hegel's and Marx's philosophical motives to those of Aristotle, for example. Aristotle philosophizes out of "wonder," out of an intellectual curiosity which is half awe, half the desire to adjust man's existence to the order of being, the cosmos. Both Hegel and Marx, on the contrary, philosophize out of unhappiness and dissatisfaction, out of the "experience" that the world is not as it ought to be. Accordingly, while Aristotle primarily aims at understanding, at discovering structures and laws to which man's thought and actions have to adjust, Hegel and Marx aim at "reconciling" and/or "revolutionizing." In Aristotle nothing is or even can be wrong as it is in its natural state. The problem for Aristotle does not consist in correcting the universe or in making it rational; it consists in discovering its inherent order and rationality and in adjusting oneself to it. In Hegel and Marx almost everything is wrong and consequently has to be *aufgehoben*, transfigured, transformed, revolutionized. In this respect the only truly important difference between Hegel and Marx is that Hegel is still enough committed to the Greek philosophical tradition to believe it possible to reconcile man with the universe by teaching him adequately to understand it, while Marx, disappointed with Hegel's speculative transfiguration, has lost all faith in the healing and reconciling power of mere thought.

Only from this point of view, it seems to me, does it become truly intelligible why Marx views his negation of philosophy as a prolongation of Hegel's exaltation of speculative thought—and why he discovers an alienation where Hegel saw none or almost none. For Marx's central argument against Hegel consists in saying that Hegel's speculative "transfiguration" cannot succeed in achieving what Hegel claims it does achieve, namely, an all-embracing reconciliation of man with reality both inside and outside himself. He accuses Hegel of camouflaging man's alienation and claims that this camouflage has been achieved by ascribing to speculative thought healing powers which it does not have, indeed, by reinterpreting both man and reality so as to make of speculative thought more than it ever can be. This accusation against Hegel obviously entails a rejection of a number of premises of Hegel's philosophy (such as that man is essentially a self-consciousness[247]), and this rejection of Hegelian premises in turn affects the notion of labor. However, it has to be repeated that the central issue is the role of labor as against that of speculative transfiguration, not the notion of labor by itself.

Marx describes the essence of labor as *Vergegenständlichung*, objectification.[248] Though he never explains what the expression 'objectification' means, it is not overly difficult to state its basic connotations. 'Objectification' first means externalization: man externalizes himself in labor in that he makes of his inner life a form of exterior objects. He confers his life on objects.[249] How-

---

[247] *Ibid.* 154 ff.; tr. Milligan, 148 ff.
[248] *Ibid.* 83 ff., 156; tr. Milligan, 69 ff., 151.
[249] *Ibid.* 84; tr. Milligan, 70.

ever, this externalization must not be taken to be a translation of pre-existing ideas into reality. Rather, the inner life conferred to outer objects must be viewed as a potentiality which becomes actual in and for man by becoming the form of a reality outside man. Accordingly, 'objectification' also connotes self-actualization: by externalizing his inner life through labor, man labors and creates, in short, brings out of himself his human potentialities, *schafft seine Gattungskräfte heraus*.[250] The products of his labor exemplify and in a sense are the actuality of his human potentialities, so much so that Marx can describe industry as the "open book of man's essential powers, the exposure to the sense of human psychology."[251] Two secondary connotations articulate further the ones just mentioned. First, the externalization of man's inner life is at the same time an appropriation, both of nature—which man transforms into his "anorganic body,"[252] into an "anthropological nature"[253]—and of man himself, who gets a hold on himself by bringing out his potentialities. Secondly, this actualization of human potentialities—an actualization which is of course only possible through the combined action of all men, that is, as a "result of history"[254]—entails and in a sense is the actualization of man's "species essence," of his social being.

However, relatively easy as it may be to state the basic connotation of 'objectification,' it is difficult to discover exactly in which way Marx understands the relation between labor *qua* objectification and alienated labor. On the one hand, contrary to what superficial readers sometimes believe, Marx quite obviously does not want to say that the externalization entailed by labor is by itself alienation. For this is precisely of what he accuses Hegel: a confusion of objectification and alienation, objectivity and being alien. Marx repeatedly stresses that man is a being to which it is essential to be in need of *independent* objects: without such objects and a need for them man would be something "un-

---

250 *Ibid.* 156; tr. Milligan, 151.
251 *Ibid.* 121; tr. Milligan, 109.
252 *Ibid.* 87; tr. Milligan 87.
253 *Ibid.* 122; tr. Milligan, 111.
254 *Ibid.* 156; tr. Milligan, 151.

natural," a monster. "A being which does not have its nature outside itself is not a natural being.... A being which has no objects outside itself is not an objective being.... An unobjective being is an unbeing (*Unwesen*)."[255] On the other hand, however, it is equally obvious that Marx wants to say that alienation is a character intrinsic to objectification at one of the stages of its development. Sometimes Marx even seems to say that *up to now* all externalization in terms of labor has been alienation. At one point he even goes as far as to intimate that labor is by its very essence alienation: "labor is only an expression of human activity within alienation, of expressing one's life by alienating it (*Lebensäusserung als Lebensentäusserung*)."[256]

At this point it becomes virtually impossible to understand what Marx means as long as one does not take into consideration his criticism of Hegel. We have already pointed out several times that, notwithstanding the appearances, Marx never touches upon those texts in which Hegel explicitly takes up the subject of labor. Instead he analyzes the structure of the *Phenomenology* as a whole and intimates that it contains an alienated description of alienated labor as well as an alienated description of the transcendence of alienated labor. Moreover, Marx hails the *Phenomenology* for having indicated that man is the outcome of his own labor and that the history of this labor has two phases: a phase of alienation and another phase in which alienation is overcome.[257] To what he objects is Hegel's claim that alienation can be surmounted by speculative thought and that Absolute Knowledge—that is, Hegel's own philosophy—is the embodiment of the phase of the transcendence of all alienation. Hegel, according to Marx, could make that claim only because he had in the first place described all alienation as one of thought alone. Identifying man with self-consciousness, Hegel had described the "alienation of the human essence" as an alienation of self-consciousness. No wonder, then, that in Hegel "the whole process of the withdrawal of alienation is nothing but

---

[255] *Ibid.* 161; tr. Milligan, 157.
[256] *Ibid.* 139; tr. Milligan, 129.
[257] Cf. *ibid.* 156; tr. Milligan, 151.

the history of the production of ... logical, speculative thought."[258]

In order to fathom this criticism it may be useful to ask a question which Marx himself never explicitly asked, although it would seem to be quite a natural question, Why did Hegel never or hardly ever dwell upon anything such as an alienation of labor, and this in spite of the fact that he was aware of most of the problems and facts which induced Marx to advance his theory of alienated labor? Why did Hegel not see the "phenomenon" around which Marx's *Manuscripts* turn? Actually, the answer would seem to be quite simple. Hegel did not see in labor taken as such an alienation worth mentioning because for him labor was neither the central moving force of history nor the ultimate means of reconciliation. To state this more precisely, Hegel did not believe that the course of history could be understood and the ultimate reconciliation achieved in terms of a "making" or "doing," in term of *praxis*. Of course, as we have tried to indicate, he was well aware that labor has its share in the humanization of mankind. But he always considered labor a tool subordinated to man's most proper means of achieving his completion—rational insight, speculative thought.

In short, Hegel did not bother with an alienation of labor because he did not consider labor as man's only and ultimate means of completion—because he ascribed to rational insight the power to achieve what labor, by its very nature, leaves undone. He was far from underestimating the importance of labor. In particular he was far from arguing that man should leave the world just as he had found it and restrict himself to understanding it. However, he was of the opinion that from a certain point it no longer is meaningful to transform the world—that at a certain point speculative thought has to take over. In other words, though Hegel was far from reducing all labor to "abstract mental labor," he undoubtedly viewed rational insight as a consummation of the liberating transformation effected by labor. Accordingly he was inclined to seek alienation as well as its ultimate transcendence in the realm of thinking rather than in that of acting. For example,

[258] *Ibid.* 154; tr. Milligan, 149.

if there was anything such as an alienation of the products of labor from their producer (a phenomenon of which Hegel was aware at least to some extent), it was not necessary to overcome all of this alienation in terms of labor itself; nor was it necessary to locate the essence of such an alienation in the very act of labor. For whatever alienation there remained in human labor could be overcome by rational insight, by speculative thought, by an ultimate dissolution of *all* alienation in the self-transparent medium of Absolute Knowledge.

Before we go on, it may be useful to point out that this aspect of Hegel's thought can be evaluated in two quite different ways. Marx's evaluation is of course a negative one. To solve *real* problems in terms of a speculative transfiguration in his view amounts to camouflaging the real problems, in particular, since it entails a translation of real problems into thought problems, of real alienation into an alienation of thought. However, this unqualified rejection of Hegel's attitude would seem to be justified only as long as one shares Marx's Promethean conception of human *praxis*, that is, as long as one agrees that *praxis* really can bring about a salvific transformation of man's condition. If, on the contrary, one does not believe that labor is the panacea for *all* alienation, if one admits that it is not possible to transform the world bodily so as to make *all* facets of alienation disappear, then it becomes meaningful to say that an all-embracing reconciliation only can be achieved if the "material" transformation effected by labor is capped by an adequate understanding of reality. Hegel, it is true, was already enough of a Promethean to view his speculative penetration of reality as a deed which succeeds in dissolving all irrationality into reason and all restraints into freedom. Also, one might argue that because of his overweening opinion of the power of rational insight he tended somewhat to underestimate the "reconciliatory" power of *praxis*. Nevertheless it remains true that Hegel's whole philosophy is still committed to the Greek insight that man's ultimate reconciliation consists in understanding the universe and his own position in it rather than in creating a perfect universe. Hegel, contrary to Marx, is still aware that to *make* the universe other than it is may be possible to a god—

but that man, ultimately at least, has to be satisfied with understanding it. "To recognize reason as the rose in the cross of the
present and thereby to enjoy the present, this rational insight is
the reconciliation ... which philosophy offers."[259]

Marx, on the contrary, has lost all faith in the reconciliatory
power of contemplation and theoretical insights, precisely because
Hegel had extolled it so much. He has realized that speculative
thought cannot achieve the ultimate reconciliation intimated by
Hegel. But instead of concluding that Hegel's all-embracing
reconciliation cannot be achieved *either* by thought *or* by *praxis*,
that within this world man cannot feel completely at home and
always remains a "stranger," he concludes that *praxis* can and
does achieve what speculative thought cannot achieve. In any
case he believes it of no use to prolong transformatory *praxis*
into a "merely speculative" reconciliation. In order that a reconciliation be real, Marx argues that it must be palpable, present
to the senses, in short, "practical." And this means that it only
can be achieved by *praxis*. All reconciling transfiguration has to be
achieved *in praxi*, or it is no reconciliation at all. But this in
turn entails that all insufficiencies with respect to man's reconciliation, indeed the very absence of salvation, have to be explained
in terms of a deficiency of *praxis* itself. The only way to achieve
ultimate completion, indeed the only way to overcome all alienation, consists in transforming the world better and more completely—in further developing labor and what in the "Theses on
Feuerbach" is called "revolutionary practice." *Praxis*, not theory,
is the lever of salvation; consequently all human alienation must
be reducible to an alienation of human *praxis* as well as surmountable
in terms of this *praxis* alone.

But this means that, contrary to what Hegel believed, alienation
cannot consist in the very existence of objects outside and independent of man, in nature's "objectivity." For if this were the
case, the only way to overcome alienation would be a dissolution
of nature into self-consciousness—a speculative transfiguration.
This is how Hegel had seen the problem, at least according to

[259] Hegel$_2$, VII, 35; tr. Knox, 12.

Marx. Alienation for Hegel consisted in the very existence of nature. "Objectivity as such is regarded as an alienated human relationship which does not correspond to the essence of man, of self-consciousness. The reappropriation ... has therefore the meaning to annul objectivity, not only alienation. That is to say, man is regarded as a purely spiritual being without objects (*als ein nicht-gegenständliches, spiritualistisches Wesen*)."[260]

Marx's fundamental argument against this conception may be paraphrased as follows. Hegel's speculative transfiguration of man and reality does not succeed in establishing an ultimate reconciliation, in bringing about salvation. But if Hegel were correct in assuming that man essentially is self-consciousness and that nature is nothing but an externalization of this self-consciousness, a purely speculative reconciliation would have to succeed. Therefore, Hegel cannot be right in claiming that nature is an externalization of man *qua* self-consciousness. Alienation must consist in something less speculative than in nature's being outside and independent of self-consciousness; it must consist in something which human *praxis* can surmount by its very development.

In short, alienation can consist only in the process whereby through acting upon nature man produces things over which he has no control. In these products of his labor man objectifies himself; they are the actuality of his human powers. Yet as the products escape his control, as they frustrate his needs rather than satisfy them, all objectification inevitably amounts to alienation and all self-actualization amounts to a deactualization.

However, to have no control over its products is not a character intrinsic to the very essence of *praxis*. It is only a stigma of a phase of the history of *praxis*. This stigma obviously cannot be abolished in terms of a speculative transformation; it can only be overcome by a further development of labor, that is, by a progress of production. Marx believes that there must come a moment after which production will amount to a thorough control over all products. When this point is reached, the most basic of all alienation is overcome—man's self-objectification has become a thorough control

---

[260] *MEGA* I, 3, 157. Cf. 172; tr. Milligan, 152; cf. 170 ff.

over nature both within and outside himself. Objectification has become pure self-expression. Thereby all labor has lost its character of a burden. In a sense it even has ceased to be labor properly speaking and has become pure self-contained creativity.

This is perhaps the most puzzling feature of Marx's treatment of labor both in the *Manuscripts* and in the *German Ideology*: on the one hand, Marx describes labor as man's "life activity" and, on the other hand, he argues that the consummation of history will abolish labor. H. Arendt has argued that Marx contradicts himself and tried to trace back this contradiction to Marx's failure to distinguish between two quite distinct human activities, *Arbeit* and *Herstellen*, the "labor of our body" and the "work of our hands," to use Locke's words.[261] However it does not seem necessary to accuse Marx of a confusion. What he wants to say is in fact quite simple: the labor of our body can achieve so radical a transformation of man and his world that it ceases to be a burden and becomes a full expression of man's freedom. "Labor is man's coming-to-be for himself within alienation, or as alienated man"[262]; it transforms man's condition to the extent that eventually man will no longer have to labor in order to satisfy his needs. As far as I can see, Marx never intimated how this might happen. But one has only to imagine that one day man will produce machines which service and even reproduce themselves to acknowledge that this idea is far from being wildly Utopian.

[261] Arendt, 90.
[262] *MEGA* I, 3, 157; tr. Milligan, 152.

23: ALIENATION IV: MAN'S "SPECIES ESSENCE" AND PRIVATE PROPERTY

Thus far we have discussed three aspects of Marx's notion of "alienation." We saw first that the term 'alienation,' as Marx uses it, connotes the phenomenon that the results or products of human activities may be and in fact are independent of the producer, beyond his control, not adequately satisfying his needs. Next we have seen that Marx views this phenomenon as a historically inevitable, though only temporary, feature of the self-development of mankind. Finally, we have tried to indicate how this concept of alienation ties in with the other central notion of the *Manuscripts*, that of labor. There remains a fourth aspect both of labor and of its alienation to be discussed: the social, indeed socialist, implications of alienated labor.

We may begin by pointing to a problem which one may have noticed while reading the preceding pages. If alienation consists in a lack of control over those things to which man communicates his "life" and in which he actualizes his human potentialities, why is it that alienation becomes increasingly severe as man's productive transformation of nature develops? How can Marx say that the "increase in the quantity of objects," that is, of human products, is "accompanied by an extension of the realm of alien powers which subjugate man"[263]? Actually it would seem that in the beginning of its career humanity had little or no control over what it produced but that this control improved as humanity's transformation of nature through labor became more embracing and thorough. In fact, this is how Engels sometimes describes the situation: alienation is

[263] *Ibid.* 127; tr. Milligan, 115.

a lack of technological mastery both of nature and of society. Yet Marx quite obviously intends to say that there was little or no alienation at the beginning of history. Alienation emerged, and then grew like a slow fever as history developed, and presently, under the conditions dealt with by the political economy of Smith and Ricardo, is about to reach a last climax, soon to be followed by a millenium in which all alienation will irrevocably belong to the past.

Obviously it would be too easy to say here that Marx simply adheres to the romantic view of history which viewed the age of the ultimate restoration of harmony and freedom as the outcome of an agelong crescendo of disorder and bondage. To put it more precisely, it is perfectly obvious that Marx *does* and *always will* adhere to this romantic scheme; but the real question is how he succeeds in rationalizing it. The answer is simple enough, although eventually it may turn out to be more intricate than expected: the lack of control over man's products which Marx has in mind when he is speaking of "alienation" is a *social* consequence of the development of man's production and his mastery of nature. In other words, when he is speaking of "alienation," Marx does not primarily have in mind the fact that things escape man's control at the technological level, for example, because they become too complex to be easily mastered or because they are too mechanical to reflect the human qualities of their producers. As far as he notices such aspects of "alienation" at all, he reduces them to something more fundamental, namely, to the fact that consequent to the progress of production there emerges a peculiar kind of socioeconomic interrelation which hinders the producer from maintaining properly "human" relations both to their products and to nature.

Some of Marx's basic ideas about this curious development are contained in his excerpts from and comments on J. Mill's *Elements of Political Economy*, which appear to have been written about the same time as the *Manuscripts*. Commenting upon a page in which Mill explained that demand presupposes both the desire to possess a commodity and the possession of an equivalent object, Marx advances here an ingenious analysis of barter (*Austausch*).

First he notices an odd contradiction in the phenomenon of barter. Man barters only when he produces more than he immediately needs, that is, when his production has reached a level at which it is no longer "selfish" (in the sense that man now works in order to satisfy the needs of others). But this means that as soon as he has become able to serve other human beings by his labor, instead of thinking of the needs of others man is more than ever interested in the satisfaction of his own selfish needs.

It must of course be added that Marx is not interested in the moral side of the question. What interests him is the fact that the actual development of human relationships does not correspond to the deployment of man's productive activity, which, as we have seen, Marx considers *the* humanizing process. The development of labor seems to point toward an increasing unification of mankind—man increasingly produces for the sake of the satisfaction of the needs of others; but barter, an immediate consequence of the development of labor, increases the isolation of man from man—man now is even more self-centered than he was when he could satisfy only his own needs.

Moreover, and this is what interests Marx most, as soon as he begins to produce for the sake of barter, man forfeits the "natural" relation of his labor to human needs and thereby permits human interrelations to become thing mediated. For if I produce for the sake of barter, I obviously do not want to satisfy my needs by what I produce; nor am I interested in the needs of another. More precisely, I am interested in the needs of another only insofar as it is the need for a thing which I produce, which in turn is equivalent to a thing which I need. In other words, my production aims at a human need only insofar as it is refracted by a thing, not insofar as it is the need of a human being. I care not for the other, but only for "his goods"; just as he cares not for me, but only for "my goods." Instead of recognizing in the other a needy human being, a man who needs me, I see only a thing which I desire to have and with respect to which the human character of its producer and owner are perfectly incidental. In other words, the social consequences of labor do not tie us to each other; they tie us to things, while they isolate us from other men. "Our mutual value is for us the value of our mutual objects. That is, we mutually consider man as having no value."[264]

Marx impressively illustrates one of the consequences of this situation by describing the language which men in a bartering society are likely to use with each other. For example, if someone was to ask me for the results of my overproduction, even though he has nothing to offer in return, he inevitably would humiliate himself and I probably would reject his request as sheer impudence. "So much are we mutually alienated to our human essence that the immediate language of our nature would appear to us an infringement of human dignity, whereas the alienated language of thing values (*sachliche Werte*) appears to be justified, self-satisfied and self-respecting human dignity." The only language which everyone understands in such a society is the language which things speak to each other.

But this means nothing less than that we have come into the power and possession of our products. We no longer own them; they own us. And they own us because we have failed to produce them socially, that is, for each other, not because in some mythical way they become disobedient. In fact it is we ourselves who produce this power of our products over ourselves. For as we produce under the conditions of private property—that is, in a society in which products belong to us, even though we do not need them—we inevitably produce things which control our relations to each other. "We are excluded from real property because our property excludes another man."[265] We do not control our products because we do not permit other men to control them. We are alienated from our products and even from nature because our production is asocial.

At the end of the passage in question Marx opposes to the kind of production just described his ideal, "social production": "Had we produced *qua* men, each of us would have affirmed (*bejaht*) in his production both himself and the other." For each of us, by actualizing his individual human potentialities, by objectifying

---

[264] *Ibid.* 546.
[265] *Ibid.* 545.

himself, would have satisfied others; self-actualization would
have been an act of kindness to another. Thus each of us constantly would have mediated between ourselves and all other men,
between individual men and the human community. Those whose
needs we would have satisfied by satisfying his own productive
and creative needs would have recognized in us a completion of
their essence, just as we would have seen ourselves sanctioned
in their thought and love. In short, by strictly individual activities
each of us would have actualized the ultimate essence of all of
us, the "species essence"; and our products and eventually the
whole of nature would have been "so many mirrors out of which
our essence would shine forth."[266]

This concluding passage, and in fact the whole text in question,
once more reminds us that Marx's primary intent is a *critical* one.
When he speaks about alienation, when he describes the contradiction inherent in barter as well as the fact that human interrelations have become thing mediated, Marx is not simply advancing an objective sociological analysis. Certainly he would
argue that his analysis squares with the facts. But his intent is to
show that there is something wrong with these facts.

What exactly is it that Marx considers wrong? We have reached
the point at which we may try to articulate the exact meaning
of Marx's early "humanism." That Marx is not per se interested
in justice has been pointed out several times already; we have also
indicated that his main concern is not the real suffering of the
real proletariat, even though occasionally Marx does state that
the first criticism of private property will have to start from its
most painful expression, "from the fact of poverty, of misery."[267]
However, the preceding analysis might suggest that Marx's central
objection to modern society amounts to saying that man is more
interested in things than in men and that all human relations
have become thing mediated, or "reified."[268] Yet even this is

[266] *Ibid.* 547. For a slightly different analysis see Popitz, 152 ff.

[267] *MEGA* I, 3, 204; tr. Dixon, 49 ff.

[268] Lukács, and later Marcuse and other students of Marx, have used the
expression '*Verdinglichung*,' 'reification,' to describe objectification within
alienation. However, as Popitz, 154, rightly points out, this expression is

only a part of Marx's criticism. For his main objection to civil
society, the reason why he advances his analysis of alienation,
is that in modern society man fails more than ever before to actualize
his ultimate nature, *which is social.*

In order to appreciate this more fully, one will have to take into
account Marx's idea and ideal of *man's nature.* We may start by
pointing to the eminent role which his conception of man ascribes
to human needs. Marx, following Feuerbach, argues that "sensibility (*Sinnlichkeit*) must be the basis of all *Wissenschaft.*"[269]
It would be very misleading to translate, as some have done,
the expression '*Sinnlichkeit*' by 'sense perception.' For even
though Feuerbach had argued that philosophy has to proceed
from sense data, not from abstract ideas, and even though Marx
basically agrees with Feuerbach on this point, he is far from sup-
porting the empiricist-positivist claim that all scientific knowledge
has to proceed from or even be reduced to sense observation.
Rather, what Marx seems to have in mind is Kant's notion of
Sinnlichkeit as receptivity, that is, man's essential dependence
upon external objects.[270] Thus the point which interests him is an
anthropological rather than an epistemological one. What he
means is simply that all *Wissenschaft* has to proceed from the one
basic fact that man depends upon, has a need of, desires, and
therefore also acts upon objects independent of himself.

As we have already indicated, this is one of Marx's fundamental
disagreements with Hegel. For Hegel's suggestion that man is
essentially spirit seemed to imply to Marx that man's dependence

somewhat misleading. For it suggests that the *Verdinglichung* is a special
type of objectification, while Marx in fact would seem to say that there is no
objectification at all under the condition of alienation. See the negative particle
'*Ent-*' in '*Entäusserung,*' '*Entfremdung,*' '*Entgegenständlichung.*' The last
expression which literally means de-objectification would seem to correspond
to Marx's thought better than 'reification.' In our text, 'reified' refers to the
hypostatization of social relations which Marx, in *Das Kapital*, discusses in
the chapter on the "fetishism of commodities."

[269] *MEGA* I, 3, 123; tr. Milligan, 111.

[270] Cf. Bockmühl, 242, who in turn refers to Marcuse$_1$, 148. As to Kant, see
also my article "Deduction of Sensibility," *International Philosophical Quarterly*
3 (1963) 201 ff.

upon external objects is only a dialectical moment or even a transitory phase of man's self-development. Hegel was of course aware that man depends upon nature; even Marx does not deny that he knew this. However, Hegel's whole philosophy and also History as described by Hegel seemed to aim at overcoming this dependence; Hegel's ideal man seemed to be a philosopher whose mind had reached Absolute Knowledge, who had become the creative or at least the recreative source of the universe, and who therefore no longer depended upon anything outside himself. For Marx, on the contrary, to say of man that he has no real need of anything outside himself amounts to treating him as a mere "creature of abstraction." If man is truly real, neither can his self-development be due to a purely mental dialectic nor can he ever become independent of nature. By his very essence he must depend upon external objects, indeed have his own nature outside himself in nature. This of course does not mean that man is only passive. Marx opposes both idealists such as B. Bauer, who ignore any "impact of another distinct from one's activity"[271]—that is, describe all passivity in terms of a *self*-determination—and naturalists such as Feuerbach, who do not see that in spite of his basic passivity man is eminently active. Man is both an "*active* natural being" and a "*passive*, conditioned, and limited creature."[272] Still, if he is passive at all in the proper sense of the term, his dependence upon external objects as well as his need of them must be an integral aspect of his existence.

"But man is not merely a natural being; he is a *human* natural being." According to Marx this means that man is a being whose dependence upon and need of nature develop, for neither nature outside himself nor his own nature is "directly given in a form adequate to the human being."[273] With this Hegel would have agreed. However, he would have added that man reaches true humanity by transfiguring all his needs into a contemplative recognition of the One Reason in everything. If in the following passage from the *Encyclopaedia* one substitutes 'man' for 'Spirit,'

[271] *MEGA* I, 3, 319; tr. Dixon, 190.
[272] *Ibid*. 160; tr. Milligan, 156.
[273] *Ibid*. 162; tr. Milligan, 158.

and a phrase such as 'truly human deed' for 'Wissenschaft'—
a substitution which, as far as Marx is concerned, hardly requires
justification—it becomes quite obvious what in Marx's eyes were
the "humanistic ideals" of Hegel:

> Thus all activities of Spirit are only a grasping of itself; and the
> end of all true *Wissenschaft* is nothing but to make Spirit re-
> cognize itself in whatever exists in heaven and on earth. As
> far as Spirit is concerned, there simply cannot be a thing radically
> different from it.... The bud of a plant ... terminates its deploy-
> ment with an actuality equal to itself—by yielding a seed.
> The same applies to Spirit; its development, too, has reached
> its end ... when Spirit has reached a complete consciousness
> of its concept.[274]

In this view nature is only an externality which as such is devoid
of sense, or rather whose only meaning is to mediate the self-
completion of a consciousness[275]; similarly the only meaning of
man's needs is to awaken the drive which eventually leads consciousness to recognize itself in whatever exists. Marx, on the
contrary, views the development from the biological entity "man"
to a truly human being as an articulation and *change in direction*
of man's needs, not as their *Aufhebung* in contemplation. Primitive
man desires and needs things of nature; the more he develops,
the more all his needs of things are transformed into and embraced
by one central need—*the need for another human being*. The whole
of history is a prehistory of the gradual emergence of truly human
needs, and the entelechy of this development is a man who experiences another man, precisely *qua* man, as the object which he
needs most of all.[276] This is why Marx, in this respect following
Feuerbach, several times argues that the relation of man to woman
is an almost empirical criterion of the degree of man's having
become human; for the sexual relationship, in its immediacy,
naturalness, and necessity, is a paradigmatic instance of needs
which aim at another human being—either as at the "spoil and
handmaid ... of lust" or at a human being. "From this relationship

[274] Hegel₂, X, 10 and 16.
[275] Cf. *MEGA* I, 3, 170 ff.; tr. Milligan, 169.
[276] Cf. *ibid.* 123 ff.; tr. Milligan, 111 ff.

one can ... judge man's whole level of development."[277] For man is human to the extent to which "another man as man has become a need for him."[278] The first premise of Marx's early humanism is probably best expressed in a sentence by Count Holbach, whom Marx quotes in the *Holy Family*: *de tous les êtres le plus nécessaire à l'homme c'est l'homme.*[279]

This may be the place to say a few words about Marx's notion of *Gattungswesen*, which time and again recurs in the *Manuscripts*. It has a rather involved prehistory which is relevant to its adequate understanding. Once more this prehistory is theological. In the sixteenth and seventeenth centuries certain Lutheran theologians developed a conception which has its origins in Luther's potential monophysism and which has aptly been described as a "theology of the *kenosis.*" According to this conception, in order to do justice to St. Paul's claim that God "emptied himself (ἐκένωσεν), taking on the form of a servant" (Epistle to the Philippians 2:7), it is not sufficient to say that the Second Divine Person "assumed" a human nature; one will have to add that the Divine Logos *turned* into a man, at least in the sense that a number of attributes of Christ's divine nature became attributes of his human nature. That this raised serious questions about Christ's being truly a man is obvious. Some of the Lutheran theologians in question argued that Christ's humanity possesses divine majesty but "renounces its use"—which ultimately amounted to saying that Christ's humanity possesses attributes such as omnipresence, omnipotence, and omniscience only potentially (the school of Giessen); others went so far as to claim that Christ's humanity does not renounce the actual use of such attributes but only hides them (the school of Tübingen).[280]

---

[277] *Ibid.* 113; tr. Milligan, 101. On this point see the analyses by G. Fessard in *Marx and the Western World*, ed. N. Lobkowicz (Notre Dame, 1967) 337-370.

[278] *Ibid.* cf. 124; tr. Milligan, 101, cf. 112.

[279] *Ibid.* 309; tr. Dixon, 179.

[280] See P. Henry's article "Théologie de la kénose," *Supplément au Dictionnaire de la Bible*, Vol. V (Paris, 1957) col. 136 ff.; also (with numerous references) K. Barth, *Kirchliche Dogmatik*, 4th ed. (Zürich, 1948) I, 2, 181 ff.

As G. M.M. Cottier has convincingly shown, the basic ideas contained in this conception had an important influence upon Hegel, who, playing moreover on the processual connotation of the German expression '*Menschwerdung*' ('incarnation'), extended the Lutheran interpretation of Christ's humanity to mankind as a whole and eventually described History as a processual kenotic incarnation, that is, as a process in which God's attributes are step by step given up by God and communicated to humanity.[281] As we have indicated earlier, this conception found its ultimate articulation in D. F. Strauss' *Life of Jesus*. While Hegel was still inclined to describe mankind's becoming divine as an expansion of God's originally having become a definite man, Strauss explicitly argued that no individual could possibly be the bearer of divine attributes, since it is contrary to the "Idea" of a union of God and man for it to become actual in one individual alone "and to be niggardly against all others":

> Thought in an individual ... the properties and functions which the church doctrine ascribes to Christ contradict each other; in the idea of the species[282] they harmonize. Mankind is the union of both natures, God incarnate, infinite Spirit externalized into finiteness and finite Spirit remembering its infinity. It is the thaumaturgist ... it is the one who dies, is resurrected, and ascends to heaven. ... Through faith in this Christ, above all in his death and resurrection, man becomes justified before God, that is, by resuscitating in himself the idea of humanity....[283]

We cannot discuss here why Strauss chose precisely the human species as the true subject of traditional Christology; it may suffice to point out that already Fichte had argued that Reason, "which in its worldly aspect divides itself in various individuals," has its totality in the "life of the species."[284] Nor can we discuss Strauss' identification of the "*idea* of the species" with concrete mankind,

---

[281] Cottier$_1$, 27 ff.

[282] Literally 'genus.' Following the common English usage, I have everywhere translated '*Gattung*' by 'species,' even though this generates some difficulties in the case of adjectives corresponding to the German '*Gattungs-*.'

[283] Strauss, II, 734 ff.

[284] Cf. Fichte, IV, 419, 429 ff.

an identification which, it has been argued, prefigures the later concern of the Left Hegelians, namely, to return from speculation to earthly reality.[285] What is more important is that four years after the publication of the *Life of Jesus* Strauss' argument reappeared in Feuerbach's pamphlet *On Philosophy and Christianity*. However, Feuerbach's version of the "idea of the species" differed from that of Strauss in at least two respects. First, while Strauss saw in this notion only the rational core of Christology and still viewed the species or mankind as a sort of mediator between a quasi-transcendent Absolute and individual man, Feuerbach already saw in mankind the "secret" both of religion in general and of its ultimate rationalization in Hegelian philosophy and therefore simply identified the "human species" with God. Secondly, he gave to Strauss' arguments a distinctly empirico-psychological twist which is highly characteristic of his anthropocentric materialism: while Strauss had argued that it is contrary to the nature of an "idea" to become actual in an individual, Feuerbach simply applied his general principle that no being, neither man nor an animal, can acknowledge values which transcend the species of which it is a member. "What, if not species concepts, are all the predicates which speculation and even religion may attribute to the deity— concepts which man gathers from his species?"[286]

It is not easy to decide to what extent this Feuerbachian notion of "species" has a social connotation. Most of the time Feuerbach simply argues that the species is man's Absolute because, even though no individual embodies all human perfections, there is no perfection lacking to the sum total of all individuals. Sometimes, however, Feuerbach gives to this notion a connotation which is social at least in a vague way. Thus, for example, he argues that people need and love each other because each man finds in fellow men perfections which he lacks. But as far as I can see he never succeeded in elaborating this idea beyond the rather elementary principle that man finds his completion when "I and thou" en-

[285] Cf. Bockmühl, 32.
[286] Feuerbach, VII, 70.

counter each other in love and friendship—an idea which, slightly changed, has been taken up by Martin Buber in our century.

It was Moses Hess who first articulated the social, indeed socialist, implications of the notion of species while at the same time completely disregarding its theological origin. For Feuerbach the species still had divine attributes; in Hess the attributes are exclusively human. To use Marx's words, it had becomes unnecessary to explicitly presuppose atheism, not to speak of religion, in order to exalt man.[287] Moreover, while Feuerbach saw the perfection of the species in a sort of cumulative togetherness of men, Hess already argued that man has his ultimate perfection in "productive cooperation." In an article "On the socialist movement in Germany," which was written in the early summer of 1844 and published in K. Grün's *Neue Anekdota* in 1845, he described Feuerbach's version of the notion of *Gattungswesen* as "rather mystical" and argued that, adequately understood, it means an "acting together (*Zusammenwirken*) of individuals." Identifying selfishness with animality, he spelled out what also underlies Marx's notion of "species essence," namely, that social collaboration, cooperation in all respects, is the ultimate fulfilment of man's human potentialities.[288]

Hess even accused Feuerbach of still being bogged down in idealism. For though Feuerbach had recognized that man's Supreme Being is the species, not an individual, he still mainly saw the unity of mankind in mental activities. Had he seen that cooperation in thinking entails and presupposes cooperation in practical, everyday life, Feuerbach would have discovered that his reduction of theology to anthropology is only part of the truth. He would have added, as Hess in fact did add, that man's true essence is social, that is, "an acting together of different individuals for one and the same end," that true humanism is a "doctrine of human

[287] *MEGA* I, 3, 125; tr. Milligan, 114.

[288] In the *German Ideology*, the expression 'species essence' is no longer used; but the core of the meaning of this expression is present. For example, when Marx explains the meaning of the expression '*gesellschaftliches Verhältnis*,' he speaks of a *Zusammenwirken mehrerer Individuen*, a cooperation of several individuals. Cf. *MEW* 3, 29 ff.; tr. Pascal, 30.

socialization (*Gesellschaftung*)," in short, that "anthropology is socialism."[289]

On another occasion Hess even attempted a sort of cosmological grounding of his ideas. Life, he argued, is communication in production or, as he put it, "exchange of productive life activity." Thus the body is the seat of life and the air its medium, for it is by their body and in the air that animals thrive, that is, actuate their metabolism with nature. Similarly, the seat of man's truly human life is society; only by communicating in production do men reach full life. "Just as earth's air is the workshop of earth, the communication and commerce (*Verkehr*) of men is the human workshop in which individual men reach the actualization and the actual use of their life and riches."[290]

Marx's notion of "species essence" differs from Hess' conception only in that Marx is constantly trying to reach the rational and even empirical core of such quasi-mythical ideas. This, of course, does not mean that from the *Manuscripts* one can extract something like a "doctrine of the *Gattungswesen*" which is both truly articulate and consistent; in fact, Marx's final rationalization of the notion of "species essence" consists in abandoning it.

One way of approaching Marx's version of the notion of "species" is through his analysis of the password of the French revolutionaries, *egalité*. Both in the *Manuscripts* and in the *Holy Family* Marx describes equality as the French—that is, political—counterpart to the self-identity of man in pure thought as described by thinkers such as Fichte and Bruno Bauer.

> Self-consciousness is man's equality with himself in pure thought. Equality is man's consciousness of himself in the element of *praxis*, that is, therefore, man's consciousness of other men as his equals and man's relation to other men as his equals. Equality is the French expression for the unity of human essence, for man's species consciousness and species attitude, for the practical identity of man with man, that is, for the social or human relation of man to man.[291]

[289] Hess$_2$, 292 ff.
[290] *Ibid*. 330 ff.
[291] *MEGA* I, 3, 207; tr. Dixon, 55 ff.

In the *Manuscripts*[292] Marx adds that a transcendence of alienation will always have to proceed from that form of alienation
which is the "dominant power": in Germany an alienation of
self-consciousness; in France an alienation at the level of equality,
that is, political alienation; in England an alienation at the level
of practical needs, that is, economic alienation. This suggests
that when he describes equality as the political counterpart to
the Fichtean "I am I," Marx is far from arguing that equality
characterizes a transcendence of the abstract individualism of
the German Idealists. Equality, it is true, is the oneness in essence
of all men "in the element of practice," that is, as an effective
principle of human companionship. However, it is still too abstract
an idea to serve as a basis for the ideal society which Marx envisages; after all, men could be perfectly equal while being perfectly inhuman.

In short, the important point cannot be that men be equal,
but rather that they be equally human. And this is possible only
if everyone desires for everyone else the fullest actualization of
his human potentialities, a condition which in turn presupposes
that one's self-objectification does not exclude the self-objectification of other men, in short, the conscious collaboration of all.
In other words, man's ultimate completion emerges in a society
in which every single individual acts as the representative of
mankind as a whole as well as for the sake of mankind as a whole.

Once this social essence of man is recognized, once it is acknowledged—*in praxi*, that is, not only in man's mind—that man's
ultimate completion entails and in fact is the ultimate completion
of each and every human being, society also becomes "the con-
summated essential oneness of nature and man, the true resurrection of nature, the naturalism of man and the humanism of nature
both brought to fulfilment."[293] For what separates man from
nature even after he has mastered it at the level of technology
is his separation from other men. As long as his mastery of nature
is not a social one, whatever he produces and transforms always

[292] *Ibid.* 134; tr. Milligan, 123.
[293] *Ibid.* 116; tr. Milligan, 104.

reflects alien beings—either men from whom he is separated or himself as separated from mankind. Only when I produce *as a man*—that is, socially—only when my labor is an objectification of the human species as a whole, does nature become a mirror which reflects Man.

All this amounts to saying that man's final self-fulfilment, the emergence of man as a species being, coincides with the emergence of communism. For communism is

> the real appropriation of the human essence by and for man; the complete return of man to himself as a social, that is, human being—a return become conscious and accomplished within the entire wealth of previous development. This communism, as fully developed naturalism, equals humanism and, as fully developed humanism, equals naturalism; it is the genuine resolution of the conflict between man and nature and between man and man—the true resolution of the strife between existence and essence, between objectification and self-affirmation, between the individual and the species. Communism is the riddle of history solved, and it knows itself to be this solution.[294]

Three things should be noticed in this glorification of communist society. First of all, Marx describes it as a "return." It is a return in a twofold sense: on the one hand, it is a return in the sense in which earlier we heard Schiller argue that it is the meaning of history that man regains at a higher level the point from which he had originally started; on the other hand, it is a return in the sense that in communist society man has succeeded in reappropriating everything alien to him. These two "returns" are obviously closely connected with each other: like Schiller or Hegel, Marx views history as a process in which man articulates his potentialities in a way which seems contradictory to his very nature and eventually reintegrates these potentialities in a synthesis which is a sort of "man's nature regained," though obviously at a level infinitely exceeding the starting point. It is important to stress this in order to ward off the frequent misunderstanding that Marx is "accusing" the past as well as the present of not being communist. That communism is a "return" is neither a historical accident nor

[294] *Ibid.* 114; tr. Milligan, 102.

something due to the machinations of evil forces. The mediation between primitive man and communism, a mediation which Marx analyses in terms of the concept of alienation, is a "necessary premise" of communism.[295] As communism is "no returning in poverty to unnatural, undeveloped simplicity," it is possible only as the result of a history whose wealth could not have emerged without alienation.[296]

Secondly, though mediated both by alienation and by its transcendence, communism is more than only an *Aufhebung* of alienation. It is not merely an "empty annulment of an empty abstraction, a negation of the negation"; it is something eminently positive which, after it has been reached through the negation of the negation represented by alienation, no longer requires this mediation.[297] Marx's emphasis on this point is so strong that at one point he even goes so far as to say that as it is the negation of a negation, communism must not be understood as the ultimate actualization of man.[298] In another passage he distinguishes several *kinds* of communism, and only the last one, which is no longer mediated by a negation, is said to be the ultimate unfolding of man's potentialities.[299] This has a special application to atheism, for atheism (the militant atheism of the Left Hegelians as well as of Feuerbach, that is) postulates man's dignity by rejecting God—and "socialism as socialism no longer stands in any need of such a mediation."[300] But it also applies to the abolition of private property: although private property obviously must be abolished if communism is to emerge, communism itself is something quite different from a society "which wants to destroy everything which is not capable of being possessed by all," for example, talents.[301]

---

[295] *Ibid.* 167; tr. Milligan, 164.
[296] *Ibid.* Notice the peculiar use of 'unnatural.' 'Natural,' in this context, means 'human' or even 'humanistic,' not 'precultural' as in Hegel and in fact in other passages in Marx.
[297] *Ibid.* 125; tr. Milligan, 114.
[298] *Ibid.* 134; tr. Milligan, 124.
[299] *Ibid.* 111 ff.; tr. Milligan, 99 ff.
[300] Cf. *ibid.* 125 ff.; tr. Milligan, 114.
[301] Cf. *ibid.* 111 ff.; tr. Milligan, 99 ff.

There obviously is a certain tension between the first and the second point, a tension which might be characterized by saying that the first point has its origin in Hegel and the second in Feuerbach. We have seen earlier that one of Feuerbach's criticisms of Hegel consisted in saying that for Hegel everything positive is something mediated. Marx himself has noticed this. After having stated that Feuerbach is the only Hegelian "who has a serious, critical attitude to the Hegelian dialectics and who has made genuine discoveries in this field," he enumerates three of Feuerbach's "great achievements": first, Feuerbach showed that philosophy is nothing else but religion rendered into rational thought and that it has likewise to be condemned as another form of the "alienation of the human essence"; secondly, that Feuerbach established "true materialism and real science" by making the social relationship of man to man the basic principle of his theory; and finally that he opposed to Hegel's negation of the negation "the self-supporting positive, positively grounded in itself."[302]

At the same time, however, perhaps without really being aware of it, Marx does not follow the antidialectical conclusion which Feuerbach drew from this conception. Insisting that only that which is not mediated is really real (the sensible as opposed to the intellectual, the bodily as opposed to the spiritual, the "natural" as opposed to the "historical," and so on), Feuerbach implicitly concluded that alienation is a *culpa* by no means *felix*. Of course, Feuerbach's anthropocentric humanism is a "return" as well, but it is a return which makes good something almost exclusively negative and which restores a human nature that has never been truly absent. As we saw earlier, this basically ahistorical conception (ahistorical, since only nature, not history, explains the presence of True Man) is due to the fact that Feuerbach viewed all alienation as an error rather than as an event of the political, social, and economic order. Marx, on the contrary, who is far from viewing alienation as a mere mistake in interpretation but rather, following Hegel, considers it a happening *in rerum natura*, interprets alienation as a "deviation" with eventually salvific

[302] *Ibid.* 152; tr. Milligan, 145.

consequences, indeed as a development which is absolutely necessary to the emergence of true humanity.

As he tries to do justice both to Hegel's dialectics of historical mediation and to Feuerbach's ahistorical naturalism, it might seem that Marx describes the coming-to-be of communism in a way which is almost contradictory. For if communism could not be achieved without alienation (without the age of private property), it would seem to be mediated, in fact constituted, by a negation; and if communism is something positive, it is difficult to see in which sense alienation has a truly salvific function. However, if one takes into account the concrete terms in which Marx advances his analysis, this inconsistency turns out to be less serious than it might seem at first sight. What Marx seems to want to say, and what later he will say quite explicitly, is this: the human wealth, both material and spiritual, which communism presupposes could develop only under the conditions of private property; but once this wealth has emerged and private property has been abolished, communism stands on its own feet—it is no longer mediated either by private property or by its abolition—except in the sense that without such a past communism could not possibly have emerged. In other words, the mastery of nature and the high degree of productivity which communism presupposes could develop only in terms of the recklessness of human (or rather "animal") selfishness and the resulting competition. But once nature has been subdued to the extent that mankind produces enough to be able to satisfy fully the needs of each and every individual, a collaboration becomes possible which, even though it is built on a Golgotha of past inhumanities, develops on its own and can regard its past as something external to it, as an animalistic prehistory which communism presupposes only "historically," not "logically."

> Just as through the movement of private property, of its wealth as well as its poverty—or its material and spiritual wealth and poverty—the budding (*werdende*) society finds at hand all the material for its development; so established (*gewordne*) society produces man in this entire richness of his being ... as its enduring result.[303]

[303] *Ibid.* 121; tr. Milligan, 109.

The third point to be discussed here is Marx's idea of private property and its abolition. On several occasions Marx distinguishes between private property and "truly human and social property."[304] We may begin by characterizing the latter, for it is the kind of property which communism, far from abolishing, establishes for the first time in history. Marx describes it as "the presence for man of essential objects, both as objects of enjoyment and as objects of activity."[305]

In other words, truly human property is the immediate availability of those objects, both products of human labor and things of nature, of which man has a genuine need. In another text Marx describes this truly human property as an "inner property."[306] This expression refers back to Hegel, who in the *Philosophy of Right*[307] describes as "inner property" human skills acquired through education, study, habit, and so on, which are basically inalienable, even though a particular use of it may be alienated for a limited period of time.[308] Moses Hess seems to have made use of this notion when in 1843 he described man's activity of producing as his "actual property" and opposed it to things as "material property."[309] Marx, however, contrary both to Hegel and Hess, describes as such "inner property" everything of which man has a true need: "for the need of a thing is the most obvious and irrefutable proof that this thing belongs to my nature, that its being is a being for me ... that it is a characteristic property (*Eigentümlichkeit*) of my essense."[310]

But man quite obviously is in need of the products of the labor of others as well. Consequently the products of others and in the end also their labor, their skill, and their whole human existence are a part of my nature no less than my own labor and skill. Yet

---

[304] *Ibid.* 93, cf. 78, 145, 537; tr. Milligan, 82, cf. 64, 137.

[305] *Ibid.* 145; tr. Milligan 137. Cf. Bockmühl, 245.

[306] *Ibid.* 537.

[307] Hegel₂, VII, 97; tr. Knox, 41.

[308] *Ibid.* 123 ff.; tr. Knox, 54. On Hegel's notion of property see the excellent article by J. Ritter, *Marxismusstudien* IV, 196-218, especially 212 ff.

[309] *Einundzwanzig Bogen* 322; cf. Bockmühl, 245.

[310] *MEGA* I, 3, 537.

this means that where there is private property, a part of my nature is not my own. Is it not obvious, then, that society has to be restructured in such a way that everything which is "a characteristic property of my essence" becomes available to me, indeed mine? Is it not obvious that "truly human property" as just described is the "positive essence of private property,"[311] its true meaning,[312] the "essential relationship to objects" of which even owners of private property implicitly are aware?[313] Indeed, is it not obvious that "communism, as the *Aufhebung* of private property, is the vindication of real human life as man's property"?[314]

It is worthwhile briefly to compare this conception with Hegel's analysis of property. For Hegel's treatment of property quite explicitly abstracts from the notion of need and centers around the notion of freedom. "The rational element of property does not lie in its satisfying needs but rather in the fact that in property the mere subjectivity of the human person (*Persönlichkeit*) is transcended."[315] Of course Hegel presupposes that only things, not persons, can become property in the true sense of the term. But inasmuch as he presupposes this achievement of modern times which abolished slavery and serfdom, he can argue that to have property and to be able to dispose of it freely is an expression of man's *Herrschaft über die Dinge*, his mastery over things.[316] And as it is my individual will which becomes objective in property, property necessarily has "the character of private property"; common property (*gemeinschaftliches Eigenthum*), even though possible, is always a "*per se* dissolvable community."[317]

[311] *Ibid.* 114; tr. Milligan, 102.

[312] *Ibid.* 145; tr. Milligan, 137.

[313] *Ibid.* 537 ff.

[314] *Ibid.* 166; tr. Milligan, 163 ff.

[315] Hegel₂, VII, 95; tr. Knox, 235 ff.

[316] *Ibid.* 113; tr. Knox, 239. In his private copy of the *Philosophy of Right*, Hegel wrote on the margin: "Mensch Herr über alles in der Natur—nur durch ihn Dasein als der Freiheit"; cf. G. W. F. Hegel, *Grundlinien der Philosophie des Rechts*, ed. J. Hoffmeister, 4th. ed. (Hamburg, 1955) 327.

[317] Hegel₂, VII, 99; tr. Knox, 42.

In fact, one of the features of private property to which Marx objects—namely, that it results in a reifiation of human interrelations—is treated by Hegel as a phenomenon of significant positive value. For if in modern society human interrelations are mediated by things and even "spiritual skills, sciences, arts, indeed religion (sermons, masses, prayers, benediction), inventions, and so on"[318] can becomes *res* in the legal sense and thus "commercialized," it certainly is true that human interrelations become highly impersonal, reified, and "abstract" (in the sense of being isolated from the total human context). Yet there also remains a realm of individual freedom not entangled in the mesh of social interdependence, in which truly personal values can subsist (Hegel mentions "my universal freedom of will" as well as ethical and religious convictions[319]). What Hegel seems to imply here is that it is precisely the impersonality of human interrelations that guarantees the intangibility of the individual person and thus his freedom, for this impersonality and "abstractness" is an expression of the fact that modern man has succeeded in freeing himself from the immediacy and animality of the "natural," that is, biological. In this sense Hegel can go so far as to intimate that there is a close relationship between the "freedom of property" of civil society and the Christian "freedom of the person"; the former is an ultimate articulation of the latter.[320]

In Marx's analysis of private property, on the contrary, the notion of freedom plays virtually no role at all. In fact, in the *Manuscripts* the term 'freedom' does not so much as occur. It does occur in the *Holy Family*, it is true. But even there Marx

---

[318] *Ibid.* 96; tr. Knox, 40 ff. Hegel discusses skills, sciences, arts, etc., in connection with the alienation of property (§§ 65 ff.); for he argues that they become property at all only by being externalized and alienated. A house is a property whether I sell it or ot; my knowledge and skill enter the realm of right only by being alienated (sold, etc.). See also Hegel's marginal remarks in the quoted edition by Hoffmeister, 330.

[319] Hegel$_2$, VII, 121; tr. Knox, 53. To § 67, in which he discusses the alienation of knowledge and skill, Hegel adds: "Das Verhältnis des absoluten Innern zu dessen Äusserlichkeit"; cf. Hoffmeister's edition, 348. These marginal notes obviously served as a guide for the lecture.

[320] Hegel$_2$, VII, 117; tr. Knox, 51. Cf. J. Ritter, *Marxismusstudien*, IV, 206 ff.

tends to ridicule the "spiritualistic freedom which imagines itself to be free even in chains."[321] This is not to say that Marx has a low opinion of freedom. But he is and always does remain very sceptical about any freedom which is not based upon very palpable and "very material conditions." And the first of these "very material conditions" is that man should be able to satisfy all his needs as those of a truly human being. Liberation always entails a change of the conditions essential for life.[322]

Marx's objection to private property, then, moves at the level which Marx considers the most fundamental level of human existence: at the level of Hegel's "system of wants," which is the subject of political economy. Man is a being of needs; private property entails the frustration of needs. However one has to be careful not to take the term 'need' in too narrow a sense. For Marx obviously wants to say more than that under the conditions of private property many people remain hungry, thirsty, and without shelter. Even though Habermas is right when he claims that Marx's notion of alienation refers to a de facto encountered situation of pauperism, not to a "metaphysical accident,"[323] and even though the disappearance of this pauperism would (and in fact did) considerably weaken the persuasive power of Marx's arguments, the Marxian criticism of private property cannot possibly be reduced to the claim that private property throws a substantial part of humanity into misery. While Proudhon, for example, was almost exclusively interested in discovering ways to ameliorate *la condition physique, morale et intellectuelle de la classe la plus nombreuse et la plus pauvre*,[324] Marx's interest centered around an emancipation of the whole of humanity. Consequently he was interested in the misery of the proletariat only insofar as, on the one hand, it was particularly indicative of the wretched situation of man in general and, on the other hand, it suggested why and how the proletariat would become humanity's savior.

[321] *MEGA* I, 3, 267; tr. Dixon, 127.
[322] *Ibid.* 207; tr. Dixon, 52.
[323] Habermas₁, 181.
[324] Cf. Proudhon's letter to the Academy of Besançon, introducing *Qu'est-ce que la propriété* (1840); cf. Proudhon, I, 119.

For example, Marx was always less interested in *Elend* than in *Verelendung*; while certainly he was shocked at the misery of the proletariat, he never made the slightest effort to help the proletariat (as anyone truly interested in his fellow men rather than in abstract ideas would have been inclined to do) but rather was delighted at the proletariat's progressive pauperization, which he counted on to provoke the salvific revolution. One might of course retort that Marx saw more clearly than most of his contemporaries that only a radical transformation of society, as opposed to charitable actions, could help the proletariat to reach an existence worthy of human beings. This certainly is true. But it is equally true that he was interested in the fate of the proletariat because he expected from it the salvation of mankind, not because he could not endure to see the wretched conditions characteristic of proletarian existence.

This, incidentally, is most obvious from the fact that Marx describes the de facto encountered situation of pauperism precisely as "alienation," not simply as poverty and misery. It certainly will not do to say that his use of this notion is only indicative of a temporary infatuation with Feuerbach. For even though after 1845 Marx almost completely abandoned this notion, his central objection to private property always remained that it is both an expression of man's still not being truly human and the greatest impediment to his eventual becoming human. In fact there is a sense in which Marx does not *oppose* private property— he "criticizes" it in order to show that it *will* inevitably disappear. His "critique" of private property ultimately aims at proving that the "movement of private property" eventually will result in its self-annulment, and his "opposition" to private property amounts in the end to the insight, or rather claim, that this self-annulment is good, indeed entails man's ultimate self-completion.

As to what is wrong with private property, Marx puts it in many different ways. But the central argument is always the same: it isolates man both from other men and from nature and thus impedes the emergence of man's true social nature. "Private property does not know how to change crude need into human needs," since under the rule of private property everyone is interested in the other's needs only for selfish reasons. "Each tries to establish over the other an alien power, so as to find thereby satisfaction of his own selfish need."[325] Under the rule of private property man's humanizing activity par excellence, labor, becomes a means of satisfying the least human of all needs, the "need to maintain physical existence."[326] Indeed, the very nature of man, his "species essence," becomes a means to his individual existence,[327] which amounts to saying that man's *human* nature becomes a means to his subhuman, or prehuman, nature. Therefore, private property is the "material sensuous expression of alienated human life,"[328] a statement which means not only that man's true life is outside himself but also, and more fundamentally, that man still is not the true subject of his history,[329] that is, master both of his own nature and of nature outside himself, and of the social reality which relates the two.

[325] *MEGA* I, 3, 127; tr. Milligan, 115.
[326] *Ibid.* 88; tr. Milligan, 75.
[327] *Ibid.* 89. Cf. 72; tr. Milligan, 76, cf. 57.
[328] *Ibid.* 114; tr. Milligan, 103.
[329] *Ibid.* 153; tr. Milligan, 146.

24: PHILOSOPHY AND POLITICAL ECONOMY

We mentioned earlier that the *Manuscripts* were drafts for a book with the prospective title "Critique of Politics and Political Economy." As V. Adoratskij correctly remarked when introducing the edition of 1932, the preserved manuscripts do not contain anything resembling an explicit critique of politics or of the "political realm" in general. They restrict themselves to a critique of political *ecomony*—and to a criticism of the Hegelian dialectic. This fact is significant, and it raises a problem which is highly relevant to our discussion of Marx's notion of *praxis*. It is significant in the sense that politics, around which most of the Left Hegelians' "critiques" had been turning since about 1840, had become a rather secondary problem for Marx. His interest now centers around economics—and the truth-value of Hegel's dialectical understanding of history. Yet why precisely around these two? What is the connection between these two themes, rather disparate after all? How is Marx's turning to economic problems connected with his turning away from Hegelian philosophy, indeed from philosophy in general? Is Marx simply abandoning philosophy for an empirical inquiry? But if this was the case, why does he leave his study of economic problems unfinished to devote more than two years to the *Holy Family* and to the *German Ideology*, which instead of centering around economics take to task the "putrescence of Absolute Spirit"[330] as displayed in the philosophy of the Left Hegelians? Or is it not rather that Marx, far from abandoning philosophy for economics, believes to have

---

[330] *MEW* III, 17; tr. Pascal, 3.

found in political economy the "secret" of all philosophic speculations? And if so, what does this mean? In particular, what is the
connection between this and the idea expressed in the *Deutsch-
Französische Jahrbücher*, namely, that philosophy has to be both
"abolished" and "actualized"?

To begin with, what exactly is the meaning of Marx's "critique
of political economy" as advanced in the *Manuscripts*? We may
approach this problem by first showing that even though it obviously is connected with Marx's commitment to the proletariat,
the critique of political economy found in the *Manuscripts* is in
no way a "logical consequence" of the ideas which Marx had developed in the *Deutsch-Französische Jahrbücher*. As the reader
will remember, Marx had argued that only the proletariat could
be the source of a *"praxis à la hauteur des principes,"* that is,
only the proletariat could carry out a revolution which would
elevate Germany, and by implication the whole world, to truly
"human heights." The justification of this claim ran somewhat
as follows: even though the starting point of such a revolution is
the brain of a philosopher, the revolution also requires "a passive
element, a material foundation." The theory of true human emancipation can become a material power only by gripping the masses.
Not just any masses, it is true. For a revolutionary theory can be
actualized only by those for whom this actualization is, or rather
implies, the satisfaction of an absolutely vital need. Moreover,
as the revolution aims at overthrowing all conditions of the present
world order, the masses who will carry out the salvific revolution
must be in an all-round opposition to the existing conditions.
But only the proletariat is a social group for whom the "dissolution of the hereto existing world order" is the "secret of its own
existence." Consequently, if the real emancipation of man is to
be accomplished, the philosopher and the proletariat must join in
a common cause.

> Just as philosophy finds in the proletariat its material weapon,
> so the proletariat finds in philosophy its spiritual weapon....
> The emancipation of the Germans is the emancipation of man.
> The head of this emancipation is philosophy; its heart is the
> proletariat. Philosophy cannot actualize itself without abolishing

the proletariat; the proletariat cannot abolish itself without actualizing philosophy.[331]

In view of this argument the logical thing for a philosopher to do would seem to be to leave this study, to preach to the proletariat, and to tell it that by satisfying the philosopher's desire to see humanity emancipated—that is, by carrying out a radical revolution—it could free itself from its inhuman situation. Certainly, and this is the point which we wish to stress, to study political economy *does not* seem to be among the more obvious implications of the argument just sketched. In this sense it certainly is an oversimplification to say that the *Manuscripts* simply work out in greater detail what the articles in the *Deutsch-Französische Jahrbücher* had sketched in bold outline.[332]

Marx's sudden interest in political economy becomes truly intelligible only if one assumes that sometime between the fall of 1843 and the spring of 1844 Marx realized that the proletariat might be more than only a "passive element" of a revolution originating in a philosopher's mind. It is true that even in 1843 Marx had described this "passive element" as something which forces itself towards thought. Still he seems to have looked at the proletariat just as any "planner" would look around for someone to carry out his ideas. Nothing indicates that he was *consciously* aware of the possibility that the salvific function of the proletariat might be the result of an age-old history; rather he considered the philosopher's desire for human emancipation as such a historical result, the proletariat being little more than a sort of *causa materialis* which the philosopher had the good fortune to find at hand. Meanwhile, however, probably through Engels' "Outlines of a Critique of Political Economy" which Marx read at the end of January, 1844, Marx discovered that the proletariat's role in the history of human emancipation might be described as due to the socioeconomic nature of mankind's self-development—a discovery which obviously suggested that the philosopher's role was far less central than either he or his Left Hegelian colleagues had believed. The proletar-

[331] *MEGA* I, 1/1, 620 ff.; tr. Bottomore, 59.
[332] Friedrich, 89.

ian revolution, instead of originating in a philosopher's mind, was
the outcome of "laws" prior to and independent of philosophical instigations.

Of course one has to be careful not to overstate the point and
say that Marx discovered that the proletarian revolution might
be predictable in terms of socioeconomic laws. For even though
in a sense this is what Marx claims to have discovered and what
he will try to substantiate during the rest of his life, there remains
in his thought an element of teleology which makes it dangerous
without further ado to speak of "predictions" and "laws." In
any case Marx does not and in fact never will imply that the
philosopher, or rather the critical economist, may restrict himself
to a perfectly detached study of laws as objective as those of
natural science. Contrary to the old Engels, and in spite of a
few misleading phrases which in later writings he himself used, Marx
always seems to have known that the effectiveness of his "laws"
depended upon man's willful doing, at least in some respect. At
the very least there remains the fact, hardly deniable even though
never explicitly stated by Marx, that he always was inclined to
think of the *proletariat's knowledge* of these "laws" as something
without which the "laws" themselves might not have their full
effect. He did not of course foresee that the capitalists, too, gradually
would become aware of these "laws" and prevent their becoming
effective by not permitting the proletariat's pauperization to
become ever worse. It is ironical but certainly worth noticing
that the laws discovered by Marx were not "falsified" in the sense
in which, for example, hypotheses are experimentally falsified
in physics; they were "made false" because Marx revealed them
and thus gave the capitalists a chance which they might never
have had otherwise.

But be that as it may, it appears obvious that Marx's interest in
political economy is due to his discovery that the "passive element"
in the revolution supposed to bring about man's final emancipation
was the result of a development as old as mankind itself and that
this development was governed by laws whose knowledge made
it possible to describe the proletarian revolution as well as the
ensuing communism as something which was *bound* to happen

rather than *ought* to happen. One might of course ask why this discovery should lead one to study political economy rather than, for example, history or sociology. Yet here one simply will have to bear in mind, on the one hand, that the only social discipline of empirical orientation of which Marx knew was political economy and, on the other hand, that political economy, as Marx saw it, was a *"Wissenschaft* of History"[333] and quite obviously included what today is called "sociology."[334]

Of course political economy as it de facto existed could not possibly suffice; this point if nothing else had been convincingly shown by Engels' article. Political economy was a "science of enrichment" born of the merchants' mutual envy and greed, and bore "on its brow the mark of the most loathsome selfishness"; indeed, while the mercantilists at least had displayed a sort of "Catholic candor" by parading the mean avarice which governed all trade, the classical economy of Smith and Ricardo added "Protestant hypocrisy" to this selfishness and eulogized allegedly humanitarian aspects of civil society's economic life.[335] Yet political economy was the arsenal containing all the facts relevant both to the critique of the present world order and to the determination of the "laws" governing the development of mankind (and thus also the future victory of the proletariat). Marx's task, therefore, could only consist in critically re-evaluating whatever political economists had discovered. This critical ransacking of political economy moreover had the important aspect of being a criticism of the least encoded self-interpretation of the present age; in this sense the critique of political economy was a radicalization of the critique of religious and political consciousness which had occupied the Left Hegelians.

In fact the expression 'critique of political economy' has two connotations which one ought to distinguish, even though they are so closely connected that Marx does not seem to have been fully aware of their difference. On the one hand, this expression

[333] Cf. *MEW* III, 18; tr. Pascal, 4.

[334] In an explicit way this point was first made by K. Korsch; today, it is emphasized by a number of scholars such as G. Lichtheim, J. Habermas, and, to a lesser extent, H. Marcuse.

[335] *MEW* I, 499, 503; tr. Milligan, 175, 180 ff.

refers to a critique of the existing world order in economic terms. Marx's analysis of alienation to which we devoted so many pages is a "critique" in this sense; the same applies to many passages in Marx's mature economic writings in which he indicates the human wrongness of economic facts even while he traces their actual structure and genesis. Here the "critique" is a function of something which might be described as the peculiar type of "moral indignation" characteristic of Marx: the critique describes real situations in terms of categories which, even while they reduce the facts to their essential nature, reveal their discrepancy with a "truly human" situation; the allegedly real is shown to be an appearance (*Erscheinung*) of true reality (*Wesen*),[336] an appearance which is both a perversion of true reality and a dialectical phase of its development (and, eventually, full emergence).

On the other hand, the expression 'critique of political economy' refers to a criticism of the *Wissenschaft*, "political economics." While the first connotation refers to a criticism of facts, this second meaning refers to a criticism of a "form of consciousness" and thus stands in close relationship to the critique of ideologies first clearly articulated in the *German Ideology*. However, this is not to say that Marx's critique of political economy is a simple *Ideologiekritik*. Ideologies properly speaking—such as religion or the philosophy of the Left Hegelians as well as political theories of all ages—could be translated into a language which itself was no longer religious, philosophical, or political. The critique of such ideologies unveiled both their truth and their falsity in terms of a radical reduction which destroyed while it explained. Political economics, on the contrary, could not possibly be reduced to a more fundamental form of consciousness; as Marx put it in an article published in August, 1844, it was the "scientific reflection of ... politico-economic conditions,"[337] that is, the theoretical counterpart of those socioanthropological data which were the very foundations of civil society.

[336] Cf. Friedrich, 93.
[337] *MEGA* I, 3, 9.

This in turn does not mean that Marx viewed political economics as a science, nor does it mean that political economics could be carried over into the epoch of communism. It was akin to science in that it described and analyzed empirical facts without thoroughly concealing them, and it was similar to ideologies in that its descriptions and analyses were determined by limited, and therefore limiting,[338] socioeconomic conditions. In a sense what Marx seems to want to say is that political economics is not a true science because the facts with which it is concerned have still not reached a level of development to permit a truly "objective" analysis of these very facts. Perhaps one might put it in another way: whereas ideologies dissolved into nothing (or rather into something thoroughly different) as soon as their "false consciousness" was unmasked, political economics could cease to be the "false consciousness" which in fact it was without ceasing to exist. Of course there also is an obvious sense in which Marx aims at "abolishing" political economics: he thinks of communism as a situation where political economics no longer is the "anatomy of society," that is, where man and his society no longer are governed by "blind" economic laws.[339] Yet even so there remains a significant difference between ideologies properly speaking and political economics: while ideologies, even though their existence and genesis may be explainable, always and necessarily are falsifications of real facts, political economics, when critically analyzed, turns out to be the "anatomy of civil society."[340]

We have said that Marx does not distinguish between these two meanings of his "critique." Yet even though Marx occasionally may commit semantic blunders such as equating nature's history with the science of natural history,[341] it would be wrong to argue

[338] Cf. MEW III, 31; tr. Pascal, 19 ff.: "... everywhere, the identity of nature and man appears in such a way that the limited (bornierte) relation of man to nature determines their limited relation to one another...."

[339] On this point see Korsch, 89 ff.

[340] Cf. MEW XIII, 8, where Marx, in the foreword to A Contribution to the Critique of Political Economy, says that his critique of the Hegelian Philosophy of Right and his articles in the Deutsch-Französische Jahrbücher led him to the result that "the anatomy of civil society is to be sought in political economy."

[341] Cf. MEW III, 18: "... the history of nature and the history of man mutually

that Marx's failure to distinguish between the two meanings of his "critique" is a semantic confusion. For the ultimate secret of Marx's critique, the reason why it is both so confusing and so fascinating, is that Marx seems to want to *criticize the facts by criticizing their "scientific reflection."*

What this means may be best explained by indicating what Marx's "critique of political economy" encompasses. Even when one restricts oneself to Marx's criticism of the *Wissenschaft*, political economics, it soon becomes obvious that it moves at several quite different levels. One type of criticism which plays an important role in the *Manuscripts*, even though it seldom is spelled out very explicitly, consists in showing that classical political economics (the only one which truly interests Marx) constantly states inhuman facts without apparently noticing their inhumanity. To quote only one instance:

> Let us put ourselves now wholly at the standpoint of the political economist.... He tells us that originally and according to the concept the whole produce of labor belongs to the worker. But at the same time he tells us that in actual fact what the worker gets is the smallest and utterly indispensable part of the product—as much only as is necessary for his existence, not as a man but as a worker, and for the propagation, not of humanity but of the slave class of workers. The political economist tells us that everything is bought with labor and that capital is nothing but accumulated labor, but at the same time he tells us that the worker, far from being able to buy everything, must sell himself and his human identity.[342]

In a passage such as this one the relationship between the "criticism of facts" and the critique of political economics properly speaking is readily understood. The political economist himself, in our instance Adam Smith, very explicitly spells out the grounds on which the simple facts are objectionable—and nevertheless does not object. Adam Smith had seen that the essence of private property is labor and that capital is accumulated labor; at the same time,

determine each other. The history of nature, so-called natural science, does not concern us here ...." These sentences occur in a passage which has been deleted, it is true.

[342] *MEGA* I, 3, 43 ff.; tr. Milligan, 26 ff.

however, he explicitly admits a fact obvious to anyone who cares to look, namely, that the worker hardly gets what is necessary for his existence. In other words, the political economist himself has advanced a criticism of facts; he has to be criticized for not being aware that his analysis is such a criticism.

Another type of "critique" is similar but already reaches a more fundamental level: political economics proceeds from certain facts without explaining them; it states laws without explaining their genesis; and so on. Here the task of the "critic" is somewhat more complex: he has to supply the explanation, or genetic analysis, which the economist does not offer; and his analysis has to be such that it immediately reveals the objectionable character of the facts and/or laws which the political economist takes for granted. Marx's analysis of "alienated labor" as the essence of private property is a striking instance of this kind of criticism.

This second type of "critique" raises a methodological problem, it is true. For one might ask why the political economist, and for that matter anyone else, *should* explain these facts and laws. And even if it were obvious that he should explain them, why should he explain them just in the way in which Marx does explain them? After all, it is obvious that such an explanation could no longer be economic in the strict sense of the term (as Marx's explanation in terms of his "theory of alienation" indicates). We might do well to phrase our question in a more answerable form: Why does Marx believe that the explanations of facts and laws must be just as he advances them, both revealing the historical origin and genesis and the *"antihumanistic" character* of the facts and laws in question? For example, why explain private property in terms of "alienation" and not in terms of "freedom," as Hegel had done?

This question is answered as quickly as it is asked: because Marx "knows" that the present world order and in particular bourgeois society is "wrong"; his only real problem consists in substantiating this insight which might be described as Marx's Left Hegelian heritage, never thoroughly abandoned. Of course, contrary to all other Left Hegelians, Marx found a way to substantiate this insight which permitted him to all but forget its origin: he could always argue that the situation of the proletariat being in fact as it is, it must be considered obvious that bourgeois society is both basically inhuman and incapable of solving the problem generated by it— and consequently condemned to perish. However it should be noticed that even later Marxists were implicitly aware of the fact that the inhuman situation of the proletariat is not the only or even the main justification of the Marxist desire to "revolutionize" society and, in particular, to see civil society disappear.

For when it turned out that civil society was capable of handling the problem generated by it—namely, the ever-increasing pauperization of the proletariat—Marxism did not "wither away" (as one would expect if the Marxist revolutionary attitude was a response to the inhuman fate of the proletarians). On the contrary, as we shall try to show in a second volume, many Marxists did and still do argue that civil society was granted only a respite not foreseen by Marx, a breathing space which would result in civil society's death all the more violently and inevitably; Lenin's book on "imperialism" published in 1917 is an instance of this attitude. Here it transpires that Marx's Left Hegelian heritage has become an implicit premise of *all* genuinely revolutionary-minded Marxism: it is taken for granted that civil society is wrong and condemned to perish; the only problem consists in showing why it is wrong and for exactly what reasons it will perish. Even so intelligent a Marxist as Karl Korsch quite obviously thought in this way: when he discusses what he calls Marx's "principle of criticism,"[343] it never even occurs to him to question the general justification of this principle; he is only concerned to show that Marx applied this principle more consistently and more realistically than any social analyst before him.

The third level of "critique" to be mentioned is closely connected with the two to which we already alluded: if civil society will not survive, if it is not the end of humanity's road, as Smith and others seemed to suggest, then political economics must be wrong in assuming that the laws obtained by an analysis of civil society are irrefragable and eternal. Here Marx's "principle of criticism" results in what Korsch has aptly described as the two principles

[343] Korsch, 57 ff.

of "historical specification" and of "change." The laws of civil society, both social and economic, which political economics describes do not apply to society in general; in particular they do not apply to future communist society. But neither do they apply to primitive, to Graeco-Roman, to early medieval society. They are fundamentally historical; they have a genesis and will in turn pass away.

In the *Manuscripts*, it is true, this idea is not articulated as explicitly as for example in the 1847 criticism of Proudhon, *The Misery of Philosophy*, or in the *Communist Manifesto*. Still its elements are already present, and with them some important implications. Thus, when in the manuscript on "alienated labor" he accuses political economics of not explaining private property, Marx states that political economics expresses the "material process" through which private property actually passes in terms of "general, abstract formulae which it then takes for laws."[344] This certainly is not to say that Marx objects to political economics' attempt to discover laws. It is not the laws to which he objects, but rather the form in which these laws are expressed: as "general, abstract, formulae." Of course, in the *Manuscripts* the "generality" and the "abstractness" which Marx has in mind still are not simply the absence of a historical point of view; it was not until the *German Ideology* that he truly succeeded in sharply dissociating from each other a "logical" and a genuinely "historical" genesis.

Thus, for example, his analysis of the genesis of private property in terms of "alienated labor" certainly is *not* historical. Though he repeatedly speaks of a development, a movement, a process of private property (and in this case indeed seems to think of historical development), his theory of alienation mainly amounts to a "logical" genealogy in Hegel's sense; as Marx puts it himself, he proceeds from the "politico-economical fact" of private property and reduces it to its "concepts."[345] Similarly, when he accuses J. Mill of advancing abstract laws, of disregarding "the change (*Wechsel*) and constant annulment" in terms of which a law first

---

[344] *MEGA* I, 3, 81; tr. Milligan, 67.
[345] *Ibid.* 90; tr. Milligan, 78.

comes to be (*wodurch es erst wird*), Marx mainly seems to have in mind the fact that Mill loses sight of other laws which, even though they contradict the first ones, contributed to their emergence. The political economist overlooks the fact that each of his laws is only "an abstract, incidental, and dialectical phase" of the "real movement."[346]

However there is another train of thought in the *Manuscripts* which anticipates the later principles of historical specification and change even more explicitly: Marx's various remarks about the history of political economics and its connection with the real "movement of private property." Following a suggestion by Engels, Marx tries here to trace the development of political economics in religious terms as a gràdual *Verinnerlichung*, subjectification, intimately connected with the ever-increasing power of private property over man's mind. The mercantilists, he argues, remained similar to Catholics in that they worshiped wealth as something external to man: they considered money as *the* wealth. Compared to them, Adam Smith may be described as "the Luther of political economy": by taking labor to be the only source of wealth, he incorporated private property in man himself and thus recognized man as its essence. In this way Smith certainly represented a progress as against the mercantile system. But this progress was in a sense for the worse: just as Luther "negated the priest outside the layman because he transplanted the priest into the layman's heart," Smith incorporated the alienation represented by private property into man's very essence—thus only perpetuating man's alienation rather than overcoming it.[347] As to Ricardo, whom Marx always viewed with an odd mixture of hate and genuine admiration, he drew the cynical conclusion: contrary to Smith, Ricardo saw clearly that the ultimate end of civil society's economic life is neither man nor national interest but only net revenue. Here the abstractions of political economics have reached a "climax of infamy"; it becomes obvious that "humanity is outside political economy and inhumanity inside political economy."[348]

[346] *Ibid.* 530 ff.

[347] *Ibid.* 107 ff.; tr. Milligan, 93 ff.

[348] *Ibid.* 514 ff.; cf. 108.

In his "Outlines of a Critique of Political Economy" Engels had argued that the sophistry of economics increases with every advance of time, so as to prevent economics from revealing its true nature; "this is why Ricardo, for instance, is more guilty than Adam Smith, and MacCulloch and Mill more guilty than Ricardo."[349] Marx's ideas on this point are somewhat more subtle. Even though he would agree with Engels as far as post-Ricardian economics is concerned (which, as it was his contemporary, Marx always was inclined to view as an insincere *apologia* for capitalist society[350]), he sees in the progress of political economics from the mercantilists to Ricardo far more than only a progress in sophistry. On the one hand, he is well aware of the fact that this history of political economics is a history of a progress in knowledge; Quesnay and all the physiocrats understood more and better than the mercantilists, Smith more than Quesnay, and Ricardo more than Smith.

This progress in knowledge ultimately is due to the economic progress itself rather than to a simple accumulation of discoveries; the true nature of civil society becomes more and more articulate and therefore visible as civil society ripens. On the other hand, the same economic progress explains the increasingly misanthropic and, since Ricardo, openly cynical attitude of political economists. Each economist "advances further in his alienation from man" than his predecessor, but he does so only because in reality this alienation becomes ever more radical.[351] The increasing "abstractness" of economic theorizing is connected with the economic development as well. As truly human social laws can be obtained only by abstracting from the "specific nature" of contemporary conditions, political economics has a queer liking for "general laws"; and as these laws only hold in an "abstract form"—that is, do not apply to the *real* situation of contemporary man— political economics is interested in seeing its laws realized, whether they help man or whether "thousands of men are ruined by it."[352]

[349] *MEW* I, 501; tr. Milligan, 179.
[350] Cf. Bigo, 16 ff.
[351] *MEGA* I, 3, 108 ff.; tr. Milligan, 95.
[352] *Ibid.* 557 ff.

In particular, political economics has no interest at all in the human dimension of the proletarians:

> It goes without saying that the proletarian—that is, the man who, being without capital and rent, lives purely by labor, and by a one-sided, abstract labor—is considered by political economics only as a worker. Political economics can therefore advance the proposition that the proletarian, the same as any horse, must get as much as will enable him to work. It does not consider him when he is not working, as a human being, but leaves such considerations to criminal law, to doctors, to religion, to the statistical tables, to politics, and to the work-house beadle.[353]

At this point it becomes perfectly obvious that the kind of political economics which developed from the mercantilists through Smith to Ricardo and his pupils has to be *transcended*. But how is one to transcend a thinking which is the "scientific reflection" of the present world order? It could not possibly suffice to develop a different type of political economics; as Marx will put it in the *German Ideology*, "this demand to change consciousness amounts to a demand to interpret reality in a different way, that is, to accept it by means of another interpretation."[354] Political economics was the reflection of a society in alienation—that is, of civil society— "in which every individual is a totality of needs and only exists for the other person, as the other person exists for him, insofar as each becomes a means for the other."[355] The only way to transcend classical political economics consisted in overcoming civil society itself.

However, and this immediately leads us to the last and most fundamental level of Marx's critique of political economics, Marx is beyond the point of believing that a philosopher like he could instigate a revolution and induce the disappearance of civil society. Since 1844, and especially since 1845, to transcend political economics no longer means for him to look for an extraphilosophical partner whom he might instigate to revolutionary action. Rather it means

---

[353] *Ibid.* 45, cf. 97; tr. Milligan, 29, cf. 84.
[354] *MEW* III, 20; tr. Pascal, 6.
[355] *MEGA* I, 3, 138 ff.; tr. Milligan, 129.

to discover the "laws" in terms of which *civil society abolishes itself*.

This turn of thought already is intimated in a passage in the *Manuscripts* in which Marx himself speaks of transcending political economics: he invites the reader to "rise above the level of political economics" and identifies this transcending with asking the following two questions:

> 1. What, in the evolution of mankind, is the meaning of this reduction of the greater part of mankind to abstract labor?
> 2. What are the mistakes committed by the piecemeal reformers (*Reformatoren en detail*) who either want to raise wages, and in this way try to improve the situation of the working class, or regard equality of wages (as Proudhon does) as the goal of social revolution?[356]

Even though both questions remain unanswered (the manuscript stops short just at this point), it is not difficult to gather from other passages what kind of an answer Marx had in mind. The second question is answered with all desired clarity in the section on alienated labor: "A forcing-up of wages ... would be nothing but better payment for the slave and would not conquer either for the worker or for labor their human vocation (*Bestimmung*) and dignity."[357] In other words, Marx rebels against the very existence of wage-labor, not against low wages as such; even an equality of wages would not do, since it might amount to nothing else than an equality in alienation and inhumanity.[358]

To the first question Marx nowhere gives an explicit answer. Yet it is obvious what the answer would be. For the sense of the question is, What is the historical meaning of the fact that the greater part of mankind is no longer truly human? What is the meaning of the existence and the ever-increasing pauperization of the proletariat? The answer is that civil society, which itself is the

[356] *Ibid.* 45 ff.; tr. Milligan, 29.

[357] *Ibid.* 92; tr. Milligan, 81.

[358] Therefore, Marx will argue in the *German Ideology* that the proletarian revolution presupposes "a great increase in productive power, a high degree of its development"; for without such a development of productive forces the proletarian revolution as well as communism would only succeed in making man's want a general one—"and thus all the old crap would necessarily be reproduced," *MEW* III, 34 ff.; tr. Pascal, 24.

result of an agelong evolution of mankind, has generated in its own womb a social class which will transcend all alienation by abolishing civil society and by establishing man as man:

> In fact, private property, in its economic movement, drives itself towards its own dissolution, ... in as much as it produces the proletariat as proletariat, a misery conscious of its spiritual and physical misery, a dehumanization conscious of its dehumanization and therefore self-abolishing. The proletariat executes the sentence that private property pronounced on itself by begetting the proletariat.... When the proletariat is victorious, it by no means becomes the absolute side of society, for it is victorious only by abolishing itself and its opposite. Then the proletariat disappears as well as the opposite which determines it, private property.[359]

From what we have said, it may have become obvious that Marx's critique of political economics aims at far more than a professional criticism of some economic theorems.[360] In later years, it is true, Marx occasionally argued with other political economists on purely technical grounds. However the ultimate end of his critique of political economics is and always will remain to unveil the laws of the self-abolishing movement of private property, laws which must be known to the proletariat if it is to become aware of itself as the savior of mankind and eventually carry out its *praxis à la hauteur des principes*, the total salvific revolution. In this sense one might argue that Marx's critique of political economy is both a scientific analysis involving prediction and a message of salvation, a call to action. This is not as contradictory as it may seem at first sight. For in a sense it is not correct to say that Marx's critique of political economy predicts communism (even though this will become obvious only in Marx's mature economic writings). His critique predicts the end of the "movement of private property" and with it the end of civil society as a whole

---

[359] *MEGA* I, 3, 206; tr. Dixon, 52.

[360] Cf. Friedrich, 98. However, Friedrich only stresses that the critique of political economics entails the critique of all other "forms of consciousness." It seems to escape him that Marx aims at developing the bourgeois science, political economics, to the point where it abolishes itself in terms of the proletarian revolution, a point which is quite well made in Korsch, 91 ff.

(which Marx later will describe as a total stagnation of all economic traffic and eventually of production itself). It offers this scientific prediction as a message of salvation to the proletariat, as an invitation to carry out the revolutionary deed to which it is destined— even while it demonstrates that all socioeconomic conditions of communist society, in particular a high level of production involving the cooperation of virtually all men, are rising within civil society itself.

It is from this perspective that one has to understand Marx's bitter polemics against Bruno Bauer. For as we saw earlier, Bauer argued that all great revolutionary movements were and always will be failures "because the mass became interested in and enthusiastic over them" and that therefore the "critique" has to disassociate itself from all mass interests and become absorbed in itself alone. Marx could not argue that "all great actions of previous history" were *not* failures, for he thoroughly agreed with Bauer that the era of salvation was still in the future. But he could, and indeed did, argue that all previous revolutions were failures because the mass which carried them out was neither representative of "man as man" nor in need of the revolution as its "life principle." If a revolution was a failure, "it was so because the mass whose living conditions it did not substantially go beyond was an exclusive, limited mass, not an all-embracing one."[361]

Marx's main criticism of Bauer, however, aims at his former friend's belief that a purely philosophical critique could change the course of the world. As Marx observes time and again, this belief is based upon the false assumption that the realities to be criticized and transformed are in the order of thought. "According to the critical critique the whole evil lies in thinking"[362]; consequently it believes itself able to change the world by correcting ideas. Yet as these ideas are only a reflection of more basic *realities*, Bauer in fact is fighting windmills. He reduces all theories to which he objects to religious "forms of consciousness" instead of considering the "commercial and industrial practice" from which

[361] *MEGA* I, 3, 253; tr. Dixon, 109 ff.
[362] *Ibid.* 223; tr. Dixon, 73.

they originate.[363] Certainly Bauer is right when he argues that it is high time for man to rise against the existing world order, "but to rise, it is not enough to do so in thought and to leave hanging over our real sensuous head the real palpable yoke that cannot be subtilized away with ideas."[364]

Still there remains the question why Marx considered Bauer's haughty intellectualism important enough to devote to it a whole book (the *Holy Family* bears the subtitle *Against Bruno Bauer and Company*) and then again a section of his elaborate criticism of the "German Ideologists." Certainly not, as S. Hook would seem to suggest, because Marx was afraid of the harmful impact which Bauer's ideas might have upon the gradually maturing revolutionary movement[365]; Marx still had a long time to go before be thought in such concrete, almost "party-political" terms. Nor is it entirely satisfactory to explain his polemics with the Left Hegelians by the fact, obviously true, that at that time Marx still believed the emancipation of mankind dependent upon an "emancipation of the Germans" and consequently, even though he no longer was in Germany, was interested in the German intellectual scene more than in the French or English problem.[366] Even the circumstance that Marx and Engels began to write the *German Ideology* after their return from a trip to England—where they had taken notice of involved economic and social realities and therefore were disgusted with the never-ending Left Hegelian polemics[367]—does not fully explain the length and detailed character of their own contribution to this discussion.

The answer to this question might become more obvious after we have said a few words about Marx's[368] polemics against Johann

---

[363] Cf. *ibid.* 284; tr. Dixon, 147 ff.

[364] *Ibid.* 254; tr. Dixon, 111.

[365] Cf. Hook, 98, 112.

[366] Friedrich, 147.

[367] Arvon, 147.

[368] Here one might raise the question whether the ideas developed in the manuscript "Sankt Max" ought to be attributed to Marx alone or to Marx *and* Engels. While in the *Holy Family*, the most important sections from which we quoted (section 3 and 4 of chapter IV and all of chapter VI with the exception of the first part of section 2) are easily identified as being written by

Caspar Schmidt, alias Max Stirner, which make up almost one half of the "two thick octavo volumes" of the manuscripts today known as the *German Ideology*. Since its publication at the end of 1844, Stirner's odd book, *The Ego and Its Own*,[369] has been interpreted in many different ways. Kuno Fischer, later a famous historian of philosophy and one of the initiators of Neo-Kantianism, in 1847 described Stirner as a typical representative of "modern sophistry" issuing from philosophical dogmatism, a subject on which Fischer had written his doctoral dissertation.[370] Thirty years later Engels initiated another interpretation—followed with others by E. Bernstein, G. Adler, and V. Basch—according to which Stirner would have been a precursor of political anarchism and thus comparable to Proudhon, Bakunin, and Kropotkin.[371]

Marx alone, this question raises serious problems as far as the *German Ideology* is concerned. However, as far as the criticism against Stirner is concerned, one can say with some certainty that the central ideas are those of Marx. Engels was the first to read Stirner's book; in a letter to Marx, dated November 19, 1844, he compared Stirner's ideas to "Bentham's egoism" and argued that this egoism must *gleich in Kommunismus umschlagen*, immediately change into communism. According to Engels, only a few "trivialities" have to be stressed against Stirner; "but what is true in his principle we have to accept," *MEW* XXVII, 11. Marx's reply to this astonishingly positive evaluation of Stirner is not preserved. However, in a letter of January 20, 1845, Engels says: "As to Stirner, I thoroughly agree with you. When I wrote to you, I still was under an immediate impression of the book; since then, I had time to put it aside and to think it through, and I find the same as you do." Engels adds that Hess, after some wavering, came to the very same conclusion. Even though Engels does not specify these conclusions, they certainly were far more negative than Engels' original evaluation. Cf. *ibid*. 14. For Hess' review of *The Ego and Its Own* see Hess₂, 381-393. See also Hess' letter to Marx, January 17, 1845, Hess₃, 105.

[369] M. Stirner, *Der Einzige und sein Eigenthum* (Leipzig, 1845). The book was published late in 1844; cf. Arvon, 17.

[370] K. Fischer, "Moderne Sophisten," *Epigonen* 5 (1848) 247-316; *idem*, "Ein Apologet der Sophistik und ein 'philosophischer Reactionär,'" *Epigonen* 4 (1847) 152-165. The first mentioned article, Fischer's dissertation, originally was published in another periodical in 1847; cf. Arvon, 143 ff.

[371] *MEW* XXI, 271; tr. Moscow, II, 367: "Stirner, the prophet of contemporary anarchism; Bakunin has taken a great deal from him ..."; cf. E. Bernstein, "Die soziale Doktrin des Anarchismus," *Neue Zeit* (1891/92) 481 ff.; G. Adler, "Der moderne Anarchismus, seine Theorie und seine Taktik," *Neue*

At the turn of the century several studies suggested that *The Ego and Its Own* was an early herald of Nietzsche's "philosophy of the Superman," even though it generally was agreed that Nietzsche himself never had an occasion to read the book.[372] More recently Stirner had to endure being compared to Kierkegaard[373] and even being described as a precursor of existentialism.[374] It even has been suggested that Stirner's philosophy is simply the product of a paranoiac mind[375]—an interpretation which certainly does not seem too far-fetched in view of the fact that Stirner's mother died in a lunatic asylum and that Stirner himself failed completely as far as his own human existence was concerned (after a brief period of fame he finished his life as a grocer and twice landed in prison for debts).

All the more astonishing is the copiousness of Marx's criticism. With respect to his polemics with Bauer one at least can point out that Marx after all was disavowing ideas of a former friend and associate, ideas to which he himself had adhered. But Stirner and Marx never so much as met, and certainly Marx never was inclined to be a Stirnerian.[376] It is true that the author of *The Ego and*

Deutsche Rundschau (1898) 1090 ff.; V. Basch, *L'individualisme anarchiste. Max Stirner* (Paris, 1904). As far as I can see, there certainly is no direct influence of Stirner on Bakunin; at most, it could be a "spiritual affinity."

[372] In 1874 Nietzsche suggested to his disciple Baumgartner that he read Stirner's book; but as we have the list of books which, from 1869 to 1879, Nietzsche took out of the library at Basle—and Stirner's book does not figure among them—it is generally agreed today that Nietzsche knew about Stirner only through some history of philosophy, probably F. A. Lange, *Geschichte des Materialismus und Kritik seiner Bedeutung in der Gegenwart*, the first edition of which was published in 1873. Cf. A. Lévy, *Stirner et Nietzsche* (Paris, 1904); also Arvon, 5.

[373] E.g., M. Buber, *Dialogisches Leben* (Zürich, 1947) 195 ff., 202 ff.

[374] E.g., Arvon, 178.

[375] E. Schultze, "Stirnersche Ideen in einem paranoischen Wahnsystem," *Archiv für Psychiatrie und Nervenkrankheiten* 25 (1903) 793-818.

[376] Even though Stirner, together with Meyen, Buhl, Köppen, and others, belonged to the followers of Bruno Bauer at Berlin, Marx never met him; it seems likely that Stirner joined the group after Marx left Berlin. Stirner submitted 26 brief articles to the *Rheinische Zeitung* between March and October, 1842; after Marx became editor in chief of the newspaper, not a single article

Its Own had made several remarks, rather critical, of communism and even referred to "Mr. Marx" by name. Yet even so Marx's criticism seems to be somewhat out of proportion. Indeed it becomes understandable only if one assumes that Stirner had touched upon a sore point in Marx's own constructions.

In fact there were two such sore points. The more obvious motive of Marx's criticism, even though rather involved, is quickly stated. The *Holy Family* had claimed to defend Feuerbach's "real humanism," or in any case conclusions drawn from it, against Bauer's "spiritualism or speculative idealism"[377]; it had argued that the "brilliant arguments *(geniale Entwickelungen)*" of the author of the *Essence of Christianity* long ago had transcended even the very categories which Bauer's critique now wielded[378] and described Feuerbach's humanism as the theoretical counterpart of the practical socialism found in France and England.[379] But when Marx read *The Ego and Its Own*, he suddenly realized that Stirner's denunciation of Feuerbach as a "pious atheist" had very much truth to it. This impression was even reinforced when Marx read Feuerbach's reply to Stirner.[380] For Feuerbach quite frankly admitted that his atheism, even though radically anthropocentric, was "religious" after all; to him the statement that there is no God was only a negative form of the "practical and religious, that is, *positive*" statement that "Man is the God."[381] Moreover, when Feuerbach defended against Stirner his notion of "species being," Marx immediately saw that this certainly was not what he himself had in mind when he identified the actualization of the "species essence"—that is, cooperation in production and consumption—with communism. For Feuerbach did not even

by Stirner was published (that is, after October 15, 1842). Engels probably knew Stirner personally.

[377] *MEGA* I, 3, 179; tr. Dixon, 15.

[378] *Ibid.* 265 ff.; tr. Dixon, 125. This passage is by Engels.

[379] *Ibid.* 301, 303; tr. Dixon, 168, 171.

[380] This reply, entitled "Über das 'Wesen des Christenthums' in Beziehung auf den 'Einzigen und sein Eigenthum,'" was published in *Wigands Vierteljahrsschrift* 2 (1845) 193-205; cf. Feuerbach, VII, 294-310.

[381] Feuerbach, VII, 297; cf. 309.

mention social cooperation, nor did he speak of the necessity of changing the social order. Even though he twice used the term 'communism,' he seemed to have nothing in mind except a vague sort of community based upon mutual recognition and love. Feuerbach's man had no revolutionary drive at all; he reveled in his divinity—and was a "communist" only in so far as he saw his human essence "in the community."[382]

At this point Marx became aware of the fact that he must defend himself against two opponents. On the one hand, he had to disassociate himself from Feuerbach; on the other hand, even though he could not avoid using his denunciation of Feuerbach, he had to avoid associating himself with Stirner. In this sense the *German Ideology* basically is a defense against both the theologically inspired and passivist humanism of Feuerbach and the extreme voluntarism and subjectivist individualism of Stirner (if one disregards the appendix on the "true socialists"). When in the first of the "Theses on Feuerbach" Marx argues both against a materialism which disregards the active and *practical* dimensions of man's being sensuous and against an idealism which ignores the sensuous and therefore ultimately *social* implications of man's being active, he has in mind Feuerbach and Stirner: Feuerbach as he had revealed himself in his reply to Stirner—that is, as a "contemplative materialist"—and Stirner as he had treated Marx's communism only as another version of Feuerbach's humanism.[383]

However there would seem to be still another reason for the vehemence of Marx's reaction to Stirner, a reason which throws significant light upon Marx's polemics against Left Hegelianism in general. For Marx saw in Stirner neither an anarchist nor an

---

[382] *Ibid.* 310.

[383] Marx's dissociation from Feuerbach was important all the more as Gustav Julius, an old friend of Bruno Bauer and former editor of the *Leipziger Allgemeine Zeitung*, explicitly insisted on the Feuerbachian origins of Marx's "practical humanism"; cf. his article "Der Streit der sichtbaren mit der unsichtbaren Menschenkirche oder Kritik der Kritik der kritischen Kritik," published in the second volume of *Wigands Vierteljahrsschrift*. The same point was made a few months later by Bruno Bauer's "Characteristik Ludwig Feuerbachs" in the third volume of the same periodical, which was published only during the years 1844/45.

existentialist; he saw in him what, historically speaking, Stirner was first of all, namely, the man who had carried the profanization of all Hegelian ideas further than any other Left Hegelian.

In a sense the history of the Left Hegelians from Strauss to Marx is the history of an evermore radical disenchantment, the process of an evermore radical translation of Hegel's speculative categories and ideas into the language of common sense. Richter and Strauss had reduced Hegel's speculative interpretation of Christ and Incarnation to talk about mankind; Bauer had extended this profanization to religion in general and, with Ruge's help, to "religious" aspects of political life; Feuerbach had reduced both religion and Hegelianism to a quasi-materialistic anthropocentrism; and Hess and Marx had translated Feuerbach's still religious anthropology into the language of a revolutionary-minded socialism. And now Stirner came and reduced all this, including communism and its ideals, to an extreme individualistic egoism. Everything dissolved into "fixed ideas," "ghosts," "phantoms," "loose screws": history, mankind, society, communism, socialism, as much as Christ, the Absolute Spirit, or ideals of bourgeois society. All this was treated by Stirner from the point of view of a naked Ego which was neither committed to nor bound by anything; *Ich hab' mein Sach' auf Nichts gestellt*, as Stirner parodied Luther. The only real problem which still occupied Stirner was how to "utilize" and to "use up" such ideals for the sake of "myself," who was the only thing that really counted.

Marx must have realized immediately that this position of Stirner's was both perfectly consistent with the general development of philosophy since Hegel and a serious alternative to his own profanization of Hegelianism. As a former Left Hegelian, he was extremely sensitive to what one might call "the logical progress of ideas"; he implicitly agreed with his former Left Hegelian allies that a philosophical position was the more "progressive" the more it succeeded in desecrating the religious atmosphere of the Great Master's thought. Like Strauss, Bauer, and Feuerbach and in a way more radically than any of them, Marx had worked at a profanization of all realms which had been "transfigured" by Hegel; he had fought against what he believed to be illusions and opiates, against religion, political ideals, and eventually against Hegel's philosophy itself. But he had not given up the hidden eschatological attitude and the implicit revolutionary drive underlying Hegelianism.

Even though he viewed Hegel's *speculative* reconciliation as an idealist self-deception, he by no means had given up the general idea underlying Hegel's system, namely, that *some reconciliation* was necessary. If he worked at disillusioning man, he did so only to force man to achieve a reconciliation after all—and this time a *real* reconciliation which entailed a "material" transformation of the real world. And now came Stirner, who argued that communism only was replacing one illusion by another. In the name of his naked Ego, Stirner went further than even Marx: he declared a "phantom" even the eschatological attitude of Hegelianism and the revolutionary enthusiasm issuing from it. While Marx certainly wanted to abolish speculative philosophy, but only in order eventually to actualize a nonspeculative philosophy, Stirner simply abolished philosophy in general by declaring it all nonsense. While Marx believed it obvious that the atomism of civil society was objectionable and therefore had to be transcended, Stirner made this very egoism of modern society his principle.

It is quite amusing to see how carefully Marx avoids touching upon this issue. Besides a lot of nasty hairsplitting and cavilling which occasionally turns into downright abuse, he tries to describe Stirner's position as an extremely radical version of Bauer's intellectualism (of which of course there was very much left in Stirner). Time and again he accuses Stirner of confusing mental struggles with real social collisions, of treating history as if it were only a history of ideas, of believing that real abuses can be banished from the world by dismissing them from one's mind. All these confusions Marx in turn traces back to the real situation of contemporary civil society, a procedure which permits him to denounce Stirner as a representative of the German petty bourgeoisie as well as to elaborate on his own notion of "ideologies."

I am far from denying that much of Marx's criticism is perfectly valid. But the interesting point is that it avoids touching upon the real issue, which obviously also was the reason why Marx had at all undertaken the effort of writing hundreds of pages against this nihilistic individualism, namely, that Stirner had called in question the very motives of Marx's own position. This, in turn, throws light upon all of Marx's polemics with the Left Hegelians, for these motives were of Hegelian origin. Many years later Marx will write that he and Engels willingly abandoned the manuscript of the *German Ideology* to the "gnawing criticism of mice," since they had reached their chief object, *Selbstverständigung.*[384] Yet the very fact that Marx had to write hundreds of pages against Hegelian epigones in order to come to an understanding with himself indicates that Marx's own position depended upon an element common to him and other Left Hegelians—an element with respect to which Marx had to show that his interpretation was the only tenable one.

This common element is easily pointed out: all the philosophies which Marx was opposing were critiques of the existing human condition as much as Marx's own "critique of political economy." To be more precise: they were either a critique or else an attempt to show that in reality there was nothing to criticize. Hegel's philosophy was both: a critique of the given human condition and an attempt to show that in the end the critical attitude had to give way to an all-embracing reconciliation. Bauer's philosophy was a competing critique. Stirner's egoism ultimately was a renunciation of all critique, since it suggested that all the objectives to be fought for were only phantoms. Feuerbach's humanism, even though it came closest to Marx's anti-idealist conception of man, had all but forgotten what it meant to be critical.

Marx was quick in discovering what the fundamental difference between all these philosophical critiques and his own critique of political economy was: none of the Left Hegelians realized what had meanwhile become the basic premise of Marx's position, namely, that the critique was embodied in the real movement of empirical history. Hegel, it is true, had implicitly been aware of it; as late as 1873 Marx will admit that Hegel was the first to describe the "general forms of the movement" of history and its

---

[384] *MEW* XIII, 10; tr. Moscow, I, 364.

dialectics.[385] But even though Hegel stood on the standpoint of modern political economy,[386] and even though he was the first to grasp that history is a process in which man by his own deeds gradually becomes the "true subject" of all developments, his argumentation was through and through vitiated by his assumption that the real movement of history ultimately has to be understood in terms of a conceptual dialectic. Yet while Hegel at least gave "in many instances the elements of a true description of the human condition," in spite of his original sin of speculation, his Left Hegelian pupils only provided an empty caricature

> which is satisfied with deriving some determination out of a product of the mind or even out of real situations and movements, changing that determination into a determination of thought, into a category, and declaring that category the *standpoint* of the product, the situation, or movement, in order then to look down on this determination with triumphant, precocious wisdom from the standpoint of abstraction.[387]

As opposed to this, Marx's task consisted in showing that his own critique, far from ineffectively condemning the present world order in terms of abstract categories or principles, only revealed the fact that the present world order was condemned in terms of immanent laws of history itself. To show this two things had to be done. On the one hand, the critique of political economy had to be embedded in a conception of history which demonstrated the end of civil society both in terms of the past and in terms of the very nature of historical development. Marx had to show that the *real movement of history*, as it was empirically given, was the "actuality" of all the abstract criticizing of the Left Hegelians—and the *Aufhebung* of their merely *philosophical* critique. On the other hand, it had to be shown that a purely philosophical critique— a critique which pretended to be presuppositionless, as it depended upon nothing except itself—could not possibly succeed. And how else could this be shown if not by suggesting that the philo-

---

[385] *MEW* XXIII, 27; tr. Aveling-Moore, I, 20.
[386] Cf. *MEGA* I, 3, 157; tr. Milligan, 151.
[387] *MEGA* I, 3, 371; tr. Dixon, 255.

sophical critique of the Left Hegelians was only an "ideology" reflecting the present world order?

In a word, what was required was the elaboration of a "materialistic conception of history," of a conception which explained both why a philosophical critique was ineffective and why the present world order was condemned to perish independently of what philosophers said—and a denunciation of the Left Hegelians as "ideologists." The fact that the "historical materialism" advanced in the *German Ideology* succeeded in handling both these problems, and in handling them in a very suggestive way, explains why communists today describe the *German Ideology* as a most important stage in the working out of the "philosophical foundations of the Communist Party."[388]

[388] Cf. the editors' remarks in MEGA I, 5, p. xvii, and *MEW* III, p. v ff.

25: HISTORICAL MATERIALISM

It has often been remarked that Marx's famous summary of his position in the foreword to *A Contribution to the Critique of Political Economy* far from succeeds in indicating the wealth and suppleness of ideas that make up his original "historical materialism." But it is seldom noticed that this summary, at least in one respect, is also very misleading. For it suggests that the "materialistic conception of history" is nothing else than a theoretical analysis issuing from purely theoretical research.

> I was led by my studies to the conclusion that legal relations as well as forms of state could neither be understood by themselves nor explained by the so-called general progress of the human mind, but that they are rooted in the material conditions of life which are summed up by Hegel ... under the name 'civil society'; and that the anatomy of civil society is to be sought in political economy.[389]

This statement certainly describes the conclusions which Marx had reached when in September, 1845, he began with Engels to write the *German Ideology*. But it completely conceals the fact that these conclusions were not the result of a detached and objective study of socioeconomic realities but rather were motivated by Marx's desire to defend against Stirner's philosophy of total disillusionment the revolutionary passion and idealism issuing from the dissolution of Hegel's philosophy of Absolute Knowledge. Considered from the point of view of its "subjective origins," Marx's "materialistic conception of history" is an attempt to show that the "putrescence of Absolute Spirit" need not go as far

---

[389] *MEW* XIII, 8; tr. Moscow, I, 362.

as Stirner believed; more precisely, that one could be a Hegelian of revolutionary inspiration without succumbing to intellectualist extravagances of people such as Bruno Bauer and exposing oneself to the threat from the "extreme Left" represented by Stirner.

It has often been remarked that the first part of the *German Ideology*, which carries the title "Feuerbach," never was completed and certainly does not contain any systematically developed criticism of Feuerbach. Actually, however, if one scrutinizes the original manuscript with all its deletions and variants,[390] one clearly gets the impression that in spite of its title this first part was not intended as a direct criticism of Feuerbach to begin with. For after briefly characterizing the "putrescence of Absolute Spirit," in a passage which abounds with corrections and deletions and eventually was deleted completely, Marx[391] writes that he intends to introduce his criticism of the individual representatives of Left Hegelianism with a few general remarks

> which will suffice to characterize the point of view of our criticism in so far as this is necessary for an appreciation of the subsequent detailed criticisms. We address (*stellen gegenüber*) these remarks to Feuerbach, for he is the only one who at least made progress and whose ideas one can take up in good faith.[392]

[390] As published in *MEGA* I, 5, 566 ff.

[391] Actually, the preserved manuscript is written by Engels, with numerous insertions by Marx's hand. We cannot discuss here the almost unsolvable problem whether in the *German Ideology* Marx's "materialistic conception of history" was significantly influenced by original ideas of Engels. For a brief, if somewhat inconclusive discussion, cf. Friedrich, 154 ff.

[392] *MEGA* I, 5, 567; *MEW* III, 18. See also the letter to Leske, in which Marx writes that he considers it important to premise to his positive analyses a criticism of German philosophy (originally, Marx added to 'criticism of German philosophy' the expression 'from Bauer,' then deleted 'Bauer' and wrote 'from Feuerbach to Stirner,' and then deleted everything except 'criticism of German philosophy'; cf. *MEW* XXVII, 448 ff.; for the deletion, *MEGA* I, 5, p. xvi). Thus the *German Ideology* would seem to be conceived by Marx as a *negative philosophical* discussion preparing a *positive economic* discussion; cf. *ibid.*: "Thus [a polemical negative treatment] is required in order to prepare the public for the point of view of my economics which is radically opposed to the hitherto existing German Science." On the other hand, however, in his letter to Annenkov, December 28, 1846, Marx refers to the

After this paragraph there immediately follows the first part, originally entitled "Ideology in general; in particular, German philosophy" and later renamed "Ideology in general, especially the German," which without further ado concentrates on Marx's *own* views and then, with occasional innuendos against Feuerbach, remains with them through the ninety-two sheets which comprise this first part of the manuscript. Instead of containing a direct criticism of Feuerbach later followed by an analogous criticism of Bruno Bauer, Stirner, and others, the first part of the *German Ideology* actually consists of a brief summary of Marx's objections to the Left Hegelians, already outlined in the preface, and an extremely elaborate exposition of the point of view from which this criticism (as well as all criticisms later developed in the *German Ideology*) is advanced. The first part deals with Feuerbach only to the extent that Marx acknowledges that the author of the *Essence of Christianity* had come closest to the heart of the matter and therefore considers it opportune to develop his own views by contrast with those of Feuerbach.

This seemingly insignificant fact is decisive for a correct evaluation of the *German Ideology* and the origin of Marx's "materialistic conception of history" as a whole. For it suggests that the usual interpretation according to which the *German Ideology* is nothing but a second attack against the Left Hegelian movement (an enlarged version of the *Holy Family* as it were) is mistaken. Apart from anything else, this interpretation does not succeed in explaining why the *German Ideology* was written; if Marx and Engels believed Left Hegelianism to be nonsense, as they tried to show in the *Holy Family*, it is incomprehensible why they should have written another manuscript on the same question. Mehring's obvious embarrassment as to how to explain this fact[393] is quite significant here.

Actually the *German Ideology* is no genuine attack at all. Rather it is a defense. Due to the extremely esoteric character of the whole discussion, there was of course no need to show the public

German Ideology as "my book on political economy"; cf. *MEW* XXVII, 462; tr. Moscow, II, 452.
[393] Cf. Mehring, 110 ff.

at large that the Left Hegelians were wrong. But to Marx it seems
to have appeared necessary to defend the Left Hegelian revolutionary spirit against the radical trivialization which it had encountered
through Stirner's book. Even if he would not convince any one
else, Marx *had* to convince *himself* that Stirner was wrong. For
if Stirner was right, the whole development of Hegelianism since
Hegel's death was a complete farce—and the revolutionary drive
around which Marx's thought had centered since the very beginning
of his career could not possibly be upheld. Yet to show that Stirner
really was wrong, Marx had to dissociate himself from Feuerbach
and once more denounce Bruno Bauer; for Marx was quick in
realizing that Stirner quite obviously was right as far as all Left
Hegelians besides himself were concerned. In fact, if Marx did
not succeed in reformulating his own position, he was lost, too.
For Stirner's book had advanced a radical criticism of any revolutionary mentality which relied upon "moral postulates," an
ought, or ideals.

Let us try to be somewhat more specific. We may begin by
briefly summarizing Marx's views on Feuerbach, Bauer, and Stirner
as advanced in the preface to the *German Ideology*. The Left
Hegelians, so Marx argues, reduce all evils to the simple fact that
people invent false conceptions and thus "limit (*beschränken*)"
and misguide themselves. Accordingly they believe that to save
the world amounts to liberating it from the "chimeras, ideas,
dogmas, and imaginary beings," under the yoke of which it is
pining away. Feuerbach, believing that all evil results from the
fact that man ascribes the perfections of his own species to a nonexistent Absolute, argues that such false imaginations should be
replaced by correct ideas about man's divine nature; Bauer, reducing all evil to a lack of a critical self-awareness, demands that
man take up a critical attitude toward his engrained dogmatic
presuppositions; and Stirner, believing the evil to consist in the
very existence of abstract ideas and ideals, argues that one ought
simply to forget everything that does not serve one's self-centered
individuality.[394]

[394] Cf. *MEW* III, 13; tr. Pascal, 1.

This summary of the Left Hegelian position, together with the line of criticism which it entails, is remarkable on two accounts. First, it leads to a criticism only if one assumes that there really *is* something to be fought against and that it is meaningful to advocate a redemption from existing reality. Marx certainly is correct when he claims that the Left Hegelian conception amounts to a demand "to interpret reality in another way" and that this in turn amounts to asking for a recognition of existing reality by means of another interpretation.[395] As reality cannot be transformed by changing one's ideas about it, a salvation in terms of a change of ideas alone must end in an accommodation to existing reality.

But this obviously is an *objection* only if one assumes that reality should *not* be recognized. In other words, Marx shares in the one fundamental assumption common to all Left Hegelians, namely, that existing reality is evil and therefore, to use Marx's own expression, must *zusammenbrechen*, "collapse." Of course, as Marx will explain in detail, his own views on the nature of the evil in question, and therefore also his views concerning the adequate remedy, significantly differ from those of all other Left Hegelians. But this in no way changes the fact that Marx shares in the basic Left Hegelian conviction that man must be liberated and saved— a conviction, it may be added, which in its present form results solely from the "putrescence of Absolute Spirit," from the dissolution of Hegelian ideas which has been discussed throughout the last two hundred pages.

Yet precisely this basic conviction had been challenged by Stirner's radicalism. Even though he proceeded from the same assumption as all other Left Hegelians and argued along the same lines as they, Stirner had come to the conclusion that the Left Hegelian revolutionary idealism and the whole revolt against existing reality were bogus. As he put it in his book,

> Man, you are not quite right in your head; you have a screw loose! You imagine great things and picture for yourself a whole world of gods who exist for you—a spiritual empire to which you are summoned, an ideal which beckons to you. You

---

[395] *Ibid.* 20; tr. Pascal, 6.

> have a fixed idea! Do not believe that I joke or use only symbols
> when I declare that all people pursuing higher aims ... are
> veritable fools, fools in a lunatic asylum.[396]

Marx had to show that it was neither necessary nor possible
to dismiss the revolution against reality as nonsense; he had to
show that there existed ideals which man simply *could not* give
up. This leads us to a second point which is even more remarkable
than the fact that Marx, far from attacking Left Hegelianism as a
whole, actually defends the basic Left Hegelian insight against
what he considers a hopelessly wrong treatment. It is the fact
that Marx throws Stirner into the same pot as all other Left Hegelians. To some extent this treatment of Stirner is of course justifiable.
Stirner cannot be understood except in connection with the "putrescence of Absolute Spirit." But the same quite obviously applies
to Marx. By throwing Stirner into a heap with Feuerbach and
Bauer, Marx misleads the reader into believing that he himself
stands on the one side of the fence, while all other Left Hegelians
stand on the other side. This might be correct if one considers
Marx *after* he had found a way of defending himself against Stirner's
challenge. But it certainly is not correct if one considers him at
the moment at which he still had to decide how to tackle Stirner's
ridicule of ideals. For at this moment Marx clearly was an ally
of Bauer and all the more of Feuerbach: he felt that he had to
defend the Left Hegelian "ideal-ism" against Stirner's cynical
egoism. Indeed, while his objection to Bauer, and in a sense to
Feuerbach as well, only amounted to saying that their haughty
intellectualism prevented them from realizing the ideal which he,
Marx, shared with them, against Stirner he had to defend the
far more basic claim that it was at all meaningful to seek a realization of such an ideal rather than simply letting go all ideals and
the whole conception of a salvation of man.

It is worth noticing that when he begins to explain "the point
of view of our criticism," that is, his own position, Marx puts
greatest emphasis upon the fact that his own presuppositions
"are not arbitrary ones, not dogmas, but real presuppositions

---

[396] Stirner, 57.

from which abstraction can only be made in the imagination."[397]
Marx's line of defense consists in arguing that he really is not
pursuing an ideal after all; that which Bauer and Feuerbach
describe, and Stirner denounces, as ideals, Marx describes as
empirical facts which it is beyond man's power to disregard.

Marx reverts to this subject several times in the *German Ideology*.
Stirner had argued that his own position was presuppositionless,
since "I presuppose only myself—and since it is me who presupposes
myself, I have no presuppositions."[398] Marx tries to make fun
of this passage, it is true, and argues that Stirner's analyses of
a *voraussetzungslose Selbstsetzung* are copied from Hegel's discussion
of the category of Essence in the *Logic*. But the point made by
Stirner obviously bothers him. He takes some pain to show that
Stirner himself has ideals, be it only by proclaiming that one ought
to become something which one still is not, namely, an egoist.[399]
Marx argues at some length that even if Stirner really could free
himself from all "dogmatic presuppositions," he could not possibly
get rid of the "real presuppositions." For these "real presuppositions" determine Stirner's "dogmatic presuppositions," at least as
long

> as he [Stirner] has not succeeded in obtaining different real
> presuppositions... or rather as long as he does not materialistical-
> ly recognize the real presuppositions as presuppositions of his
> thinking—whereby the dogmatical presuppositions simply cease
> to exist.[400]

Similarly Marx tries to argue that Stirner's attack against
ideals takes the latter more seriously than they deserve. Thus
he accuses Stirner of believing that the "measure of freedom which
people win for themselves is determined by the corresponding
conception of the ideal of man" and opposes to this conception
his own view according to which people always liberated themselves only to the extent "to which the existing forces of produc-

---

[397] *MEW* III, 20; tr. Pascal, 6.
[398] Cf. Stirner's anonymously published article, "Recensenten Stirners," in
Wigands Vierteljahrsschrift 3 (1845) 183. Cf. *MEW* III, 248 ff.
[399] Cf. *MEW* III, 250.
[400] *Ibid.* 419.

tion prescribed and permitted it."[401] When Stirner denounces ideals
as a form of "enjoying oneself (*Selbstgenuss*)," Marx counters
that all tasks and ideals are in fact "conceptions of the revolutionary tasks which are ... materially prescribed," "the conscious
expression of the necessity to defend ... the position in which
individuals, classes, and nations are found in each and every
moment,"[402] and so on. At first sight, it is true, this materialistic
reduction of ideals to historical necessities very closely resembles
an abandoning of ideals. But one only has to remember in which
direction, according to Marx, the laws imposed by "material
necessities" lead the development of history, and one immediately
realizes that, far from giving up his revolutionary ideals, Marx
believes he has succeeded in preserving them by *incorporating
them into actual history.*

For this is what his defense against Stirner and therefore also
the essence of Marx's "materialistic conception of history" amounts
to: the ideals pursued by the Left Hegelians are declared to be
the immanent $\tau\acute{\epsilon}\lambda o\varsigma$ of history itself so that the Left Hegelian
revolutionary drive becomes an immanent law of objective his-
torical reality. The *ought* really is an *is*, a potentiality of history
which reaches its maturity quite independently of whether people
have ideals or do not have them. More precisely, history's *is*
appears as an *ought* only because it still is only a potentiality,
that is, because man still did not succeed in getting control of the
real conditions of his life. "The all-round actualization of the
individual will cease to be imagined as an ideal ... only when the
moving force of the world (*der Weltanstoss*) which solicits the
individual's capacity for real development will have come under
the individual's control—as the communists desire it."[403]

We must refrain from discussing further the various details
of the "materialistic conception of history" developed in the *German Ideology*. On the one hand, they are too well known to require an elaborate treatment; on the other hand, a critical discus-

---

[401] *Ibid.* 417.
[402] *Ibid.* 405.
[403] *Ibid.* 273.

sion would require far more space than we have at our disposal
and therefore must be postponed to another volume. However,
I should like to add a few remarks about where all this leaves us as
far as Marx's notion of "practice" is concerned—a topic which in
turn requires that first a few words be said on the "Theses on
Feuerbach," which generally are recognized to be the text in
which Marx speaks about "practice" more explicitly than anywhere else in his writings.

The first point which I should like to make here is that the importance of these "Theses" seems to be vastly overrated today.
It certainly is a questionable way of proceeding when Sidney
Hook, for example, minimizes the importance of the *Philosophic
and Economic Manuscripts* on the grounds that to take seriously an
early writing which Marx himself never published would "violate
accepted and tested canons of historical scholarship,"[404] and then
devotes no less than thirty pages to the "Theses on Feuerbach."
After all, the *Manuscripts* comprise more than one hundred seventy
pages of the *Historisch-kritische Gesamtausgabe*, while the "Theses"
consist of only a few sentences; the *Manuscripts* are drafts for a
book which Marx intended to publish and for which he had signed
a contract with a publisher, while the "Theses" are brief notes
for analyses never written; in fact, the same notebook which
contains the "Theses" also contains two other notes which are
not uninteresting but at which most people do not even care to
glance. And the suggestion that the *Manuscripts* represent Marx's
early and immature thought is wholly a matter of interpretation,
not a statement made on the ground of "accepted and tested
canons of historical scholarship," especially if one considers that the
"Theses on Feuerbach" were probably written only a few months
after the *Manuscripts*, that is, within a period so brief as to make
appear highly implausible the claim that while the latter writing
is immature, the "Theses" are expressive of Marx's mature thought.
In this respect the recent study by Nathan Rotenstreich, who carefully takes account of the *Manuscripts* even while analyzing the
"Theses," certainly does more justice to Marx than Hook's attempt

---

[404] Hook, 4.

to identify the Father of Communism as a precursor of Dewey and thus indirectly of himself. Yet even with respect to Rotenstreich's study one wonders why the "basic problems of Marx's philosophy" should be sought in a few remarks which have become famous only because Engels published them at a time when merely a few could still remember the feverish discussions of the 1840's and no one, including Engels himself, had a clear idea about Marx's early philosophical thought.

Another and somewhat more complex issue is the difficult question as to when *exactly* Marx wrote the "Theses." They are found on pages 51 and 55 of a notebook consisting of exactly one hundred pages which Marx used between 1844 and about the middle of 1847. However, as this notebook originally consisted of loose sheets which were fastened together only later, its pagination is unfortunately not indicative of the date of composition of the notes it contains. For example, on the second page one finds a draft for the conclusion of the first paragraph of the second chapter of *The Misery of Philosophy*, a note which cannot have been written before the spring of 1847, several months after the *German Ideology* had been completed[405]; and no one has ever suggested that the "Theses" were written after the *German Ideology*.

The real question, however, is whether they were written significantly earlier than the major (especially the first) parts of the *German Ideology* or simultaneously with them. When Engels first published the "Theses" in 1888, he suggested that they were notes for a never-written final section of the first part of the *German Ideology*—which, on the one hand, seems to be the main reason why today everybody believes that this first part originally was intended as a direct criticism of Feuerbach comparable to the criticism of Bauer and Stirner and, on the other hand, seems to be about the only reason why V. Adoratskij,[406] when he republished

---

[405] Cf. *MEGA* I, 5, 547 ff., 6, 621 ff., and D. Rjazanov's description of the manuscript in *Marx-Engels-Archiv*, Vol. I (Frankfurt, n.d. [1927]) 222.

[406] Actually, already Rjazanov; see fn. 405. The reasoning would seem to resemble the following. After having established friendship with Marx in the fall of 1844, Engels returned to England; in April, 1845, he joined Marx in

the "Theses" in 1932, suggested March, 1845, as the most likely date of composition. If Adoratskij is right (and there are no convincing reasons why he should be wrong, even though his suggestion seems to be little more than an educated guess), the "Theses" would have been written about five months before Marx and Engels began to write the *German Ideology*; for about the latter work we know with some certainty that it was not begun until after the two friends returned from their trip to England, that is, after the end of August, 1845.

The reason why this question is of some importance is that there is a rather striking difference between the basic insights alluded to in the "Theses on Feuerbach" and the "materialistic conception of history" advanced in the *German Ideology*. The two texts do not contradict each other, but they seem to be animated by quite a different spirit: at first sight at least the "Theses" are much more activistic than anything suggested in the *German Ideology*. If this first impression is deceptive, then the "Theses" certainly would have to be interpreted differently from what offhand they seem to suggest and how usually they are interpreted.

In a sense, however, this contrast between the activistic spirit of the "Theses" and the more theoretical attitude represented by the *German Ideology* is a contrast (and conflict) found in the *German Ideology* itself as well. In order to explain this let us briefly consider the famous eleventh and last of the "Theses on Feuerbach": "The philosophers have only *interpreted* the world differently; the point

Brussels. Concerning his arrival in Brussels, Engels wrote in 1885 that when he met Marx, the latter already had "worked out the materialistic conception of history in its essential traits," cf. "Zur Geschichte des Bundes der Kommunisten," *MEW* XXI, 212; tr. Moscow, II, 344. The *German Ideology* was begun only five months later; and as Engels, when he published the "Theses" in 1888, introduced them as a "first document in which is deposited the brilliant germ of the new world outlook" (*ibid.* 264; tr. Moscow, II, 359), it would seem natural to suggest that the "essential traits" of the "materialistic conception of history" which Engels learned from Marx early in 1845, were precisely the "Theses on Feuerbach." Of course, this reasoning is somewhat shaky. Engels never suggested that he *saw* the "Theses" in 1845; in fact, when he writes that he found the "Theses" in an "old notebook" (*ibid.*), he possibly means only that at that time (in 1888) he saw them for the first time.

is to change it." As it stands (and one cannot well consider it
otherwise than as it stands, since it is a single sentence not inserted by Marx into any context), this thesis sounds as if Marx
wanted to invite man to revolutionary actions. Until now, so
this thesis seems to say, philosophers have only changed their
mind about a world which remained totally unaffected by such
ideas; what matters is to cease to change one's mind about the
world and instead to change the world itself.

This leads of course immediately to the Stirnerian question,
"But why ought we change the world?" As we have seen, Marx
could not reply to this question by reminding Stirner of obvious
ideals. For Stirner precisely had shown that all nonegoistic ideals
are far from obvious and that people who pursue them are "fools
in a lunatic asylum." In fact Marx himself explicitly spells out
that he does not pursue any ideals. In the manuscript of the
first part of the *German Ideology*, the final copy of which was written
by Engels, Marx inserted by his own hand the following passage:

> Communism is for us not a *state* (*Zustand*) which ought to
> be established, an *ideal* to which reality will have to adjust
> itself. We call communism the *real* movement which abolishes
> the present state [originally, as one can see from the deletions,
> Marx intended to write: "which is the practical *Aufhebung*
> of the present state"]. The conditions of this movement result
> from the presuppositions now in existence.[407]

But this means that Marx is not advancing an invitation to
action at all, contrary to what the eleventh "thesis" seems to
suggest. Rather he states as a *fact* that people *do* change the
world in a definite way and thus push history in a definite direction.
Instead of *urging* people to act he predicts that they *will* act. But
what does then the eleventh of the "Theses on Feuerbach" mean?
As it seems impossible to construe it in such a way as to make it
say that ideals are irrelevant, the only plausible answer would
seem to consist in saying that it means just what it says, namely,
something incompatible with Marx's dismissal of ideals, and that
it therefore reveals a basic ambiguity in Marx's thought.

---

[407] *MEW* III, 35; tr. Pascal, 26. For the fact that this passage is a later in-
sertion by Marx's own hand see *MEGA* I, 5, 572, sub 25, line 5.

To be more precise, this thesis reveals the fact already mentioned, namely, that almost against his will Marx has been pushed into this dismissal of ideals by Stirner. By his very nature and certainly by his Left Hegelian tradition Marx is an idealist and a fighter against the existing order; but Stirner spoiled the game for him by showing that such an idealism contradicts the intrinsic logic of the profanization of Absolute Knowledge and therefore cannot be justified. The much discussed ambiguity which obtains between Marx the determinist, who later speaks of laws and tendencies which work "with iron necessity towards inevitable results"[408] and even condones an interpretation according to which he would have considered social developments as a "process of natural history,"[409] and Marx the voluntarist, who his whole life incited the proletariat to rebellion and occasionally even organized secret associations supposed to carry out revolutions, is the outcome of this very problem. For it would be much too easy to claim that in March, 1845, Marx still wanted to change the world, while several months later he already believed that the world would change by itself. As we have seen, Marx *always* had the tendency to translate the Left Hegelians' revolutionary mentality into objective laws; already in his dissertation he had spoken of a "psychological law" in terms of which spirit in certain situations becomes an "energy." On the other hand, the activistic spirit certainly is not completely absent from the *German Ideology*. For Marx argues there against the Left Hegelians as follows:

> Since according to their fantasy the relationships of men, all their goings on, their chains, and their limitations are products of their consciousness, the Young Hegelians logically put to men the moral postulate of exchanging their present consciousness for human, critical, or egoistic consciousness and thus of removing limitations. This demand to change consciousness amounts to a demand to interpret the existing order (*das Bestehende*) in another way, that is, to recognize it by means of another interpretation. The Young Hegelian ideologists ... are the staunchest conservatives.[410]

[408] *MEW* XXIII, 12; tr. Aveling-Moore, I, 8 ff.
[409] *Ibid.* 26; tr. Aveling-Moore, I, 18.
[410] *MEW* III, 20; tr. Pascal, 6.

Since we have seen that Marx no longer asks us to pursue ideals but rather predicts their more or less automatic actualization, this certainly is a very curious criticism. For Marx's objection amounts to saying that the Left Hegelians are willing to change only their ideas about the world, not the world itself. But as we just saw, Marx himself does not want to change the world either; he believes to have discovered that it *does* change. Thus it is somewhat difficult to see why from his point of view the Left Hegelians should be called "conservatives" rather than simply fanciful dreamers, for example. As he is not inviting to action but rather speaking about its necessary development, Marx intends to change reality even less than the Left Hegelians, who at least wanted to change it by developing their ideas; moreover Marx's "materialistic conception of history" is in a sense nothing but a change of consciousness, namely, a new theory of reality and thus a new "recognition of the existing order by means of another interpretation." The only real difference between Marx and the other Left Hegelians consists in that the latter pretended to save the world by changing their ideas, while Marx has reached an idea no longer to be changed, which amounts to saying that the world *saves itself independently of* philosophical speculations.

I may do well to add that the point under discussion has to my mind nothing to do with the question as to whether according to Marx man is free or not, that is, whether Marx is a determinist with respect to human freedom. To be more precise, Marx's translation of "moral postulates" into "historical laws," of the *ought* into an *is*, might quite well be compatible with the claim that individuals have free will and thus are responsible for their actions. As long as it is not linked with a materialistic theory of being, as it is the case in Engels' *Anti-Dühring* and *Dialectics of Nature*, Marx's "materialistic conception of history" simply amounts to saying that human freedom is not unlimited—an obvious truth which no one ever denied. That philosophical conceptions and legal patterns are determined by socio-economic conditions, or that the ideals which people pursue are "materially prescribed," by itself only amounts to saying that the sphere of truly free human acts is somewhat more limited than people usually believe. It does *not* amount to saying that there exists no free will. As contemporary Marxist-Leninists rightly point out,[411] a historical necessity (and be it ever so "iron") might very well be "statistical" in nature, that is, apply and therefore also be verifiable only with respect to relatively long periods of time and a relatively great number of individuals—and thus be perfectly compatible with what ordinarily is called "free will."

This is all the more so as Marx's "materialistic conception of history," even though it is not an appeal to realize certain ideals and therefore is not a summon to practice, contains an elaborate theory *about* human practice and its relevance to historical development. One must indeed be careful to distinguish these two points. On the one hand, Marx counters Stirner's challenge by declaring that the Left Hegelian ideals and their revolutionary drive are but an alienated expression of a dynamics *immanent to real history* itself. On the other hand, however, he does *not* describe this dynamics of history in such a way as to make of history an organism which develops *independently of what people do*. Rather he argues that because of their "physical organization ... and their consequent relation to the rest of nature,"[412] human individuals act in a definite way and thus set history going in a certain direction. To put it in other terms, even though history does not depend upon man's conscious intentions, it depends, and thoroughly so, upon what humans do. The question as to whether people acting in this way deserve to be called "free" in the sense of having a "free will" obviously does not interest Marx; what interests him is the (alleged) fact that their actions as well as the rationality inherent to these actions are not dependent upon the ideas and ideals which people make up for themselves.

Marx's "historical materialism" often has been described as an "economic determinism," that is, a conception according to which economic patterns and laws thoroughly determine man's historical existence. This interpretation is not wrong, it is true, but it is misleading since it refers only to one part of Marx's conception.

---

[411] E.g., *Filosofskaja Enciklopedija* (Moscow, 1960 ff.), the article "Determinism," I, 466 b.

[412] *MEW* III, 21; tr. Pascal, 7.

It undoubtedly is correct to say that political formations, legal relationships, human theories about them, and all "ideologies" in general are, according to Marx, determined by and thus have to be explained in terms of "material conditions of life," that is, technological achievements and the consequent economic relationships. But the technological achievements and economic relationships, in turn, are brought about by man himself. It may be true that man does not bring them about purposefully; even though his practice may be purposeful, it usually is not his conscious purpose to bring about definite economic relationships. But, on the other hand, these relationships clearly do not resemble "laws of nature," entirely independent of whether people exist and what they do. This is what Marx seems to have in mind in the third of the "Theses on Feuerbach":

> The materialistic teaching concerning the changing of circumstances and education forgets that the circumstances are[413] changed by men and that the educator himself must be educated. This teaching therefore is bound to split society into two parts, one of which is above [taking seriously] society.[414]
> The coinciding of the changing of circumstances and human activity, or self-changing, can only be expressed and rationally understood as *revolutionary practice*.[415]

Again, we must ask the reader not to take too seriously the normative connotation which at least the first paragraph of this "Thesis" seems to convey. Marx is not asking that the circumstances *be* changed or the educator himself be educated, nor, at least so it seems, is he bothered by the incompatibility of over-

---

[413] ... *dass die Umstände von den Menschen verändert und der Erzieher selbst erzogen werden muss.* After 'verändert' there obviously is a word missing; as the 'muss' at the end of the sentence is singular, it cannot also refer to the plural in 'Umstände.' We do not know whether Marx would have inserted 'werden' or 'müssen,' that is, whether he meant to say that the circumstances *are* changed by men or *ought* to be changed by men.

[414] What Marx seems to mean by this odd sentence (supposing that one really has to read 'ihr' as referring to 'Gesellschaft,' not 'ihn' which then would refer to 'Teil'), is this: the materialists who consider men determined by circumstances have to consider their own ideas (and thus themselves who oppose the given order) outside society, outside the historical determinants.

[415] *MEW* III, 5 ff.

simplified theories of "a causal dependence of mind upon matter" with a "programme of reform or revolution."[416] Rather his point seems to be that materialists such as the philosophers of the French Enlightenment, who considered man a creature of circumstances and education, miss a crucial point by overlooking the fact that circumstances and education are not natural entities like climate or food but for the most part are created by man himself. As Marx puts it in the *German Ideology*, "circumstances make men as much as men make circumstances."[417] And this is the case, not in the sense that although man is determined by circumstances, he also can change them at will (which clearly would be contradictory), but rather in the sense that the circumstances which determine man today were created by other men yesterday, just as the man of today inevitably creates new circumstances of tomorrow.

> History is nothing but the succession of the separate generations, each of which exploits the materials, deposits (*Kapitalien*), the productive forces handed down to it by all preceding ones, and thus, on the one hand, continues the traditional activity in completely changed circumstances and, on the other hand, modifies the old circumstances with a completely changed activity.[418]

All the seemingly definite sociopolitical relationships, even the economic relationships which underlie them, are a result of human practice. In this vein Marx later will write against Proudhon that economists only explain how within given relationships production is carried out but they do not try to understand how these relationships themselves were produced, "that is, the historical movement which has created them,"[419] the history of human *praxis* which brought them about. Thus all revolutionary-minded economists and philosophers consider their own programs as something outside history and society; as they cannot very well explain their revolutionary ideas in terms of the circumstances which they fight against, they have to assume that, unlike all

[416] Hook, 286.
[417] *MEW* III, 38; tr. Pascal, 29.
[418] *Ibid*. 45; tr. Pascal, 38.
[419] *MEW* IV, 126.

other conceptions, their own ideas are independent of circumstances, education, and the like. Marx, on the contrary, can argue
that his ideals are as determined by the circumstances as these
circumstances determine the limited and unredeemed man of
today: as it is man himself who created the circumstances, the
latter are embodied *praxis*, and thus at one and the same time
the source of all evils and the preconditions of future salvation,
the inhumanity of the present and the embodied ideal of a more
human future.

It is in this perspective that the expression 'revolutionary
practice' must be understood. Marx is far from suggesting "that
human beings cannot change the world without changing themselves, and that actual social struggles ... are the best school for
acquiring an education in social realities"[420]; in any case he is
far from advancing the imperatives which such an interpretation
suggests. His point simply is that human practice is revolutionary
by its very nature. It is what men do that is decisive in history,
not what they do by willfully engaging in social struggles aimed
at destroying the existing order, but rather what they constantly
and inevitably do as determined by what past generations have
done. In other words, the fact that men are dependent upon their
circumstances and nevertheless constantly succeed in overthrowing
them can only mean that human practice by its very nature leads
to and results in an overthrow of existing circumstances and the
creation of new and less "limited" ones. This is why in the *German
Ideology* Marx without further ado identifies "material practice"
and "revolution"[421]; far from arguing that man *should* rise and
overthrow existing conditions, he argues that "material practice"
necessarily *does* overthrow them.

Of course one will immediately have to add that when he speaks
in this way of a "material practice," Marx has more in mind than
only labor or even production in the wide sense of the term. As

[420] Hook, 289.
[421] Cf. *MEW* III, 38; tr. Pascal, 28 ff., where there is a clear parallel between
"explaining practice from the idea" and "criticism as the moving force of
history," on the one hand, and "explaining the formation of ideas from material
practice" and "revolution as the moving force of history," on the other hand.

far as it seems evident, there is nowhere in his writings anything resembling a definition of '*Praxis*'; in fact, considering how central this notion is to his thought, one time and again is astonished to see how relatively seldom Marx uses it. But it is not too difficult to gather from the *German Ideology* what Marx means by '*Praxis.*' It might be described as a relatively homogeneous human activity which can take on many different forms; it may range from bodily labor of the most humble sort to political revolutions; and it may be anything in between as long as it results in a transformation of mind-independent realities which entails a humanization of man.

Here emerges an important ambiguity, however. Marx often uses the expression '*Praxis*' simply in the sense of 'what man does' as opposed to 'what man thinks,' and in this connection he even does not shrink from making quite derogatory remarks about *certain kinds* of practice. Thus, for example, he speaks of possible contradictions between the consciousness of one nation and the practice of another[422]; about Christian moral commands he says that they remain without result "in practice"[423]; he mentions the "French practice" according to which the wife is considered the private property of the husband[424]; he speaks of the "*Praxis* of the bourgeois" who accepts as payment everything as long as it can be made into money[425]; decries the "petty, shopkeeperlike, and mechanical *praxis*" of the German bourgeoisie[426] and complains that Feuerbach knows only the "dirty-Jewish form of appearance" of practice and does not apprehend the significance of the "revolutionary, practical-critical activity."[427]

There is of course nothing to object against Marx's using the expression '*Praxis*' both in a technical and in a vernacular sense, nor is the fact necessarily problematical that he distinguishes between a revolutionary *praxis* and a petty, or vulgar, practice.

[422] *MEW* III, 32; tr. Pascal, 21.
[423] *Ibid.* 237.
[424] *Ibid.* 322.
[425] *Ibid.* 381.
[426] *Ibid.* 458.
[427] *Ibid.* 5.

As we already said, only those activities which contribute to the humanization of man are *Praxis* in the strong sense of the term. But how is one supposed to decide which practice is "revolutionary" and which is not "revolutionary"? One may object that this is a badly put question, since it is irrelevant to practical purposes; as Marx once says it, to believe that the changing of circumstances depends upon people's good will is nothing but an "old illusion."[428] Still, even if it were true that if one is "materialistic" enough, one never may find oneself in the embarrassing situation of having to decide about an *intended* practice whether it is "revolutionary" or not (simply because if it really is "revolutionary," it eventually will occur, with or without us), this notion is too central to Marx's thought simply to leave it at that. Marx himself would of course object, even if we were to rephrase the question and ask, In terms of which *norms* is a practice "critical" and "revolutionary," that is, humanizing? For he believes to have demonstrated a *fact* as opposed to which all norms and ideals are insignificant, namely, "that the contemporary individuals *necessarily will* (*müssen*) abolish private property, since the productive forces have developed so far that under the rule of private property they have become a destructive force, and since the opposition of classes has been carried to ultimate extremes."[429] But may one not simply ask, then, what the expression 'revolutionary practice' means?

As far as I can see, Marx nowhere gives a clear answer to this question, either in his early or in his late writings. One might of course simply say that a practice is "revolutionary" if it brings closer the ultimate completion of humanity, communism. But this is a very unsatisfactory answer. For communism, according to Marx, is not an ideal, not even truly a task, but a predictable fact necessarily entailed by "existing circumstances" and ultimately, by the first premise of all human history, "the physical organization of individuals and their consequent relation to the rest of nature." Thus all activities which lead up to it are in a very fundamental sense predetermined and necessary. But who would dare to call necessary events "critical" and "revolutionary"?

[428] *Ibid*. 363.
[429] *Ibid*. 424.

Marx once says that by wanting to establish a correct consciousness about the existing fact that people do and always did
need each other, Feuerbach did go as far as a theoretician can
go without ceasing to be a theoretician and a philosopher.[430] Applying the dialectical structure of this phrase to Marx himself,
one might argue that by trying to incorporate ideals into actual
history, Marx has gone as far as someone trying to rationalize the
Left Hegelian revolutionary drive can go without giving up what
one might call the "basic Left Hegelian insight." Unfortunately,
however, and quite unlike Feuerbach or even Bauer with his
"critical critique," Marx has landed himself in a hopeless dilemma
which has haunted his more intelligent disciples until today.
This dilemma may be summed up as follows: if ideals play no
genuine role in history, it hardly is meaningful to speak of a *revolutionary* practice and, in fact, to be a revolutionary or even
"progressive" at all. Practice in this case is as little "revolutionary"
as biological evolution or the movement of stars. On the other
hand, if there really exists a truly "'revolutionary,' critical-
practical activity," as Marx suggests in the first of the "Theses
on Feuerbach," then not only must it be possible to be guided
by some ideals but moreover there must exist some norms, an
ought which transcends existing reality more radically than the
"consciousness of existing *Praxis*" to which Marx in the *German
Ideology* reduces all theoretical consciousness.[431] It may be added
that it would not help here to revert to what we said earlier about
the notion of alienation, namely, that when they use this notion,
Hegel and Marx imply that it is possible to measure man's present
existence by a potentiality revealed by this existence itself. For
alienation is something like a negated *ought* embodied in facts,
a kind of existence which reveals an ideal to be pursued and which,
precisely in the light of this ideal, appears as denying man his
ultimate completion. In 1844 the notion of an *Aufhebung* of alienation still was an "ideal" for Marx, in the sense of a possible fulfilment which not only de facto would but also *ought* to be achieved

[430] *Ibid.* 42; tr. Pascal, 33.
[431] *Ibid.* 31; tr. Pascal, 20.

and therefore ultimately could be predicted only with "psychological certainty." Yet by trying to show that this *ought* is not an empty one, a "fixed idea," as Stirner claimed, Marx eventually has reached the point at which the ought has becomes a sheer *is*. All revolutionary drive has been transformed into sheer facts, and therefore the history of practice was turned into a *necessity* which has swallowed up everything truly "revolutionary."

Of course in the *German Ideology* Marx still is inconsistent enough not to carry his ideas to their ultimate logical conclusions. Thus he writes that while Feuerbach knows only a theoretician's relationship to the world, for real man and his exponent, "the *practical* materialist, that is, communist, the point is to revolutionize the existing world, of practically attacking and changing given things."[432] This statement about what the real man, in particular the proletariat, *does*, is of course perfectly compatible with the "materialistic conception of history." But insofar as Marx expresses this idea as an imperative, a *request* to "attack" and to "change" the existing world, he clearly contradicts his own basic conception. Or perhaps it would be better to say, not that he contradicts himself, but rather that passages such as the one just quoted once more reveal the basic ambiguity of "historical materialism." If ideas formed in the human mind are "materially prescribed," nothing but the expression of objective necessities, then there is no need to urge people to be "practical," to act. On the other hand, if there really is a "point" in purposefully revolutionizing the existing world, if it matters whether people "practically attack and change given things"—that is, freely decide to do it rather than do it under the pressure of existing circumstances—then undoubtedly there must exist ideals which are more than only a reflection of circumstances themselves. To cooperate with what in the long run necessarily happens anyway is no meaningful imperative, except in the vague sense which became so prominent in the minds of later Marxists and communists, namely, that to ride with the relentless escalator of history is preferable to standing idly beside it and watching it pass.

[432] *Ibid.* 42; tr. Pascal, 33.

Considered from this point of view, Marx's criticism of Feuerbach, as developed both in the "Theses" and in a few passages in the first part of the *German Ideology*, is extremely misleading. For this criticism contains two quite different components, one of which is thoroughly in line with the "materialistic conception of history," while the other is a remnant, *never* completely abandoned, of Marx's earlier conception which is incompatible with the former. When in the first "Thesis" Marx accuses Feuerbach of being a contemplative materialist in the sense that he considers reality only insofar as it is an object of theoretical attitudes, not insofar as it is something done and made by man,[433] he simply develops his notion that the circumstances which determine man and in fact the whole environment in which man finds himself are the result of human action. As the parallel passage in the *German Ideology* indicates, Marx's point is, not that Feuerbach only contemplates while in fact he ought to act, but rather that Feuerbach overlooks that

> the sensuous world which surrounds him is, not a thing given immediately from all eternity, ever the same, but the product of industry and the state of society, and this in the sense that it is the result of the activity of a whole succession of generations, each standing on the shoulders of the preceding one, developing its industry and its intercourse, modifying its social organization according to the changed needs.[434]

In other words, Marx accuses the author of the *Essence of Christianity* of overlooking the fact that virtually everything which

---

[433] "The main shortcoming of all materialism up to now (including that of Feuerbach) is that the *object*, the reality, sensuousness, is conceived only in the form of the object or of the intuition (*Anschauung*); not however as *sensuous human activity*, *Praxis*; not subjectively. Hence the *active* side was developed abstractly in opposition to materialism by idealism, which obviously does not know the real sensuous activity as such. Feuerbach wants sensuous objects really distinct from the objects of thought; but he does not conceive of human activity itself as an activity *aimed at objects (gegenständliche Tätigkeit)*. Consequently, he considers in the *Essence of Christianity* only the theoretical attitude as the genuinely human one, while practice is conceived and determined only in its dirty-Jewish form of appearance. He therefore does not comprehend the significance of 'revolutionary,' practical-critical activity," *MEW* III, 5.

[434] *MEW* III, 43; tr. Pascal, 35.

man may *contemplate today* has been *generated by human activities
in the past.* Feuerbach certainly was right in emphasizing against
Hegel and the Hegelians that the really real is the empirical, the
immediate, the sensuously given. But contrary to Hegel, who
had grasped that everything except bare nature is a creation of
man, Feuerbach is so fascinated by the "natural" as opposed to
the "historical" that he forgets that even the objects of the simplest
sense certainty are given to human observation only through
"social development, industry, and commercial intercourse." The
cherry tree which Feuerbach always used as an instance of a really
real because palpable object exists in Europe only because a few
centuries ago it had been transplanted into our zone "and therefore
only *through* this action of a definite society in a definite age."
Indeed, this "unceasing sensuous labor and making (*Schaffen*)"
is so much the foundation of the objects of all sense certainty
that if it was interrupted only for a year, Feuerbach would hardly
recognize the things which today he contemplates and probably
would not even exist himself. It is of course true that underneath
all this man-made world there is a nature which is independent
of man, but as far as human contemplation is concerned, this
nature no longer exists anywhere, "except perhaps on a few Austral-
ian coral islands of recent origin." In short, Feuerbach's materialism
constantly overlooks history, the fact that the empirical foundations
from which derive all human ideas have been created by man himself. "As far as Feuerbach is a materialist, history does not exist for
him, and insofar as he considers history, he is not a materialist."[435]

So far everything which Marx says is certainly compatible with
the "materialistic conception of history." But Marx also says
(or at least implies) other things which are of a completely different
inspiration. Already his accusation that Feuerbach is only a
"contemplative materialist," a "theoretician," hardly is justified
from the over-all point of view of the *German Ideology.* After
all, Marx himself contemplates no less than Feuerbach; he has
developed a new interpretation of a contemplated world, but
certainly not replaced theory by practice. He has advanced a

---

[435] *Ibid.* 43 ff.; tr. Pascal 35 ff.

theory of reality as molded by human practice; but he contemplates this world just as much as Feuerbach contemplates his. Accordingly it hardly makes sense when in the *German Ideology* he accuses Feuerbach of having only a "conception" of the sensuous world which confines itself to contemplating the world,[436] as if Marx himself would have anything else! The only difference consists in that Marx contemplates a world which according to his conception owes its form to human practice, while Feuerbach contemplates a world from which he has dismissed as improper everything practical.[437]

There is of course a tenuous sense in which one may grant that the "materialistic conception of history" is genuinely "practical," not merely a theory *about* historical practice. For Marx's claim that all economic, social, legal, and political patterns are results and sediments of human practice permits him to describe man's *ultimate* completion, communism, as a situation where all circumstances will be "liquidated," that is, brought thoroughly under man's conscious control, and thus no longer will be "circumstances" properly speaking. Even though Marx's conception is as contemplative as that of Feuerbach, it predicts a social formation in which history will no longer be something which one merely *has to watch* (for presently one can "make" it only quite incidentally), but rather something which one performs with the same ease and self-aware spontaneity with which a great artist creates his masterpiece.

> Communism differs from all previous movements in that it overturns the basis of all previous relations of production and intercourse and for the first time consciously treats all natural (*naturwüchsige*) presuppositions as creatures of previous men, strips them of their natural character, and subjugates them under the power of united individuals.... in communist society where nobody has one exclusive sphere of activity but each

---

[436] *Ibid.* 42; tr. Pascal, 34.

[437] Marx's remark that Feuerbach reduces *Praxis* to its "dirty-Jewish form of appearance" probably alludes to the passage in the *Essence of Christianity* in which Feuerbach argues that the commandments of the Jewish God extend to vulgar external activities, such as keeping oneself clean; cf. Feuerbach VI, 39.

can become accomplished in any branch he wishes, society makes it possible for me to do one thing today and another tomorrow, to hunt in the morning, fish in the afternoon, rear cattle in the evening, criticize after dinner, just as I have a mind, without ever becoming hunter, fisherman, shepherd, or critic.[438]

But this society cannot artificially be brought about. Even the communist revolution depends, not upon "social institutions of inventive social talents," but solely upon the productive forces and their development.[439] Of course the proletariat eventually will knock down capitalist society with all its institutions. But it cannot possibly do so before its time has come, and even then it will do so mainly, not because someone incited it to rebellion, but rather because it is driven by a "conscious awareness of a necessity." "If the material elements of a total revolution ... are not given, it is absolutely irrelevant to the practical development whether the *idea* of this revolution has been expressed a hundred times already—as the history of communism proves."[440]

This volume might well conclude with a warning. To describe, as it has been, Marx's "historical materialism" as the result of an attempt to preserve the Left Hegelian heritage in spite of Stirner's challenge does not by itself amount to denouncing as ideology whatever Marx has to say about history and human practice. By this it is not meant to say that Marx's conception is true, whatever 'true' may mean in philosophical discourse. Yet it has to be emphasized that, contrary to what Marx himself believed and what contemporary Marxists maintain, the *subjective genesis* of an idea does not by itself throw light upon its truth value. As Aristotle says, even the conclusions of syllogisms with false premises quite accidentally may be correct. It is left to the reader, and hopefully to a few critical reflections in another volume, to decide to what extent Marx's ideas give one an insight into the infinite complexity and wealth of reality—quite independently of the obvious fact that the *genesis* of these ideas makes them appear in a somewhat dubious light.

[438] *MEW* III, 70 and 33; tr. Pascal, 70 and 22.
[439] Cf. *ibid*. 364. The phrase "social institutions, etc." is from Stirner, 422.
[440] *Ibid*. 38 ff.; tr. Pascal 29 ff.

BIBLIOGRAPHY AND
FOOTNOTE GUIDE

1. Since in the *first* part of this volume most of the works referred
    to in the footnotes are mentioned only a few times, in many
    cases only once, it seemed unnecessary to use abbreviations
    (except for Greek and Latin sources, which are abbreviated in
    the usual way). The only exceptions may be the abbreviations
    PL for *Patrologia Latina*, ed. Migne (Paris, 1857 ff.) and *PG*
    for *Patrologia Graeca*, ed. Migne (Paris, 1844 ff.). If not otherwise
    indicated, the references throughout are to the Greek or Latin
    original; whenever appropriate, the particular edition was cited
    (e.g., Aristotle, Fragment 16 Walzer; Euripides, Fragment 910
    Nauck; etc.).
2. In the *second* and *third* parts of this volume, on the contrary,
    the same sources had to be quoted repeatedly. Thus, the references
    were reduced to the author's last name, volume if applicable,
    part or section if applicable, and page. The full reference may
    be found in *Section A* of this bibliography. If several different
    works, or editions of the works, by the same author were used, the
    author's last name is followed by a number (e.g., Hegel$_1$, Hegel$_2$,
    etc.), as it is in the bibliography.
3. If it is at all possible, the sources are cited in the original language.
    In the case of Hegel and Marx, however, it seemed opportune
    to refer to existing translations. Whenever a reference to Hegel's
    and Marx's writings is followed by the abbreviation "tr.", and
    in turn by a name (e.g., tr. Milligan), it applies to *Section B*
    of this bibliography, where such translations are listed by the
    translator's name. This made it possible to refer in the footnotes
    only to the volume and page of the German edition; by looking
    up the translation, the reader will have no difficulty in discovering
    which of Hegel's or Marx's works is involved.
4. The only abbreviations in the strict sense of the term are those
    referring to the two standard editions of Marx's writings:

MEGA[1] for Karl Marx-Friedrich Engels, *Historisch-kritische Gesamtausgabe*, ed. D. Rjazanov and (from volume 3) V. Adoratskij
(Frankfurt, 1927 ff.).

---

[1] Followed by part, volume, section if applicable, page.

MEW[2] for Karl Marx-Friedrich Engels, *Werke* (Berlin: Dietz Verlag, 1961 ff.). In most instances I have translated the texts myself so that the reference to a translation usually indicates only the *corresponding passage* in the translation.

A

Arendt, H. *The Human Condition.* Anchor Paperback, 1958.

Arvon, H. *Aux sources de l'existentialisme: Max Stirner.* Paris, 1954.

Axelos, K. *Marx, penseur de la technique.* Paris, 1961.

Baader, Franz von. *Sämtliche Werke*; ed. F. Hoffmann. Leipzig, 1854.

Balthasar, H. U. v. *Prometheus. Studien zur Geschichte des deutschen Idealismus.* Heidelberg, 1947.

Barth, K. *Die protestantische Theologie im 19. Jahrhundert.* 2nd ed. Zürich, 1952.

Bauer, Bruno$_1$. *Die evangelische Landeskirche Preussens und die Wissenschaft.* Leipzig, 1840.

Bauer, Bruno$_2$. *Kritik der evangelischen Geschichte der Synoptiker.* Vol. I. Leipzig, 1841.

Bauer, Bruno$_3$. *Die Judenfrage.* Braunschweig, 1843.

Beyer, W. R.$_1$. *Hegel-Bilder, Kritik der Hegeldeutungen.* Berlin (East), 1964.

Beyer, W. R.$_2$. "Der Begriff der Praxis bei Hegel." *Deutsche Zeitschrift für Philosophie* (1958) 749-779.

Bell, D. "The Rediscovery of Alienation." *The Journal of Philosophy* 56 (1959) 933-952.

Benz, E.$_1$. *Swedenborg in Deutschland.* Frankfurt, 1947.

Benz, E.$_2$. "Die Mystik in der Philosophie des deutschen Idealismus." *Euphorion* 46 (1952) 280-300.

Benz, E.$_3$. "Johann Albrecht Bengel und die Philosophie des deutschen Idealismus." *Deutsche Vierteljahrsschrift für Literaturwissenschaft und Geistesgeschichte* 27 (1953) 528-554.

Benz, E.$_4$. *Schellings theologische Geistesahnen.* Abhandlungen der Ak. d. Wissensch. u. d. Literatur, geistes- und sozialwissenschaftl. Klasse, 3. Wiesbaden, 1955.

Benz, E.$_5$. *Nietzsches Ideen zur Geschichte des Christentums und der Kirche.* Leiden, 1956.

Bezold, F. V. *Geschichte der Rheinischen Friedrich-Wilhelms-Universität.* Bonn, 1920.

---

[2] Followed by volume and page. As far as possible, this more recent edition has been used for all writings after the *Holy Family.*

Bigo, P. *Marxisme et humanisme: introduction à l'oeuvre économique de Karl Marx.* Paris, 1954.

Bockmühl, K. E. *Leiblichkeit und Gesellschaft. Studien zur Religionskritik im Frühwerk von L. Feuerbach und K. Marx.* Forschungen zur system. Theologie und Religionsphilosophie, 7. Göttingen, 1961.

Burkhardt, J. *Gesamtausgabe.* 12 vols. Berlin-Leipzig, 1930.

Butler, W. M. *The Saint-Simonian Religion in Germany.* Cambridge, 1926.

Cieszkowski, A. v.$_1$. *Prolegomena zur Historiosophie.* Berlin, 1838.

Cieszkowski, A. v.$_2$. *Gott und die Palingenesie.* Berlin, 1842.

Cornu, A.$_1$. *Moses Hess et la Gauche Hégélienne.* Paris, 1934.

Cornu, A.$_2$. *Karl Marx et la révolution de 1848.* Paris, 1948.

Cornu, A.$_3$. *Karl Marx et Frederick Engels.* Vol. I, *Les années d'enfance et de jeunesse. La Gauche Hégélienne. 1818/20—1840,* Paris, 1955. Vol. II, *Du libéralisme démocratique au communisme. La "Gazette Rhénane." Les "Annales Franco-Allemandes." 1842—1844.* Paris, 1958. Vol. III, *Marx à Paris.* Paris, 1962.

Cottier, G. M.-M.$_1$. *L'athéisme du jeune Marx et ses origines Hégéliennes.* Paris, 1959.

Cottier, G. M.-M.$_2$. *Du romantisme au Marxisme.* Paris, 1961.

Demetz, P. *Marx, Engels und die Dichter.* Stuttgart, 1959.

Derbolav, J. "Die kritische Hegelrezeption des jungen Marx und das Problem der Emanzipation des Menschen." *Studium Generale* 15 (1962) 271-288.

Dicke, G. *Der Identitätsgedanke bei Feuerbach und Marx.* Wissenschaftl. Abhandlungen der Arbeitsgemeinsch. für Forschung d. Landes Nordrhein-Westfalen, 15. Köln-Opladen, 1960.

Doctrine de Saint-Simon. Exposition. Première année, 1829; ed. C. Bouglé and E. Halévy. Paris, 1924.

Dubský, I. *Hegels Arbeitsbegriff und die idealistische Dialektik.* Rozpravy ČSAV, sešit 14, ročník 71. Prague, 1961.

Dupré, L. K. *Het vertrekpunkt der marxistische wijsbegeerte.* Amsterdam-Antwerpen, 1954.

Einundzwanzig Bogen aus der Schweiz; ed. G. Herwegh. Zürich-Winterthur, 1843.

Evans, D. O. *Social Romanticism in France, 1830-1848.* Oxford, 1951.

Feuerbach, L. A. *Sämtliche Werke;* ed. W. Bolin and F. Jodl. 2nd ed., 13 vols. Stuttgart, 1960.

Fichte, J. G. *Werke;* ed. F. Medicus. 6 vols. Leipzig, 1922.

Friedrich, M. *Philosophie und Ökonomie beim jungen Marx.* Berlin, 1960.

Gebhardt, J.$_1$. *Politik und Eschatologie. Studien zur Geschichte der Hegelschen Schule in den Jahren 1830-1840.* Münchener Studien zur Politik, 1. München, 1963.

Gebhardt, J.₂. "Karl Marx und Bruno Bauer." *Politische Ordnung und menschliche Existenz. Festschrift E. Voegelin.* München, 1952, 202-242.

Gehlen, A. "Über die Geburt der Freiheit aus der Entfremdung." *Archiv für Rechts- und Sozialphilosophie* (1952/53) 338-353.

Grégoire, F. *Études Hégéliennes.* Louvain-Paris, 1958.

Gurvitch, G. *La vocation actuelle de la sociologie.* Paris, 1950.

Habermas, J.₁. "Zur philosophischen Diskussion um Marx und den Marxismus." *Philosophische Rundschau* (1957) 165-235.

Habermas, J.₂. *Theorie und Praxis.* Politica, 11. Neuwied a. R., 1963.

Haering, Th. L. *Hegel, sein Wollen und sein Werk.* Vol. I, Leipzig-Berlin, 1929. Vol. II, Aalen, 1963.

Halévy, E. *Histoire du socialisme européen.* 6th ed. Paris, 1948.

Hallische Jahrbücher für deutsche Wissenschaft und Kunst. From July, 1841, *Deutsche Jahrbücher für Wissenschaft und Kunst*; ed. A. Ruge and Th. Echtermeyer. Leipzig, 1838-1843.

Haym, R. *Hegel und seine Zeit*; photo reprint of 1857 Berlin ed. Darmstadt, 1962.

Hegel, G. W. F.₁. *Werke*; ed. G. Lasson and J. Hoffmeister. 30 vols. Leipzig, 1905 ff.

Hegel, G. W. F.₂. *Sämtliche Werke (Jubiläumsausgabe)*; ed. H. Glockner 22 vols. Stuttgart, 1932 ff.

Hegel, G. W. F.₃. *Berliner Schriften* (1818-1831); ed. J. Hoffmeister. Hamburg, 1956.

Hegel, G. W. F.₄. *Briefe*; ed. J. Hoffmeister, 4 vols. Hamburg, 1952 ff.

Heine, H. "Zur Geschichte der Religion und Philosophie in Deutschland," in *Heinrich Heines Sämtliche Werke*; ed. E. Elster. Vol. IV. Leipzig-Wien, 1887 ff., 160-296.

Heiss, R.₁. "Das Verhältnis von Theorie und Praxis bei Hegel." *Blätter für deutsche Philosophie* (1935) 75-84.

Heiss, R.₂. *Die grossen Dialektiker des 19. Jahrhunderts (Hegel-Kierkegaard-Marx).* Köln-Berlin, 1963.

Heiss, R.₃. "Hegel und Marx." *Symposion.* Vol. I. Freiburg, 1949, 169-206.

Hepner, B.-P. *Bakounine et le Panslavisme Révolutionnaire.* Paris, 1950.

Hertz-Eichenrode, D. *Der Junghegelianer Bruno Bauer im Vormärz.* Berlin, 1959. Doctoral Dissertation.

Hess, Moses₁. *Sozialistische Aufsätze 1841-1847*; ed. Th. Zlocisti. Berlin, 1921.

Hess, Moses₂. *Philosophische und sozialistische Schriften 1837-1850*; ed. A. Cornu and W. Mönke. Berlin (East), 1961.

Hess, Moses₃. *Briefwechsel*; ed. E. Silberner. Quellen und Untersuchungen zur Geschichte der deutschen und österr. Arbeiterbewegung, 2. The Hague, 1959.

Hoffmeister, J.₁. *Dokumente zu Hegels Entwicklung.* Stuttgart, 1936.
Hoffmeister, J.₂. *Die Heimkehr des Geistes. Studien zur Dichtung und Philosophie der Goethezeit.* Hameln, 1946.
Hook, S. *From Hegel to Marx. Studies in the Intellectual Development of Karl Marx.* 2nd ed. Ann Arbor, 1962.
Hyppolite, J.₁. *Genèse et structure de la Phénoménologie de l'Esprit de Hegel.* 2 vols. Paris, 1946.
Hyppolite, J.₂. "Aliénation et Objectivation." *Études Germaniques* 6 (1951) 117-124; 7 (1952) 37-43.
Hyppolite, J.₃. *Études sur Marx et Hegel.* Paris, 1955.
Joly, R. *Le thème philosophique des genres de vie dans l'antiquité classique.* Académie Royale de Belgique, classe des mémoires et lettres. Vol. 29; part 3. Bruxelles, 1955.
Kant, I. *Werke*; ed. E. Cassirer. 11 vols. Berlin, 1922 ff.
Kaufmann, W. "Hegel: Legende und Wirklichkeit." *Zeitschrift für philosophische Forschung* (1956) 191-226.
Klages, H. "Das Verhältnis von Theorie und Praxis bei Karl Marx." *Soziale Welt* 13 (1962/63) 267-278.
Kofler, L. "Das Prinzip der Arbeit in der Marxschen und in der Gehlenschen Anthropologie." *Schmollers Jahrbuch für Gesetzgebung, Verwaltung und Volkswirtschaft* 78 (1958) 71-86.
Kojève, A. *Introduction à la lecture de Hegel.* Paris, 1947.
Korsch, K. *Karl Marx.* New York, 1963.
Kühne, W. *Graf August Cieszkowski.* Veröffentl. des Slawischen Institutes der Universität Berlin, 20. Leipzig, 1938.
Labry, R. *A. I. Herzen.* Paris, 1928.
Lauth, R. "Einflüsse slawischer Denker auf die Genesis der Marxschen Weltanschauung." *Orientalia Christiana Periodica* (1955) 399-450.
Lenz, M. *Geschichte der kgl. Friedrich-Wilhelms-Universität zu Berlin.* Halle, 1918.
Lewalter, E. "Zur Systematik der Marxschen Staats- und Gesellschaftslehre." *Archiv für Sozialwissenschaft und Politik* 68 (1933) 641-675.
Löwith, K.₁. "L'achèvement de la philosophie classique par Hegel et sa dissolution chez Marx et Kierkegaard." *Recherches philosophiques* 4 (1934/35) 232-267.
Löwith, K.₂. "Man's Self-Alienation in the Early Writings of Marx." *Social Research* 21 (1954) 204-229.
Löwith, K.₃. *Von Hegel zu Nietzsche.* 4th ed. Stuttgart, 1958.
Lukács, G.₁. *Geschichte und Klassenbewusstsein.* Berlin, 1923.
Lukács, G.₂. *Moses Hess und die Probleme in der idealistischen Dialektik.* Archiv für die Geschichte des Sozialismus und der Arbeiterbewegung; ed. C. Grün, 12. Leipzig, 1926.
Lukács, G.₃. *Der junge Hegel. Über die Beziehung von Dialektik und Ökonomie.* Zürich-Wien, 1948.

Marcuse, H.$_1$. "Neue Quellen zur Grundlegung des histor. Materialis-
    mus." *Die Gesellschaft* (1932) 136-174.
Marcuse, H.$_2$. "Über die philosophischen Grundlagen des wirt-
    schaftswissenschaftlichen Arbeitsbegriffs." *Archiv für Sozial-
    wissenschaft und Sozialpolitik* 69 (1933) 257-292.
Marcuse, H.$_3$. "Über den affirmativen Charakter der Kultur."
    Zeitschrift für Sozialforschung 6 (1937) 54-94.
Marcuse, H.$_4$. *Reason and Revolution. Hegel and the Rise of Social
    Theory.* Boston, 1960.
Marxismusstudien; ed. E. Metzke. 2nd vol. I. Fetscher, Tübingen.
    Vol. I, 1954. Vol. II, 1957. Vol. III, 1960. Vol. IV, 1962.
Mayer, G.$_1$. "Die Anfänge des politischen Radikalismus im vor-
    märzlichen Preussen." *Zeitschrift für Politik* 6 (1913) 1-114.
Mayer, G.$_2$. "Die Junghegelianer und der preussische Staat." *His-
    torische Zeitschrift* 121 (1920) 413-440.
Mehring, F. *Karl Marx, the Story of his Life.* Ann Arbor, 1962.
Michelet, G. L. *Geschichte der letzten Systeme der Philosophie in
    Deutschland von Kant bis Hegel.* Berlin, 1837.
Mueller, G. E. "The Hegel Legend of 'Thesis-Antithesis-Synthesis.'"
    Journal of the History of Ideas 19 (1958) 411-414.
Neher, W. *Arnold Ruge als Politiker und politischer Schriftsteller.*
    Heidelberger Abhandlungen zur mittleren und neueren Geschichte,
    64. Heidelberg, 1933.
Neubauer, F. "Die Bedeutung der Praxis in den Schriften von
    Marx und Engels." *Archiv für Rechts- und Sozialphilosophie*
    (1961) 179-191.
Nohl, H. *Hegels theologische Jugendschriften.* Tübingen, 1907.
Novalis. *Werke, Briefe, Dokumente*; ed. E. Wasmuth. 3 vols. Hei-
    delberg, 1953 ff.
Nüdling, G. *Ludwig Feuerbachs Religionsphilosophie.* 2nd ed. Pader-
    born, 1961.
O'Neil, J. "The Concept of Estrangement in the Early and Later
    Writings of Karl Marx." *Philosophy and Phenomenological
    Research* 25 (1964) 64-84.
Peperzak, A. T. B. *Le jeune Hegel et la vision morale du monde.*
    The Hague, 1960.
Popitz, H. *Der entfremdete Mensch. Zeitkritik und Geschichts-
    philosophie des jungen Marx.* Philosophische Forschungen,
    Neue Folge, 2. Basel, 1953.
Proudhon, P. J. *Œuvres complètes.* 18 vols. Paris, 1923 ff.
Ramm, Th. *Die grossen Sozialisten als Rechts- und Sozialphiloso-
    phen.* Vol. 1. Stuttgart, 1955.
Ritter, J.$_1$. *Die aristotelische Lehre vom Ursprung und Sinn der
    Theorie.* Arbeitsgemeinschaft für Forschung des Landes Nord-
    rhein-Westfalen, 1, Köln-Opladen, 1953.

Ritter, J.$_2$. *Hegel und die französische Revolution*. Arbeitsgemein-schaft für Forschung des Landes Nordrhein-Westfalen, 63. Köln-Opladen, 1957.

Rohrmoser, G. "Zur Vorgeschichte der Jugendschriften Hegels." *Zeitschrift für philosophische Forschung* 14 (1960) 182-208.

Rosenkranz, K. *G. W. F. Hegel's Leben*. Berlin, 1844.

Rotenstreich, N. *Basic Problems of Marx's Philosophy*. New York, 1965.

Röttcher, F. "Theorie und Praxis in den Frühschriften von Karl Marx." *Archiv für Philosophie* 11 (1961) 246-311.

Rubel, M.$_1$. *Bibliographie des oeuvres de Karl Marx (avec en appendice un répertoire des oeuvres de Friedrich Engels)*. Paris, 1956. *Supplément à la Bibliographie*, etc. Paris, 1960.

Rubel, M.$_2$. *Karl Marx, Essai d'une biographie intellectuelle*. Paris, 1957.

Ruge, A. *Aus früherer Zeit*. 4 vols. Berlin, 1863 ff.

Seeberger, W. *Hegel, oder die Entwicklung des Geistes zur Freiheit*. Stuttgart, 1961.

Schelling, F. W. J. v. *Sämtliche Werke*; ed. K. F. A. Schelling. Stuttgart-Augsburg, 1856 ff.

Scheibert, P. *Von Bakunin zu Lenin*. Vol. I. Leiden, 1956.

Schieder, Th. "Das Problem der Revolution im 19. Jahrhundert." *Historische Zeitschrift* 170 (1957) 233-271.

Schiller, J. C. F. v. *Sämtliche Werke*; ed. E. v. d. Hellen. 16 vols. Stuttgart-Berlin, 1904.

Schnabel, F. *Deutsche Geschichte im 19. Jahrhundert*. 2nd ed. 4 vols., Freiburg, 1949.

Schmidt, A. *Der Begriff der Natur in der Lehre von Marx*. Frankfurter Beiträge zur Soziologie, 11. Frankfurt, 1962.

Schulz, R.-E. "Geschichte und teleologisches System bei Karl Marx." *Wesen und Wirklichkeit des Menschen. Festschrift H. Plessner*. Göttingen, 1957, 153-194.

Schulze, W. A. "Oetingers Beitrag zur Schellingschen Freiheitslehre." *Zeitschrift für Theologie und Kirche* 54 (1957) 212-225.

Schweitzer, A. *Geschichte der Leben-Jesu Forschung*. 6th ed. Tübingen, 1951.

Staatslexikon oder Enzyklopädie der Staatswissenschaften; ed. C. von Rotteck and C. Welcker. 15 vols. and 4 suppplementary vols. Altona, 1834 ff.

Stace, W. T. *The Philosophy of Hegel*. Dover Paperback, 1955.

Stein, L. v. *Der Socialismus und Communismus des heutigen Frank-reich*. Leipzig, 1842.

Stirner, M. *Der Einzige und sein Eigentum*. Leipzig, 1845.

Strauss, D. F. *Das Leben Jesu kritisch bearbeitet*. 2 vols. Tübingen, 1835 ff.

434

Theory and Practice

Stuke, H. *Philosophie der Tat. Studien zur Verwirklichung der Philosophie bei den Junghegelianern und Wahren Sozialisten.* Industrielle Welt, 3. Stuttgart, 1963.

Tucker, R. C. *Philosophy and Myth in Karl Marx.* Cambridge, Mass., 1961.

Tschiżewskij, D., ed. *Hegel bei den Slawen.* 2nd ed. Darmstadt, 1961.

Wackenheim, Ch. *La faillite de la religion d'après Karl Marx.* Paris, 1963.

Wahl, J. *Le malheur de la conscience dans la philosophie de Hegel.* 2nd ed. Paris, 1951.

Weil, E. *Hegel et l'état.* Paris, 1950.

Weiss, J. *Moses Hess, Utopian Socialist.* Detroit, 1960.

Zelený, J. "Problém základů vědy u Hegela a Marxe (The Problem of the Foundation of Science in Hegel and Marx)." *Filosofický Časopis*, Prague (1964) 478-494; (1965) 204-212.

B

tr. Aveling-Moore: Karl Marx. *Capital. A Critical Analysis of Capitalist Production.* 3 vols. Moscow: Foreign Languages Publishing House, 1954 ff. This is a reproduction of the 1881 English edition, ed. Engels. Corresponds to Vols XXIII/XXV of *MEW*.

tr. Baillie: G. W. F. Hegel. *The Phenomenology of Mind*; tr. J. B. Baillie. 2nd rev. ed. London, 1964. Corresponds to Vol. II of Hegel$_2$.

tr. Bottomore: Karl Marx. *Early Writings*; tr. T. B. Bottomore. London, 1963. According to this edition, the two articles in the *Deutsch-Französische Jahrbücher* are quoted, corresponding to *MEGA* I, 1/1, 576-621. The *Manuscripts* are quoted according to the edition by Milligan.

tr. Dixon: Karl Marx and Friedrich Engels. *The Holy Family.* Moscow: Foreign Languages Publishing House, 1956. Corresponds to *MEGA* I, 3, 175-388.

tr. Haldane-Simson: *Hegel's Lectures on the History of Philosophy*; tr. E. S. Haldane and F. H. Simson. 3 vols. New York, 1955. Corresponds to Vols. XVII/XIX of Hegel$_2$.

tr. Johnston-Struthers: *Hegel's Science of Logic*; tr. W. H. Johnston and L. G. Struthers. 2 vols. London, 1951. Corresponds to Vols. IV and V of Hegel$_2$.

tr. Knox: *Hegel's Philosophy of Right*; tr. T. M. Knox. Oxford, 1953. Corresponds to Vol. VII of Hegel$_2$.

tr. Knox-Kroner: *On Christianity. Early Theological Writings by Friedrich Hegel*; tr. T. M. Knox; introduction by R.

Kroner. Harper Torchbooks, 1948. Partial edition of Nohl.

tr. Milligan: Karl Marx. *Economic and Philosophic Manuscripts of 1844.* Moscow: Foreign Languages Publishing House, 1961. Corresponds to *MEGA* I, 3, 33-172. Contains also Engels' "Outlines," corresponding to *MEW* I, 499-524.

tr. Moscow: Karl Marx and Frederick Engels, *Selected Works in Two Volumes.* Moscow: Foreign Languages Publishing House, 1955.

tr. Pascal: Karl Marx and Friedrich Engels. *The German Ideology, Part I & III*; tr. R. Pascal. New York: International Publishers, 1960. Does not contain the manuscript on Stirner or mention passages that have been deleted. Corresponds to *MEW* III, 13-77 and 441-530.

tr. Speirs-Sanderson: G. W. F. Hegel. *Lectures on the Philosophy of Religion*; E. B. Speirs and J. B. Sanderson. 3 vols. London, 1962. Corresponds to Vols. XV ˙and XVI of Hegel₂.

tr. Sibree: G. W. F. Hegel. *The Philosophy of History*; tr. J. Sibree; introduction by C. J. Friedrich. Dover Paperback, 1956. Corresponds to Vol. XI of Hegel₂.

INDEX

200698